The 1966 Green Bay P

The 1966 Green Bay Packers

*Profiles of Vince Lombardi's
Super Bowl I Champions*

EDITED BY GEORGE BOZEKA

Associate Editors
Mark Ford, Denis Crawford and *John Maxymuk*

GREAT TEAMS IN PRO FOOTBALL HISTORY

McFarland & Company, Inc., Publishers
Jefferson, North Carolina

LIBRARY OF CONGRESS CATALOGUING-IN-PUBLICATION DATA

Names: Bozeka, George.
Title: The 1966 Green Bay Packers : profiles of Vince Lombardi's Super Bowl I champions / edited by George Bozeka ; associate editors, Mark Ford, Denis Crawford and John Maxymuk.
Description: Jefferson, North Carolina : McFarland & Company, Inc., Publishers, 2016. | Series: Great teams in pro football history | Includes bibliographical references and index.
Identifiers: LCCN 2016015955 | ISBN 9781476662039 (softcover : acid free paper) ∞
Subjects: LCSH: Green Bay Packers (Football team)—History. | Lombardi, Vince. | Football coaches—United States.
Classification: LCC GV956.G7 A17 2016 | DDC 796.332/64097756109046—dc23
LC record available at https://lccn.loc.gov/2016015955

BRITISH LIBRARY CATALOGUING DATA ARE AVAILABLE

ISBN (print) 978-1-4766-6203-9
ISBN (ebook) 978-1-4766-2442-6

Front cover: MVP quarterback Bart Starr and the Green Bay Packers facing off against the Kansas City Chiefs in the first Super Bowl on January 15, 1967 (Photograph by Vernon Biever)

Printed in the United States of America

McFarland & Company, Inc., Publishers
Box 611, Jefferson, North Carolina 28640
www.mcfarlandpub.com

To Bob Carroll, founder of the Professional Football Researchers Association and the father of professional football research

Acknowledgments

George Bozeka

This book project has been a collaborative effort of the Professional Football Researchers Association. I would like to thank our board of directors and membership for accepting my vision of a "Great Teams in Pro Football History" book series and making this book about the 1966 Green Bay Packers the initial book in this planned series. Special thanks to Chris Willis and Mark Durr for their helpful guidance through the development and completion of this project.

Thanks to all our contributors for their commitment and for the many hours they spent researching, writing, and rewriting the biographies and features included in this book.

I would like to thank Jon Kendle of the Ralph Wilson, Jr., Pro Football Research and Preservation Center at the Pro Football Hall of Fame and Cliff Christl, the Packers team historian, for their help in providing archived files to our contributors. I would also like to thank Aaron Popkey, the director of public affairs for the Packers, and his public affairs intern Katie Hermsen for their help in compiling head shots from the Packers archives for use in this book. An additional thank you to Steve Raymer and the Pavek Museum of Broadcasting for providing a head shot of broadcasting legend Ray Scott.

Heartfelt thanks to Jim Biever and the Biever family for giving us special access to the extraordinary archives of the late Packers photographer Vernon Biever and for allowing us to use his images in this book. Special thanks to Matt Foss for acting as our liaison to Jim and the Biever family.

I would like to thank Kenneth R. Crippen for organizing interviews of many of the surviving members of the 1966 Packers. Donny Anderson, Zeke Bratkowski, Carroll Dale, Willie Davis, Dave Hathcock, Jerry Kramer, Bob Long, Red Mack, Jim Taylor, Phil Vandersea, Steve Wright, and Packers journalist Bud Lea generously made time in their busy schedules to share their recollections with our contributors. Further thanks to former Packer Bob Hyland and Bob Jeter's son Rob, the former head basketball coach at the University of Wisconsin–Milwaukee, for making themselves available for interviews.

Thanks to Rick Schabowski for spending countless hours researching newspaper and video archives for the project and making his detailed work available to our contributors. Thanks also to Tracy Thibeau for the research work he did on Packer Tom Brown.

Finally, thanks to associate editors Denis Crawford, Mark L. Ford, and John Maxymuk for their help during the editing process. Special thanks to Mark for providing additional research materials to many of our contributors, and a very special thank you to John, my right hand throughout this project.

Table of Contents

Part 4: The Stadiums

Part 5: The Press

Preface

George Bozeka

It is impossible to chronicle professional football in America without huge chapters on Vince Lombardi and his great Green Bay Packers teams of the 1960s. His 1966 squad is key to the narrative as the winners of the first AFL/NFL World Championship Game, ushering in the Super Bowl era of the National Football League. From its rather humble beginning during the 1966 season, the Super Bowl has morphed into the largest carnival in professional sports.

What makes the history of the 1966 team so compelling is not only Lombardi but the great cast of players. From Lionel Aldridge to Tommy Joe Crutcher to Willie Davis to Dave Hathcock to Ray Nitschke to Bart Starr to Willie Wood, the people and their exploits on the field are enlightening, entertaining, and inspirational.

The "winning isn't everything, it's the only thing" mantra attributed to Lombardi and his great Packer teams is only part of the narrative. Striving for excellence is without question the foundation of the Lombardi Packers, but there are other prevalent themes: the importance of team over the individual, the shared love, faith, and respect of the Packer teammates and their coaches, and the color blind culture of the team and their coach.

Lombardi ultimately taught his players life lessons. They were philosophies that served them well on the gridiron and in life after football. Player after player went on to lead accomplished and successful lives after their playing careers were over. They not only won championships on the field, they were also Super Bowl winners in life.

This book project had its beginning in 2012 when I purchased a book at my local Barnes and Noble about the 1947 Brooklyn Dodgers. It was part of a Memorable Teams in Baseball History series produced by the Society for American Baseball Research (SABR). That book and series got me thinking that a similar series on football teams would be a great project for the Professional Football Researchers Association (PFRA). The PFRA is a nonprofit corporation that was founded and organized in 1979 in Canton, Ohio, at the Pro Football Hall of Fame. The purposes of the organization are to foster the study of professional football as a significant cultural and athletic institution; to establish an accurate historical account of professional football; and to disseminate research information. I presented my idea to the PFRA board of directors and membership at the 2014 Biennial Meeting, which was held in Cleveland at the Browns Training Facility and FirstEnergy Stadium. The board and membership generously approved the project and decided that a book about the 1966 Green Bay Packers should be the first in the planned series. The 1966 Packers, winners of the first AFL-NFL World Championship Game (Super

Bowl I), seemed an obvious choice, as the PFRA planned to hold its 2016 Biennial Meeting at Lambeau Field in Green Bay, in honor of the 50th anniversary of the Packers' Super Bowl victory.

This book offers a complete history of the 1966 Packers, including coach and player biographies, game summaries and statistics, and thematic essays about the Packers ownership structure, training camp and the preseason, the draft, how the team was built, the taxi squad, Lambeau Field, Milwaukee County Stadium, and race and the Packers. Finally, biographies of key media personalities that covered the team, including photographer Vernon Biever, make up the remainder of the book.

Contributors to the project thoroughly researched the 1966 Packers, poring over newspaper articles, magazines, media guides, yearbooks, internet sites and books written by and about the team and its members; consulting the research center at the Pro Football Hall of Fame as well as team archives; and conducting interviews with surviving members of the team.

The book has truly been a labor of love for the PFRA and its membership. We hope that it adds to the scholarship on this great team, and its renowned coach, Vince Lombardi.

PART 1

The Organization

Head Coach Vince Lombardi

Gary Sarnoff

"Who the hell is Vince Lombardi?" asked a member of the Packers executive committee when hearing that the Green Bay Packers had hired a new coach.[1] In late January 1959, it was a common question being asked by Green Bay players and football fans throughout Wisconsin. By a vote of 26–1, the Green Bay Packers executive committee approved the hiring of the New York Giants assistant coach as the new head coach and general manager of their team.

It was clear from the start that "Lombardi will be the boss. He'll do the firing and hiring," said Green Bay Packers president Dominick Olejniczak. "He'll run this football team."[2] That authority assured Lombardi's success in building something special in the little city known for its packing and paper plants. At his first meeting with his players, he told them what they could expect: "Gentlemen, we're going to have a football team here, and we're going to win some games. Do you know why? You are going to have confidence in me and in my system. By being alert, you are going to make fewer mistakes than your opponent. By working harder, you are going to out-execute, out-work, and out-tackle every team that comes your way."[3]

Vincent Thomas Lombardi was born on June 11, 1913, in Brooklyn, New York. He was the first of five children of Harry and Matilda Lombardi. Harry Lombardi was a hard worker, a strong believer in self-discipline, and a devout Catholic who arrived in America at the age of two. "He was a perfectionist," said his eldest son. "He was a perfectionist if there ever was one."[4] Harry Lombardi owned and operated a wholesale meat company, located near the Hudson River in Manhattan. His strong principles and values were important necessities in creating a successful business.

During his childhood, Vince Lombardi spent time working at his Dad's company—cutting meat, hauling the loads of beef, learning the salesmanship of the wholesale meat market—to get a head start in the family business. But after getting caught on one of the belt hooks in the meat house, Vince vowed that he would never work for the family meat company.[5]

In 1928, Vince finished his grammar school education at Brooklyn's P.S. 206, and made a decision to continue his education by enrolling in a six-year program at Cathedral Prep in Brooklyn aimed at the priesthood. Following his first four years at Cathedral Prep, Lombardi decided "he was not intended to be a priest" and dropped out.[6]

Having ruled out a career in the family business and the priesthood, Lombardi turned his attention to football. He knew he loved football, often playing the game during his free time in local sandlots and sometimes persuading a friend or two to take a long subway ride to the Polo Grounds to watch the New York football Giants or Fordham

University. He also followed the game through the sports pages, and became aware of scholarship opportunities to play football in college. He decided to pursue a football scholarship by, in effect, repeating his senior year at St. Francis Prep. He played football at St Francis and did well, making All-Scholastic Honorable Mention as a 175-pound halfback/guard to win a scholarship to Fordham University.[7]

The Fordham Rams had a successful football tradition, and were coached by Jim Crowley, a former member of Knute Rockne's famed Four Horsemen. Crowley had tasted success in his first head coaching job at Michigan State, compiling a 22–8–3 record that included an upset win over the Rams, before accepting the head coaching job at Fordham in 1933. His first freshman class included fullback Vince Lombardi, although he would not be at that position for very long. During a preseason drill, Rams assistant coach Frank Leahy (who would later become the head coach of Notre Dame) motioned for Lombardi to line up against him to demonstrate a blocking drill. The coach threw a hard block that knocked down Lombardi. Lombardi quickly got up and invited the coach to try again. When he did, it was Leahy who hit the ground this time, and Lombardi was switched from the backfield to right guard, his position throughout his collegiate career.[8]

The strength of the Rams was their line, known as the Seven Blocks of Granite, including number 40, Vince Lombardi, at right guard. Although not the most talented player, Lombardi made up for the lack of talent with heart, courage, and a desire to win. After a difficult loss to NYU dashed Fordham's Rose Bowl hopes during Lombardi's senior year Fordham teammate Alex Wojciechowicz recalled, "We were all disappointed—we wanted to dig a big hole and climb into it—but Vince took it the hardest."[9]

Lombardi also excelled in his studies, and had established a vibrant social life. Through a cousin of his roommate, he was introduced to Marie Planitz, who was impressed by his maturity and liked his curly dark hair. One day after the two began to date, Vince visited Marie at her family's home in the Bronx. After Lombardi said good-bye and walked out the door, Marie announced that she was going to marry that man one day.[10]

In June of 1937, Lombardi graduated from Fordham University. He was now in the real world, but jobs were scarce. He decided to continue his education by enrolling in Fordham's law school, but tired of law school quickly and dropped out.[11] Lombardi played semipro football for the Brooklyn Eagles, and then the Wilmington (Delaware) Clippers. Following his decision to drop out of law school, he worked for a finance company collecting debts, a tough job, especially in the depth of the Depression. Then in 1939, the door opened to the path that would lead to Lombardi's Promised Land.

In the summer of 1939, Andy Palau, a teammate of Lombardi's at Fordham, accepted the head coaching job at St. Cecilia, a small Catholic high school in Englewood, New Jersey. When Palau's assistant coach resigned less than a week before the start of the school, Andy began the task of finding a replacement. His old Fordham baseball coach, Jack Coffey, suggested that he call Lombardi.

Palau called the Lombardi residence and spoke with Vince's mother. "He's not here right now. He's working at a finance company. What do you want him for?" she asked. "To coach football," replied Palau. "To coach football!" said Mrs. Lombardi. "Why would he want to do anything as silly as that?"[12]

Palau got in touch with Lombardi. The two met to talk about the job, and Lombardi accepted for a salary of $1,700. However, the job required more than just coaching football. He would have to teach chemistry, Latin, and physics, and become the head coach for the school's basketball team.

The coaching duo of Palau and Lombardi made an immediate impression. "If the Saints lose, it won't be any fault of Palau and Lombardi," penned sportswriter Marv Hyman of the *Englewood Press*.[13] Before the third game of the first season, Palau called on Lombardi to give the pregame speech. Inspired by Lombardi's pep talk, St. Cecilia defeated Tenafly High, 13–0. The Saints would not lose another game that season and were declared the North Jersey Group Two Parochial School state champions of 1939.

Lombardi had a promising position and had launched his coaching career successfully. He now felt secure enough to propose to his long-time girlfriend. Vince and Marie were married on August 31, 1940.

Under the direction of Palau and Lombardi, St. Cecilia captured the North Jersey state championship

Vince Lombardi (photograph by Vernon J. Biever).

during the next two seasons to establish the small school as a powerhouse and to gain recognition throughout the state. According to the *Englewood Press*, assistant coach Lombardi stressed sound fundamentals to build a strong line on both sides of the ball—with linemen known for toughness, technique, and their speed in charging fast and low off the line of scrimmage.[14]

In 1942, Palau left St. Cecilia to take a coaching job at Fordham University. Lombardi was now the head coach of the football team at St. Cecilia. Also during that year, Marie gave birth to the couple's first child, a boy, named Vincent Henry.

After an extremely successful run at St. Cecilia which included a 32-game unbeaten streak in football and a New Jersey state championship in basketball, Lombardi accepted a job coaching the freshman football team at Fordham. During his last semester as a high school teacher and coach in 1947, he became a father for the second time when Marie gave birth to a girl, named Susan.

Following his second season at Fordham, Lombardi became an assistant coach for one of the best college programs in the country when he was hired by Red Blaik, the head coach at Army in 1949. With Lombardi as the offensive coach, the Cadets went undefeated during his first season. A year later, the Cadets won every game leading up to their last game of the season, versus Navy. In a shocker, the Midshipmen upset Army, 14–2.

In 1951, a cheating scandal rocked West Point. The scandal decimated the program, resulting in an inexperienced team of mostly freshmen players, but Blaik and Lombardi were not discouraged. They continued to be enthusiastic and hopeful and worked to develop the young players. The 1952 team made terrific progress by improving to a 4–4–1 record, followed by an impressive 7–1–1 season in 1953 to win the Lambert Trophy, given to the season's best college football team in the East.

By this time, the New York Giants were calling. Longtime Giants head coach Steve Owen had been fired after a disappointing run since the Giants' last appearance in the NFL championship game in 1946. The Giants ownership was clear on who they wanted

as their next head coach—Red Blaik. Blaik wanted to remain at Army, but he recommended his fiery offensive assistant for the Giants head job. The Giants ownership passed on Lombardi, feeling that they needed a name with head coaching experience. Jim Lee Howell, a former Giants player and coach who had head coaching experience at a small college, was given the job. The Giants, however, had a job for Lombardi on the coaching staff. He would run the offense while a promising up-and-coming coach named Tom Landry would handle the defense.[15]

Lombardi struggled at the beginning. He wanted to run the same offensive system he used at Army—a split-T option play that required the quarterback to either pitch out or run with the ball while running along the line of scrimmage. "Well, that might work with a college quarterback," said Giants halfback Frank Gifford, "but we had Charlie Conerly," who was 33 years old.[16] When Lombardi sent in that play during his first exhibition season with the Giants, Conerly would change the play. The New York linemen also had problems adjusting to the new coach's blocking scheme.

In addition to disliking the new offense, the players considered Lombardi to be "loud and arrogant—a total pain in the ass."[17] They would mock him in private calling him Little General and Little Mussolini and joke about his flashing teeth.[18]

Lombardi knew he wasn't communicating with his players. One evening during training camp, he paid a visit to the players in their dorm. He explained that he was new to the NFL and could use a helping hand. After hearing that, Gifford said that it changed the team's opinion; they now wanted to help Lombardi. "We would listen to him and he would listen to us,"[19] said Charley Conerly. "It didn't take long for us to realize that Vinny's approach to football was very basic—fundamentals: hit, block, and tackle—he was somebody special. His enthusiasm, his spirit, was infectious," said Gifford.[20]

The Giants' fortunes began to change under the new coaching staff. By Vince's third year, the Giants were NFL champions, following a 47–7 win over the Chicago Bears in the 1956 championship game.

Lombardi had established himself as a talented NFL assistant, but what he really desired was to be a head coach. Disappointed over being overlooked time and time again, he began to believe he was destined to be an assistant coach. He did receive one head coaching opportunity, from the Philadelphia Eagles, but after being forewarned that the owners were too involved with coaching decisions, he declined the offer. However, his time was about to come.

The Green Bay Packers had been doormats in the NFL through the 1950s; a team that had not tasted a championship since World War II, had not posted a winning season since going 6–5–1 in 1947, and did not have a direction. The Packers' executive committee, which governed the city-owned Packers, was in dire need of someone who could turn things around. Scooter McLean had been the latest hope of changing the team's fortunes. Hired as the head coach prior to the 1958 season, McLean said his team would be going for a championship, but after a dismal 1–10–1 season, Packers were looking for a new head coach. "We liked Scooter, and we really wanted to win for him," said Packers guard Jerry Kramer, "but we didn't know how to win."[21] When the season ended, the assumption was that McLean would be fired. As it turned out, Scooter resigned, or as the press put it, "Scooter scooted" and took a job as an assistant with the Lions.

Lombardi was contacted by the Packers and went to Green Bay to interview for the position. He made it clear that he wanted a dual job of head coach and general manager. He also insisted on being in complete command with no interference from the executive committee. Once, the executive committee may have balked at that, but they were now desperate and hearing grief from other stockholders. A commander of an American Legion Post who owned a share of the team spoke out by asking the members of the executive committee to resign. Other shareowners, fed up after a decade of losing, believed that the team needed a fresh start, beginning with a new executive board.[22]

Lombardi was hired as the Packers' new head coach, but he was not a popular choice. "When I found out that he was an assistant for the New York Giants, I thought the Packers made the dumbest move in the world," said Jerry Kramer. "They hired a guy who had never been a head coach in his life."[23]

But Kramer and the others found out otherwise after they reported for Lombardi's first training camp. By the end of that first training season, the Packers were Lombardi's team. The defeatist attitude that had haunted the organization for so many years was gone, and so were 15 players from the 1958 Packers. "Some retired, and some Lombardi traded, and some he cut, but one way or another, he got rid of people who had grown comfortable with defeat."[24]

The new Packers began the new season with a surprising 3–0 start, beating the Bears, Lions, and 49ers. Five consecutive losses followed, but the team rebounded to win their last four games to end the season with a 7–5 record for Green Bay's first winning season in 12 years.

The Green Bay players knew what to expect when they arrived for training camp in 1960. "Nobody showed up at training camp even a little bit out of shape," according to Jerry Kramer. "Lombardi had made physical fitness nuts out of all of us."[25]

Despite losing their first game of the season in 1960, the Packers won the Western Conference and headed to the NFL championship game versus the Eagles at Franklin Field in Philadelphia. The Eagles defeated the Packers 17–13 in a hard fought title game. In the locker room following the game, Lombardi addressed his team without criticism. "Perhaps you don't realize that you could have won this game," he calmly said. "We are men and we will never let this happen again. Now we can start preparing for next year."[26]

Like 1960, the Packers lost their first game the following season, then won 11 of their next 13 to wrap up their second straight conference championship. In the championship game, they were to meet the New York Giants, but there was a problem: Star halfback Paul Hornung was serving in the army and would have to miss the game. In the wake of the Berlin crisis, several military reservists were summoned during the season, including Packers middle linebacker Ray Nitschke and flanker Boyd Dowler. "They're doing a good job on us," said Lombardi. "You can't lose three frontliners and keep winning."[27]

Nitschke and Dowler would play in the 1961 championship game, but not Hornung, who was instructed to remain at Fort Riley, Kansas, much to Lombardi's dismay. But the Packers head coach had an idea. He had met President Kennedy earlier in the month at the National Football Foundation Hall of Fame dinner in New York. The president had given Lombardi the number of his personal private phone line and told him to call if he needed anything. Vince called the president and explained the situation. "Hornung isn't going to win the game on Sunday," the president said, "but football fans of this country deserve the two best teams on the field that day."[28]

In the 1961 championship game, at Green Bay, Hornung, freed to play by the president, led the Packers to a 37–0 rout of the Giants.

The 1962 Packers went 13–1 to win their conference for a third straight season. In the championship game at Yankee Stadium, the Giants were hungry to avenge their humiliating championship defeat from the year before. But neither the fired-up Giants nor the frigid weather and swirling winds could stop Lombardi's Packers. A touchdown run by Jim Taylor and three Jerry Kramer field goals lifted the Packers to a 16–7 win.

The 1963 Packers were expected to win again, but they were hamstrung before the season began when Paul Hornung was suspended for the entire season for gambling. The Packers went 11–2–1 that season, but those two losses, both to the Chicago Bears, were the difference. Bears head coach George Halas said before the season that his team had to beat Green Bay twice in order to win the championship, and that proved to be true. The Bears, who finished 11–1–2, went on to defeat the Giants, 14–10, in the championship game.

In 1964, Paul Hornung returned, but Lombardi was unable to disrupt the downward spiral. Green Bay finished with a disappointing 8–5–1 record to place second in their conference for the second consecutive season. Most coaches would be content with second place, but not Lombardi. To him it was either first place or last, with no in-between. Before the next season, he made it clear that he did not want to finish in second place ever again. He told his team that the reason for the two second place seasons was they had become "fatheaded" and stopped paying the price for success. He made it clear that his team would pay the price in 1965.[29]

When the Packers tied the 49ers in the last game of the 1965 season, they had achieved a 10–3–1 record to finish tied for first with the Baltimore Colts in the NFL's Western Conference. In a playoff at Green Bay to determine the best in the West, Don Chandler booted the game-winning field goal in overtime to lift the Packers to a 13–10 win over the Colts and propel the Packers into the championship game against the defending champs, the Cleveland Browns.

On a snowy day and a muddy field at Green Bay, the Green Bay offense used the well-known Lombardi power sweep as the main weapon to consistently gain yardage. Following playbook-type blocking, Paul Hornung and Jim Taylor carried the ball for over 200 yards to help pave the way to a 23–12 Green Bay win over the Browns.

In 1966, the Packers went 12–2 to capture their second straight Western Conference championship. In the championship game, they traveled to Dallas to meet the Cowboys. The Cowboys were a young, talented and well-coached team, headed by Tom Landry, the former defensive coordinator of the New York Giants during the days when Lombardi ran the New York offense. The Packers took a 14–0 lead, and then led 34–20 late in the contest. But the Cowboys rallied to cut the score to 34–27, and then drove to the Packers two-yard line with a little over a minute to play.

On fourth down and goal, and with the ball two yards from the Green Bay end zone, Cowboys quarterback Don Meredith rolled to the right as Packers outside linebacker Dave Robinson blitzed on the play. Number 89 of the Packers grabbed the Dallas quarterback around the neck, but Meredith was able to get off a desperation pass that Green Bay safety Tom Brown intercepted in the end zone to clinch the NFL championship. "Vince knew what I did was successful," Robinson would later say, "but he would never say that. He graded everyone's performance with plusses and minuses. He gave me a minus two on that play."[30]

For the first time ever, the NFL champions would play the AFL champions in Los Angeles in the world championship game, AFL versus NFL, before the name Super Bowl became official.

At stake was the pride of the National Football League. All other NFL team owners, executives, and players, who had cursed and hoped to beat the Packers every season, were now wishing Lombardi and the Packers the best in their matchup versus the Kansas City Chiefs. Lombardi felt the pressure leading up to the big game. In a five-minute interview before the big game, television announcer Frank Gifford said that Lombardi kept holding onto him and "was shaking like hell."[31] Not only were his Packers representing the entire NFL, they were playing for the Packers dynasty, and everything that Lombardi's Packers stood for. After a tight first half, the Packers turned it on in the second half to thump the Chiefs, 35–10.

The Lombardi Packers were now the class of all professional football. They had won four championships in the 1960s, including two in a row on two occasions, and they had also won the first matchup against the best of the AFL. The pressure of winning every season was taking its toll, though. Lombardi was tired. He suffered from dizziness, diarrhea and constipation. He had given up smoking in 1963 and took a physical every year, but refused his doctor's request to have a proctoscopy exam.

Could the Lombardi Packers win a third successive championship? Only one team in NFL history had done it: The Packers had won three in a row, from 1929 to 1931, although that did not count according to the coach. "The Little Sisters of the Poor could have won then," said Lombardi.[32] The 1967 season started off with a tie and three wins, but those wins were close games and unimpressive. The Packers then lost to the winless Vikings for their first loss of the season. Following the defeat, Lombardi called for a meeting with 14 of his players who had been with the team since their 1961 championship season. "Frankly, I'm worried," he told them. "I just don't know what to do." He warned the veterans that it was up to them to bring the "new boys" along, and to help him. This baffled the players. Lombardi had always known exactly what to do.[33]

The Packers responded by winning six of their next seven to clinch the Central Division of the Western Conference. But with two weeks remaining, the Packers went into the playoffs on a low by dropping the last two games of the season to finish with an unimpressive 9–4–1 record. The first of those two losses was to the Rams in Los Angeles when the Rams blocked a punt in the game's closing minutes and went on to score a game-winning touchdown for a 27–23 win. "That one really bothered Lombardi, because we lost on a fundamentals play," said Packers wide receiver Carroll Dale. "He was generally easier on us after a loss. He was toughest when we were winning, but after a loss he would make some adjustments and a few changes. He acted differently after the loss in Los Angeles. 'You don't deserve to be the winners that you are,' he told us the week after the game."[34]

In the Western Conference playoff game, the Packers played the Rams in Milwaukee. Los Angeles scored first to take a 7–0 lead, but the Packers rebounded to score four unanswered touchdowns for a 28–7 win to avenge the loss in Los Angeles and advance to the NFL championship game.

History was in Lombardi's grasp as the Packers hosted the Dallas Cowboys for the NFL title on December 31, 1967, at Lambeau Field, on the coldest New Year's Eve in Green Bay history. A win meant that Lombardi's quest to win three consecutive NFL championships would be fulfilled.

The temperature was a frigid 13 below zero, with a stiff wind that dropped the wind chill factor to minus 36, but that did not seem to affect the Packers offense, as Green Bay stormed to a 14–0 lead. But the Cowboys fought back, and then took the lead on the first play of the fourth quarter when a halfback option pass caught the Green Bay secondary flatfooted to produce the go-ahead score.

With the score 17–14, and with less than five minutes to play, the Packers went on a 68-yard scoring drive that would make history. The drive ended with 16 seconds to play, when guard Jerry Kramer and center Ken Bowman blocked Cowboys tackle Jethro Pugh to open a gap for quarterback Bart Starr to sneak through with the winning touchdown in a 21–17 Packers win—for the third consecutive NFL championship.

The Packers went on to beat the Oakland Raiders in the anticlimactic second Super Bowl, 33–14; that would be Lombardi's last game as head coach of Green Bay. A few weeks later, he announced his retirement. He would remain as Green Bay's general manager, but Phil Bengtson, the defensive coordinator during the Lombardi regime, was now the new head coach of the Packers.

In 1968, General Manager Lombardi would watch the practices while keeping his distance. He wanted to give Bengtson the same distance and freedom that he had requested when he took control of the Packers in 1959. He felt like an outsider. He was bored. Contract negotiations and other aspects of the general manager position proved not to be as challenging as he had thought.[35] The 1968 Packers finished out of the playoffs. Some said that age had caught up to the team. Others cited that it was due to Lombardi's retirement.

In February of 1969, Lombardi decided to seek new challenges by accepting the position of head coach of the Washington Redskins. Like the Packers job in 1959, the franchise had not had a winning season in over a decade. Unlike the old Packers, the Redskins, featuring a good passing game led by quarterback Sonny Jurgensen and wide receiver Charley Taylor, were far from being the worst team in professional football.

Under Lombardi's leadership, the Redskins finished with a 7–5–2 record for their first winning record since 1955. The future of the team seemed bright under the direction of Lombardi, and everyone looked forward to the 1970 season.

One day after the season, Washington linebacker/assistant coach Sam Huff encountered Lombardi in the Redskins office. Huff noted that the head coach was pale and looked ill. Startled by Lombardi's appearance, he suggested to the head coach to go and see a doctor. Lombardi agreed. In the spring the coach's stomach was bothering him. He began to take pills to ease his gastric distress. A few months later, he checked into the Georgetown Hospital. An examination revealed that he had a lesion in his left colon. Exploratory surgery performed a few days later revealed a malignant tumor. When the Redskins' 1970 training camp began in July, Lombardi was not there. He was released from the hospital and allowed to go home to recuperate. He was tired, fatigued, and getting weaker. He also was restless and wanted to get back to the job. One day he made a visit to training camp and addressed the rookies. He spoke but was hard to hear. "It was a moving experience," said Sam Huff. Lombardi had said something to the effect that they should be proud to wear the uniforms of the Washington Redskins.[36]

Lombardi went back to the hospital, and on September 3, 1970, the legendary coach died at the age of 57.

Vince Lombardi created a winning legacy and changed sports forever. Voted the greatest coach in NFL history by an ESPN panel of experts in 2013, Lombardi was once unknown and questioned about his lack of head coaching experience, but he left a blueprint for all leaders to follow. Even today, nearly half a century since his passing, people of all occupations examine his winning methods, hoping to create better teams and winning organizations.

NOTES

1. John Eisenberg, *That First Season* (Boston: Houghton Mifflin Harcourt, 2009), 45.
2. *Milwaukee Sentinel,* February 3, 1959.
3. Eisenberg, 91–92.
4. Robert J. Wells, *Vince Lombardi: His Life and Times* (Madison: Wisconsin House, 1971), 26.
5. David Maraniss, *When Pride Still Mattered: A Life of Vince Lombardi* (New York: Simon & Schuster, 1999), 24.
6. *Ibid.,* 27.
7. "All Scholastic Selections," *Brooklyn Daily Eagle*, December 4, 1932.
8. Wells, 30.
9. Jerry Kramer, *Lombardi: Winning Is the Only Thing* (New York: Pocket Books, 1971), 18.
10. Maraniss, 40.
11. *Ibid.,* 68.
12. Kramer, 26.
13. *Englewood Press*, September 21, 1939.
14. *Englewood Press,* November 13, 1941.
15. Wells, 56–57.
16. Kramer, 53.
17. Maraniss, 156.
18. *Ibid.*
19. *Ibid.,* 158.
20. Kramer, 53.
21. Jerry Kramer, *Jerry Kramer's Farewell to Football* (New York: World Publishing, 1969), 125.
22. Eisenberg, 41–42.
23. Kramer, 126.
24. *Ibid.,* 131.
25. *Ibid.,* 136.
26. Donald T. Phillips, *Run to Win: Vince Lombardi on Coaching and Leadership* (New York: St. Martin's Press, 2001), 44.
27. Bud Lea, *Magnificent Seven: The Championship Games That Built the Lombardi Dynasty* (Chicago: Triumph Books, 2002), 6.
28. *Ibid.*
29. Phillips, 157.
30. Lea, 103.
31. *Ibid.,* 106.
32. Jerry Kramer, *Instant Replay: The Diary of Jerry Kramer*, ed. Dick Schaap (New York: Signet, 1968), 208.
33. *Ibid.,* 139.
34. Carroll Dale interview with author, August 2014.
35. Wells, 139.
36. Sam Huff, *Tough Stuff* (New York: St. Martin's Press, 1988), 225.

Assistant Coaches

ED BRYANT

Six men assisted Vince Lombardi in 1966, the year the Green Bay Packers were the first team to claim what is now the Lombardi Trophy.[1] Three of them helped with the defense: Phil Bengtson, Dave Hanner, and Jerry Burns. On the offensive side of the ball were Red Cochran, Ray Wietecha, and Bob Schnelker.

Lombardi, who had never lived in a climate like Green Bay's, must have taken com-

Head Coach Vince Lombardi, assistant coaches Jerry Burns, Red Cochran, Ray Wietecha, Dave Hanner, Phil Bengtson, Bob Schnelker (NFL Illustrated Green Bay Game Program).

fort knowing that Phil Bengtson had grown up in Roseau, Minnesota, with its equally serious winters, when he hired Bengtson as a chief defensive assistant in 1959. For Bengtson, an All-American and All-Big Ten tackle at the University of Minnesota, the position meant a job, which he needed, but it also meant leaving lovely San Francisco for the cold weather and yet another job as an assistant, and this after Bengtson had recommended himself for the same head coaching position the Packers had conferred on Lombardi. Except for his military service with the Navy from 1942 to 1945 during World War II, Bengtson had been living in the Bay Area since 1940, when his Minnesota connections to the legendary Clark Shaughnessy brought him to Stanford.

Bengtson and Shaughnessy both played college football for Minnesota, but the bridge between them was Bernie Bierman. For Bierman, Shaughnessy was first teammate, then coach, then boss, and then benefactor, when Shaughnessy facilitated Bierman's first job as a head coach, as Shaughnessy's successor at Tulane. Bierman was Bengtson's head coach at Minnesota, and then his boss there, until Bengtson left him for Shaughnessy and Stanford.

In Bengtson's career, he would assist both Bierman and Shaughnessy. His first coaching job in 1935 took him to the University of Missouri, but in 1938, Bierman hired him, and Bengtson would remain as a Minnesota assistant until he joined Shaughnessy in moving to Stanford in 1940.[2]

Bengtson was an assistant at Stanford from 1940 to 1941 and 1946 to 1950, moving to the NFL and San Francisco 49ers in 1951. He assisted three different 49er head coaches from 1951 to 1958.[3]

Lombardi's defensive line coach in 1966 was Dave "Hawg" Hanner, long familiar to Packer fans as a member of Green Bay's 1961 and 1962 champions. Hanner was a defensive tackle at Arkansas, drafted in the fifth round of the 1952 NFL Draft by the Packers with the 52nd pick. Hanner played on the line for the Packers from 1952 to 1964. Following his playing career he was an assistant coach with the Packers from 1965 to 1979 and 1982, serving under Lombardi, Bengtson, Dan Devine and Bart Starr. He also later served as a scout for Green Bay.[4]

After quarterbacking Michigan to a 1951 Rose Bowl win over California, Jerry Burns began his long coaching career serving as both head baseball coach and assistant football coach at the University of Hawaii in 1951. Burns joined George Allen at Whittier in 1952, as an assistant football coach. He also served as head basketball coach at Whittier, and he must have liked being a head coach, because in 1953, Burns stepped down and took a job as head coach of both basketball and football at St. Mary's of Redford High School in his native Michigan.[5]

The step down paid off just a year later, when his fellow former Michigan Wolverine, Forest Evashevski, hired Burns to assist him at the University of Iowa. After one year as freshman coach and two years coaching the backs on both sides of the ball, Burns succeeded Bump Elliott as the coach of Evashevski's defense. Then, in 1961, Burns was rewarded, succeeding Evashevski as head coach of the Hawkeyes. In 1962, he became the first Iowa head coach who could claim wins over both Michigan and Ohio State in the same season. Five years into his tenure, though, with *Playboy* predicting a number one national ranking, Burns' 1965 team failed to live up to the pre-season hype, and unimaginably so, turning in a 1–9 record that cost Burns his job. Burns became an assistant again in 1966, but at the highest level, as a defensive secondary coach with the defending NFL champion Packers.[6]

Burns served on Lombardi's staff in 1966 and 1967. After Lombardi retired following the 1967 season, Burns joined the Vikings as offensive coordinator under Head Coach Bud Grant. He served under Grant for the next 17 seasons. Burns hoped to be chosen to succeed Grant who led the Vikings to four Super Bowls, but he was passed over in favor of Les Steckel in 1984 when Grant retired. Burns had to settle for succeeding the second Bud Grant, the one who came back in 1985 when Steckel lost the job after a single season; only in 1986 did Burns finally get his wish to succeed Grant coaching the Vikings. Burns coached the Vikings for the next six seasons fashioning a 55–46 record.[7]

John Thurman "Red" Cochran Jr., was a fine all-around athlete at Wake Forest. After serving as a B-24 Liberator pilot during World War II he played three seasons for the Chicago Cardinals from 1947 to 1949. Red was a cornerback, punter, return specialist, and running back for the Cardinals. His career was cut short by a knee injury but he was a member of the 1947 NFL champion Cardinals. Red was an assistant coach at Wake Forest from 1951 to 1955, and an assistant with the Detroit Lions from 1956 to 1958. George Wilson, Cochran's boss in Detroit, hired Scooter McLean to fill Cochran's job in 1959, and Cochran went to work for Lombardi as his offensive backfield coach.[8]

Harland Svare, a linebacker with the Rams and Giants, went into coaching after his playing career was over. Although Svare never coached a minute of Packer football, as coach of the Rams from 1962 to 1965, he played an indirect role in shaping the 1966 Packers staff. When Svare played under Tom Landry in New York, Lombardi, the other key Giants assistant, had on his side of the ball Ray Wietecha at center and Bob Schnelker at end. When Svare became head coach of the Rams, he hired both as assistants; Wietecha to coach the offensive line and Schnelker the receivers.

Both Wietecha and Schnelker would in time be reunited with Lombardi in Green Bay, but their departures from the Rams occurred a year apart. In 1965, Ray Wietecha essentially swapped the Rams and Packers offensive line jobs with yet another former Giant, Bill Austin, and a year later, with Svare out as Rams coach, Schnelker left Los Angeles and joined the Packers, just in time for the first Super Bowl.

Before anyone can punt or place-kick, the ball has to come back fast and clean, and the 1966 Packers had an offensive line coach in Ray Wietecha who was one of the best long snappers ever. Wietecha didn't call attention to his snaps during games, but he told proudly a story that made it into his obituary. It was before the 1958 Pro Bowl, and Cleveland immortal Lou Groza was practicing, with Tommy McDonald as his holder. The Hall of Famer Groza was astonished by Wietecha's no-look snaps, perfect every time, and Wietecha carried the praise with him like a badge of honor.[9]

Before Wietecha became a Giant, he served in the Marines, attended two colleges, and played baseball professionally, but he found his niche in life on the offensive line, the football birthplace of Bengtson and Lombardi as well. Wietecha was the Giants center from 1953 to 1962. He was a key member of the 1956 NFL Champions, and was named to multiple Pro Bowls and All-Pro Teams.

The job of coaching the Packers offensive line required repetition and attention to detail. Vince Lombardi's philosophy was to do the simple perfectly, no matter that the defense could come to know what to expect. The Packer sweep, for instance, was one percent chalk and 99 percent execution. Cochran's backs would follow Austin and then Wietecha's charges on the sweep, and it attests to their success that Forrest Gregg and Jerry Kramer and Fuzzy Thurston are nearly as well-known as Jim Taylor and probably better known than Carroll Dale or Boyd Dowler, whose job it was to catch the ball.

Dale and Dowler's position coach was Bob Schnelker. Schnelker played his college ball at Bowling Green when it was still possible to be the 377th player chosen in the draft, as Schnelker was in 1950 by the Browns, but he didn't enter the NFL until 1953, when he played eight games as a Philadelphia Eagle. Schnelker worked with Lombardi in New York and Green Bay, and with Wietecha in New York and Los Angeles and Green Bay, but spent even more years working with Jerry Burns, beginning in 1966 in Green Bay. Schnelker was Burns' offensive coordinator in Minnesota from 1986 to 1990.[10]

Schnelker had the fewest catches in his seven years with the Giants in 1956, when the Giants were champions, and the most in 1960, when his 38 catches were not enough to overcome the Giants getting swept by the Eagles. The Giants had been conference champions three out of the four previous seasons, but 1960 hurt for another reason. With the retirement of Jim Lee Howell after the 1960 season, the Giants offense went in a new direction in 1961, with Y.A. Tittle and Joe Walton brought in to replace Charlie Conerly and Schnelker.[11]

Schnelker stayed on with the Packers after Lombardi, through Phil Bengtson's time as head coach, and then in 1972, he was re-united with Harland Svare as the San Diego's Chargers "head offensive coach," what today we would call coordinator. Working his way from San Diego to Miami to Kansas City to Detroit, Schnelker returned to Green Bay in 1982 and worked under Bart Starr and Forrest Gregg for four years, which were followed by five years as the offensive coordinator in Minnesota under Jerry Burns.

NOTES

　1. www.profootballarchives.com.

　2. americanfootballdatabase.wikia.com; James W. Johnson, *The Wow Boys: A Coach, a Team, and a Turning Point in College Football* (Lincoln: University of Nebraska Press), 2006.

　3. www.profootballarchives.com; www.pro-football-reference.com.

　4. www.pro-football-reference.com.

　5. Eight days before the Super Bowl, the *Appleton Post Crescent* reported that Kansas City Chiefs tight end Fred Arbanas had been coached at St. Mary Redford High School in Detroit by Jerry Burns; Wikipedia reports that Burns was St. Mary's head coach for baseball and basketball as well as football.

　6. cfbdatawarehouse.com; J.A. Allen, "Iowa Football: 5 Seasons More Disappointing than 2010," bleacherreport.com, December10, 2010, bleacherereport.com.

　7. www.pro-football-reference.com.

　8. The Associated Press reported that McLean would join the Lions on December 18, 1958, and on February 4, 1959, announced the hiring of Cochran and Bengtson by Green Bay. Martin Hendricks, "Red Cochran Joined Packers Organization in 1959, Helped It Become Dynasty," jsonline.com, August 4, 2015, www.jsonline.com.

　9. Richard Goldstein, "Ray Wietecha, Key to Giants' Glory Days, Dies at 74," nytimes.com, December 22, 2002, www.nytimes.com.

　10. www.pro-football-reference.com.

　11. *Ibid.*

Ownership

JOHN MAXYMUK

When the New England Patriots won Super Bowl XLVIII over the Seattle Seahawks, NFL Commissioner Roger Goodell did what commissioners have been doing for decades: he awarded the Vince Lombardi Trophy to the victorious team's owner, in this case, Robert Kraft. When the Green Bay Packers won the pro football championship for the 1966 season, three things were very different about the celebration.

First, the game officially was called the AFL-NFL World Championship Game; the term Super Bowl would not be adopted until the third iteration of the game following the 1968 season. Second, the championship trophy was not renamed the Vince Lombardi Trophy until after the coach's death in 1970. Third, Commissioner Pete Rozelle could not award the first championship trophy to the Packers' owner because the team is publicly-owned. Green Bay is the only NFL franchise owned by shareholders and operated by an elected board of directors, and it will remain the only one since that ownership model was banned by the league in 1960, with the Packers grandfathered into the league's by-laws.

The origins of this unique ownership structure date almost to the origins of the team itself and to the team's patron saint, Curly Lambeau. After dropping out of Notre Dame, Lambeau took a job with the local Indian Packing Company in 1919 and got married to his high school sweetheart Marguerite. That fall, Curly joined up with the men reorganizing Green Bay's town football team. Lambeau was elected captain, and he arranged with his boss at Indian Packing, Frank Peck, for the company to sponsor the team by paying for uniforms. A year later, the Indian Packing Company was taken over by the Acme Packing Company, run by brothers John and Emmett Clair, and Acme continued to sponsor the semipro Packers.

In 1921 at Lambeau's urging, the Clairs successfully applied for a franchise in the American Professional Football League as the NFL was then called. Lambeau's arrangement with Acme Packing was similar to George Halas' set up with the Staley Starch Company at the time. Halas, however, was able to acquire full ownership of the Bears over time; Lambeau was not able to muster the financial clout to do that. The Packers went 3–2–1 in the NFL that year, but then had their franchise revoked because Lambeau had used underclassmen for a game late in the season. That was not an unheard of practice at the time, but it was against the rules. At this point the Clairs bowed out of the picture.

Lambeau himself was granted a new franchise by the league in July 1922 and was running the team, but not backing it. With the assistance of publicity man George Calhoun of the *Green Bay Press Gazette*, he raised money from local backers to stake the team. However, by the middle of the 1922 season, the undercapitalized Packers were in financial turmoil again. Calhoun brought in *Press Gazette* publisher Andrew Turnbull who used a stock sale to generate money and get the team on firm financial footing by converting them into a nonprofit publicly-owned corporation—the Green Bay Football Corporation. That first stock sale sold shares at $5 apiece and raised over $7,000.

Turnbull, Lambeau and three other community leaders (businessman Leland H. Joannes, Dr. W. Weber Kelly, and attorney Gerald Clifford) became known as "The Hungry Five," and they managed the fortunes of the team for several years to come, although the team actually was owned by the community. Lambeau continued as the front man. There were other small-town teams in the league during these years that relied on local boosters to financially back the team, such as the Rock Island Independents, Pottsville Maroons and Portsmouth Spartans, but only the Packers survived. Historian Craig Coenen makes the point in *From Sandlots to the Super Bowl* that the biggest difference between the Spartans, the last small town team to disappear from the NFL, and the Packers was the local economy. Portsmouth, Ohio, was ravaged by a flood and by the failure of the local shoe manufacturing industry, while Green Bay fared better through the Depression because its local industry of toilet paper was sturdier. Thus, local businesses and fans were better able to support the team in those tough times.

That's not to say that there weren't more financial crises to endure. In the midst of the Great Depression in 1931, an allegedly inebriated fan fell through the wooden bleachers in old City Stadium and broke two vertebrae in his back. He sued the team and won a $5,000 judgment that the team could not pay once its insurance company went bankrupt. The team was placed into receivership to protect it from creditors. In order to climb out of that hole, the original corporation was dissolved and a limited stock sale was held in 1935 to create Green Bay Packers, Inc. Once again the fans bought shares in the Packers, shares that would never pay a dividend and could only be sold back to the corporation at the original sale price. That sale price was $25 in 1935, and over $13,000 was raised.

With the team in deep decline on the field in the late 1940s, a third stock sale was arranged in 1950 and netted roughly $125,000. Again, shares were offered at $25 each, but this time it was stipulated that no one could buy more than 200 shares. The team's fourth stock sale occurred in 1997 following a Super Bowl triumph. That year 106,000 shares were sold at $200 each and netted $24 million for the team's capital improvements. The most recent stock sale sold 268,000 shares at $250 each and gained $67 million for renovations of Lambeau Field in 2012. There are now over 360,000 shareholders of Green Bay Packers, Inc., and the corporation's annual meeting drew 15,000 to Lambeau Field in 2015.

So there is no single owner, but there is a team president, hired by the board of directors, who also leads the team's seven-person executive committee. So in 2011, Commissioner Goodell could present the Vince Lombardi Trophy to Packers president Mark Murphy. Murphy is the eleventh team president: Andrew Turnbull (1923–27); Ray Enrard (1928); Dr. W. Weber Kelly (1929); Lee Joannes (1930–47); Emil Fischer (1948–52); Russ Bogda (1953–57) Dominic Olejniczak (1958–81) Robert Parins (1982–88) Bob Harlan (1989–2007); John Jones (2007); and Murphy (2008–).

In 1966, though, the situation was different. Yes, Dominic Olejniczak was president, but Lombardi ran the team and thus accepted the trophy that would later bear his name. Lombardi insisted on complete control when he accepted the job of coach/general manager in 1959 and rewarded Olejniczak's faith by winning five championships in the 1960s.

Ultimately, no matter what ownership structure is in place, a team's success or failure depends on the abilities of those in charge. If a team owner hires the right football people who make the right decisions about the team, then winning will follow. Similarly, losses will ensue from a team whose leaders are ineffectual or incompetent. The Packers declined in the late 1940s as Lambeau lost his touch. They continued losing under a series of coaches in the 1950s, but it also should be pointed out that those coaches were undermined by self-important board members meddling in the day-to-day operations on the field. Lombardi, strong and capable, ended that, and the team succeeded.

After Lombardi, the team was led poorly at all three levels of management: president, general manager and coach. Olejniczak, who picked the right man in Lombardi, did not do so in his ensuing hires, and the team declined again. It took the leadership of Bob Harlan, Ron Wolf and Mike Holmgren to restore the luster to the Green and Gold. No matter what, the publicly-owned Green Bay Packers cannot be sold and will never be moved. No other franchise can make those claims to its devoted fans.

REFERENCES

Coenen, Craig. *From Sandlots to the Super Bowl: The National Football League, 1920–1967*. Knoxville: University of Tennessee Press, 2005.

Names, Larry. *The History of the Green Bay Packers: Book I: The Lambeau Years Part One*. Wautoma: Angel Press of Wisconsin, 1987.

_____. *The History of the Green Bay Packers: Book II: The Lambeau Years Part Two*. Wautoma: Angel Press of Wisconsin, 1989.

_____. *The History of the Green Bay Packers: Book III: The Lambeau Years Part Three*. Wautoma: Angel Press of Wisconsin, 1990.

_____. *The History of the Green Bay Packers: Book IV: The Shameful Years*. Wautoma: Angel Press of Wisconsin, 1995.

Building the Team

JOHN MAXYMUK

It's not a stretch to say that putting together the 1966 world champion Green Bay Packer roster was a process over a decade in the making. When legendary team founder Curly Lambeau was forced out following the 1949 season, the cupboard was bare. The only players from that 1949 team to receive any All-Pro consideration in the 1950s were centers Ed Neal and Jay Rhodemyre, and by 1953 both of those players were retired. New coach Gene Ronzani was building from scratch as an expansion team would. The smartest move that Ronzani made was hiring Jack Vainisi, a 23-year-old former Notre Dame lineman whose playing career ended when he contracted rheumatic fever in the army, as the team's talent scout and head of player personnel.

It was a laborious process, but over ten drafts, Vainisi acquired a boatload of talent that coaches Ronzani, Lisle Blackbourn and Scooter McLean failed to use to its full potential. The coaches also were hindered by a meddling and incompetent board of directors. Vainisi took a proactive role in the 1959 search for a new coach, contacting Paul Brown and George Halas for their insight. In fact, Jack was a major orchestrator behind-the-scenes of the hiring of Lombardi and recommended to Vince that he insist on total control of the franchise to ward off the meddlers. Under Vince Lombardi, all that talent began to win games. Packer fans owe much to what the unsung Vainisi was able to accomplish during the wan decade of the 1950s.

In the ten NFL drafts from 1951 to 1960, Vainisi selected 19 players who would become All-Pros or Pro Bowlers as Packers, and five of them would be elected to the Hall of Fame. If you add in undrafted free agent Willie Wood, whom Jack signed, and Herb Adderley, drafted by Lombardi on Jack's recommendation prior to his sudden demise late in 1960, that makes seven Hall of Famers. Eighteen of the 22 starters on Lombardi's first championship team in 1961 were either drafted by Vainisi or signed by him as free agents; the other four were acquired by Lombardi via trade. Even the 1966 championship team five years later featured Jack's players as nine of the 22 starters.

Chronologically, the first member of the 1966 Packers to come to Green Bay was end Max McGee, a fourth round draft pick in 1954. He was followed in 1956 by second round pick Hall of Fame tackle Forrest Gregg, fifth rounder All-Pro tackle Bob Skoronski and 17th round shot-in-the-dark Hall of Fame quarterback Bart Starr. 1957 top pick Paul Hornung was finishing his Hall of Fame career in 1966. The 1958 draft brought two Hall of Famers and an All-Pro for the 1966 team: fullback Jim Taylor in round two, linebacker Ray Nitschke in round three and guard Jerry Kramer in round four. Vainisi drafted receiver Boyd Dowler in the third round in 1959 before Lombardi arrived. Vince made two key trades that year that brought two starters for the 1966 champs. Guard Fuzzy Thurston was acquired from Baltimore for linebacker Marv Matuszak, and defensive tackle Henry Jordan came from Cleveland for a fourth round draft pick.

Lombardi's second season of 1960 brought two more Hall of Famers: undrafted free agent safety Willie Wood and defensive end Willie Davis, acquired from Cleveland for end A.D. Williams. When Vainisi died of a heart attack in December 1960, his position was filled first by Dick Voris and then by Pat Peppler, but Lombardi also took on more responsibility for the player drafts. In 1961, Vince selected three men who would be starters in 1966: Herb Adderley in round one, defensive tackle Ron Kostelnik in round two and halfback Elijah Pitts in round 13. Nineteen sixty-two was a washout, but four 1966 starters and one key reserve arrived in 1963. Defensive back Bob Jeter had been the team's second round pick in 1960, but chose to play Canadian football instead; he came south to Green Bay in 1963. The 1963 draft produced linebacker Dave Robinson in the first round, defensive end Lionel Aldridge in the fourth and tight end Marv Fleming in the 11th. Quarterback Zeke Bratkowski came over from the Rams in midseason with center Ken Iman going to Los Angeles in exchange at the end of the year.

The second round pick from 1963, safety Tom Brown, played major league baseball with the Washington Senators in 1963 before returning to the gridiron in 1964. Another defensive back, Doug Hart, was acquired on waivers from the Cardinals in 1963 and spent that season on the Green Bay taxi squad before making the team in 1964. A major trade with Philadelphia brought linebacker Lee Roy Caffey and a 1965 first round pick to the Packers in exchange for center Jim Ringo and fullback Earl Gros. The 1964 draft brought several key reserves for the 1966 team: linebacker Tommy Joe Crutcher in round three; receiver Bob Long in round four; tackle Steve Wright in round five and center Ken Bowman in round eight.

A "future" draft pick in round 20 of 1964 brought center Bill Curry who joined the team in 1965. Three trades delivered three more essential pieces for the championship run. Receiver Carroll Dale was acquired from the Rams for Dan Currie; tight end Bill Anderson came from the Redskins for a sixth round pick and kicker Don Chandler arrived from the Giants for a late round pick. The 1965 draft only produced one 1966 player who made the team in 1965—tight end Allen Brown—and he was on injured reserve that year.

There were three "future" picks in the 1965 draft who reported to the Packers in 1966: first rounder halfback Donny Anderson, 11th rounder defensive end Jim Weatherwax and 16th rounder linebacker Phil Vandersea. The 1966 draft delivered first rounders fullback Jim Grabowski and guard Gale Gillingham as well as 17th rounder defensive back Dave Hathcock. Minor leaguer defensive tackle Bob Brown was signed as a free agent off the Wheeling Ironmen of the Continental Football League, and receiver Red Mack was picked up on waivers during the season from the Falcons.

Altogether, 29 of the 1966 Packers were drafted by Green Bay, eight were acquired in trades, two came from the waiver wire, one from the minor leagues and one was an undrafted free agent. Four of the 29 draftees were selected as "futures" while they were still underclassmen. Eight of the starters (six on offense and two on defense) were drafted by Jack Vainisi and eight (three on offense and five on defense) by Vince Lombardi. Five of the starters came via trade (two offense and three defense), and one defensive player was signed as an undrafted free agent.

The 1966 champions were following on the heels of the 1965 champions. Eight players from that team were replaced in 1966, and all were upgrades. Three players were lost to the Atlanta Falcons in the expansion draft: guard Dan Grimm, halfback Junior Coffey and third quarterback Dennis Claridge. Grimm was replaced by future All-Pro Gale Gillingham, Coffey was replaced by the versatile rookie Donny Anderson and Claridge was replaced on the roster by special teams gunner Red Mack, with new third quarterback Kent Nix being held on the taxi squad. Four players were traded: halfback Tom Moore to the Rams for Ron Smith, Dick Arndt and a second round pick; fullback Allen Jacobs to the Giants for a seventh round pick; defensive end Lloyd Voss to the Steelers with 1966 draft pick Tony Jeter for a number one pick in 1967; and defensive back Hank Gremminger to the Cowboys for a fifth round pick. Moore was replaced by rookie Phil Vandersea as Lombardi added a fifth linebacker rather than a fourth halfback; Jacobs was replaced by top draft pick Jim Grabowski; Voss was replaced by rookie Jim Weatherwax; and Gremminger was replaced by rookie Dave Hathcock. Finally, defensive tackle Bud Marshall was cut and replaced by free agent rookie Bob Brown.

Training camp began on Wednesday, July 13, with 22 of 26 rookies reporting and 26 of 35 veterans. There was actually a lot more NFL talent in that 1966 Green Bay training camp than the Packers could use, so draft picks Fred Heron, Tony Jeter, Ron Rector and Ralph Wenzel as well as holdover taxi squad member Ray Schoenke were all traded for future draft picks. As noted above, the team's third quarterback, Kent Nix, was assigned to the taxi squad. Nix was joined there by receivers Jeff White and Sonny Redders, guard Roy Schmidt and defensive back/kicker Larry Moore. White and Schmidt were future draft choices from 1965, while Nix, Redders and Moore were undrafted free agents. None would ever play with Green Bay although Nix and Schmidt would play in the NFL.

Quarterback Ron Smith, acquired from the Rams, lost out to free agent Kent Nix and was traded to the Steelers for whom he went 2–5 as a starter in 1966. Two members of the 1965 Packers' taxi squad, guard Eli Strand and halfback Bill Symons, were both cut in August, but landed elsewhere. Strand spent 1966 with Pittsburgh and started in New Orleans in 1967 before his reputation as a clubhouse lawyer ended his career. Symons signed with the BC Lions of the Canadian Football League in 1966, and then had a Hall of Fame CFL career with Toronto from 1967 to 1973. He was the Most Outstanding Player in the CFL in 1968 and one of three players cut by Lombardi to make the Canadian Hall, along with George Dixon cut in 1959 and Garney Henley cut in 1960.

Trades of excess talent for more draft picks, used in conjunction with futures draft picks, were Lombardi's attempt to keep the Packers on top. The "futures" rule, initiated in 1949 according to *Total Football*, allowed teams to draft a player who had eligibility remaining if his original class had graduated. Because of this rule, there are several discrepancies between the year a player was drafted and the year he joined the Packers. A good team that did not need as many immediate reinforcements could take advantage of the rule and draft players a year early that might not be available in their actual draft class. All-American halfback Donny Anderson is the most famous example, in that he was drafted in the first round in 1965, but finished his Texas Tech eligibility that year before signing with Green Bay in 1966. The futures rule ran counter to the egalitarian purpose of the draft and was rescinded with the 1967 merger between the leagues. By draft class, these are the 29 players originally drafted by the Packers.

> 1954—Max McGee
> 1956—Forrest Gregg, Bob Skoronski and Bart Starr
> 1957—Paul Hornung
> 1958—Jim Taylor, Ray Nitschke and Jerry Kramer
> 1959—Boyd Dowler
> 1960—Bob Jeter
> 1961—Herb Adderley, Ron Kostelnik and Elijah Pitts
> 1963—Dave Robinson, Tom Brown, Lionel Aldridge and Marv Fleming
> 1964—Tommy Joe Crutcher, Bob Long, Steve Wright, Ken Bowman and Bill Curry
> 1965—Donny Anderson, Allen Brown, Jim Weatherwax and Phil Vandersea
> 1966—Jim Grabowski, Gale Gillingham and Dave Hathcock

On the whole, Vince Lombardi was very skilled in using trades to improve his club. He was able to obtain two Hall of Fame defensive linemen (Willie Davis and Henry Jordan) from Cleveland for a mid-round draft pick and a poor receiver, an All-Pro guard (Fuzzy Thurston) from Baltimore for a journeyman linebacker and other key players (Carroll Dale, Don Chandler and Bill Anderson) for late draft picks and spent veterans. His trade of aging center Jim Ringo and disappointing fullback Earl Gros for Lee Roy Caffey and a first round draft pick gave Green Bay a chance to get younger. Lombardi was continually swapping players he couldn't use for draft picks and stockpiled multiple first round picks from 1965 to 1968 in this way.

The draft pick stockpiling should have allowed the dynasty to continue beyond the final title in 1967, but Vince's draft choices did not pan out as well as they could have. Green Bay managed to maintain a top defense in the wake of Lombardi, and its rebuilt offensive line, which included tackle Dick Himes, guards Gillingham and Bill Lueck and center Ken Bowman, was pretty solid, but the offensive skill positions were never properly replaced. Donny Anderson proved to be a very good player, but he was not Paul Hornung, and Jim Grabowski's career was derailed by injuries. All the young receivers were completely substandard, but the biggest deficit was at quarterback where Dennis Claridge, Kent Nix, Don Horn and Billy Stevens all proved to be failures in the NFL and couldn't replace aging and ailing Bart Starr.

REFERENCES

Carroll, Bob, Michael Gershman, David Neft, and John Thorn. *Total Football.* New York: Harper, 1997.
Green Bay Press Gazette.
Milwaukee Journal.
Milwaukee Sentinel.
www.pro-football-reference.com.

The 1966 Draft

CHRIS WILLIS

As the Packers were finishing up the 1965 NFL season, which would end with their first of three consecutive NFL championship wins (1965–1967), Vince Lombardi and his staff were also preparing for the 1966 NFL draft in an odd place. Unlike today when the NFL draft is a year-round TV spectacle that lasts until April or May, the 1966 draft was held near the end of the 1965 season. On Thanksgiving weekend—Saturday, November 27—the NFL held their annual players selection draft, and the Packers front office brass was sitting in a hotel conference room in the city of Los Angeles as they prepared to play the Rams that Sunday. Because the merger was seven months away the rival American Football League (AFL) also held its draft on the same day. The two leagues were still in the midst of a money-grubbing battle over players. In the 1966 draft the top player both leagues wanted was Texas linebacker Tommy Nobis, who ultimately was taken number one overall by the expansion Atlanta Falcons, who signed the All-American away from the AFL's Houston Oilers.

As for the Packers, they planned a simple strategy for their draft. Vince Lombardi knew his team was getting old at some positions—although the roster was still very talented and very deep. But two positions looked to be getting long in the tooth: offensive line and, of more importance, running back. Paul Hornung (rookie in 1957) and Jim Taylor (rookie in 1958) had combined to play 16 years with the Packers with over 2,400 rushing attempts. Lombardi looked to replace his two future Hall of Fame running backs, and both Hornung and Taylor would play their last season in Green Bay in 1966.

The plan to replace his star running backs started a year earlier in the 1965 draft when Lombardi drafted Texas Tech running back Donny Anderson as a future pick, number seventh overall. Anderson became an All-American in 1965, finishing fourth in the Heisman Trophy, with over 1,500 yards from scrimmage and 17 touchdowns. After his senior season, he signed with the Packers.

As Lombardi looked deeper at the 1966 draft, he found some very talented running backs coming out of college. He watched film of West Virginia fullback Dick Leftridge, and he also watched speedy Mike Garrett of USC, who ran for 1,440 yards, scored 13 touchdowns and won the 1965 Heisman Trophy. But Garrett lacked the size for Lombardi's power sweep; he was only five-feet-nine and weighed 190 pounds. The player that grabbed Lombardi's attention was Illinois running back Jim Grabowski.

Grabowski had both size, at six-feet-two and 220 pounds, and speed. He was a perfect fit for Lombardi's offense, and Saint Vince envisioned Anderson and Grabowski as his new Taylor-and-Hornung. The only problem was that nobody knew for whom Grabowski wanted to play, either the NFL or AFL. During the AFL draft, the expansion Miami Dolphins selected Grabowski in the first round with the number one overall pick. At the end of the day, young Grabowski had the upper hand on the two rival leagues. He actually wanted to stay close to home but kept that information to himself.

When the draft started on November 27 the Packers had two first round picks, the pick at number nine that they got for losing end Ron Kramer to the Detroit Lions as a free agent, and their own pick, number 13 overall. As the first round unfolded, Lombardi liked his chances of getting Grabowski. Nobis went number one to the Falcons; Michigan offensive tackle Tom Mack (as of 2015, the only Hall of Famer selected in the 1966 NFL draft) was selected number two overall by the Los Angeles Rams; the Steelers selected running back Leftridge third; Indiana defensive end Randy Beisler went fourth to the Eagles; Iowa guard John Niland fifth to the Cowboys; the Redskins surprised everyone by taking Princeton kicker Charlie Gogolak sixth; Purdue tackle Jerry Shay went seventh to the Vikings; and Oklahoma linebacker Carl McAdams went eighth to the Cardinals.

Now the Packers were on the clock. Lombardi didn't waste much time in selecting Jim Grabowski with the ninth overall choice. Three picks later Lombardi was back on the clock. This time he went for help on the offensive line. When the 1966 Packers season started four of the five Packers offensive linemen were 30 years or older—RT Bob Skoronski (32), LG Fuzzy Thurston (33), RG Jerry Kramer (30) and RT Forrest Gregg (33). Only center Bill Curry (who was 24) was younger. So Lombardi loaded up on young offensive linemen.

At 13 in the first round of the 1966 NFL draft, the Packers selected Minnesota offensive tackle Gale Gillingham who turned out to be a gem. At six-feet-three, 255 pounds, Gillingham was quickly moved to guard by Lombardi. After playing mostly as a backup in 1966, Gillingham became a starter at left guard, then right guard, and played the next nine years for the Packers.

After drafting Gillingham, the Packers selected two more tackles, future pick junior Tom Cichowski (Maryland) in the second round and Fred Heron (San Jose State) in the third round; Heron would play mainly defensive tackle. Then Lombardi went back to the running backs position, as he selected five backs over the next eight draft choices. Sadly, only Grabowski would make the team and make plays for the Packers.

Over the draft's 20 rounds, Lombardi would eventually select 20 players. Sticking to his game plan, Lombardi would pick six running backs and six offensive linemen/tight ends- more than half the draft choices.

1966 Green Bay Packers NFL Draft Choices

Round	Overall	Name of Draft Choice	Position	School
1st	9	Jim Grabowski	FB	Illinois
1st	13	Gale Gillingham	T	Minnesota
2nd	30	Tom Cichowski	T	Maryland*
3rd	45	Fred Heron	T	San Jose State
3rd	46	Tony Jeter	E	Nebraska
4th	62	John Roderick	HB	Southern Methodist
7th	108	Ray Miller	E	Idaho*
8th	124	Ken McLean	HB	Texas A&M
9th	138	Ron Rector	HB	Northwestern
10th	154	Sam Montgomery	HB	Southern
11th	168	Ralph Wenzel	C	San Diego State
12th	184	Jim Mankins	FB	Florida State*
13th	198	Ed King	LB	USC*
14th	214	Ron Hanson	E	North Dakota State
15th	228	Grady Bolton	T	Mississippi State
16th	244	Robert Schultz	DE	Wisconsin–Stevens Point
17th	258	Dave Hathcock	DB	Memphis State
18th	274	Jim Jones	DE	Nebraska–Omaha
19th	288	Dave Moton	TE	USC
20th	304	Ed Maras	E	South Dakota State

*Selected as Juniors

Three weeks after the draft, first round pick Jim Grabowski chose the NFL's Green Bay Packers over the AFL's Miami Dolphins. On December 20 at the Drake Hotel in Chicago Grabowski was introduced to the media. "I choose the National League because I've lived in Chicago and want to play around home," said Grabowski. "Lombardi is a great coach and Green Bay a great team." In the end, the Dolphins didn't have a chance. Lombardi had his guy. "Real happy to have Grabowski. He's a real fine running back," Lombardi replied quietly about his rookie running back.[1]

Unfortunately, Vince Lombardi didn't pick many good players in the 1966 NFL draft. One of his problems was that he had such a talented and deep roster there just weren't many open spots on his team. Another problem was that 1966 was a weak draft class. Out of the 20 players selected only three made the 1966 Packers roster: both first round picks, Jim Grabowski and Gale Gillingham, as well as 17th round pick defensive back Dave Hathcock. The roster was just too deep and talented for the rest of the 1966 draft class.

Maybe the draft distracted Lombardi and his staff because the day after selecting 20 players the Packers played their worst game of the 1965 season. Facing an awful Los Angeles Rams team that was just 1–9, and had lost eight games in a row, Lombardi's offense was smothered by the Rams' defense. The Fearsome Foursome front four held the Packers rushing game to just 22 yards to upset Green Bay 21–10.

As the Packers' 1966 training camp went on at St. Norbert College in De Pere, Wisconsin, Lombardi could see some of his draft picks would not make the team. He ended up trading a few of the choices away. Third round selection defensive lineman Fred Heron was dealt (along with a fourth round pick) to the St. Louis Cardinals for a third round choice in the 1968 draft. Heron, nicknamed "Sweet Pea," went on to play seven years with the Cardinals.

Ninth round halfback Ron Rector was sent to the Washington Redskins and 11th round draft pick guard Ralph Wenzel was sent packing to the Cleveland Browns. Soon after arriving at the Browns Wenzel was on the move again this time going to the Pittsburgh Steelers where he played five seasons before finishing up his career by playing two years with the San Diego Chargers.

As for Ron Rector he had the saddest end to his career of anyone in the Packers' 1966 draft. Midway through the 1966 season Rector was sent from the Redskins to the expansion Atlanta Falcons where he played through the 1967 season. Then in the summer of 1968 right before training camp was to start Rector and a few of his friends were driving their motorcycles on an Ohio highway to go to a concert in Columbus. The speeding Rector was involved in a motorcycle accident and suffered a fractured skull and concussion. A few weeks later on July 14, 1968, he died in the hospital at the age of 24. He played in just 14 NFL games.[2]

In the end, the Packers' 1966 draft yielded just two meaningful players, Jim Grabowski and Gale Gillingham, as Dave Hathcock played just one year with the Packers. Needless to say, it was not one of Vince Lombardi's best drafts, although he was able to turn several of his lower picks into future draft choices through astute trades.

NOTES

1. *Long Beach* (CA) *Press-Telegram,* December 20, 1965. *Manitowoc* (WI) *Herald-Times*, December 20, 1965.

2. *Mansfield* (OH) *News-Journal*, July 15, 1968. *Oakland Tribune*, July 1, 1968.

PART 2

The 1966 Season

Training Camp and Preseason

Rick Schabowski

The 1966 Green Bay Packers training camp opened on Wednesday, July 13, on the campus of St. Norbert College in De Pere, Wisconsin, five miles from Green Bay. On that day, 22 rookies and free agents reported to Sensenbrenner Hall. The veterans weren't required to check in until Saturday, though 29 of them were eager enough to start early. Three first round draft choices weren't yet in camp since they were practicing with the College All-Stars in Evanston, Illinois: Donny Anderson, Jim Grabowski, and Gale Gillingham. Also missing was taxi squad holdover Larry Moore who couldn't report until released from the army in another ten days.

Asked by the *Milwaukee Sentinel*'s Bud Lea what advice he would give these new-comers, veteran defensive end Lionel Aldridge said, "The rule to follow for a rookie is to keep your mouth shut and don't quit. Don't go out of your way to talk to a veteran. He's not interested in a rookie until he's sure he can make the club."[1]

Founded in 1919, the Packers spent their first 27 seasons training in Green Bay. On Curly Lambeau's insistence, the team purchased Rockwood Lodge, located just south of Dyckesville on the shores of Green Bay in 1946. The team practiced and lived there until it was destroyed by fire in January 1950. The following summer, the Packers practiced on fields beyond East High School in Green Bay. They stayed at the old Northland Hotel and ate at the YMCA, which had a cafeteria. Then in 1951, Coach Gene Ronzani decided to take the team out of town. He chose a small agricultural college in Grand Rapids, Minnesota, but it was like the team dropped off the face of the earth. When Liz Black-bourn replaced Ronzani in 1954, he moved the team to Stevens Point, Wisconsin, and it remained the summer home for four years. The Packers moved to St. Norbert College in 1958, Scooter McLean's one and only coaching year. The team lived at Sensenbrenner Hall, ate at the school's cafeteria, and had all team meetings at St. Norbert. The team would bus to Green Bay for practice twice a day. Vince Lombardi, a devout Catholic, loved St. Norbert. He made a habit of attending Mass every day, and it was only a short distance to his home in Allouez.

One thing that typified the 1966 Packers early on was that the players had worked out on their own during their time off, and were in good shape when they reported to work. Two weeks into camp, Ray Nitschke would comment on his team, "It's the best I've ever seen at this stage…. It's all due to everyone coming back in condition. We didn't have to waste time getting into shape."[2] Vince Lombardi was pleased with the first workout on July 14. "Nobody was puffing in our grass drill this morning. That's the way I like to see it."[3] That was almost true; rookie center Steve Buratto, a free agent from Idaho, col-lapsed after agility drills, exhausted from the 40-hour bus trip to camp.

The schedule was standard fare for an NFL training camp, with wakeup call at 7:00 am, breakfast at 7:30, rookies to board the bus for Lambeau Field by 8:30 and veterans by 8:45, practice drills from 10 to 11:30, lunch at noon. Afternoon meant another drill from 3:00 to 4:30, dinner at six, the evening team meeting at 7:30 p.m., and lights out at 11:00—six days a week, Monday through Saturday, although Saturday dinner meant entertainment before getting the rest of the weekend off. Keeping with tradition, a rookie was made to sing that first night, and Ron Rector warbled out "Strangers in the Night." "One thing here," admonished Fuzzy Thurston, "we dedicate a song to our coach and general manager.... Vince Lombardi." Thurston started off with "He's Got the Whole World in His Hands" and then began to adlib some new lines ("He's got bonus babies, in his hands.... The greatest stars. The oldest ends"). At that evening's end, Lombardi dismissed his exhausted players, telling them that the best was yet to come. "These last three days have been all for fun. Monday, we go to work."[4]

Mondays also meant cuts. At the beginning, there were 59 players in camp. Lombardi would be required to let 19 of them go over the next several weeks, in order to get to the NFL roster limit of 40 men on the active roster. The first cuts were made on Monday the 18th, and the coach spoke to two players, offensive tackle Jim Chevilott of Boston College, a free agent, and defensive tackle Bob Schultz of Wisconsin-Stevens Point, a 16th round draft pick. Now, there were 21 rookies and 36 veterans left. On Thursday the 21st came the first team scrimmage, lasting 65 minutes. Lombardi told the press, "It was a little sloppy, but there was some good hitting."[5] The roster was trimmed further, with North Carolina free agent quarterback Junior Edge waived on the 23rd.

Veteran defensive end Lloyd Voss and third round draft choice Tony Jeter (whose older brother, Bob, was on the Packers) were traded to Pittsburgh for a number one pick in 1967. Indeed, the 1966 Packers had so much surplus talent that they could use it to prepare for the future, with eight of their extras becoming valuable bargaining chips that could get more draft picks in the future, leading *Sentinel* columnist Lloyd Larson to write, "The Packers don't keep up with the Joneses. They ARE the Joneses."[6]

The Packers annual intrasquad game took place on Thursday, July 28, at Lambeau Field. Tickets were one dollar apiece, and the proceeds went to charity. A crowd of 21,722 fans came out to watch the Packers offense blank the defense, 24–0. It wasn't that the defense was lacking, but under the rules, the defense almost always got shut out. The ball would be placed on the 20-yard line, and the defense would try to stop the offense. If the defense stopped the drive, whether on fourth down or a turnover, it was back to the 20, and everyone started over. The only way the defenders could score at all would be on a safety, a pick six, or by returning a fumble to the end zone. Herb Adderley, Bill Curry, Tom Brown and Bob Jeter each intercepted one of Bart Starr's 16 pass attempts, but Starr completed ten others for 125 yards, including a touchdown to Boyd Dowler.

Backup Zeke Bratkowski completed 13 out of 22 attempts for 168 yards, and had a touchdown pass to Marv Fleming. Don Chandler missed a 31-yard field goal, but hit from the 15 and had two extra points, while taxi squad kicker Larry Moore converted after the Dowler touchdown. The rookies did their part, with Ron Rector passing to Sonny Redders for the other score on a halfback option. Jim Taylor led the ground attack, netting 79 yards in ten carries. Lombardi was satisfied with the result, observing, "I think we'll have a workmanlike team this year. I was pleased considering it was the first game-like scrimmage where they were on their own."[7]

Next, came the preseason, but first free agent defensive lineman Marty Sica was cut, tenth round defensive back Sam Montgomery was sent to Atlanta, 1965 taxi squadder Ray Schoenke was traded to Cleveland and third rounder Fred Heron was traded to St. Louis.

Chicago, August 5, 1966

As the reigning NFL champions, the Packers kicked off the preseason with the Chicago College All-Star Game in Soldier Field on Friday, August 5. The 1966 game against the College All-Stars meant more to the Packers than it might have for any other team since Green Bay had suffered the humiliation of being the last NFL champion to *lose* to the college kids three years earlier by a score of 20–17. Packers linebacker Dave Robinson had been one of the college kids in that 1963 game, and recalled later, "I never thought we were going to win. The idea was to look as good as possible because your future employer was watching. At halftime the score was ten to ten and we were the most surprised guys in the stadium. In the third, we went ahead 13–10. Otto [Coach Otto Graham] was satisfied with that lead and told us to hold on to the ball." Then "a Green Bay defender made a wrong move," and (Pat) Richter ran past him for the touchdown.

The Packers weren't about to take anything for granted. The 1966 All-Stars were humbled, 38–0, the worst defeat since 1949. Bud Lea commented later, "That duel was as one-sided as a firing squad." A crowd of 72,000, the largest in nine years, watched the Packers extend their shutout to 38–0 after three quarters before letting up. For the entire game the All-Stars only managed ten first downs and 157 total yards.

After the game, Lombardi, at a loss for words, said, "I really don't know what to say about this one. Yes, I think we were up, but I don't believe in this revenge business." When it was pointed out that the huge victory matched an All-Star game record he replied, "No, I wasn't aware of it. I don't give a damn, either."[8] On the Monday after the game, 1965 taxi squad man Wally Mahle was cut. Now, came the NFL opposition.

Milwaukee, August 12, 1966

Since 1959, the Midwest Shrine Game in Milwaukee had been a matchup between the Packers and the Bears. Milwaukee isn't a bad midway point between the two cities, being 90 miles north of the Bears and 120 miles south of the Packers. On Friday, August 12, they met at the '66 Shrine Game at Milwaukee County Stadium, in front of 47,034 fans.

It was a big deal for the Bears, who had lost six consecutive Shrine games to the Packers, and had beaten them only once in regular season play since Chicago's 1963 championship. The Packers lead 3–0 at halftime, but in the second half, the Bears kept playing their starters, while the Packers began rotating the rest of their players into the action. As a result, the Packers lost to the Bears 13–10.

The Packers had outgained the Bears in total yards, 332 to 289, but as Lombardi told reporters after the game, "A fumble, pass interception and an offsides penalty stopped our drives. I don't like to lose, but I'm not displeased with what we saw out there. We played a lot of young people." He added, with a smile, "I think the Bears are a good football team and I'm glad to see it. I've turned over a new leaf this year. I'm going to be pleasant."[9] Why the good mood after losing to his archrival? It turned out that Lombardi really was "glad to see" what a good football team the Bears could be. By playing his first string for the entire game, George Halas had inadvertently provided Lombardi with some valuable film footage to study for their two regular season meetings.[10] Up next was a trip to Dallas to meet the Cowboys.

Dallas, August 20, 1966

The Packers didn't know it, but they would be meeting the Cowboys in the NFL championship at the end of the season. For now, however, it was just an exhibition match between two former coaching colleagues, Vince Lombardi and Tom Landry. Upon landing in Dallas, "they were greeted by blast furnace temperatures" and … mosquitos! Dallas was fighting an outbreak of encephalitis, with 68 cases of the sleeping sickness having been diagnosed already. The city had been sprayed by low-flying Air Force aircraft to eliminate the mosquito population, and when the Packers arrived at the Cotton Bowl for a late afternoon workout, Lombardi broke out dozens of cans of insecticide and helped spray the players.

In front of an enthusiastic, packed house of 75,404 at the Cotton Bowl, the Packers played very poorly, giving up interceptions, fumbles, and dropped passes, and lost to the Cowboys 21–3. Lombardi, commenting at the club buffet after the game said, "We played a poor game. Nothing I can say will erase the pain. We're not a cohesive team yet. We're trying too many things. We played poorly, but I'm not taking anything away from the Cowboys, they looked great. I'm sure they put a great deal of emphasis in this game, but that's no alibi. We certainly didn't come here to lose."[11]

On the Cowboys side, Coach Tom Landry commented. "You'll hear a lot from Green Bay before this season is over. The Packers are a good team and have strengthened themselves with the addition of these new runners. Don't worry about the Packers, they'll be all right. Winning these exhibitions is probably more important to us than it is to them. After all, they've built up a winning tradition. They know how to win. I know that when Vince and I were both with the Giants, we approached the exhibitions that way. The club has a lot of confidence in itself, so we could experiment because we knew we could win when we had to."[12]

So, the Packers now had back-to-back losses, even if the games didn't count. "Three years ago we lost to the College All-Stars and won all our other preseason games," said Lombardi. "This year we beat the All-Stars and lost our next two preseason games. Now you draw your own analogy…. I can still tell you we'll have a good football team."[13] Undrafted free agent Steve Buratto was cut the following day, and ninth round pick Ron Rector was traded to Washington for a fourth rounder.

Green Bay, August 27, 1966

Now, it was back to Green Bay, for the only preseason meeting scheduled for Lambeau Field, and the 50,837 available seats were already sold out. It was the annual Bishop's Charities Game, set for Saturday, August 27, and the guests were the Pittsburgh Steelers. This one would be a homecoming for Steelers Head Coach Bill Austin, who had been part of Lombardi's original staff in 1959 as his line coach, serving through the 1964 season. After a stint as a Rams assistant, Austin had been hired to rebuild the Steelers, who had finished 1965 as the NFL's worst team, at 2–12–0. "It's a lot like the challenge Vince faced when he took over the Packers in 1959," Austin told reporters when he came back to his former home. "We've got a lot of problems but we're coming along."[14] Although he wanted to make a good showing in front of his former boss and mentor, Austin had no illusions about winning, telling the *Pittsburgh Press*, "It will be difficult, but nothing is hopeless. Vince doesn't like to lose, let alone losing two in a row. He'll work the daylights out of the Packers for this game. You can bet on that."[15]

The Packers notched their first 1966 preseason victory over an NFL team besting the Steelers 17–6 in a hard-hitting defensive affair. The Steelers' defense broke through the line five times to bring Bart Starr down, but the Steelers offense was kept out of the end zone the entire game.

Lombardi pulled his regulars late in the third period, and gave rookies Jim Grabowski and Donny Anderson an opportunity to play and make up for the time lost to their appearance in the College All-Star game. In the victory, Bob Long reinjured his knee and center Ken Bowman suffered a dislocated shoulder. "When the Packers want to play," the Steelers' quarterback Bill Nelsen said afterward, "watch out. Take our game tonight. We wanted this one badly, but we made too many mistakes and you can't err against a defense like Green Bay and expect to win." The Packers definitely wanted to play, and Lombardi's comments on the win were laconic. "It was fair. That's all. We're all right."[16]

Milwaukee, September 3, 1966

Before the Packers' final preseason game, they would have to trim their roster to 43 players. Still with 47 players during the next day's work out, Lombardi lost his temper and suddenly halted the practice. Despite the humid weather, he ordered everyone to go through a full-scale scrimmage that went for ten minutes before being called off just as abruptly. During the full-speed drills, Lombardi lashed out at rookies and veterans alike. Only the injured Bowman and Long were excused from the sudden evaluation. Ostensibly, the full-speed, full-tackling, scrimmage placed emphasis on the running game and on timing, but it also would be the final practice for at least four players.

Lombardi apparently saw enough after ten minutes to draw a conclusion, and things went back to normal for the rest of the session. Word came down the next morning that Jeff White, Bill Symons, and Rich Marshall were out, and that Ron Smith had been traded. Smith and taxi squad guard Eli Strand were sent to Pittsburgh, joining their recent camp-mates, Lloyd Voss, Tony Jeter and Ralph Wenzel. Wenzel had been traded first to Cleveland, but then was cut and signed by the Steelers. All five would make the Steelers' 1966 roster, with Smith and Voss becoming starters. White, Larry Moore, Kent Nix and Roy Schmidt would all be signed to the Packers' taxi squad for 1966.

The final preseason game, in Milwaukee again, with the New York Giants visiting, would take place on Saturday, September 3. As with the other Milwaukee games, the players would be driven down from Green Bay the day before, so that they could get in their practice at County Stadium. On Friday morning Vince Lombardi and staff were ready for the players to step off the buses at noon for a workout designed around what would be expected from the Giants. But 12:00 arrived, and nobody was in sight. Reporters noticed the tension when Lombardi looked over at the clock that read 12:30. "Where are they? They should have been here at noon!"

Finally, at 1:00, an hour late, one of the two buses rolled in and the players walked into the stadium. "Where in the blazes have you been?" Lombardi demanded (the press may have paraphrased it a bit for the readers). "Bus broke down," a veteran muttered, as he kept moving, knowing better than to stay for a conversation with his angry coach. Max McGee tried to lighten the mood. "It wasn't so bad going downhill," he said. "But Fuzzy Thurston and the others had a heck of a time pushing us uphill." The coach was not amused. Of course, his full wrath was reserved for two bus drivers, and when the second bus rolled in at 1:15 with the rest of the team, its driver gave his best explanation. Not long after pulling out of Green Bay for the 110-mile trip, his bus broke down, so they both pulled over and radioed for help, then waited for another set of wheels to arrive. Somehow, nobody thought to call Vince Lombardi. Whatever else Lombardi told the driver, the press reduced it to "I don't like this kind of treatment."[17]

There were no problems in the Packers last pre-season game on Saturday September 3, as the Packers were in high gear in a 37–10 rout over the New York Giants in front of 47,102 fans at Milwaukee County Stadium.

"Green Bay's a tough crew," Giants quarterback Earl Morrall commented afterward. "The ends, particularly Willie Davis, were giving me trouble all night. The Packers are the best defensive team we've faced." After the game, Lombardi shooed away the press. "You don't want me. You only want me when I lose," he said, pointing them in the direction of the stars of the night. "The team's over there. Go talk to them." Max McGee summed it up. "We needed a little lift like that. It came at the right time."[18]

The preseason was over. Lombardi had tested all of his men during the game. "They've all played a great deal of football and that was the purpose of it. If they are called on to play now, they know their jobs. Notice that I said 'if.'"[19] The regular season kickoff was now less than a week away, set for Saturday afternoon at Lambeau against the team they had beaten in the 1965 Western Conference playoff, the Baltimore Colts. Were they ready? "I can't answer that until next week," Lombardi told the press. "This is a big opener for us, but we have to remember, it's not the entire season. We're preparing for 14 tough games, not just one."[20] For most observers, though, it wouldn't take a week to answer whether the Packers were ready to face Baltimore.

They were ready.

NOTES

1. "Packer Rookies Told: Keep Quiet, Don't Quit," *Milwaukee Sentinel*, July 13, 1966.
2. "'66 Offense Looks Good—'Best at This Stage,' Packers Nitschke," *Daily Northwestern* (Oshkosh, WI), July 30, 1966.
3. "Packers 'Cool' First Day," *Milwaukee Sentinel*, July 15, 1966.
4. "Lombardi Cracks Whip Early," *Milwaukee Sentinel*, July 19, 1966.
5. "Sloppy, but Good Hitting," *Milwaukee Sentinel*, July 22, 1966.
6. "Lloyd Larson Column," *Milwaukee Sentinel*, August 18, 1966.
7. "Packer Intrasquad Game Featured by 3 TD Passes," *Appleton* (WI) *Post-Crescent*, July 29, 1966.
8. "Vince Says Pack Was 'Up'; Sauer Admits 'Weaknesses,'" *Appleton* (WI) *Post-Crescent*, August 6, 1966.
9. "Mistakes Cost Us Game—Lombardi," *Milwaukee Sentinel*, August 13, 1966.
10. "Halas Did Packers Favor by Sticking with Starters," *Milwaukee Sentinel*, August 15, 1966.
11. "Lombardi Admits Packers Not a Cohesive Team Yet," *Milwaukee Sentinel*, August 22, 1966.
12. "Packers Are in Midseason Form, Although That's No Compliment," *Milwaukee Journal*, August 22, 1966.

13. "Played Poor Game ... Nothing Will Erase Pain—Vince," *Green Bay Press Gazette*, August 22, 1966.

14. "Striking Steel Could Be Spark," *Milwaukee Sentinel*, August 22, 1966.

15. "Steelers Optimistic for Packers," *Pittsburgh Press*, August 26, 1966.

16. "Packer Win Gives Little Indication of Future," *Milwaukee Sentinel*, August 29, 1966.

17. "Vince Slightly Perturbed by Packers' Late Arrival," *Janesville Daily Gazette,* September 3, 1966.

18. "Packers Needed Lift, Got It," *Milwaukee Sentinel*, September 5, 1966.

19. *Ibid.*

20. *Ibid.*

Regular Season Game Summaries

Rupert Patrick, Neal Golden
and Rich Shmelter

September 10, 1966—Game 1: Baltimore Colts vs. Green Bay Packers

Milwaukee County Stadium

	Baltimore	Green Bay
First downs	11	17
Yards rushing	112	155
Yards passing	106	138
Total yards (Net)	213	292
Passes	14–21	14–19
Intercepted by	3	1
Punts	3–141	3–134
Fumbles lost	0	0
Yards penalized	0	5

Baltimore	0	3	0	0	3
Green Bay	0	14	10	0	24

Baltimore—Field Goal, Michaels 26
Green Bay—Caffey 52, interception return (Chandler kick)
Green Bay—Jeter 46, interception return (Chandler kick)
Green Bay—Starr 8, run (Chandler kick)
Green Bay—Field Goal, Chandler 15
A—48,650

Rushing
(Attempts, Yards)
Baltimore—Hill 13–51; Lorick 7–25; Moore 8–21; Unitas 3–12; Matte 1–3
Green Bay—Taylor 16–76; Starr 3–36; Hornung 14–34; Anderson 1–6; Grabowski 1–3

Passing
(Attempts, Completions, Interceptions, Yards)
Baltimore—Unitas 20–14–3–106; Cuozzo 1–0–0–0
Green Bay—Starr, 19–14–1–138

Receiving
(Receptions, Yards)
Baltimore—Berry 5–40; Mackey 4–34; Hill 2–10; Moore 2–10; Richardson 1–12
Green Bay—Dowler 6–73; Taylor 1–21; Hornung 3–16; Fleming 3–16; Dale 1–12

Interceptions
Baltimore—Stonebreaker
Green Bay—Caffey, Jeter, Tom Brown

Fumbles Recovered
Baltimore—None
Green Bay—None

The 47th NFL regular season began on the evening of Saturday, September 10, when the Baltimore Colts visited County Stadium in Milwaukee. The game was nationally televised on CBS and played in front of a then-record County Stadium crowd of 48,650 spectators.[1] It was also a battle between future Hall of Fame Head Coaches as Don Shula of Baltimore squared off against Green Bay's Vince Lombardi. There were a total of 15 future Canton enshrinees amongst the players in the game, ten from the Packers and five from the Colts.

This was the anticipated rematch of the tiebreaker playoff game from 1965, which was played at Lambeau Field, as the Colts and Packers finished the previous season tied at 10–3–1. In the elimination game to settle the Western Conference crown and decide who would face the Cleveland Browns for the 1965 NFL title, the Packers won a 13–10 sudden death thriller. The game featured a major controversy, as regulation ended with a 25-yard field goal by Green Bay's Don Chandler that was high and veered right and many thought was no good. Baltimore felt they had been robbed and were out for Packer blood.

The Colts received the opening kickoff and drove to the Packers 19-yard line thanks to three first downs on the ground by Jerry Hill.[2] After coming up just short of the first down marker on a scramble, Johnny Unitas gambled, going for it on fourth-and-one, but Ray Nitschke stopped Hill in his tracks for no gain.

After the Packers were unable to move the ball, Baltimore started driving again, moving the ball 54 yards, with Unitas connecting on passes to Lenny Moore, John Mackey and Raymond Berry. Once again, the Packers defense bent but did not break, forcing a 26-yard FG by the left-footed Lou Michaels to put the Colts in front 3–0 two and a half minutes into the second period.

Starr finally got the Packers offense in motion, connecting with Jim Taylor on a screen for 21 yards and a toss to Boyd Dowler for ten more, and Taylor picked up 12 more on a run. Green Bay worked the ball inside the Baltimore ten-yard line but came up short of the goal line. Chandler came in to attempt a 16-yard FG, but it was blocked by Michaels.

Four plays later, Unitas threw a short pass over the middle but it was swiped by Lee Roy Caffey. Aided by some nice blocking from Nitschke and Henry Jordan, Caffey returned the interception 52 yards to paydirt to give the Pack a 7–3 lead with 2:43 to go in the half. "I just didn't see Caffey," said Unitas after the game.[3] Less than two minutes later, Unitas went to the air again, throwing for Berry on a square-out pattern to the left.[4] Bob Jeter (starting in his first game)[5] stepped in front of the pass at the Baltimore 46 and ran untouched down the sideline to put the Packers ahead by 11 points at the midway point.

The Packers took the second half kickoff, and Starr methodically drove them 79 yards in ten plays, keyed by Starr connecting with Dowler on a pass that was good for 25 yards to midfield. Passes to Dowler and Paul Hornung were followed by Starr dropping back to pass, seeing a gap on the right side, and running it in from eight yards out to make it 21–3 on the Packers' only offensive touchdown in the contest.

Later in the third, the Packers were moving again, with Taylor breaking off an 18-yard scamper and Starr connecting with Dowler for nine yards and Carroll Dale for 12 more. The drive ran out of steam, but Chandler topped off the scoring with a 15-yard FG, giving the Green and Gold a commanding 24–3 lead with a minute to play in the third period.

In the fourth quarter, a deep pass from Unitas was intercepted by Tom Brown at the goal line, and two plays later, Starr was picked by Steve Stonebreaker, who returned the ball to the Green Bay 24-yard line. Unitas threw to Berry at the 13, and a pass to Mackey put the pigskin at the five. However, the Baltimore scoring threat was snuffed when a Unitas pass intended for Berry on fourth-and-goal was broken up in the end zone by Jeter.

The Packers ate up what remaining time they could, and turned the ball over to the Colts with about two minutes to play. Baltimore waved the white flag during their final drive when Unitas was replaced with backup Gary Cuozzo.

Green Bay began the 1966 season with a 24–3 victory, their fourth straight victory over the Colts. The Packers players awarded the game ball to Coach Lombardi, who commented after the game, "Defensively, we did an outstanding job. It was superb."[6]

About the offense, Vince quipped, "On offense, we didn't get the ball into the end zone as much as we would have liked."[7]

One odd bit of trivia is that this game was only one of two times in his career that Unitas had two of his interceptions returned for touchdowns in the same game; the other occasion was on December 6, 1958, against the Los Angeles Rams.

In the West, the Rams and Lions kept pace with the Packers by winning their openers on Sunday.

September 18, 1966—Game 2: Green Bay Packers vs. Cleveland Browns

Cleveland Municipal Stadium

	Green Bay	Cleveland
First downs	22	16
Yards rushing	118	110
Yards passing	238	184
Total yards (Net)	356	266
Passes	20–30	15–24
Intercepted by	0	0
Punts	3–118	5–190
Fumbles lost	2	1
Yards penalized	31	50

Green Bay	0	7	7	7	21
Cleveland	7	10	0	3	20

Cleveland—Collins, 11 pass from Ryan (Groza kick)
Cleveland—Collins, 24 pass from Ryan (Groza kick)

Green Bay—Hornung, 44 pass from Starr (Chandler kick)
Cleveland—Field Goal, Groza 42
Green Bay—Taylor, 1 run (Chandler kick)
Cleveland—Field Goal, Groza 46
Green Bay—Taylor, 9 pass from Starr (Chandler kick)
A—83,943

Rushing
(Attempts, Yards)
Green Bay—Hornung 14–51; Taylor 17–42; Starr 4–17; Pitts 3–8
Cleveland—Green 9-52; Kelly 11–51; Ryan 2–7

Passing
(Attempts, Completions, Interceptions, Yards)
Green Bay—Starr 30–20–0–238
Cleveland—Ryan 24–15–0–184

Receiving
(Receptions, Yards)
Green Bay—Hornung 3–69; Taylor 8–64; Dowler 4–61; Dale 2–23; Fleming 2–15; Bill Anderson 1–6
Cleveland—Collins 4–70; Warfield 3–54; Green 5–33; Kelly 3–27

Interceptions
Green Bay—None
Cleveland—None

Fumbles Recovered
Green Bay—Aldridge
Cleveland—Wiggin, Modzelewski

The season's second week featured a rematch of the 1965 NFL championship (won by Green Bay, 23 to 12) as the Packers traveled to Cleveland and played before nearly 84,000 fans at Municipal Stadium. The Browns were still a very formidable team, even without the mighty Jim Brown, who left Cleveland for the bright lights of Hollywood following the 1965 season. His replacement was Leroy Kelly, who led the NFL in punt return average in 1965. The Browns were led by Dr. Frank Ryan, a mathematician (he designed the Tudor NFL Strategy board game that was based on actual NFL data) and deadly accurate passer. His favorite target was Paul Warfield, who was one of the top deep threat receivers of his generation. Blanton Collier assumed the coaching duties in Cleveland following the ouster of Paul Brown following the 1962 season, and his Browns won the 1964 NFL championship, still the last for the franchise.

Five minutes into the first period, Ryan hit Gary Collins on the right sideline for 19 yards to put the ball just across midfield, then, hooked up with Warfield on a pass for 37 more to the 11-yard line. From there, Ryan went back to Collins underneath the goal posts[8] to give the Browns a 7–0 lead midway through the first frame.

After the kickoff, the Packers drove into Cleveland territory, but Taylor coughed up the ball to Cleveland's Paul Wiggin. After an exchange of punts, it only took the Browns three plays to get into the end zone again; passes from Ryan to Collins for 16 yards, to Kelly for 21 more to the Green Bay 24, and back to Collins again in the end zone on the first play of the second period. The Packers found themselves in a hole, down 14–0 after 15 minutes of play.

Green Bay picked up a first down when Starr swept left for 11 yards on third-and-one. A pass to Taylor for nine yards and a smash through the middle by Taylor for ten more put the Pack near midfield, and Hornung carried the ball into the Cleveland end of the field. Starr ran for it on third-and-four but came up a yard short at the Cleveland 44. Facing a fourth-and-one, Bart rolled the dice and threw a play-action pass to an open Hornung at the 30, with the Golden Boy taking it the rest of the way. With four minutes elapsed in the second quarter, the Cleveland lead was cut in half.

Cleveland picked up a first down and moved just across midfield, but a sack from Lee Roy Caffey derailed the drive, and the punt from Collins went for a touchback. The short passing game was working for Starr, connecting with Dale for 11 yards, Dowler for nine more and Hornung for six. A couple short runs by Elijah Pitts gave Green Bay a first down at the Cleveland 44. Starr dropped back to pass when he was sacked by Dick Modzelewski at midfield and fumbled, with Little Mo recovering with less than four minutes remaining before intermission.

An offensive interference penalty undid the Browns drive, but Lou "The Toe" Groza came in and booted a 42-yard FG that was partially blocked,[9] bounced off the cross bar, and fell over to make it 17–7 Cleveland at the midway point.

A short punt from Collins left the Packers with good field position early in the second half. Hornung ran for nine yards, and Taylor got loose on the right side for 19 yards to the Cleveland 31-yard line. A pass to Dowler gained 16 yards, and Taylor carried it in from a yard out to cut the deficit to three points with seven minutes to play in the third.

Ryan scrambled for 17 yards, and a run by Ernie Green up the middle put the ball at the Green Bay 41. The Packers' front four put up a stand, as Henry Jordan and Lionel Aldridge sacked Ryan on second down while Aldridge registered a solo sack on third down, forcing a punt. Green Bay got a break on a personal foul penalty against the Browns, and Starr hit on passes to Dale for 12 yards and Dowler for 17 more, putting the Pack into Cleveland territory. A clipping penalty cost the Packers 15 yards, setting up a first-and-26, but Hornung made up 19 of those on a pass play. A third down pass fell incomplete, and Chandler's 34-yard FG attempt went wide to the right. With 13 minutes to play in the fourth quarter, the Browns clung to a 17–14 lead.

Cleveland took over at their 20 after the missed field goal, and three plays later, Kelly swept left, picking up 32 yards worth of real estate to the Green Bay 42. The Browns were unable to convert another first down, and Groza boomed a 46-yard FG to widen the Cleveland lead to 20–14 with 11:18 remaining.

The Packers began from their 15, and Starr promptly fired to Dowler on a crossing pattern for 19 yards, followed by a screen to Taylor for 18 more to put the Packers across midfield. Bart was caught behind the line but ran for it, gaining nine yards on a keeper, and then, threw to Marv Fleming for seven more. After a short pass to Taylor, Starr lobbed a screen to Bill Anderson for six yards, just enough for a first down at the Cleveland 11-yard line. Hornung hit the line for a yard, and Fleming took a pass to the two. Facing a third-and-one, Taylor swept to the left but Johnny Brewer got to Taylor and took him down for a seven-yard loss. Six points down and nine yards from victory, Starr went back to Taylor again, throwing a safety valve pass[10] to him in the right flat at the five, with Taylor getting past Erich Barnes, Ross Fichtner and Jim Houston[11] and going in to tie the game. Starr said after the game, "My primary receiver was covered like a blanket and I went to Jimmy."[12] Following the 14-play, 85-yard drive that ate up nearly nine minutes, Chandler tacked on the extra point to give the Packers a 21–20 lead with 2:34 to play.

With enough time to get into range for Groza, Ryan began with a handoff to Kelly that gained nine yards to the Cleveland 27 as the two-minute warning stopped the clock. A short toss to Warfield for six yards was followed by Kelly blowing through the middle for nine more to the 44. After an incompletion intended for Collins brought up a fourth-and-six at the Cleveland 48, Ryan threw a screen to Green that gained six yards and a couple inches as less than a minute remained. Ryan dropped back to pass but Willie Davis got through and sacked him, and on second down Ryan was unable to find Warfield and threw it away. On third down from the Packer 48, Ryan dropped back into the pocket but Aldridge got to him and applied the sack, with the ball coming loose, and Aldridge recovered to seal the 21–20 Green Bay victory.

In the standings, Green Bay stayed tied with the Rams at 2–0, with both the Colts and Lions at 1–1.

September 25, 1966—Game 3: Los Angeles Rams vs. Green Bay Packers

Lambeau Field

	Los Angeles	Green Bay
First downs	12	14
Yards rushing	106	94
Yards passing	124	262
Total yards (Net)	173	327
Passes	14–28	13–21
Intercepted by	0	1
Punts	7–293	4–165
Fumbles lost	1	5
Yards penalized	21	40

Los Angeles	0	6	7	0	13
Green Bay	7	10	0	7	24

Green Bay—Hornung 6, pass from Starr (Chandler kick)
Green Bay—Hornung 4, run (Chandler kick)
Green Bay—Field Goal, Chandler 14
Los Angeles—Field Goal, Gossett 13
Los Angeles—Field Goal, Gossett 35
Los Angeles—Bass 8, run (Gossett kick)
Green Bay—Pitts 80, pass from Starr (Chandler kick)
A—50,861

Rushing
(Attempts, Yards)
Los Angeles—Bass 13–59; Moore 17–41; Josephson 1–6
Green Bay—Taylor 15–42; Hornung 11–33; Donny Anderson 1–8; Starr 2–5; Grabowski 1–4; Pitts 3–2

Passing
(Attempts, Completions, Interceptions, Yards)
Los Angeles—Gabriel 28–14–1–124
Green Bay—Starr 21–13–0–257; Hornung 1–1–0–5

Receiving
(Receptions, Yards)
Los Angeles—Truax 7–62; Snow 3–45; Moore 4–17
Green Bay—Pitts 1–80; Dale 6–76; Hornung 2–45; Fleming 2–42; Dowler 1–16; Taylor 1–3

Interceptions
Los Angeles—None
Green Bay—Robinson

Fumbles Recovered
Los Angeles—Baughan, Cross, Jones, Lamson, Meador
Green Bay—Tom Brown

The Packers hosted the Los Angeles Rams in Week 3. Rams rookie Head Coach George Allen installed Roman Gabriel as the starting quarterback and the team seemed to respond to the change, winning their first two games over Atlanta and Chicago. Jack Snow was his favorite deep threat receiver and Dick Bass was the primary ball carrier. The Rams' strength was their defensive front four, "The Fearsome Foursome" Deacon Jones, Merlin Olson, Rosey Grier and Lamar Lundy, a unit that struck fear in the hearts of quarterbacks across the NFL. The winner of this game would sit atop the NFL Western Conference with a 3–0 record.

The Packers got across midfield in the early going, but they were forced to attempt a 45-yard FG by Chandler. Deacon Jones got through and blocked the kick, and that was the only serious scoring threat until late in the quarter when the Packers offense came alive again. The seven-play, 70-yard drive included passes from Starr to Dale for 12 and 11 yards to move the ball across midfield. The big play was a pass to Fleming over the middle that covered 37 yards to the Rams six-yard line. Two plays later, Starr flipped a pass to an open Hornung in the end zone, and the Packers led 7–0 with two and a half minutes to play in the first period.

The Packers defense got to Gabriel twice on the next drive, the two sacks setting up a fourth-and-long. Things got worse when Rams punter Jon Kilgore shanked a 28-yard punt, giving the Pack outstanding field position at their 33-yard line as the first quarter neared its end.

Passes by Starr and Hornung (Hornung's last pass in the NFL, as it turned out), along with a keeper from Starr, were followed by a run by Taylor and a pass to Dale for ten more to set up a first-and-goal at the seven. On third down, Hornung went off right tackle and four yards later, it was 14–0 Packers with just over three minutes gone in the second quarter.

On the Rams' second play from scrimmage after the kickoff, Dave Robinson made a leaping snag of a Gabriel pass, returning it to the Rams' 13-yard line. The Rams defense shut down Starr and company, which led to a 14-yard FG by Chan-

Packers vs. Rams, September 25, 1966. Quarterback Bart Starr #15 hands the ball off to halfback Paul Hornung #5. The Packers won 24–13. Photograph by Vernon J. Biever.

Packers vs. Rams, September 25, 1966. Quarterback Bart Starr #15 hands off to halfback Paul Hornung during this 24–13 victory. Rams Hall of Fame defensive tackle Merlin Olsen #74 is in pursuit. Photograph by Vernon J. Biever.

dler as Green Bay widened their lead to 17–0 with six and a half minutes elapsed in the second frame. It seemed the rout was on.

The worm began to turn later in the first half, when Starr was sacked by Maxie Baughan, who forced the ball loose and recovered for the Angelinos at the Packers 19. The Packers got a big defensive play when Bob Jeter broke up a Gabriel pass for Snow in the end zone, which led to a Bruce Gossett 13-yard FG to put the Rams on the board. With time running out in the half, a bungled handoff to Pitts was recovered by Irv Cross at the Packers 23. A sack from Ron Kostelnik brought Gossett back into the game to kick another FG (this time from 35 yards out) to make it 17–6 at the half.

After both teams failed to do anything and punted it away, the Rams made their only successful drive of the day. Starting from their 46, a couple of short passes to Billy Truax and Tom Moore, along with two runs by Bass, put the ball into Gossett's FG range, but three points weren't going to be enough to stay in the game. Another run by Moore and pass to Truax gave the Rams a first-and-goal at the nine. Two plays later, Bass took a handoff through the middle and it was a 17–13 game midway through the third period.

A Starr pass to Hornung over the middle picked up 39 yards, but Hornung was hammered by Chuck Lamson and fumbled it away at the LA 36, with Lamson recovering. The Golden Boy injured his neck on the play and would miss the rest of the game, with Pitts coming in to replace him. The Rams were unable to take advantage of the turnover, but at the end of the period, Starr was sacked by Deacon and fumbled, with the Packers hanging onto a four-point lead.

After a run by Moore put the ball at the 50, the drive sputtered, and Gossett's 48-yard FG was kicked into the wind and fell ten yards short.[13] Starr and company began from their eight-yard line after Willie Wood tried to return the missed field goal, but a Los Angeles sack led to a punt. The Rams started from excellent field position at the Green Bay 35, but the defense made a stand and Gossett tried another three-pointer, which again failed.

Two plays later, from the Packers 20, Starr faked a handoff to Taylor and went deep to Pitts at the LA 45, with Elijah outrunning Cross to the end zone. "Actually I was trying to throw to my end," said Starr after the game. "Pitts was wide open. They ignored him."[14] The 80-yard TD pass made it 24–13 Packers following the extra point from Chandler with less than nine minutes remaining.

Los Angeles embarked on a ball control drive that ended when Les Josephson fumbled and Tom Brown recovered at the GB 16 in fourth quarter and returned it four yards. With two and a half minutes to play, Green Bay just needed a couple first downs to salt it away. Two runs by Pitts were enough to move the chains, and Lombardi felt confident enough to bring in the rookies—Donny Anderson and Jim Grabowski, to run out the clock. After a short run by Grabowski, Anderson lost the handle on the ball and Ed Meador recovered at the Green Bay 35-yard line.

Gabriel was unable to do anything in the remaining seconds, and when the gun sounded, the Packers had a 24–13 victory.

The Packers defense was the difference as they overcame the five turnovers and sacked Gabriel eight times. It was also the first loss by George Allen as an NFL head coach,[15] and he gave the Packers their due after the game when he said, "Green Bay always comes through and they deserved to win … they played a better game."[16]

The Packers were now alone at the top of the West at 3–0, the Rams, Colts and Lions trailing at 2–1.

October 2, 1966—Game 4: Detroit Lions vs. Green Bay Packers

Lambeau Field

	Detroit	Green Bay
First downs	17	10
Yards rushing	174	66
Yards passing	193	212
Total yards (Net)	349	251
Passes	15–24	11–19
Intercepted by	0	2
Punts	6–233	7–259
Fumbles lost	3	0
Yards penalized	123	12

Detroit	0	7	0	7	14
Green Bay	10	7	3	3	23

Green Bay—Fleming 53, pass from Starr (Chandler kick)
Green Bay—Field Goal, Chandler 14
Green Bay—Dale 78, pass from Starr (Chandler kick)
Detroit—Nowatzke 1, run (Walker kick)
Green Bay—Field Goal, Chandler 22
Detroit—Marsh 8, run (Chandler kick)
Green Bay—Field Goal, Chandler 31
A—50,061

Rushing
(Attempts, Yards)

Detroit—Marsh 21–89; Nowatzke 14–61; Studstill 1–15; Plum 1–9

Green Bay—Taylor 12–34; Hornung 15–22; Donny Anderson 1–7; Starr 1–3

Passing
(Attempts, Completions, Interceptions, Yards)

Detroit—Plum 24–15–2–193

Green Bay—Starr, 19–11–0–212

Receiving
(Receptions, Yards)

Detroit—Studstill 5–89; Nowatzke 4–44; Cogdill 3–32; Ron Kramer 2–20; Marsh 1–8

Green Bay—Dale 2–99; Fleming 3–72; Dowler 2–16; Taylor 2–15; Bill Anderson 1–8; Hornung 1–2

Interceptions

Detroit—None

Green Bay—Robinson, Tom Brown

Fumbles Recovered

Detroit—None

Green Bay—Kostlelnik, Hart, Jeter

The Lions traveled to Titletown to visit the Packers in Week 4, and played before a full house at Lambeau Field. Lion stars included defensive tackles Alex Karras and Roger Brown, linebacker Wayne Walker and future Hall of Famer Dick LeBeau at corner. The

Packers vs. Lions, October 2, 1966. Following a handoff from quarterback Bart Starr #15, Paul Hornung #5 carries the ball behind blockers (from left to right) #64 Jerry Kramer, #75 Forrest Gregg, and #31 Jim Taylor. The Packers won 23–14. Photograph by Vernon J. Biever.

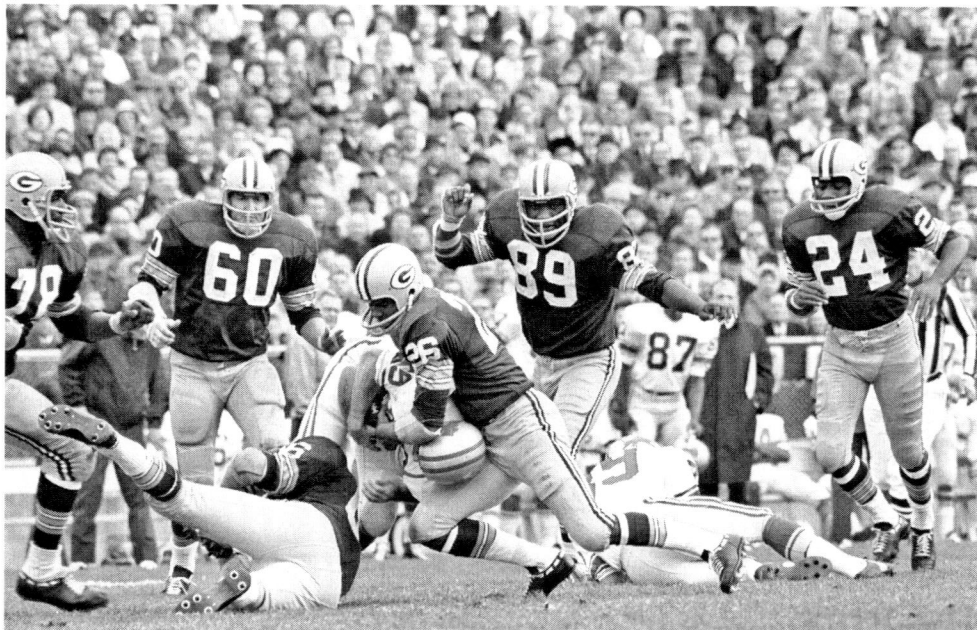

Packers vs. Lions, October 2, 1966. Ray Nitschke (on the ground), along with Herb Adderley #26, tackles a Lions player during the Packers' 23–14 victory. Other Packer defenders, including Robert Brown #78, Lee Roy Caffey #60, Dave Robinson #89 and Willie Wood #24, surround the action. Photograph by Vernon J. Biever.

quarterbacking duties were shared by Milt Plum and rookie Karl Sweetan, with Plum getting the start against the Packers. Their head coach was former Redskins and Lions signal caller Harry Gilmer, who was in the second and final season of his NFL head coaching career.

On the fourth play from scrimmage, Starr threw a short slant pass to Fleming, with Fleming breaking a tackle from Bruce Maher and outrunning the Lions defense to complete a 53-yard touchdown pass. After the Lions punted following the kickoff, Chandler shanked a punt 15 yards into a strong wind to the Packers 35, but the Lions were unable to capitalize thanks to a key sack from rookie Bob Brown. Wayne Walker attempted a 49-yard FG but the boot went wide to the left.

On the subsequent Detroit drive, an Amos Marsh fumble on first down was forced by a jarring hit from Jordan and recovered by Kostelnik at the Lions 39. The Pack benefitted from a roughing-the-passer call against the Lions, but a third down run by Green Bay came up a yard short. Chandler connected on a 14-yard FG to give the Packers a 10–0 lead after one period.

Early in the second quarter, Starr aired it out to Dale on a post pattern,[17] with Dale catching the ball at the Detroit 45 and taking it to the house. The 78-yard touchdown pass gave the Packers a 17–0 lead. A 47-yard pass from Plum to Pat Studstill put the Lions just inside the Packers 29. From that point, Plum connected with Gail Cogdill for 12 yards before scrambling for nine more to put the ball at the 12-yard line. The Lions ran it in from there, with Tom Nowatzke bursting across from a yard out for the score. The 12-play, 80-yard drive put Detroit on the board with over two minutes to play before intermission.

With time running out in the half, Plum hooked up with Nowatzke on a 24-yard pass. However, a Plum pass intended for former Packer Ron Kramer was intercepted by

Tom Brown at the Green Bay 32 and returned 15 yards. After 30 minutes of play, the Packers led 17–7.

The Lions were unable to do anything to start the second half and punted, with Green Bay getting a 15-yard bonus when Detroit was flagged for interfering with a fair catch, putting the ball at the Detroit 47. A pass to Dowler gained 14 yards, but Karras got to Starr, dropping him at the 40. The sack took the wind out of the Packers drive, and Chandler was unsuccessful on a 43-yard FG that went wide right.

The teams traded punts, and then, Plum dropped back and was hit by Willie Davis as he released the ball. The lame duck pass dropped to Dave Robinson at midfield and was returned to the Detroit 43. An interference call against the Lions gave Green Bay the ball at the 22-yard line. The Detroit defense put up a stand, forcing a 22-yard FG by Chandler to increase the Packers lead to 20–7.

The Lions running game moved them into Packers territory, with Cogdill running for 11 yards, and Studstill taking an end-around for 15 more, putting the Lions at the Packers 28. After Nowatzke ran for six yards, Kostelnik and Tom Brown double-teamed Plum for a sack, setting up a fourth-and-14 at the 32-yard line. Plum dropped back and connected with Studstill for 17 yards to the 15, with Detroit getting additional yardage when Robinson was flagged for a late hit on Studstill. The Lions found themselves with a first-and-goal at the Green Bay eight-yard line. The ball went to Marsh, who went off left tackle, going through several Packers before falling into the end zone. With less than 13 minutes to play, it was a one-possession game at 20–14.

With the Packers needing a score to give them some breathing room, Starr responded with a pass to Dale for 21 yards to midfield, but the drive stalled. However, the punt from Chandler was muffed by Jim Todd, with Doug Hart recovering for Green Bay at the Detroit 22-yard line. The Packers moved to the 15 before Karras got to Bart again, this time on third down. Chandler came in and toed a 31-yard FG to give the Packers a 23–14 lead midway through the final frame.

Both teams were unable to do anything, and they exchanged punts. Plum threw to Studstill, but the ball came loose, and Bob Jeter snatched it out of the air at the Lions 31-yard line, which was the last gasp for the Lions as the Packers improved to 4–0.

After the game, Lombardi said, "I don't think we played one of our better games today … but there is no team in this league that can play a good football game week after week after week. It cannot be done."[18] He added, "This is the kind of game you have to win if you're going to be champions."[19] It certainly wasn't one of the Packers' better games, but the key number, besides the 5–0 turnover ratio, was the 123 penalty yards for Detroit against 12 for Green Bay.

The first place Packers were now trailed by the Rams at 3–1 and the Colts at 2–1, with the Lions dropping back to 2–2.

October 9, 1966—Game 5: Green Bay Packers vs. San Francisco 49ers

Kezar Stadium

	Green Bay	San Francisco
First downs	17	17
Yards rushing	106	154

	Green Bay	San Francisco
Yards passing	287	121
Total yards (Net)	368	248
Passes	18–26	12–25
Intercepted by	1	1
Punts	3–118	6–270
Fumbles lost	1	0
Yards penalized	61	50

Green Bay	3	0	10	7	20
San Fran	0	7	7	7	21

Green Bay—Field Goal, Chandler 18
San Francisco—Crow 27, pass from Mira (Tommy Davis kick)
San Francisco—Hazeltine 22, fumble return (Tommy Davis kick)
Green Bay—Hornung 43, pass from Starr (Chandler kick)
Green Bay—Field Goal, Chandler 22
San Francisco—Crow 8, pass from Mira (Tommy Davis kick)
Green Bay—Dale 38, pass from Starr (Chandler kick)
A—39,290

Rushing
(Attempts, Yards)
Green Bay—Taylor 16–54; Hornung 11–30; Pitts 6–20; Starr 1–2
San Francisco—Mira 3–46; Willard 14–43; Kopay 4–42; Crow 9–23

Passing
(Attempts, Completions, Interceptions, Yards)
Green Bay—Starr 26–18–1–287
San Francisco—Mira 21–9–1–104; Brodie 4–3–0–17

Receiving
(Receptions, Yards)
Green Bay—Dale 4–86; Hornung 3–51; Taylor 4–39; McGee 1–39; Pitts 2–27; Fleming 2–27; Dowler 2–18
San Francisco—Crow 5–53; Parks 2–26; Stickles 2–20; Kent Kramer 1–13; Willard 1–6; Casey 1–3

Interceptions
Green Bay—Robinson
San Francisco—Kimbrough

Fumbles Recovered
Green Bay—None
San Francisco—Hazeltine

Kezar Stadium in San Francisco was the site of the Packers' fifth game of the season, and 39,290 fans turned out on a warm afternoon with temperatures in the upper 70s. The Packers came into the game undefeated at 4–0, while the 49ers were winless at 0–2–1. Odds makers tabbed the Packers 13-point favorites to beat San Francisco.[20]

Jack Christiansen, who had a Hall of Fame career as a safety with the Lions in the 50s, was the 49er head coach. Backup quarterback George Mira would get his only start of the 1966 season in this contest as starter John Brodie would see limited action due to a groin injury.[21] Their running game consisted of a pair of guys who were both selected second overall in their respective drafts; John David Crow (1957 Heisman Trophy winner, second overall pick in the 1958 NFL draft) and Ken Willard (the second selection in the 1965 NFL draft). Their receiving corps included Dave Parks, who led the NFL in pass receptions, receiving yards and TD catches in 1965, and Bernie Casey, who later went into acting.

Starting from his 15 after a Tommy Davis punt, Starr connected on a pass to Dale, who took a pass along the left flat for 19 yards. Twice, Hornung got the call on third-and-short and carried for the first down, but on a third-and-a-foot at the SF 31, the Niners knew what was coming, and they stopped the Golden Boy short. The 39-yard FG try by Chandler was wide right midway through the first.

Later in the first quarter, Starr hit Max McGee over the middle on third-and-inches, with Max getting loose for a total of 39 yards to the Niners 26. Runs by Taylor and Hornung put the ball into the red zone, but the drive stalled, and Chandler nailed an 18-yard FG, giving Green Bay a 3–0 lead with a minute to play in the first period.

Following an exchange of punts, Mira completed passes to Monty Stickles and Parks, each for 14 yards. From the Packers 27, Mira bootlegged to his right, then scrambled left, and found an open Crow at the two-yard line, with Crow going in for the TD. The conversion from Davis gave the 49ers a 7–3 lead in the middle of the second stanza.

The teams traded punts until Kermit Alexander returned Chandler's punt to midfield as two minutes remained in the first half. A pass to Parks was good for 12 yards, and Kent Kramer hauled in a pass on a crossing pattern for 13 more. With time running out, Davis attempted a 41-yard FG that was short. After two quarters, the Packers trailed seven to three.

Starr began the second half with a pass to Fleming that gained 14 yards and a first down, but things quickly went from bad to worse. After a sack set up a third-and-20, the 49ers sent the blitz, and Starr was sacked again with the ball coming loose. Matt Hazeltine scooped up the fumble at the 22 and ran it into the end zone to give the 49ers a 14–3 lead as three minutes were elapsed in the third period.

Herb Adderley broke off a 28-yard return on the ensuing kickoff, giving the Packers excellent field position at their 44. A short run by Taylor was followed by a pass to Dowler that put the ball at the SF 43. Bart put it up for Hornung, who was alone on the right sideline at the 30 and took it the rest of the way to cut the Niners lead to 14–10 with four and a half minutes played in the third.

After a Davis punt, the Packers took over again at their 42-yard line. A screen to Taylor garnered 14 yards and moved the ball across midfield, and Dale took a pass 24 yards to the Niners 15-yard line. After the drive ran out of steam, Chandler split the uprights from 22 yards out. With six minutes to play in the third quarter, the Packers pulled to within a point as they trailed 14–13.

Following another punt from Davis, a screen to Taylor gained 18 yards, with a personal foul against the 49ers giving the Packers a first down at their 44. A pass to Fleming covered 13 yards as the third quarter drew to a close. The fourth quarter began with Starr throwing a pass intended for Dowler in the right flat at the SF 19, but it was snatched by Elbert Kimbrough, who returned it 44 yards to the Packers 37-yard line where Taylor made a touchdown-saving tackle.

On first down, Mira was sacked for nine yards, but on the next play, he dropped back again, could not locate a receiver and ran for it. Thanks to some fancy moves and a nice block from Stickles, Mira covered 38 yards before he went down at the eight yard line. On first-and-goal, Mira arched the pass over Lee Roy Caffey, with Crow hauling in another touchdown pass to widen the 49ers lead to 21–13 a minute into the final quarter.

Donny Anderson returned Jim Norton's kickoff to the Packers 31. Starr worked the ball down the field in four plays, starting with a pass over the middle to Pitts that gained 20 yards and put the ball just across the midfield stripe. Bart flipped another pass to Pitts for seven yards, and Taylor swept left for four more, setting up a first-and-ten at the Niners 38. Dropping back in the pocket, Starr uncorked a deep pass for Dale at the five and Carroll took it the rest of the way. The PAT from Chandler left the Packers a point behind at 21–20 with 11:27 to play.

The Packers got a huge break when Mira went to the air on third-and-seven, and his pass was intercepted by Dave Robinson at the Niners 32 and returned to the nine-yard line. On third down, Dowler was called for offensive pass interference against Alexander in the end zone and the Packers were penalized 15 yards. Chandler attempted a 26-yard FG but the ball drifted a couple feet too far to the left.

With seven minutes on the clock, Brodie was in at quarterback after Mira was kicked in the forearm tackling Robinson on the interception.[22] Runs by Willard and Crow and Dave Kopay, along with a couple screens by Brodie, moved the ball inside the 20 as two minutes remained. The Packers started burning time outs, and Green Bay finally stopped the 49ers at the two-yard line, but they only had 30 seconds left and no time outs left.

San Francisco held on for the 21–20 victory, and the Packers fell from the ranks of the unbeaten, finding themselves tied with the Rams at 4–1 atop the Western Conference. This was arguably the biggest upset of the 1966 NFL season.

"We should have won by 20," Coach Lombardi said after the game. "We did have chances. We just failed to take advantage of them."[23]

Elsewhere, the Bears beat the Colts so that each was now 2–2 and tied for second behind the Packers and Rams. The Lions dropped to 2–3.

October 16, 1966—Game 6: Green Bay Packers vs. Chicago Bears

Wrigley Field

	Green Bay	Chicago
First downs	12	6
Yards rushing	121	42
Yards passing	80	69
Total yards (Net)	180	94
Passes	8–19	12–23
Intercepted by	1	3
Punts	6–209	6–241
Fumbles lost	1	1
Yards penalized	23	74

Green Bay	0	0	10	7	17
Chicago	0	0	0	0	0

Green Bay—Hornung 1, run (Chandler kick)
Green Bay—Field goal, Chandler 30
Green Bay—Wood 20, interception return (Chandler kick)
A—48,573

Rushing
(Attempts, Yards)
Green Bay—Taylor, 17–66; Pitts, 8–40; Starr 1–0; Hornung, 6–11; Grabowski 1–3; Anderson 2–1
Chicago—Sayers, 15–29; Bukich 2–4; Arnett 5–3; Piccolo 1–5; Marconi 1–2; Bull, 6–(-1)

Passing
(Attempts, Completions, Interceptions, Yards)
Green Bay—Starr, 18–8–1–80; Pitts 1–0–0–0
Chicago—Bukich, 23–12–3–69

Receiving
(Receptions, Yards)
Green Bay—Taylor 4–42; Dowler 1–15; Dale 1–13; Pitts 1–6; Hornung 1–4
Chicago—Arnett 4–3; Sayers 3–21; Ditka 2–26; Jones 2–10; Allen 1–9

Interceptions
Green Bay—Adderley, Nitschke, Wood
Chicago—Atkins

Fumbles Recovered
Green Bay—Aldridge
Chicago—Butkus

For the first time in 1966, the 4–1 Packers came off a loss. How would they respond? Perhaps there was no team they would rather play in that circumstance than their old rivals, the Chicago Bears. After starting the season with losses to Detroit and Los Angeles, George Halas' crew won their next two over the Vikings and Colts. The Bears took the pressure off journeyman quarterback Rudy Bukich by giving the ball frequently to running back Gale Sayers (322 yards on 62 carries so far in 1966). Sayers was also an excellent receiver along with tight end Mike Ditka, whom the Packers would double cover.

The 95th edition of Packers-Bears resulted in the first shutout by Green Bay in Wrigley Field in 34 years. Neither team threatened in the first 30 minutes until Bukich hit Sayers with a 12-yard pass to the Packer 30. But a penalty nullified the play. On the next snap, Adderley intercepted and returned 43 yards to flip the field and give the Packers a chance to score before intermission, but Chandler missed a 29-yard field goal try.

Green Bay took the second half kickoff and produced the only sustained drive of the afternoon. The Pack marched 65 yards in 12 plays to a touchdown, with Hornung smashing over from the one behind a good block by Taylor. Hornung suffered a shoulder injury on the play, and Pitts replaced him the rest of the way.

The defense had a hand in the last ten points. Nitschke intercepted a Bukich pass to set up Chandler's 30-yard field goal in the third quarter. Then, midway through the final period, Wood returned an interception 20 yards to pay dirt to put the victory on ice.

With the Packers' front four harassing Bukich all day, the Bears offense crossed midfield just twice.

The game took just two hours and 14 minutes—a short one even by 1966 standards. When he took over the Packers in 1959, Lombardi told the press, "I am not a funny

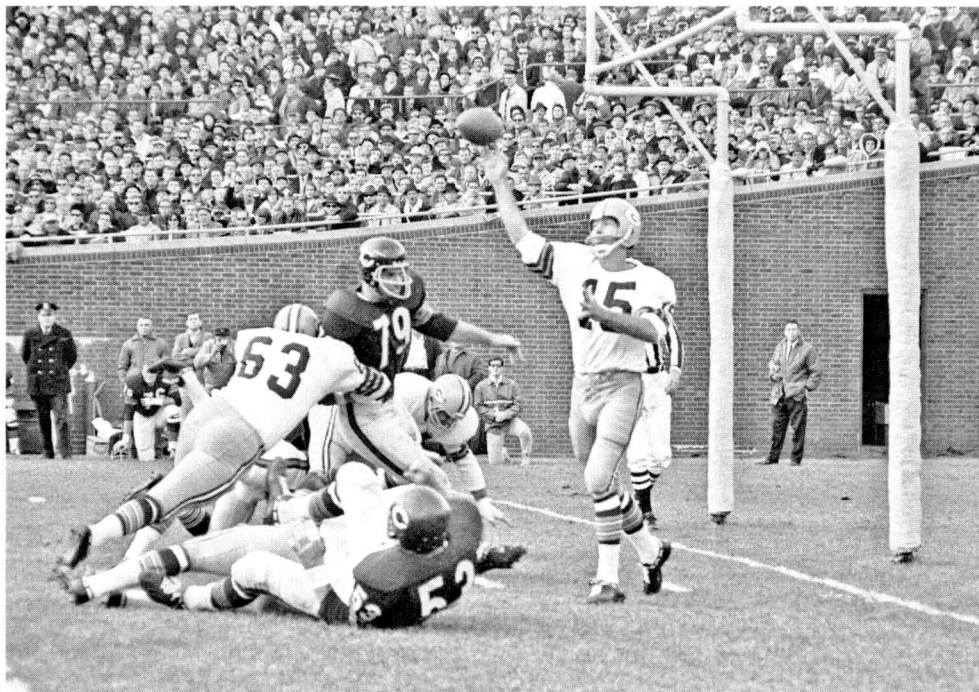

Packers at Bears, October 16, 1966. Quarterback Bart Starr #15 attempts a pass against the Bears defense at Wrigley Field. Fuzzy Thurston #63 attempts to protect Starr from Bears defensive lineman Dick Evey #79. The Packers won 17–0. Photograph by Vernon J. Biever.

man." But he produced chuckles when asked about his defense after the whitewash. "I thought they were lousy." Then he offered a serious response. "I thought we got ready to play a football game…. It was that simple." He also provoked smiles when he confessed, "Every time I see Sayers make a move out there, I lose another year of life." Did this mean he preferred to see Sayers run inside? "Sayers will kill you inside too…. I'd rather have him sitting on the bench, frankly."[24] Davis explained the Pack's strategy that held Gale to only 29 yards on 15 carries. "You have to keep him changing his direction. Keep turning him in so that the guys in pursuit have a crack at him. You can't make mistakes on Sayers. Last year we did, and he killed us."[25] Willie gave credit to the secondary. "We had good coverage from our deep men … this gave the linemen an extra step … and I think we gave some extra effort too. I can't remember our last shutout, but I can guarantee I'll remember this until Tuesday."[26]

In the other locker room, Halas pronounced the game "the worst offensive effort we've had in many, many years. Yes … many, many years. We made more mistakes than I can remember … fumbles, interceptions, penalties…. Our defense was great, and our offense was miserable…. You must rate their defensive effort and our offensive ineptness as equal factors in the result." When asked if the Bears could still win the Western Conference with three losses, Halas refused to take the bait. "I'm too old for that prognostication and conjecturing. I leave that to the young coaches … to Don Shula."[27]

With Los Angeles losing to Minnesota, Green Bay was back in sole possession of first place with a 5–1 record. They were followed by the Rams at 4–2 and the Colts at 3–2.

October 23, 1966—Game 7: Atlanta Falcons vs. Green Bay Packers

Milwaukee County Stadium

	Green Bay	*Atlanta*
First downs	19	15
Yards rushing	126	140
Yards passing	251	142
Total yards (Net)	357	216
Passes	10–19	11–29
Intercepted by	4	0
Punts	4–159	6–234
Fumbles lost	0	0
Yards penalized	64	48

Green Bay	7	21	7	21	56
Atlanta	0	0	3	0	3

Green Bay—Pitts 3, run (Chandler kick)
Green Bay—Taylor 1, run (Chandler kick)
Green Bay—Dale 51, pass from Starr (Chandler kick)
Green Bay—Anderson 5, run (Chandler kick)
Atlanta—Field Goal, Kirouac 41
Green Bay—Adderley 68, interception return (Chandler kick)
Green Bay—McGee 24, pass from Bratkowski (Chandler kick)
Green Bay—Anderson 77, punt return (Chandler kick)
Green Bay—Hart 40, interception return (Chandler kick)
A—43,623

Rushing
(Attempts, Yards)
Green Bay—Grabowski 7–52; Taylor, 10–50; Pitts, 6–9; Anderson 5–15
Atlanta—Wheelwright 8–51; Coffey 11–41; Claridge 3–22; Johnson 2–20; Scales 2–3; Johnson 3–3

Passing
(Attempts, Completions, Interceptions, Yards)
Green Bay—Starr, 13–8–0–220; Bratkowski 6–2–0–31
Atlanta—Johnson   17–5–3–91;   Claridge   11–6–1–51; Lothridge 1–0–0–0

Receiving
(Receptions, Yards)
Green Bay—Dale 4–110; Pitts 2–66; Dowler 2–41; McGee 1–24; Fleming 1–10
Atlanta—Martin 4–42; Hawkins 2–36; Burke 2–22; Coffey 1–21; Anderson 1–16; Wheelwright 1–5

Interceptions
Green Bay—Adderley, Hart, Crutcher, Jeter
Atlanta—None

Fumbles Recovered
Green Bay—None
Atlanta—None

The Pack's next game was as close to a breather as you could get in the NFL. The Atlanta Falcons, a first-year expansion team, had yet to win in six outings. The closest they had come to victory was the opener at home against the Rams, 19–14. Since the baseball Braves had just moved to Atlanta after the 1965 baseball season, the city of Milwaukee was not likely to welcome the Falcons with anything but thunderous boos.

Atlanta was coached by Norb Hecker, a former Green Bay defensive backfield coach. His roster included three former Packers: QB Dennis Claridge, HB Junior Coffey, and G Dan Grimm. The only chance the visitors had lay in the Western Conference leaders having a letdown after an emotional win at Chicago. But defensive captain Willie Davis vowed that wouldn't happen in flawless Lombardi-speak. "There's no question we're going to be in for one of our toughest games of the year. Atlanta has got to be high and really after us. I know I'm approaching this ball game with all the seriousness I've had in preparing for any game this season."[28]

When the score was only 7–0 after one period, Packers fans may have thought their heroes had overlooked the winless foe. But a flurry of three touchdowns before halftime ended that anxiety. Pitts, starting for the ailing Hornung, ran in from the three to cap the first quarter scoring drive. In the second quarter, Taylor plunged over from the one, Starr threw a perfect 51-yard pass to Dale, and Anderson slid outside his right tackle for a five-yard touchdown, his first as a Packer.

Lombardi played backups wherever possible in the second half, but the onslaught continued thanks mostly to the defense and the special teams. After a field goal spoiled the shutout, Adderley scampered 68 yards with an interception. Then veteran Max McGee hauled in a 24-yard pass from Zeke Bratkowski. Anderson struck again with a 77-yard punt return before Doug Hart returned another pick 40 yards to top off the 56–3 rout.

The 53-point margin of victory was the largest in Packers history while the 56 points were the highest since a 57–21 walloping of the Lions in 1945. The eight touchdowns tied a club record, and Chandler's eight extra points set a new standard in that department.

Halfway through the 1966 season, Green Bay led the West with a 6–1 mark, followed by the Colts at 4–2 and the Rams at 4–3. Over in the East, St. Louis topped the conference with a 5–1–1 record, followed closely by Dallas at 4–1–1 and Cleveland at 5–2. Both the Eagles and Redskins were still alive at 4–3.

October 30, 1966—Game 8: Green Bay Packers vs. Detroit Lions

Tiger Stadium

	Green Bay	Detroit
First downs	19	19
Yards rushing	174	84
Yards passing	170	271
Total yards (Net)	344	317
Passes	13–15	21–45
Intercepted by	3	0
Punts	3–124	4–186
Fumbles lost	2	2
Yards penalized	33	52

Green Bay	0	17	7	7	31
Detroit	0	7	0	0	7

Green Bay—Pitts 4, run (Chandler kick)
Green Bay—Field Goal, Chandler 40
Detroit—Nowatzke 2, run (Walker kick)
Green Bay—Pitts 24, pass from Starr (Chandler kick)
Green Bay—Taylor 1, run (Chandler kick)
Green Bay—Pitts 3, run (Chandler kick)
A—56,594

Rushing
(Attempts, Yards)
Green Bay—Pitts, 21–99; Taylor, 16–50; Starr 2–16; Anderson 2–15; Grabowski 2–6
Detroit—Marsh 13–32; Nowatzke 9–52

Passing
(Attempts, Completions, Interceptions, Yards)
Green Bay—Starr, 13–11–0–154; Bratkowski 2–2–0–16
Detroit—Sweetan 45–21–3–271

Receiving
(Receptions, Yards)
Green Bay—Dowler 3–30; Fleming 3–28; Pitts 2–31; Taylor 2–13; Dale 1–52; Anderson 1–11; Grabowski 1–5
Detroit—Studstill 7–164; Kramer 5–51; Nowatzke 3–4; Cogdill 2–23; Henderson 2–8; Malinchak 1–13; McLenna 1–8

Interceptions
Green Bay—Tom Brown, Caffey, Nitschke
Detroit—None

Fumbles Recovered
Green Bay—Davis, Adderley
Detroit—Rasmussen, LeBeau

Green Bay played their return engagement at Detroit after beating the Lions 23–14 in Green Bay October 2. Because the Packers objected to being the Lions' opponent every year for the annual Thanksgiving Day clash in Detroit, the NFL agreed to rotate the visiting team starting in 1966.

Following a scoreless first period, Green Bay broke the ice on the first of Pitts' three touchdowns, a four-yard burst that climaxed a 55-yard, eight-play drive that started when Tom Brown intercepted a Karl Sweetan pass that tipped off the hands of diminutive flanker Pat Studstill. Elijah gained all but ten of the yards on the march, with his 17-yard run being the largest gainer. Soon after, Nitschke tipped up a pass and returned it 21 yards to the Detroit 39 to set up Chandler's 40-yard field goal to move the lead to 10–0.

But the Lions struck back quickly. A 63-yard pass from Sweetan to Studstill, who took the ball away from two Packer defenders, put Detroit in business at the 21. Amos Marsh and Tom Nowatzke hammered to the two from where Nowatzke scored to make it 10–7.

Adderley took Garo Yepremian's kickoff on the six and raced 65 yards to the Detroit 29. Two plays later, Fleming fumbled a pass from Starr and Dick LeBeau recovered for the Lions. But a personal foul penalty negated the turnover and put the ball on the 15. However, two plays later, Taylor lost the ball when hit by Alex Karras, and Wayne Rasmussen fell on it.

Detroit drove close enough for Wayne Walker to try a field goal that went wide from the 40. The Packers responded with an 80-yard drive in seven plays to extend the lead back to ten before the half. Starr scrambled 21 yards to the Detroit 24, and then hit Pitts on the goal line for six.

The second half brought more Packer power. Continuing the pattern of staying mostly on the ground with Starr passing sparingly but with deadly precision, Green Bay stormed 78 yards in nine plays. The big gainer was a 51-yard pitch to Dale to the 18. Taylor's one-yard plunge made it 24–7.

Finally, Pitts contributed 19 yards to a fourth touchdown drive that he finished himself with a three-yard bolt in the last period. The possession started when linebacker Lee Roy Caffey stole an aerial at the Packers 46. Starr passed only once during the march, a ten-yarder to Dowler. Bart turned the helm over to Bratkowski after completing 11 of 13 for 154 yards in the 31–7 romp.

As the score mounted, Lions fans expressed their displeasure with Head Coach Harry Gilmer by waving signs saying "Bye Bye Harry" and singing the tune "Good Night, Ladies" with "Harry" inserted for "Ladies."[29]

For the second week in a row, Lombardi was able to flood the field with reserves in the final quarter and hold Hornung out of action while the pinched nerve in his neck healed. Vince called it "our best all-around game of the season" and praised his starting halfback. "Pitts has been a good back for us the last six years. You've got to think of him like a first stringer." Elijah, who missed the magic 100-yard mark by one, admitted he was concerned about his place on the roster when the Packers paid an estimated $1 million in bonuses to rookies Anderson and Grabowski. "You work hard to try to earn a spot," Pitts said. "I know Lombardi is going to give everybody a chance and play the best man."[30]

Green Bay continued to cruise alone in first place in the West at 7–1. Baltimore beat Los Angeles to keep pace at 5–2, but the surprising Rams at 4–4 were falling out of the race.

November 6, 1966—Game 9: Minnesota Vikings vs. Green Bay Packers

Lambeau Field

	Green Bay	Minnesota
First downs	18	20
Yards rushing	158	126
Yards passing	140	172
Total yards (Net)	292	290
Passes	11–18	16–26
Intercepted by	0	0
Punts	2–91	3–106
Fumbles lost	1	0
Yards penalized	20	19

Green Bay	7	3	7	0	17
Minnesota	0	10	0	10	20

Green Bay—Taylor 1, run (Chandler kick)
Minnesota—Brown 1, run (Cox kick)
Green Bay—Field goal, Chandler 11
Minnesota—Field goal, Cox 31
Green Bay—Pitts 2, run (Chandler kick)
Minnesota—Field goal, Cox 16
Minnesota—Brown 1, run (Cox kick)
A—50,861

Rushing
(Attempts, Yards)
Green Bay—Pitts 18–89; Taylor 16–68; Starr 1–1
Minnesota—Brown 21–51; Mason 10–23; Osborn 9–28;
Tarkenton 5–22; Lindsey 1–2

Passing
(Attempts, Completions, Interceptions, Yards)
Green Bay—Starr, 18–11–0–140
Minnesota—Tarkenton 26–16–0–172

Receiving
(Receptions, Yards)
Green Bay—Taylor 5–44; Pitts 4–58; Dowler 1–25; Dale 1–13
Minnesota—Phillips 4–72; Carpenter 4–45; Brown 4–30;
Flatley 3–26; Mason 1–(-1)

Interceptions
Green Bay—None
Minnesota—None

Fumbles Recovered
Green Bay—None
Minnesota—Kassulke

Norm Van Brocklin's Minnesota Vikings came to Green Bay with confidence based on their last two trips to Lambeau Field: a 24–23 win in 1964 and a close 24–19 loss in 1965. Like the Packers, the Vikes came off an impressive victory, 28–3 over the 49ers. The purple defense had allowed slightly over ten points in the last four games, and quarterback Fran Tarkenton had connected on 75 percent of his passes in the last three contests. Fran gave defenses trouble with his scrambling ability and would kill the Pack on third downs on a sunny afternoon with temperatures in the low 40s.

The teams traded 80-yard mirror-image drives to start the game. The Packers took 12 plays after forcing Minnesota to punt to start the game. Seven snaps were runs by Pitts and Taylor, the longest being 14 by Elijah. Starr passed twice, to Taylor for 23 and to Pitts who burst away from two defenders on the 12 and raced to the one. Jimmy scored from there.

A key play on the Vikings' 15-play touchdown march came on third-and-four at the Packers 30. After dancing around, Fran stepped forward and underhanded the ball to Bill Brown who gained 23 to the seven. After Aldridge threw Brown for a loss of three, Tarkenton raced back as far as the 35 before hitting Red Phillips on the one. Brown took it over from there.

Before halftime, the teams traded field goals to make it ten all at the half.

The Packers held the ball for 7:36 of the third quarter while moving 86 yards in 15 plays to take a 17–10 lead. After Pitts and Taylor gained seven each, Starr passed to Elijah for 15, Jimmy for nine, and Dale for 13 to the 15. The Pack traveled by land the rest of the way: Taylor four, Pitts seven, two, and two.

Mixing passes and runs, the Vikings controlled the pigskin the rest of the quarter to gain a 16-yard Fred Cox field goal on the second play of the final quarter and the 16th of the possession to cut the lead to 4.

Green Bay missed moving the chains by a yard, and Chandler punted. Ed Scharockman took it to the 12, but a facemask penalty gave Minnesota a 15-yard head start for their possession. After two runs gained seven, Tarkenton worked some more third-down magic. He flipped a pinpoint pass behind a cluster of three Packers to Phillips for a 38-yard gain to the 29. Dave Osborn and Brown crashed to the 17. After Kostelnik dropped Osborn for a loss of three, Fran hit Paul Flatley for ten. On third-and-three, Osborn got double what he needed. Dave ran again to the one, and Brown plunged in to put Minnesota on top 20–17 with 6:53 remaining.

Green Bay's next possession went nowhere after Gary Larsen threw Starr for a six-yard loss to the 14 to force a punt with 4:13 to play. The Vikings ran Osborn three times for a key first down but soon had to kick. The Pack started on their 11 with 1:42 on the clock. But Bart had no magic wand this time. He threw four times but completed only one, to Taylor for just four. So Minnesota took over and stalled for four plays, not even taking a chance of getting a field goal blocked. With just nine ticks left, Starr connected with Dowler for 25 and Pitts for 17 when the gun sounded.

Lombardi was succinct in his assessment. "They did a great job of possessing the ball.... We did too. We drove for points every time we got the ball, except once ... but we never got the ball back." Vince, who long since labeled Tarkenton "a great athlete," admitted "he hurt us, certainly, but they did other things, too. They ran the ball on us very successfully."[31]

Van Brocklin spoke in the same vein. "Both teams looked like they had the same plan—three, four six, move the sticks." Asked about his quarterback, Norm grinned. "Sensational, incredible.... Whatever adjectives you want to use.... I think he made 11 third down plays, somebody told me. That's the name of the game."[32]

With the loss, Green Bay's lead dropped to a half-game over the 6–2 Colts, with the Rams continuing to fall to 4–5.

November 20, 1966—Game 10: Chicago Bears vs. Green Bay Packers

Lambeau Field

	Green Bay	Chicago
First downs	15	9
Yards rushing	69	75
Yards passing	240	98
Total yards (Net)	296	160
Passes	17–31	9–22
Intercepted by	3	1
Punts	5–204	6–281
Fumbles lost	1	1
Yards penalized	85	93

Green Bay	0	7	0	6	13
Chicago	0	0	0	6	6

Green Bay—Dale 6, pass from Bratkowski (Chandler kick)
Chicago—Sayers 2, run (kick failed)
Green Bay—Dale 33, pass from Bratkowski (kick failed)
A—50,861

Rushing
(Attempts, Yards)
Green Bay—Taylor 20–49; Pitts 10–14; Starr 1–6; Bratkowski 2–0
Chicago—Sayers 20–68; Bull 3–10; Kurek 2–0; Bukich 1–(-3)

Passing
(Attempts, Completions, Interceptions, Yards)
Green Bay—Bratkowski 25–14–1–190; Starr 5–3–0–50; Pitts 1–0–0–0
Chicago—Bukich 17–7–2–79; Wade 4–2–0–19; Sayers 1–0–1–0

Receiving
(Receptions, Yards)
Green Bay—Dale 6–87; Taylor 3–17; Dowler 2–49; Pitts 2–33; Fleming 2–28; Long 2–26
Chicago—Bull 3–33; Ditka 3–29; Gordon 2–22; Sayers 1–14

Interceptions
Green Bay—Adderley, Jeter, Robinson
Chicago—Petitbon

Fumbles Recovered
Green Bay—Caffey
Chicago—Butkus

After an off week due to the uneven number of teams in the league, the Packers hosted the Bears. Chicago had won one, lost one, and tied two since Green Bay beat them 17–0 on October 16. The Pack came into the game 7–2, now tied with the Baltimore Colts atop the Western Conference after the Colts disposed of the Falcons 19–7 on November 13. Despite an extra week of rest, Hornung would not return to the starting lineup, especially after it was revealed that he had a broken nose. "I'm not going to risk a serious injury," explained Coach Lombardi.[33]

The teams engaged in another defensive struggle in which two of the three touchdowns, one for each side, were set up by the defenses.

The Packers suffered a setback right away. Starr pulled a hamstring on his first pass of the game, after which he went to the sidelines and told Bratkowski to start cranking up. Bart toughed it out for three more series before leaving for good. Zeke had replaced Bart for three crucial wins in the hectic 1965 championship campaign, and the former Georgia quarterback led another victorious effort. But it wasn't easy.

The Bears often deployed an eight- or nine-man line and red dogged from almost anywhere. However, the Packer line and backs did an excellent job, limiting Chicago to one sack, a 13-yard loss by Bratkowski in the fourth period. With the Bears openly inviting them to pass, Green Bay threw 31 times, completing 17. The 227 net aerial yards compensated for gaining just 69 on the ground.

The tone was set on the first play from scrimmage. Taylor tried the middle, but the Bears stormed through and hurled him for a five-yard loss. On the next snap, Starr dropped a beautiful throw into Dowler's arms 40 yards upfield. However, the drive ended with Chandler missing a field goal from the 39. The rest of the quarter consisted of a punting duel between Chandler and Bobby Joe Green.

The home team launched an advance in the second quarter that started with Taylor running for six and Bratkowski throwing to Dale for 11. The drive stalled, but Charley Bivins belted Chandler on the punt. The penalty gave the Pack new life on the Chicago 35. Zeke hit Pitts for 16, but the next four plays moved the ball only nine yards and the Packers turned the ball over on downs. However, three plays later, Green Bay regained possession when Caffey recovered a fumble on the 18. After a delay of game penalty, Zeke pitched 14 yards to Taylor to the eight. Following two runs, Bratkowski threw a six-yard pass to Dale for a 7–0 lead. Carroll juked Roosevelt Taylor and took the ball on the goal line.

Dave Robinson gave the Bays another chance when he intercepted a pass in front of Ditka and returned six yards to the 29. But a holding penalty took the steam out of the advance, and Chandler's field goal try from the 37 sailed wide.

Bill Wade, the signal caller for the Bears' 1963 championship team, replaced the ineffective Bukich early in the third quarter but couldn't spark the offense. Late in the quarter, Bob Jeter snared a halfback pass by Sayers on the Green Bay 39. Zeke connected with Pitts for 17, Taylor for six, Dowler for nine, and Dale for 14 to the 19. But Taylor fumbled, and Butkus recovered.

Early in the final period, the Bears got their sack of Bratkowski. Richie Petitbon intercepted Zeke's next pass and returned 20 yards to the Packers five. Bukich re-entered at that point, and three plays later Sayers ran wide for six. However, Bears kicker Roger LeClerc made like a duffer and kicked behind the ball, which dribbled into the line to keep the Pack in front, 7–6.

The Packers responded with a time-consuming touchdown march. Taylor and Pitts ran on first and second downs, and Bratkowski, emulating Starr's third-down efficiency, completed passes of 16 to Dale and 15 to Fleming to reach the 18. A holding infraction set the pigskin back to the 32, but Zeke overcame that in one swoop. Dale juked Dave Whitsell on the ten, gathered in the pass on the five, and ran in untouched. As Carroll crossed the goal line, the score from Detroit went final on the stadium scoreboard: Lions 20 Colts 14. The Packers had only to hold on to secure undisputed first place in the West. However, the struggling Chandler made the task more difficult by missing the extra point.

The Green and Gold defense stuffed the Bears, the offense ran the clock down with six rushing plays for 16 yards, and the defense finished off the 13–6 victory.

Packers vs. Bears, November 20, 1966. Fullback Jim Taylor #31 is about to make contact with Bears defensive back Bennie McRae #26. Bears defensive lineman Bob Kilcullen #74 is in the background. The Packers won the game, 13–6, and never lost again in the 1966 season. Photograph by Vernon J. Biever.

Calling it "a typical Bear-Packer game," Lombardi lauded the work of Bratkowski. "I think Zeke deserves a great deal of credit. It's pretty hard to come in there when you haven't been playing much." Vince also bragged about the defense, which held Sayers to 68 yards on 20 carries. "We held 'em two games with one touchdown." As usual, the coach refused to mention individuals. "It's hard to single out anybody on the defense when they all played so well."[34]

With the Colts losing to the Lions, Baltimore dropped out of a tie for first with a 7–3 record, one game behind the Packers' 8–2 mark. The only other team in the West with fewer than five losses was San Francisco at 4–4–2.

November 27, 1966—Game 11: Green Bay Packers vs. Minnesota Vikings

Metropolitan Stadium

	Green Bay	Minnesota
First downs	20	18
Yards rushing	164	128
Yards passing	149	229
Total yards (Net)	304	322
Passes	20–31	15–27
Intercepted by	1	0
Punts-Yards	5–203	3–74
Fumbles lost	1	1
Yards penalized	72	68

Green Bay	7	14	0	7	28
Minnesota	3	0	6	7	16

Minnesota—field goal, Cox 27
Green Bay—Elijah Pitts 1, run (Don Chandler kick)
Green Bay—Jim Taylor 14, pass from Bart Starr (Chandler kick)
Green Bay—Marv Fleming 10, pass from Starr (Chandler kick)
Minnesota—field goal, Cox 30
Minnesota—field goal, Cox 22
Minnesota—Dave Osborn 38, pass from Fran Tarkenton (Cox kick)
Green Bay—Jim Grabowski 36, run (Chandler kick)
A—47,426

Rushing
(Attempts, Yards)
Green Bay—Jim Grabowski, 7–61; Elijah Pitts, 12–41; Don Chandler, 1–33; Jim Taylor, 8–20; Bart Starr, 3–9
Minnesota—Bill Brown, 17–40; Jim Lindsey, 11–40; Dave Osborn, 2–20; Fran Tarkenton, 6–18; Phil King, 3–6; Billy Ray Barnes, 1–4

Passing
(Attempts, Completions, Yards, Interceptions)
Green Bay—Bart Starr, 31–20–149—0
Minnesota—Fran Tarkenton, 27–15–229—1

Receiving
(Receptions, Yards)

Green Bay—Marv Fleming, 4–37; Boyd Dowler, 4–35; Elijah Pitts, 4–31; Jim Taylor, 4–25; Jim Grabowski, 3–8; Carroll Dale, 1–13

Minnesota—Red Phillips, 5–98; Jim Lindsey, 3–37; Paul Flatley, 2–29; Preston Carpenter, 2–20; Bill Brown, 2–7; Dave Osborn, 1–38

Interceptions
Green Bay—Herb Adderley
Minnesota—None

Fumbles Recovered
Green Bay—Ray Nitschke
Minnesota—Carl Eller

Coming into this contest, the Vikings had a 3–6–1 record and were losers of their two previous games. The Packers were mean and hungry for revenge after their loss to the Vikings on November 6. Green Bay was tough in rematches against teams that beat them earlier in the same season. Only two teams were able to accomplish a series sweep since Vince Lombardi became head coach. The Baltimore Colts achieved the feat in both 1959 and 1964, and the Chicago Bears did it in 1963. The 1959 Colts won the NFL title for the second straight year, made it to the NFL title game in 1964, and the 1963 Bears went on to win the NFL crown.

At game time, the temperature was 33 degrees with a wind chill making it feel like 22 degrees, which seemed perfect for the Nordic-like clashes of teams from that region of the United States in November. The Vikings got on the board first thanks to a balanced offensive attack. Tarkenton connected on short passes, and running back Bill Brown pounded the ball, but the Green Bay defense prevented Minnesota from getting into the end zone. Fred Cox was called upon to salvage the drive, and delivered with a 27-yard field goal that gave Minnesota an early 3–0 lead.

With Starr still nursing a tender hamstring injury suffered one week earlier, the offense made it to midfield before stalling. On fourth down, Chandler came on to punt. The snap from center Bill Curry went high and wide, but Chandler was able to get control of the ball, and Chandler decided to run instead of punt. Getting a good block from Steve Wright, Don picked up 33 yards before being stopped at the Minnesota 17. Pitts carried for nine yards on first down; Taylor added three more for a new set of downs inside the ten. Starr then mixed things up with a four-yard pass to Dowler that placed the ball on the one. On second-and-goal, Pitts capped off the drive to put the Packers up by a 7–3 margin at the end of the first quarter.

With the clock ticking down the opening 15 minutes of play, team captain Willie Davis broke free from the man blocking him and got his hands on Tarkenton. In the process of bringing him down, Davis stripped the ball from the quarterback's grasp, and linebacker Ray Nitschke quickly pounced on the fumble at the Minnesota 37.

On the first play of the second quarter, the Packers kept the chains moving by running for a first down on a fourth-and-one situation. During this drive, Starr completed four passes to Taylor with the final reception resulting in a 14-yard touchdown. Taylor rammed through two would-be tacklers on the five, and Green Bay was up, 14–3.

The Vikings made an attempt to cut into the 11-point deficit, but Cox missed on a 34-yard field goal try. The Packers stalled on their next possession, and Chandler got off a punt that pinned the Vikings on their own 15-yard line. Once again, Davis got to Tarkenton, this time dropping him for a loss of nine yards. On the day, the Green Bay defense sacked Tarkenton four times for 35 yards. A penalty then pinned the Vikings back even deeper, and Bobby Walden was forced to punt from his own end zone with time running out in the first half.

Just as Walden's foot was about to connect with the ball, Adderley broke through. The ball hit him in the side, causing it to carry a mere four yards to give Green Bay possession on the Minnesota 11. After Taylor ran for one yard, Starr threw into coverage, but tight end Marv Fleming emerged from the crowd with the ball in his hands. The ten-yard scoring strike was Starr's second of the game, and the Packers headed to the visitor's locker room with a commanding 21–3 halftime advantage.

The Viking defense clamped down in the third quarter and forced two Chandler punts that produced a pair of Cox field goals from 30 and 22 yards out to make it a 21–9 game.

Starr connected with Pitts for a 14-yard reception, and Dale for 13 more yards. Pitts then ran for a pickup of 11 to take Green Bay to the Minnesota 30. Starr ran for ten yards, but fumbled, and the Vikings' Carl Eller recovered the ball. The Vikings could not capitalize on the turnover and had to punt. The Packers failed to move the ball as well, and returned possession back to Minnesota via a Chandler punt that Lance Rentzel called a fair catch on at the four.

Tarkenton threw for 229 yards during the course of this game. Ninety-nine of those yards came on the ensuing offensive series. Red Phillips made the highlight reel with an incredible 61-yard catch that saw him stretch his body to secure. After Nitschke dropped running back Bill Brown for a loss of three yards, Tarkenton threw to Minnesota's other running back, Dave Osborn, who broke a tackle by Tom Brown on the Green Bay 25, and he then crossed the goal line to pull the Vikings to 21–16 in the fourth quarter.

After seeing an 18-point advantage cut drastically with the clock ticking down in the final stanza, Starr got a drive going with a seven-yard pass to rookie Jim Grabowski, who came on to replace Taylor at fullback after Jimmy was hit in the head on the second to last play of the third quarter. After throwing to Grabowski, Starr connected with Dale for another 16 yards as the clock now showed five minutes remaining. On six straight plays, Grabowski and Pitts crashed into the defense, getting the ball to the Minnesota 30. Unfortunately, the drive stalled and a 37-yard Chandler field goal attempt went wide.

The missed field goal gave Minnesota renewed hope of coming all the way back with 3:25 left to play. Bill Brown started the drive off with a 12-yard run, which was followed by Jim Lindsey running for three more. A Tarkenton to Phillips pass gained 11 yards, and a two-yard run by Brown had the ball at midfield with two minutes left.

On second-and-eight, Phil King took a pitchout from Tarkenton. He stopped and looked to throw an option pass, but could not find an open receiver. He threw the ball back to Tarkenton, who then let a pass fly toward Preston Carpenter. Adderley intercepted the ball and returned it 13 yards to the Minnesota 45.

With 1:14 left, Green Bay stayed on the ground. On third down, Grabowski spun away from two tacklers, and was sprung loose by a block from Dowler on Earsell Mackbee. The result was a 36-yard touchdown run, and Chandler then added the final point of the game on a conversion kick that made the final score 28–16.

This proved to be a hard-fought game by both teams. However, the aches and pains suffered by the Packers were made a little easier to deal with after finding out that Baltimore lost to the Rams. Baltimore's loss allowed Green Bay to increase their lead in the West by two games over the Colts with three games left in the regular season.[35]

Over in the Eastern Conference, the St. Louis Cardinals had been sole possessors of the lead for eight straight weeks until a new contender came on the scene. The Dallas Cowboys climbed up the ranks to share the conference lead with St. Louis at the climax of Week 11.

As Week 12 unfolded, the struggle for control of the Eastern Conference remained the same. The Cowboys hosted the Browns on Thanksgiving, and came away with a 26–14 win to keep them even atop the conference with an 8–2–1 record. The Cowboys were assisted by quarterback Don Meredith's 94.3 completion percentage against the Browns, and Don Perkins 111 yards rushing. The Browns, winners of the past two conference titles, still had hopes of obtaining a third straight conference crown with a 7–4 record. St. Louis managed to hold on its share of the lead thanks to a pair of Jim Bakken field goals in a 6–3 victory over the 3–7–1 Steelers.

December 4, 1966–Game 12: San Francisco 49ers vs. Green Bay Packers

Milwaukee County Stadium

	Green Bay	San Francisco
First downs	20	17
Yards rushing	107	140
Yards passing	236	183
Total yards (Net)	311	321
Passes	13–24	14–33
Intercepted by	2	0
Punts-Yards	8–335	5–197
Fumbles lost	1	2
Yards penalized	30	66

San Francisco	0	0	0	7	7
Green Bay	7	0	0	13	20

Green Bay—Carroll Dale 83, pass from Bart Starr (Don Chandler kick)

Green Bay—Starr 1, run (kick blocked)

San Francisco—Dave Parks 65, pass from John Brodie (Tommy Davis kick)

Green Bay—Elijah Pitts 2, run (Chandler kick)

A—48,725

Rushing
(Attempts, Yards)

Green Bay—Jim Taylor, 18–84; Elijah Pitts, 14–27; Jim Grabowski, 1–1; Bart Starr, 1–1; Donny Anderson, 2–(-6)

San Francisco—Ken Willard, 14–52; John David Crow, 9–52; Tommy Davis, 1–22; Gary Lewis, 3–8; Dave Kopay, 4–5; George Mira, 1–1

Passing
(Attempts, Completions, Yards, Interceptions)

Green Bay—Bart Starr, 24–13–236–0

San Francisco—John Brodie, 33–14–183–2

Receiving
(Receptions, Yards)
Green Bay—Marv Fleming, 4–36; Carroll Dale, 3–142; Elijah Pitts, 3–31; Jim Taylor, 2–14; Boyd Dowler, 1–13
San Francisco—Dave Parks, 6–138; John David Crow, 2–27; Bernie Casey, 2–13; Monty Stickles, 2–7; Gary Lewis, 1–4; Dave Kopay, 1–6

Interceptions
Green Bay—Bob Jeter, Dave Robinson
San Francisco—None

Fumbles Recovered
Green Bay—Tom Brown; Ron Kostelnik
San Francisco—Stan Hindman

For the second week in a row, the Packers were looking for revenge on a team that beat them in 1966. In addition to evening the season series out, the Packers also had the opportunity to clinch at least a tie for their fifth conference crown during the Lombardi era. It seemed that playing San Francisco proved to be lucky for the Packers in three of their last four tie-clinching conquests. En route to conference titles in 1960, 1962, and 1965, Green Bay clinched a tie in wins against the 49ers. They also had the chance to clinch the conference title outright if the Colts lost to Chicago.

The 49ers were at 5–4–2 coming into this game, and looking for their second straight winning season under Head Coach Jack Christiansen. Since recording their first win of the season against Green Bay two months earlier by a narrow 21–20 decision, the 49ers became a solid football team. They posted a 4–2–1 record during the time leading up to this rematch with Green Bay, and had averaged over 400 yards of offense in their three previous games. They entered this clash with the Packers fresh off a convincing 41–14 victory over Detroit on Thanksgiving Day.

A record crowd of 48,725 came out to County Stadium to witness this game. Freezing rain coupled with a 27-degree temperature and a 16-mile per hour wind made this an afternoon game under the lights. Tommy Davis got off a short kickoff that bounced around the field before rookie Donny Anderson scooped the ball up and was tackled deep in Green Bay territory at the eight. Jim Taylor, recovered from his head injury suffered one week earlier, gave the Packers some breathing room by running for nine yards. Green Bay then faced a third-and-one situation from the 17.

Starr faked a handoff to Pitts, and with the defense ready for a plunge into the line, Starr took the ball from Pitts at the last second and threw a short pass across the middle to Dale, who outran the opposition en route to an 83-yard touchdown. The Packers led, 7–0, with a mere 1:56 expired from the game clock. However, Dale's long scoring trek was the lone tally in the scoring column until the fifth play of the fourth quarter.

The Niners offense looked to be on their way to quickly tying the game. The backfield tandem of Willard and Crow moved the chains on the ground, and quarterback John Brodie balanced the running attack with short pass completions. The result was a first down on the Packers 18. But Aldridge hit Brodie on third-and-seven, causing a fumble that Kostelnik recovered. The 49ers came back again on a 35-yard pass from Brodie to Dave Parks, but another fumble, this time recovered by Tom Brown at the Green Bay 33, killed the momentum.

The 49ers made three more serious attempts to get on the board in the first half but failed each time, while Chandler had to punt four times in the second quarter. Even though the 49ers were down by seven points at the end of the first half, they dominated the stats. They had a 15 to four advantage in first downs, and outgained Green Bay 206 to 138 in total yards.

The third quarter was a punting duel between Davis and Chandler. With the quarter coming to a climax, the Packers went on the move. Starting at their own 17, Taylor ran for seven combined yards on the final two plays of the third quarter. Starr then took to the air, hitting Taylor for eight, Dale for 11, Pitts for 11, and Fleming for 17, which got the Packers down to the San Francisco 12-yard line. Starr then handed off to Pitts on five straight plays. With the ball on the one, Starr kept the ball on a quarterback sneak for a touchdown to complete the 16-play drive. Chandler's extra point attempt on the icy infield section of County Stadium was blocked, and the Packers led, 13–0.

Three minutes after Starr's touchdown, the 49ers struck to cut into the 13-point deficit. From the San Francisco 35, Brodie threw a deep pass to Parks. Parks shoved off Jeter, made a juggling catch and ran the rest of the way for a 65-yard touchdown to tighten the score to 13–7.

Donny Anderson returned the ensuing kickoff to the Packers 30. With solid blocking up front, Starr threw down the middle to Dale for a 48-yard gain to the Niners 22. Taylor ran for a gain of ten, and the Packers received extra yardage when defensive end Clark Miller was called for a late hit on Taylor after the fullback was already on the ground. The penalty moved the ball to the six. Pitts then carried for four, and got scoring honors on the following play when he ran for a two-yard touchdown with 2:55 left in the game to up the score to 20–7.

San Francisco did not go quietly, as they came back to get a first down at midfield. Linebacker Dave Robinson then silenced the 49ers by intercepting a Brodie pass to seal Green Bay's victory. On the second to last play, Starr was taken out of the game to a standing ovation from the Packer faithful after completing 13 of 24 pass attempts for 236 yards and one touchdown pass, plus running for one score himself. The Packers improved to 10–2 on the year and maintained their two game conference lead over Baltimore after the Colts rallied in the final 39 seconds to beat Chicago when Unitas connected with Berry on a 24-yard touchdown pass. The win ended a two-game losing streak for Baltimore.[36]

While the Packers disposed of the 49ers in Week 13 to clinch at least a share of the Western Conference title, the Cowboys made a major move in seeking their first title of any kind. With heavy fog and a light rain coming down at the Cotton Bowl, the Cowboys improved to 9–2–1 with a 31–17 win over the Cardinals, who dropped into sole possession of second place in the Eastern Conference with an 8–3–1 record. Elsewhere in the Eastern Conference, the Browns stayed in third place with an 8–4 record after beating the Giants, 49–40.

December 10, 1966–Game 13: Green Bay Packers vs. Baltimore Colts

Memorial Stadium

	Green Bay	Baltimore
First downs	14	15
Yards rushing	97	153

	Green Bay	Baltimore
Yards passing	183	140
Total yards (Net)	242	283
Passes	12–23	11–25
Intercepted by	4	0
Punts-Yards	6–291	3–121
Fumbles lost	1	1
Yards penalized	19	25

Green Bay	7	0	0	7	14
Baltimore	0	10	0	0	10

   Green Bay—Elijah Pitts 42, pass from Bart Starr (Don Chandler kick)
   Baltimore—Tony Lorick 1, run (Lou Michaels kick)
   Baltimore—field goal, Michaels 26
   Green Bay—Pitts 2, run (Chandler kick)
   A—60,238

Rushing
(Attempts, Yards)
   Green Bay—Jim Taylor, 17–43; Elijah Pitts, 11–43; Bart Starr, 1–8; Zeke Bratkowski, 1–3
   Baltimore—Jerry Hill, 25–88; Tony Lorick, 10–35; Tom Matte, 3–18; Johnny Unitas, 5–12

Passing
(Attempts, Completions, Yards, Interceptions)
   Green Bay—Bart Starr, 15–7–96–0; Zeke Bratkowski, 8–5–87–0
   Baltimore—Johnny Unitas, 24–11–140–3; Gary Cuozzo, 1–0–0–1

Receiving
(Receptions, Yards)
   Green Bay—Elijah Pitts, 4–79; Jim Taylor, 3–34; Carroll Dale, 2–29; Marv Fleming, 2–23; Max McGee, 1–18
   Baltimore—Raymond Berry, 4–59; Lenny Moore, 2–18; John Mackey, 2–15; Tom Matte, 1–25; Tony Lorick, 1–18; Jimmy Orr, 1–5

Interceptions
Green Bay—Wood, Caffey, Tom Brown
Baltimore—None

Fumbles Recovered
Green Bay—Dave Robinson
Baltimore—Barry Brown

From 1958 to 1968 the Green Bay Packers or the Baltimore Colts won the NFL's Western Conference every year except 1963. This time around, the Colts would be hosting this most crucial matchup inside "the Old Grey Lady of 33rd Street," Memorial Stadium. The Colts' only hope of being conference champions was if they beat the Packers, and then won their regular season finale while Green Bay lost theirs to Los Angeles. The lone notable injury was Packers guard Fuzzy Thurston, who was nursing an ankle injury. He was replaced by rookie Gale Gillingham. The Colts reported no injuries, but John Unitas had some discomfort due to a sore passing shoulder.

The kickoff went to Donny Anderson who received the ball on the Green Bay eight and returned it 22 yards to give the Packers their first offensive series starting on the 30.

Green Bay moved close to midfield before being forced to punt. Chandler got off a 51-yard punt that pinned Baltimore deep on the 12. Unitas attempted to pass on first down, but Willie Wood intercepted to give Green Bay possession starting on the Baltimore 46.

Facing a third-and-six situation from the Colts 42, Starr threw to Pitts on the 20-yard line with Alvin Haymond and Jerry Logan surrounding him. Pitts slipped free to record a 42-yard touchdown to give the Packers a 7–0 advantage. That score held up for the remainder of the opening quarter.

After an exchange of punts, the Colts' offense got going early in the second quarter. Unitas threw to Berry for 20 yards. The Packers' defense had allowed only 130 points to be scored on it over 12 weeks, and it stiffened up once again. Unitas and company were able only to get slightly past midfield before stalling. Lou Michaels then missed a 45-yard field goal attempt. A few minutes later, Chandler missed

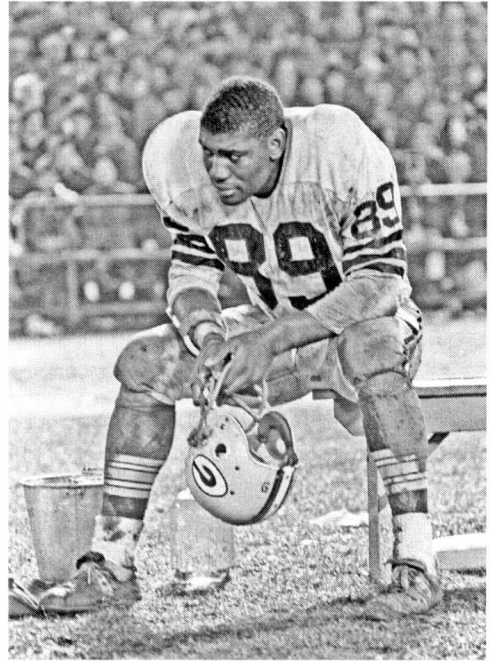

Packers at Colts, December 10, 1966. Linebacker David Robinson #89 sits on the bench, muddied. The Packers won 14–10. Photograph by Vernon J. Biever.

Packers at Colts, December 10, 1966: Running back Elijah Pitts #22 scores the touchdown that puts the Packers ahead for good. Quarterback Zeke Bratkowski #12 is in the background to the right. Guard Jerry Kramer #64 attempts to block Colts defensive end Lou Michaels #79. The Packers won 14–10. Photograph by Vernon J. Biever.

a field goal attempt from the same distance. Haymond caught Chandler's attempt at the goal line. After being trapped on the eight, he got away for a long gain that was stopped with a Willie Davis tackle at the Green Bay 47.

The Colts took advantage of Haymond's efforts by tying the score within six plays. The big play of the quick drive was a Unitas to Berry pass that covered 27 yards and placed the ball on the Packers two. Jeter was injured on the play and was replaced by third-year pro Doug Hart. Tony Lorick punched the ball over the goal line from the one at the 8:12 mark of the second quarter.

The Colts then took the lead 30 seconds after tying the game. Anderson fumbled the ensuing kickoff, and Barry Brown recovered for Baltimore on the Green Bay 21-yard line. The Packers' defensive unit rose to the challenge and prevented a touchdown, but Michaels connected on a 26-yard field goal that gave the home team a 10–7 lead. The first half ended when Starr was dropped for a loss of three yards. He suffered a rib injury early in the sec-

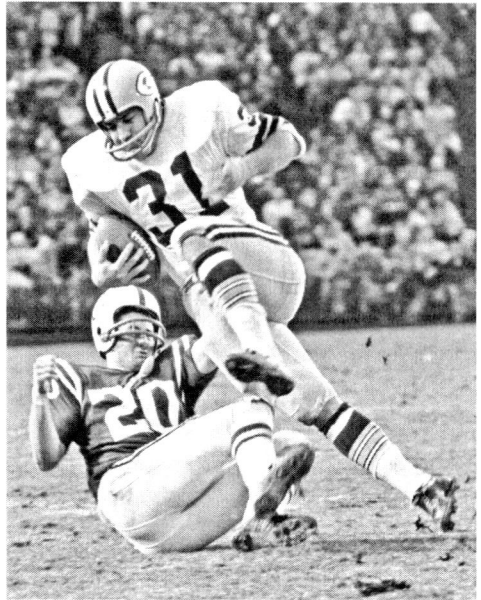

Packers at Colts, December 10, 1966. Fullback Jim Taylor #31 carries the ball while Colts defensive back Jerry Logan #20 attempts the tackle. Photograph by Vernon J. Biever.

ond quarter, and by halftime, the pain was too much and it hampered his ability to function on the field. X-Rays later showed Starr had bruised ribs. He was replaced in the second half by Bratkowski.

The players returned to the field greeted by a hard rain that was making the turf soft and messy. The first ten minutes of the second half was a saga of missed field goals. Michaels missed a 47-yarder that was returned 47 yards by Willie Wood. Chandler then tried from 47 yards out. His kick had the distance but went wide right. The Packers quickly had possession returned to them three plays later when safety Tom Brown intercepted a Unitas pass intended for tight end John Mackey on the Baltimore 39.

Pitts and Taylor went to work on the ground, advancing the ball to the Baltimore 27 in two carries. The Packers got lucky on third down

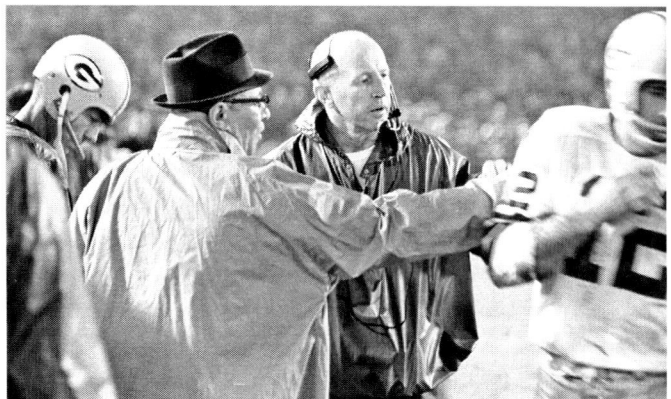

Packers at Colts, December 10, 1966. Coach Vince Lombardi and assistant coach Red Cochran talk as backup quarterback Zeke Bratkowksi #12 heads out onto the field. Quarterback Bart Starr #15 is on the left, looking down. The Packers won 14–10. Photograph by Vernon J. Biever.

when middle linebacker Dennis Gaubatz dropped a possible interception thrown by Bratkowski. Luck then shined on the home team when Chandler missed a 30-yard field goal attempt that would have tied the game.

Early in the fourth quarter, Michaels missed again from 37 yards out. Bratkowski started the following drive off with a 28-yard pass to Pitts that got the ball to the Green Bay 48. Taylor ran for four yards, Bratkowski threw across the middle for a gain of 11 to Fleming, and Pitts and Taylor combined for 12 more yards on the ground. After Pitts was stopped for no gain on first down at the 25, Bratkowski looked to pass. Unable to find an open receiver, he ran for three yards. He then went back to the air, this time looking for Max McGee. Bratkowski had called for McGee to run an outside route. The veteran receiver decided against the original route after he saw the middle of the field open up as Baltimore sent a defensive back on a safety blitz. Zeke hit McGee with an 18-yard reception with defensive backs Lenny Lyles and Jerry Logan converging on him the moment he made the catch at the four. Two plays later, Pitts went into the end zone standing up to regain the lead for Green Bay, 14–10, with 4:57 left in the game.

The Colts were not about to fold in front of their home crowd. They got down to the Green Bay 15 on the strength of passes from Unitas to Hill, Moore, and Berry. With 1:29 remaining, Unitas went back to pass, and unable to find an open receiver, he started to run up the middle but was greeted by a Willie Davis ball-stripping tackle. Linebacker Dave Robinson fell on the ball that *Sports Illustrated* would dub the "Million Dollar Fumble." The Packers then ran out the clock to clinch their fifth conference title in seven years.[37]

Over in the Eastern Conference, the race for supremacy remained the same, as the top three teams competing for the title all lost. The losses put the Cowboys at 9–3–1, and the Cardinals at 8–4–1. The Cards' only hope of winning the conference was to beat 8–5 Cleveland in the regular season finale and then hope that the Giants, owners of the worst record in the league, upset the Cowboys on the same weekend.

December 18, 1966–Game 14: Green Bay Packers vs. Los Angeles Rams

Los Angeles Memorial Coliseum

	Green Bay	Los Angeles
First downs	14	19
Yards rushing	118	100
Yards passing	245	284
Total yards (Net)	355	351
Passes	13–23	23–38
Intercepted by	1	1
Punts-Yards	3–131	6–284
Fumbles lost	3	1
Yards penalized	49	56

Green Bay	7	10	0	10	27
Los Angeles	3	6	0	14	23

    Los Angeles—field goal, Gossett 36

    Green Bay—Bob Jeter 75, interception return (Don Chandler kick)

    Los Angeles—field goal, Gossett 30

    Green Bay—field goal, Chandler 10

Los Angeles—field goal, Gossett 17
Green Bay—Donny Anderson 2, run (Chandler kick)
Green Bay—Carroll Dale 23, pass from Zeke Bratkowski (Chandler kick)
Green Bay—field goal, Chandler 47
Los Angeles—Roman Gabriel 11, run (Gossett kick)
Los Angeles—Marlin McKeever 3, pass from Gabriel (Gossett kick)
A—72,416

Rushing
(Attempts, Yards)
Green Bay—Donny Anderson, 11–58; Jim Taylor, 6–27; Paul Hornung, 5–19; Jim Grabowski, 9–9; Zeke Bratkowski, 1–4; Elijah Pitts, 3–1
Los Angeles—Dick Bass, 14–49; Roman Gabriel, 4–24; Tom Moore, 5–22; Jim Stiger, 2–3; Ken Iman, 1–2

Passing
(Attempts, Completions, Yards,
Interceptions)
Green Bay—Zeke Bratkowski, 23–13–245—1
Los Angeles—Roman Gabriel, 37–22–237—1; Jon Kilgore, 1–1–47–0

Receiving
(Receptions, Yards)
Green Bay—Carroll Dale, 3–121; Marv Fleming, 3–27; Jim Taylor, 2–0; Bob Long, 1–42; Donny Anderson, 1–22; Elijah Pitts, 1–18; Max McGee, 1–10; Paul Hornung, 1–5
Los Angeles—Marlin McKeever, 6–53; Tom Moore, 6–26; Tommy McDonald, 4–46; Dick Bass, 3–0; Jack Snow, 2–62; Steve Heckard, 1–50; Claude Crabb, 1–47

Interceptions
Green Bay—Bob Jeter
Los Angeles—Eddie Meador

Fumbles Recovered
Green Bay—Dave Robinson
Los Angeles—Chuck Lamson; Bill George; Merlin Olsen

The city of Los Angeles was one month away from hosting the first-ever Super Bowl. However, on the week before Christmas Day 1966, the Packers were in the City of Angels for their regular season finale. Their goal was to get back to Los Angeles to represent the NFL in that history-making initial Super Bowl.

Even though the Conference title was secured, Lombardi had his starters open the game. He also wanted to get as many of his rookies and reserves involved in the action. Two players that were certain not to see action were guard Fuzzy Thurston, who was hampered by an injured ankle, and Bart Starr. With the game not bearing any postseason implications for the Packers, there was no need to have Starr in the game while he was still nursing bruised ribs. The offense was turned over to the more than capable hands of Zeke Bratkowski, making his first start since 1963 when he was a member of the Rams.

The 1966 Rams were a team of streaks after the Packers handed them their first loss of the year in Week Three. They rallied for two straight wins after losing to Green Bay. It was then on to a dismal four-game losing streak that dropped them to 4–5. After that slide, they rebounded with a four-game winning streak before hosting the Packers in the regular season finale. The Rams, at 8–5, were guaranteed of finishing with a winning record for the first time since 1958.

On a 58-degree afternoon in Los Angeles, with a wind of eight miles-per-hour blowing in, the Packers kicked off to start the regular season finale. The Rams took the opening kickoff and went 42 yards in 11 plays to score on a 36-yard field goal from Bruce Gossett.

After both teams exchanged fumbles, the Rams were driving once again. After getting to the Green Bay 27, quarterback Roman Gabriel threw to receiver Jack Snow near the sideline. Jeter jumped the route, intercepted the pass at the 25, and raced 75 yards for the touchdown, the team's sixth interception return touchdown of 1966, which tied the NFL record set previously by the Browns in 1960.

Undaunted by the quick score, the Rams came back and reached the Green Bay 25 early in the second quarter on the strength of Gabriel passes to Tommy McDonald and Dick Bass. Gossett successfully booted a 30-yard field goal to close to within one point of the Packers' lead. With that field goal, his 27th, Gossett set the NFL record for most field goals in one season.

The second quarter started to become the battle of kickers. After Gossett's record-setter, Chandler kicked a ten-yard field goal to extend Green Bay's lead to 10–6. The big play of the drive came on a 45-yard pass from Bratkowski to Dale that placed the ball on the Rams' four. The Rams came right back to have Gossett extend his NFL record to 28 field goals in a single season. Snow caught a 58-yard pass from Gabriel to get the Rams close enough for Gossett to boot a 17-yard three-pointer to once again cut the deficit to one point, 10–9.

With the all-rookie backfield of Grabowski and Anderson, plus the arm of Bratkowski, the Packers went 78 yards in seven plays to produce the game's first offensive touchdown. Two Bratkowski passes allowed Green Bay to get inside the Los Angeles ten quickly. Dale caught the first pass for a gain of 22 yards at the Rams 48. The second went to Bob Long, who stretched his body out to snag a 42-yard reception at the nine. Two plays later, Anderson ran for a two-yard touchdown to give Green Bay a little breathing room before halftime, 17–9.

The Packers started the second half with Taylor gaining 20 yards in three carries. Zeke then threw to Dale for 24 yards to get the ball down to the Rams 36. Hornung, seeing his first action since October 16, ran for three yards, and Bratkowski threw to Fleming for an additional five yards. With only two yards needed for another first down, Hornung carried twice, but came up just inches shy of the required distance.

The remainder of the third quarter became a punting duel between Chandler and Kilgore. The score stayed at 17–9 going into the fourth quarter, but the Packers began a successful drive as the clock ticked away the end of the third quarter.

The old veteran tandem of Taylor and Hornung graced the backfield and helped move the Packers 62 yards in nine plays. Hornung got the drive started with a pair of seven-yard runs. Bratkowski got into the act by throwing to Fleming for 16, and then capped the drive off with a 23-yard scoring strike to Dale to make the score 24–9. Chandler then added a 47-yard field goal to increase the Green Bay advantage to what seemed to be an insurmountable 27–9 bulge.

The Rams went on to score after a fake punt got them to the Packers 15. On second-and-11, Gabriel dropped back to pass but instead took off on an 11-yard touchdown jaunt to close the margin to 27–16. Grabowski and Anderson were back in as Green Bay's running back duo. Anderson gained 33 yards in three carries to help the Packers get downfield. Grabowski then fumbled and Merlin Olsen recovered the ball and lost it to teammate Jack Pardee to give the Rams hope.

Steve Heckard caught one pass all day, but it was for 50 yards to get the ball down to the Packers three. On second down, Marlin McKeever caught a three-yard touchdown pass from Gabriel to make the score 27–23 with 24 seconds left.

The Rams came close to pulling off the impossible, but in the end, the 1966 Packers finished the regular season with an NFL-best 12–2 record. They missed out on a perfect season by a combined four points.

This game turned into a passing duel. Bratkowski and Gabriel threw a combined 61 passes, with 36 of them being completions for 529 yards. Vince Lombardi managed to get all his players some work throughout the game, and the Green Bay defense sacked Gabriel six times for 33 yards.[38]

The Browns ended the Eastern Conference race by defeating the Cardinals, 38–10. With St. Louis losing, the Cowboys officially posted their first-ever championship. Dallas then went out and gained a hard-fought 17–7 decision over the dismal Giants. The win gave Dallas the Eastern Conference crown with a 10–3–1 record.

Meanwhile in the AFL, Buffalo won the East by beating Denver in the season finale to edge out the Patriots, who lost their finale to the Jets. Kansas City had clinched the Western crown three weeks before.

Final 1966 Regular Season NFL Standings

Eastern Conference

Team	Win	Loss	Tie	Percentage	Points For	Points Allowed
Dallas Cowboys	10	3	1	.769	445	239
Cleveland Browns	9	5	0	.643	403	259
Philadelphia Eagles	9	5	0	.643	326	340
St. Louis Cardinals	8	5	1	.615	264	265
Washington Redskins	7	7	0	.500	351	355
Pittsburgh Steelers	5	8	1	.385	316	347
Atlanta Falcons	3	11	0	.214	204	437
New York Giants	1	12	1	.077	263	501

Western Conference

Team	Win	Loss	Tie	Percentage	Points For	Points Allowed
Green Bay Packers	12	2	0	.857	335	163
Baltimore Colts	9	5	0	.643	314	226
Los Angeles Rams	8	6	0	.571	289	212
San Francisco 49ers	6	6	2	.500	320	325
Chicago Bears	5	7	2	.417	234	272
Detroit Lions	4	9	1	.308	206	317
Minnesota Vikings	4	9	1	.308	292	304

NOTES

1. *Milwaukee Journal,* September 11, 1966.
2. *Appleton* (WI) *Post-Crescent,* September 11, 1966.
3. *Manitowoc* (WI) *Herald-Times,* September 12, 1966.
4. *New York Times,* September 11, 1966.
5. *Appleton* (WI) *Post-Crescent,* September 11, 1966.
6. *Fond Du Lac* (WI) *Commonwealth Reporter,* September 12, 1966.
7. *Manitowoc* (WI) *Herald-Times,* September 12, 1966.
8. *Chicago Tribune,* September 19, 1966.

9. *Elyria* (OH) *Chronicle-Telegram*, September 19, 1966.
10. *Appleton* (WI) *Post-Crescent*, September 19, 1966.
11. *Cleveland Plain Dealer*, September 19, 1966.
12. *Appleton* (WI) *Post-Crescent*, September 25, 1966.
13. *Appleton* (WI) *Post-Crescent*, September 26, 1966.
14. *Manitowoc* (WI) *Herald-Times*, September 26, 1966.
15. *Long Beach* (CA) *Press-Telegram*, September 24, 1966.
16. *Appleton* (WI) *Post-Crescent*, September 26, 1966.
17. *Milwaukee Sentinel*, October 3, 1966.
18. *Appleton* (WI) *Post-Crescent*, October 3, 1966.
19. *Chicago Tribune*, October 3, 1966.
20. *Oakland Tribune*, October 9, 1966.
21. *Chicago Defender*, October 10, 1966.
22. *Oakland Tribune*, October 10, 1966.
23. *Eau Claire* (WI) *Daily Telegram*, October 10, 1966.
24. *Maconitowoc* (WI) *Herald-Times*, October 17, 1966.
25. *Ibid.*
26. *Rockford* (IL) *Register*, October 17, 1966.
27. *Ibid.*
28. *Appleton* (WI) *Post-Crescent*, October 23, 1966.
29. *Appleton* (WI) *Post-Crescent*, October 31, 1966.
30. *Milwaukee Sentinel*, October 31, 1966.
31. *Appleton Sports Crescent*, November 7, 1966.
32. *Ibid.*
33. *Waukesha* (WI) *Daily Freeman*, November 17, 1966.
34. *Appleton* (WI) *Post-Crescent*, November 21, 1966.
35. *Green Bay Press-Gazette*, November 28, 1966.
36. *Green Bay Press-Gazette*, December 5, 1966.
37. *Green Bay Press-Gazette*, December 11, 1966.
38. *Green Bay Press-Gazette*, December 19, 1966. www.pro-football-reference.com.

1966 NFL Championship Game

Rupert Patrick

January 1, 1967—NFL Championship: Green Bay Packers vs. Dallas Cowboys

Cotton Bowl

	Green Bay	Dallas
First downs	19	23
Yards rushing	102	187
Yards passing	304	238
Total yards (Net)	367	418
Passes	19–28	15–31
Intercepted by	1	0
Punts	4–160	4–129
Fumbles lost	1	1
Yards penalized	23	29

Green Bay	14	7	7	6	34
Dallas	14	3	3	7	27

Green Bay—Pitts 17, pass from Starr (Chandler kick)
Green Bay—Grabowski 18, fumble return (Chandler kick)
Dallas—Reeves 3, run (Villanueva kick)
Dallas—Perkins 23, run (Villanueva kick)
Green Bay—Dale 51, pass from Starr (Chandler kick)
Dallas—Field Goal, Villanueva 11
Dallas—Field Goal, Villanueva 32
Green Bay—Dowler 16, pass from Starr (kick blocked)
Dallas—Clarke 68, pass from Meredith (Villanueva kick)
A—74,152

Rushing
(Attempts, Yards)
Green Bay—Pitts 12–66; Taylor 10–37; Starr 2–(-1)
Dallas—Perkins 17–108; Reeves 17–47; Meredith 4–22; Norman 2–10

Passing
(Attempts, Completions, Interceptions, Yards)
Green Bay—Starr 28–19–0–304
Dallas—Meredith 31–15–1–238

Receiving
(Receptions, Yards)
Green Bay—Dale 5–128; Taylor 5–23; Fleming 3–50; Dowler 3–49; McGee 1–28; Pitts 1–17; Long 1–9
Dallas—Reeves 4–77; Norman 4–30; Clarke 3–102; Gent 3–28; Hayes 1–1

Interceptions
Green Bay—Tom Brown
Dallas—None

Fumbles Recovered
Green Bay—Grabowski
Dallas—Livingston

There were actually two NFL championship games between Dallas and Green Bay during the year of 1967, and they served as bookends for the calendar year, if you will. The first was held on New Year's Day of 1967 to decide the 1966 NFL championship. The second championship game was played on December 31, 1967, to decide the 1967 NFL title. That game is better known as the Ice Bowl because it was played in arctic conditions in Green Bay and is one of the most famous pro football games ever played.

Because of the Ice Bowl's fame, this first championship meeting between Dallas and Green Bay is arguably the most underrated postseason game in pro football history. The winner of this game would represent the NFL in the inaugural AFL-NFL World Championship Game, unofficially the Super Bowl. Their opponent would be the Kansas City Chiefs, who soundly defeated the Buffalo Bills 31–7 earlier in the day to win the AFL title.

In their seventh season, the Cowboys had emerged as a powerhouse. Led by quarterback Dandy Don Meredith, the Cowboys led the NFL both in yards gained and points scored. The defense was fourth in fewest points allowed, and second in fewest yards allowed. They had not yet become Doomsday but they were getting there quickly, anchored by Future Hall of Famers Bob Lilly and Mel Renfro.

The champion Packers were rolling along, but they were aging and would start breaking up after the 1966 season with Paul Hornung retiring and Jim Taylor finishing his career with the expansion Saints in 1967. The legendary Packers power rushing game finished eighth of 15 teams in rushing yards, but their defense was excellent, leading the NFL in fewest points and fewest passing yards allowed.

The temperature hung around 40 degrees with a light wind, and the Cotton Bowl was filled to capacity for the 2:30 p.m. CST start. Odds makers had the Packers favored to win by seven points over a Cowboys team playing in its first postseason game. As would be the case with the Ice Bowl, this contest was decided in the final 30 seconds of regulation.

Danny Villanueva kicked off for Dallas, and Donny Anderson caught the ball at the one-yard line and returned it to the Packers 24. On the first play from scrimmage, Pitts took a handoff through a gap on the right side of the line, taking advantage of some great blocking as he picked up 32 yards to the Dallas 44, where Renfro pushed him out of bounds. Starr threw to Dale in the left flat for nine yards, and Taylor ran inside for four yards, more than enough for a first down at the 31.

On first down, Starr dropped back to pass but Lilly batted down the ball at the line. Bart tossed a screen to Taylor on second down, but Lilly caught Taylor in the backfield for a four-yard loss. Dale made a juggling catch over the middle at the 20 on third down, barely giving the Pack a

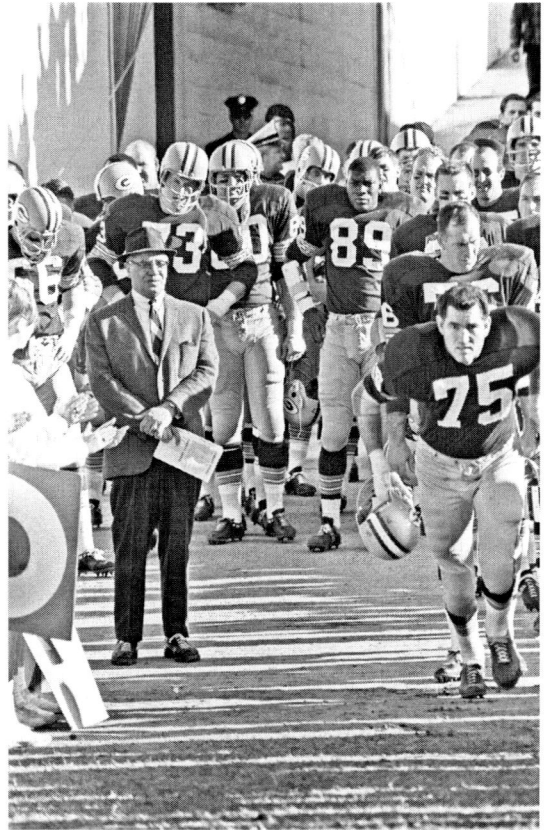

Packers at Cowboys, January 1, 1967. Coach Vince Lombardi watches as his players take the field before the 1966 NFL championship game. Forrest Gregg #75 runs on to the field to the right. Bob Skoronski #76 is behind Gregg. Behind Lombardi (from left to right) are #66 Ray Nitschke, #73 Jim Weatherwax, #80 Bob Long and #89 Dave Robinson. Paul Hornung #5, Max McGee #85, and Bart Starr #15 are in background to the right. The Packers won 34–27. Photograph by Vernon J. Biever.

fresh set of downs. Taylor picked up three yards on the ground on first down. Starr then dropped back and connected with an open Pitts at the seven-yard line, and Elijah bounced off Warren Livingston at the three and went into the end zone. The Packers had a 7–0 lead just four minutes into the game.

Chandler kicked off to Renfro, who took the kick at the goal line and returned it to the 20. There he was hit by Bob Brown, as Gillingham popped the ball free. Grabowski picked up the loose pigskin and rambled 18 yards to the end zone to give the Pack a quick 14–0 lead with 4:20 elapsed.

The ensuing kickoff went to Renfro again, who received it at the eight and returned it to the 35-yard line. Dallas went into a ball-control offense to slow the pace, with short Meredith passes and runs by Dan Reeves and Don Perkins. Reeves took a handoff up the middle for four yards, and Perkins carried for seven yards and a first down. Reeves ran the ball to midfield, and Dandy Don flipped a pass to *North Dallas Forty* author Pete Gent, who went out on the right sideline at the Packer 43 for another first down.

Pettis Norman took an end around to the right for six yards before Nitschke took him down. Meredith pitched to Reeves but he came up a little short of the first down marker. On third-and-one, Meredith gambled with a bomb to Bullet Bob Hayes inside the five-yard line, but the pass was broken up by Tom Brown, providing safety help. On fourth down, Reeves got the call, running the ball to just inside the 30-yard line and giving the Cowboys a fresh set of downs. After a pass to Hayes gained a yard (his only reception in the game), Gent took a pass 11 yards to the 18. A run by Reeves was stuffed by Nitschke for no gain, and the Cowboys took a time out. Meredith connected with Norman in the right flat, with Norman going out of bounds at the six. A late hit penalty was assessed against Dave Robinson on the play, moving the ball half the distance to the goal line. On first-and-goal from the three, Reeves went over right tackle to waltz into the end zone. With four and a half minutes left in the first quarter, Green Bay's lead was trimmed to 14–7.

Anderson returned the kickoff from Villanueva to the Green Bay 13, but the Packers went three-and-out. Dallas took over on their 41 after the punt.

After a four-yard run by Perkins, he took a pitchout and went through the right side for 11 more yards and a first down at the Packers 44. Meredith then found Reeves open on the left side for 22 yards. Following a sack by Lionel Aldridge on first down, Meredith handed off to Perkins, who burst through the right side of the line at the 23 and blew past

Packers at Cowboys, January 1, 1967. Quarterback Bart Starr #15 hands off to fullback Jim Taylor #31, with offensive linemen Jerry Kramer #64 and Forrest Gregg #75 in the background. The Packers won 34–27 for their second consecutive NFL championship and fourth under Vince Lombardi. Photograph by Vernon J. Biever.

Packers at Cowboys, January 1, 1967. Receiver Boyd Dowler #86 gets upended by Cowboys defensive back Mike Gaechter #27 after scoring a touchdown to put the Packers up 28–20 in the 1966 NFL championship game. The Packers eventually won 34–27. Photograph by Vernon J. Biever.

defenders to fall into the end zone for the touchdown. With 36 seconds remaining in the first period, Dallas and Green Bay were tied at 14.

Adderley returned the kickoff to the Packers 36-yard line. The first quarter ended with Taylor running left for eight yards before an offside penalty against the Cowboys gave Green Bay a first down just short of midfield. Starr went deep for Dale on a post pattern at the Dallas 15, with Cornell Green in tight coverage. Green tried for the interception, but the ball went through his outstretched hands. Dale reeled it in and raced into the end zone to make it a 21–14 game on the second play of the second quarter.

Meredith started from his 28-yard line following the kickoff return by Renfro. A run by Reeves picked up a yard, and Gent caught a pass over the middle for ten yards. On second down, Meredith threw to Reeves at the 50-yard line, with Dan zipping along the sideline to the Packers 21 to complete the 40-yard pass play. Reeves ran off tackle for five yards, and on second down picked up a couple more to the 14. On third-and-three, a keeper by Meredith came up a yard short of the marker, but Perkins carried the ball to the nine on fourth down, setting up a first-and-goal. Reeves carried twice for a total of five yards, but after a third down incompletion, Villanueva booted an 11-yard FG to reduce the Green Bay lead to 21–17 with 8:37 to play in the half.

Adderley returned the kickoff 24 yards to the Green Bay 30, and on the first play from scrimmage, Pitts broke off a 24-yard run to the left side before being brought down by Renfro at the Dallas 46. Starr fired to Fleming for eight yards, and a short run by Pitts set up a third-and-one. Taylor took a screen from Bart to the 25, giving the Pack another first down. Starr overthrew Dale on first down, and Pitts carried for a yard. On third-and-seven, Starr's screen to Pitts went off his hands. Chandler's 30-yard FG attempt was blocked by the right hand of George Andrie, and the Cowboys took over at their 20 as 4:44 remained before intermission.

A Dallas three-and-out led to a punt from Villanueva to the Packers 42. The Packers were unable to move, but Chandler's punt pinned the Cowboys at their seven with exactly two minutes to go before the half.

An illegal procedure penalty against Dallas moved the ball back to the three, and Reeves carried to the left, taking the ball to the nine. Meredith handed off to Perkins, who gained four yards. The Cowboys needed four yards on third down, which Perkins barely got. The first half ended with a draw to the right by Perkins to the 22, and the Cowboys went into the locker room on the short end of a 21–17 verdict.

Chandler kicked off to start the second half, and Walt Garrison caught the ball at the two and returned it to the Dallas 30. Perkins took a pitch to the left side for four yards, and on second down, Meredith handed off to Reeves but Aldridge caught Reeves for a loss of one yard. Norman caught a pass on the right sideline, going out at the 40, but the chain gang determined that he came up three inches short of the first down marker. Villanueva punted to the Green Bay 30-yard line where the ball went out of bounds.

After a short run by Pitts, a short pass over the middle was nearly picked off by Renfro, setting up a third-and-nine. Starr's left sideline pass was underthrown but Dowler dove and hauled it in for a ten-yard gain to keep the drive alive. Taylor swept left for five yards, but Pitts was taken down for a two-yard loss on second down by Mike Gaechter and Lee Roy Jordan. Bart came through again with a pass to Dale for 11 yards on third-and-seven to move the ball to the Dallas 45. A handoff to Taylor was good for five yards up the middle, and Bob Long caught a sideline pass for nine more yards, moving the chains again. Taylor ran off tackle for eight yards to the 23, and on the next play, Starr handed off to Pitts, who carried inside, but Gaechter stripped the ball loose. Warren Livingston fell on the ball for Dallas at the Cowboys 21-yard line with over eight minutes to play in the third period.

Packers at Cowboys, January 1, 1967. Coach Vince Lombardi is carried off the field after the Packers' 34–27 victory over the Cowboys in the 1966 NFL championship game. Photograph by Vernon J. Biever.

The Cowboys followed with a 13-play drive that ate up about five minutes of the clock. Willie Wood knocked away a pass to Reeves in the end zone and the drive culminated with a 32-yard FG by Villanueva. With three and a half minutes left in the third quarter, Green Bay clung to a 21–20 lead.

Anderson returned the kickoff to the Packers 26. On the first play from scrimmage, Starr aired it out to a wide-open Dale in the right flat at the Dallas 45, with Dale taking the ball to the Dallas 31 where Green took him down after a gain of 43 yards. A run by Taylor was good for four yards, and Starr dumped off a pass to Taylor in the middle that put the ball at the 22-yard line, setting up a third-and-one, but the Cowboys were flagged for being offside, giving the Packers five yards and a first down. Pitts gained a yard, and then with less than 30 seconds to play in the third quarter, Starr connected with Dowler on a crossing pattern at the five. Boyd pulled it in just out of the grasp of Renfro and crossed the goal line where he was flipped on his head by Mike Gaechter. The Packers led 28–20.

The third quarter ended with Renfro returning the kickoff to the Dallas 35. After making one first down to begin the fourth quarter, Meredith threw three straight incompletions. Villanueva's punt went out of bounds at the Green Bay 26.

Starr fired to Dowler for 23 yards to midfield, but Boyd was injured on the play, and the Packers were forced to use a time out. After a third down sack by Willie Townes and Dave Edwards, Chandler boomed a punt that went to Hayes just inside the end zone, but Hayes made the mistake of not downing it for a touchback, and he was smothered by four Packers at the Dallas one-yard line. "I really didn't know I was in the end zone," Hayes said after the game. "I just made a mistake. I was thinking about getting the ball and going."[1]

Dallas gained 12 yards on three runs, but then two incompletions and a sack by Henry Jordan at the seven led to Villanueva punting to the Dallas 48 with nine and a half minutes left.

Pitts lost a yard running and George Andrie sacked Starr for eight more. Facing a third-and-19, Bart responded with a clutch 24-yard pass to a double-covered Fleming in the middle, with Fleming taking the ball to the Dallas 33. Starr overthrew Pitts on a sure touchdown pass on first down, and a draw to Taylor lost a couple yards courtesy of Townes. On third-and-12 from the 35, Bart flipped a short pass to Taylor, with Taylor weaving his way through the middle for 16 yards, enough for a first down.

A run by Taylor gained a couple yards, but Starr was sacked at the 28-yard line. Once again, Starr came through on third-and-long as he lofted a pass toward Max McGee on an out route at the two. McGee made his only catch of the day a big one as he hauled in the pass and fell into the end zone with Livingston draped over him. On the extra point, Lilly got a hand up and blocked the attempt, and the Packers led 34–20 with 5:20 to play in regulation. The blocked kick kept it a two-possession game.

Renfro returned the kickoff 26 yards to the Dallas 29. On first down, Meredith hit Norman for eight yards, with Norman getting out of bounds, ending a streak of eight straight incompletions by Meredith. On second-and-two, Meredith scrambled to the 42, for a first down. A deep pass for an open Buddy Dial was overthrown, and on second down, Meredith completed a screen to Reeves in the left flat at the 43. Reeves was nailed by Caffey and the ball popped loose, but Wood could not hold onto the ball. Meredith knocked it out of bounds, and the Cowboys retained possession, although they lost ten yards on the play. On third-and-20, Aldridge and Davis poured in for the sack, and Meredith barely got the pass away. Frank Clarke blew past safety Tom Brown, caught the ball at the Green Bay 30 and streaked to the end zone. With 4:09 left on the clock, Dallas had trimmed the Green Bay lead to 34–27.

Adderley returned Villanueva's kickoff to the Packers 28, and Starr hit Fleming for 18 yards on the first play from scrimmage. Starr then suffered his fifth sack of the game, and it cost the Packers eight yards, pushing them back to their 38. After Dallas called their first time out, Bart went to the air on second down, but Townes batted down his pass at the line. Taylor caught a screen on third down, but Lee Roy Jordan was all over

Taylor and brought him down for a seven-yard loss. Dallas called time again, and Chandler was rushed and got off an awful punt. The ball went off the side of Chandler's foot and traveled just 16 yards to the Packers 47 with 2:19 to play.

On first down, Meredith went to Clarke again over the middle for 21 yards to the Green Bay 26. Perkins took a draw four yards to bring on the two-minute warning. Meredith put it up for Clarke in the right side of the end zone but the pass was incomplete, and there was a flag on the field at the Green Bay two-yard line. Brown was called for interference on Clarke, and Dallas had a first-and-goal, six feet away from sudden death as 1:52 was left on the clock. The stage was set for one of the great goal line stands in pro football history.

Meredith handed off to Reeves, who went off right tackle, gaining a yard to the one. On second down, Dallas lineman Jim Boeke was flagged for jumping before the snap, pushing the Cowboys back to the six. With three shots at the end zone remaining, Meredith lobbed a screen to Reeves who was having vision problems, and the pass went through his hands. A minute and 14 seconds remained when the Meredith threw low to a diving Norman in the right flat at the two, with Brown there to prevent Norman from getting up and going into the end zone.

On the last chance for the Cowboys, Meredith dropped back and rolled right. Robinson darted through the line and latched onto Meredith, pulling him to the grass. As he was falling, Meredith unloaded a wobbly desperation pass into the end zone. Brown atoned for his earlier interference penalty by intercepting the ball in the back of the end zone with 28 seconds to play. "I was looking for Bob Hayes," Meredith told reporters. "He [Robinson] had me so I threw the ball. I had to."[2]

"It was the biggest play I ever made," Brown was quoted as saying.[3]

The victorious Lombardi praised the resilient Cowboys, "I was surprised they scored that many points on us."[4] Landry said after the game, "We made too many errors and it cost us the ball game."[5] He also gave the Packers their due, "Green Bay is a real good team, and it's no embarrassment to lose to them. But we still had our chances."[6]

NOTES

1. *Dallas Morning News*, January 2, 1967.
2. *New York Times*, January 2, 1967.
3. *Dallas Morning News*, January 2, 1967.
4. *Milwaukee Sentinel*, January 2, 1967.
5. *Dallas Morning News*, January 2, 1967.
6. *Hartford Courant*, January 2, 1967.

Super Bowl I

NEAL GOLDEN

January 15, 1967—Super Bowl I: Kansas City Chiefs vs. Green Bay Packers, Los Angeles Memorial Coliseum

When the National and American Football Leagues reached a merger agreement on June 9, 1966, the provisions included an annual game pitting the champions of the two leagues. Even though the merger would not be complete until after the 1969 season, the first championship game would be played following the 1966 season. Lamar Hunt, owner of the Kansas City Chiefs and the main architect of the merger from the AFL side, began calling the championship game the "Super Bowl" as early as July. The term quickly caught on with the media and the public although it was not the official title of the first game.

The Kansas City Chiefs won their second AFL crown (the other coming as the Dallas Texans) by thumping the Buffalo Bills 31–7. Later that New Year's Day, the Packers copped their fourth NFL title in six years with a thrilling 34–27 triumph over the Dallas Cowboys.

Both teams felt the pressure of winning for their leagues but especially the Packers, who were installed as 12.5-point favorites.[1] The NFL owners had done nothing but deride the standard of play in the AFL since the upstart league began in 1960. People around the NFL besieged Vince Lombardi with telegrams and phone calls urging him not to lose to a league they considered a joke a few years earlier. Lombardi shared the league's sentiments with his players. "He told us this was for a way of life, a game of survival, a test of manhood," recalled Willie Davis.[2]

The Chiefs arrived on the West Coast four days before the Packers, a move that Coach Hank Stram regretted. "We had come too early," Hank later admitted.[3] His team "had been ready to play days earlier." The Chiefs worked in secret, adding new wrinkles to the 18 offensive sets and 350 plays they already employed. From their film study, the Packers thought the Chiefs' offense mirrored the Dallas Cowboys' attack in many ways—confusing the defense with shifting sets that disguised the formation until the last second.[4] On the other hand, preparing for the Packers was simple. "They were pure vanilla," Stram

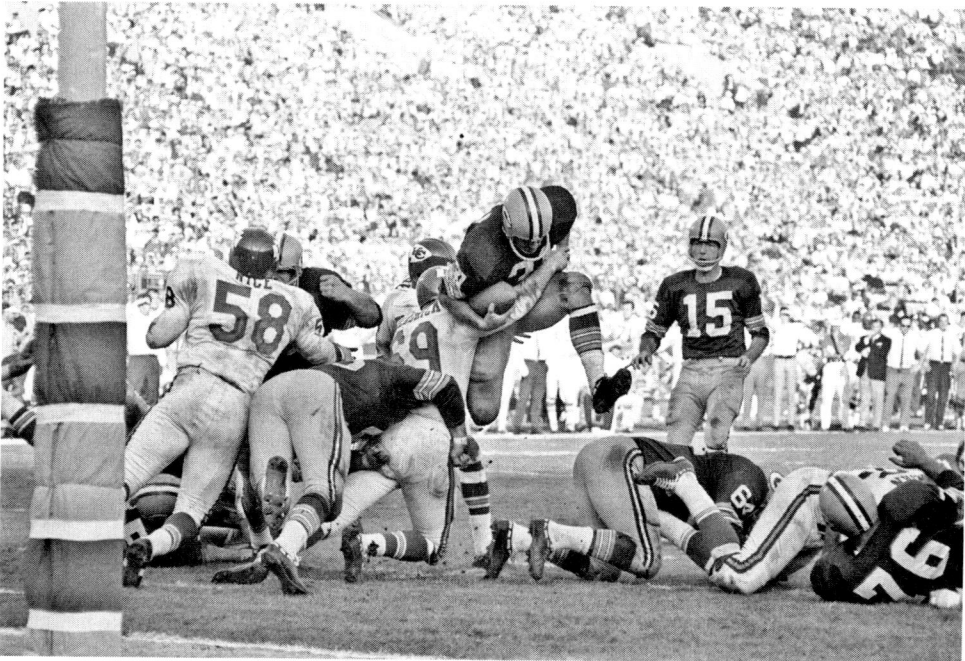

Packers vs. Chiefs, Super Bowl I, January 15, 1967. Fullback Jim Taylor #31 scores the first rushing touchdown in Super Bowl history. Quarterback Bart Starr #15 looks on from the backfield. Photograph by John Biever.

remembered. "We saw everything in the AFL, and here we were, preparing for a team that defensively used just one alignment and one coverage. It was unbelievable, but they were good enough to get by with it."[5]

Despite Stram cautioning his men to let sleeping dogs lie, cornerback Fred "The Hammer" Williamson couldn't resist. Fred loved to talk. In an article in *Life* magazine, the ex–Marine with karate training[6] disparaged the Packer receivers and vowed to use his "Hammer Tackle" on them. "If Boyd Dowler and Carroll Dale or any of those other guys have the nerve to catch a pass in my territory they're going to pay the price, man."[7] Williamson's remarks didn't sit well with his teammates and caught the attention of the opposition. Watching Kansas City films with his team, Lombardi proclaimed The Hammer the dirtiest player he had ever seen.[8]

When the Packers arrived at Santa Barbara, Lombardi worked them mercilessly. Losing was not an option for the NFL standard bearers.

Both coaches feared their teams were too tight as they left for the stadium the morning of the game, so each tried to loosen up his men. When the champions of the "Mickey Mouse" AFL arrived at their dressing room in the Coliseum, the trainers, doctors, and equipment men wore Mickey Mouse hats, and a phonograph played the Mouseketeers' theme song.[9]

Lombardi was the last man to board the Packers' bus to the stadium. He took his usual seat in the first row by the door, but, as the bus started to pull out, he stopped the driver. Vince stepped into the aisle, got the attention of his players, and did a soft shoe dance. "Go, Coach, Go!" yelled the amazed Packers. When Vince sat back down, the assistant next to him asked, "What was that?" "They were too tight," replied Lombardi.[10]

One Packer who definitely was not tense was wide receiver Max McGee. After catching only four passes all season, the 34-year-old, 12-year veteran expected to ride the bench. So he had no qualms about sneaking out after bed check Saturday night even though his roommate and best buddy, Paul Hornung, still nursing a pinched nerve in his shoulder, refused to come along. Max returned to the hotel after sunup and managed an hour nap before departing with the team.[11]

	Green Bay	Kansas City
First downs	21	17
Yards rushing	133	72
Yards passing	250	228
Total yards (Net)	361	239
Passes	16–24	17–32
Intercepted by	1	1
Punts	4–173	7–317
Fumbles lost	0	0
Yards penalized	40	26

Green Bay	7	7	14	7	35
Kansas City	0	10	0	0	10

    Green Bay—McGee 37, pass from Starr (Chandler kick)
    Kansas City—McClinton 7, pass from Dawson (Mercer kick)
    Green Bay—Taylor 14, run (Chandler kick)
    Kansas City—Field Goal, Mercer 31
    Green Bay—Pitts 5, run (Chandler kick)
    Green Bay—McGee 13, pass from Starr (Chandler kick)
    Green Bay—Pitts 1, run (Chandler kick)
    A—61,946

Rushing
(Attempts, Yards)
Green Bay—Taylor 17–56; Pitts 11–45; Anderson 4–30; Grabowski 2–2
Kansas City—Dawson 3–24; Garrett 6–17; McClinton 6–16; Coan 3–1; Beathard 1–14

Passing
(Attempts, Completions, Interceptions, Yards)
Green Bay—Starr 23–16–1–250; Bratkowski 1–0–0–0
Kansas City—Dawson 27–16–1–211; Beathard 5–1–0–17

Receiving
(Receptions, Yards)
Green Bay—McGee 7–138; Dale 4–59; Pitts 2–32; Fleming 2–22; Taylor 1–(-1)
Kansas City—Burford 4–67; Taylor 4–57; Garrett 3–28; McClinton 2–34; Arbanas 2–30; Carolan 1–7; Coan 1–5

Interceptions
Green Bay—Wood
Kansas City—Mitchell

Fumbles Recovered
Green Bay—None
Kansas City—None

The temperature at game time was in the high 70s with a thin layer of California smog hanging over the area.[12] Despite a top ticket price of just $12, one-third of the mam-

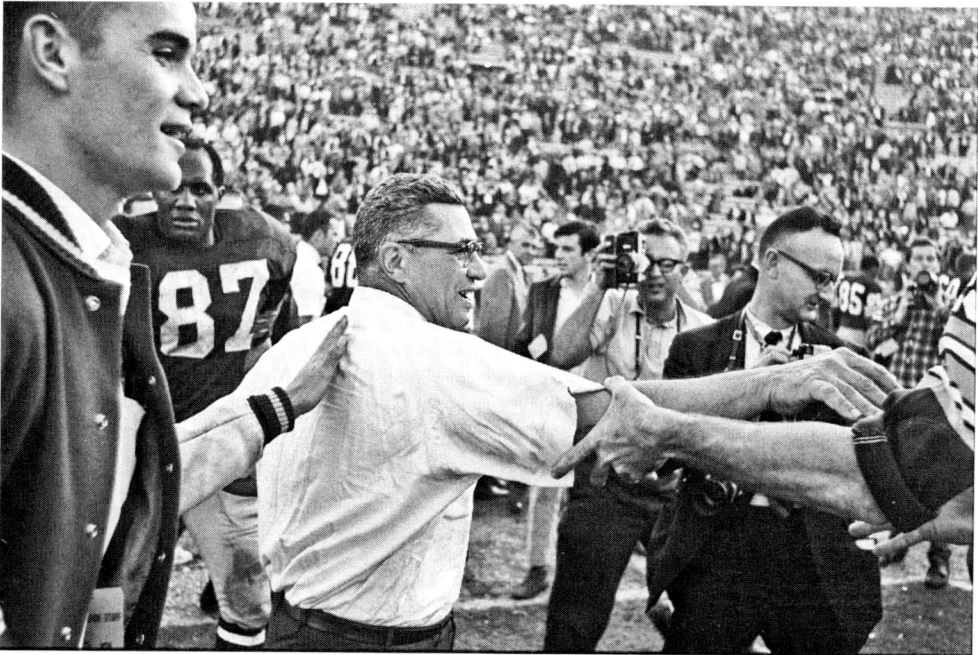

Packers vs. Chiefs, Super Bowl I, January 15, 1967. Coach Vince Lombardi on the field after the 35–10 victory in Super Bowl I. Defensive tackle Willie Davis #87 is to the right and the man looking down and to the right in the background is Packer photographer Vernon J. Biever. Photograph by John Biever.

moth Coliseum was empty. After a seven-year war fought in the courts and the newspapers, the champions of the two rival leagues were finally meeting on the field of play. Both teams displayed some nervousness in the early going, the Chiefs more so than the Pack. Green Bay won the toss and received. They unveiled nothing new on their first series. Taylor tried the left side of the Chiefs' line, and then Pitts went right. Jimmy gained three on third-and-one. After the play, Dowler, experiencing excruciating pain from a pinched nerve in his shoulder suffered in the NFL championship game, left the game never to return. On the sideline, Lombardi yelled for McGee. Max couldn't find his own helmet; so he grabbed a lineman's and hurried into the huddle. "I didn't even bother to stretch out too much [before the game]," Max later admitted, "because I figured I'd just be sitting around watching anyway. I could barely stand up for the kickoff."[13]

Starr immediately went to his new receiver but underthrew him. Then the Chiefs sacked Starr twice in a row, the first by defensive tackle Buck Buchanan and the second by blitzing linebacker Bobby Bell. When McGee returned to the bench, he told Hornung, "If Bart'll throw me the ball, I'll win the car [the Most Valuable Player Award]. They're not even covering me." Max passed the same message to his quarterback.[14]

While the Packers used the NFL football on offense, the Chiefs employed the AFL football, which was longer and thinner than the NFL ball and therefore easier to throw. ("Is it easier to intercept too?" Lombardi asked reporters before the game.[15]) Kansas City started from their 37 after Mike Garrett returned the punt nine yards. When quarterback Len Dawson moved under center, he saw Nitschke staring at him. Len thought to himself, "This is the meanest, ugliest man I have ever seen."[16] Dawson immediately rolled left behind Stram's patented "rolling pocket"[17] and threw to Chris Burford, who caught the ball out of bounds. After a four-yard run, Dawson went to Burford again for a first down at the Green Bay 47. But a stuffed run and two incompletions forced a punt.

Starr began to connect with his receivers against Kansas City's triple-stack linebacker alignments. One of the outside backers would join middle man Sherrill Headrick inside the defensive ends to stop the run. But that left no one to help a cornerback cover a receiver on one side of the field if the tight end occupied the safety.[18] So Bart hit Fleming over the middle for a first down at the Packers 34. Then Starr scrambled out of the pocket and tossed to Pitts who ran to the Chiefs 43. After linebacker E. J. Holub threw Taylor for a six-yard loss, Starr threw to Dale, who made a diving catch at the 37 in front of Williamson.

Next came the first big play of the game. Chiefs defensive coordinator Tom Bettis called a blitz. But as Starr later explained, "The Chiefs may not have realized that we loved when teams blitzed. We had a very good adjusting process for dogging linebackers and safeties."[19] McGee, flanked to the left, ran a quick post across the middle. Hit by Buchanan as he threw, Starr delivered the ball behind Max, but McGee deftly reached behind him with his right hand and pulled in the ball as cornerback Willie Mitchell, two yards behind the receiver, dove in vain. McGee continued untouched the remaining 19 yards into the end zone.[20]

Kansas City started from their 13 after multiple officials on the split crew threw flags for clipping on the kickoff return. Faking a handoff on almost every passing play, Dawson rolled out but, finding no one open, ran to the 21. A quick flat pass to Garrett produced a first down at the 23. Three plays later, Dawson hit tight end Fred Arbanas for a first down at the Chiefs 49. Garrett spun his way to the 41, inches short of a first down, before Dawson scrambled for two to move the chains. When a third down pass to Reg Carolan failed to gain the first down, Mike Mercer came on for a 40-yard field goal try that sailed just wide to the left with 1:05 left in the period.

The Packers went three-and-out, and the Chiefs began a scoring drive early in quarter two. Dawson rolled right and threw back across the field to Garrett, who meandered through six tacklers to the Green Bay 49. Three runs generated a first down at the 37. Dawson then looped a beautiful pass to Otis Taylor on a post pattern toward the right pylon. Tom Brown dragged down the 6'3" receiver at the seven. Again using play action, Len rolled right and threw to McClinton in the end zone to tie the game.

Green Bay struck back with a 73-yard, 14-play march. On third-and-one, Starr decided to go for the home run. Calling his favorite short yardage play, he faked a handoff to Taylor and fired to Dale at the Packers 40, and Carroll raced untouched to the end zone.[21] But an illegal motion penalty nullified the score. Bart came back on the next play with a completion to McGee for a first down at the 42. After two misfires, the Green Bay signal-caller threw his fourth pass in a row, Dale snagging it for a first down at the Chiefs 43. It took three downs again to move the chains, Fleming jumping between Headrick and safety Johnny Robinson to snare Starr's heave at the 27. Continuing the same pattern, Bart again converted on third down, flipping to Pitts who went out of bounds at the 14. Taylor then took a handoff and started around left end before cutting back and barreling into the end zone. Packers 14, Chiefs seven with four and a half minutes left in the half.

Beginning at the 26, Dawson led the AFL champs into field goal range. He connected

Packers vs. Chiefs, Super Bowl I, January 15, 1967: NFL Commissioner Pete Rozelle awards the NFL-AFL world championship trophy to coach Vince Lombardi following the Packers' 35–10 victory. Longtime Packer photographer Vernon J. Biever called this the best photograph he ever took. With an awareness of history, Biever recalled being the only still photographer in the room when this event took place, noting this photograph could never be taken again. Photograph by Vernon J. Biever.

with Arbanas for 17 and Taylor for six. Then Len went back to Burford for a first down at the Green Bay 32 just before the two-minute warning. When a third-down pass to Garrett missed the first down by a yard, Stram didn't hesitate to send out Mercer, whose 31-yard boot sailed through the uprights. The Packers ran off the final 50 seconds to leave the field with only a 14–10 lead.

Stram recalled his team's feeling at halftime. "The guys were up; we had done all right…. The Chiefs were confident. Fred Arbanas, walking toward the locker room, was excited. 'Hey, Coach, We can beat these guys! They're nothing like we thought they'd be!' … I felt good. The versatile, unorthodox Cinderellas were going to beat the staid old hands. We couldn't wait to get back out there!"[22]

The Packers knew they had not played their best in the first half. McGee may have been one of the few playing free and easy. Willie Wood dropped two possible interceptions. Nitschke was so keyed up he forgot his assignment on several plays. When a remarkably calm Lombardi[23] told his men they were too tight, Nitschke muttered, "Who the hell does he think got us so nervous in the first place?" Vince told them they had adjusted to Kansas City in the first half. "Now I want you to go out there and make Kansas City adjust to you.[24] Are you the world champion Green Bay Packers? Go out on the field and give me your answer."[25] Vince reminded defensive coordinator Phil Bengtson that the game plan called for delaying any blitzing until the second half to lull Dawson into a false sense of security. The change in tactics would pay off immediately.[26]

The Chiefs started promisingly when Dawson rolled right and ran for a first down. After two runs failed to gain a first down, the Chiefs faced third-and-five. Their analysis of the Packers had revealed that Green Bay blitzed on third-and-five just three times in two years.[27] But Bengtson chose this moment to launch his first red dog of the afternoon. Falling backwards to avoid linebacker Lee Roy Caffey and with Henry Jordan tipping his passing arm,[28] Dawson threw a dying quail to his left that Wood snagged at the Green Bay 45 and returned down the sideline to the five. Starr recalled his thinking as he led the offense onto the field. "It was an ideal opportunity to cross up the Chiefs' defense. I figured they'd be looking for Jimmy Taylor again, and they were. Elijah Pitts took the handoff and scored easily." Instead of Kansas City driving for a go ahead touchdown, the Packers extended their lead to 11 points just like that. Dawson called the interception the turning point of the game.[29]

Kansas City gained another first down on its next possession, but Jeter, Nitschke, and Caffey threw Bert Coan for a loss on third-and-one to bring on the punt team. The Chiefs recorded a sack of their own when Holub and Buchanan smothered Starr for a seven-yard loss to force a three-and-out. The Packers blitzed for the third time in the half on the first play of the Chiefs' next possession, causing Len to overthrow Burford. Caffey broke through on the next snap and dumped Len for a 13-yard loss to the 14. The hurt continued when Jordan, Davis, and Kostelnik knocked down Dawson on the two.

After a clipping penalty on Jerrel Wilson's punt moved the ball back to the Packers 44, Green Bay converted three straight third downs. Starr then faked a handoff and shot a pass to McGee breaking over the middle from the left. The ball bounced off the wideout's hand a stride into the end zone, but he grabbed the deflection. Touchdown number two for the guy who didn't expect to play a down, and a 28–10 Packers lead with less than a minute to go in the third period.

Little changed for the AFL champs in the final period. Wood and Adderley just missed interceptions on the first two plays. On the Pack's next possession, cornerback

Willie Mitchell, whom Starr had been targeting all afternoon, got some revenge by intercepting an underthrown pass intended for McGee. Unfortunately, the turnover gave Kansas City the ball on their own 11. But Dawson suddenly got hot. With the secondary playing back to avoid big plays, he looped a pass to McClinton who made a fine lunging catch to the 38. Two more completions brought a first down at the Green Bay 46, but Len's next three throws hit the ground to force another punt.

Not the least deterred by Mitchell's pick, Starr threw to Dale on a down-and-out in front of the cornerback for 24 yards to the 44. The next target was McGee down the middle. With Mitchell climbing his back, Max ran another ten yards to the 18. Two snaps later, the beleaguered cornerback knocked down a pass aimed at Dale. Then Pitts broke through the line and seemed headed to pay dirt until Robinson knocked him down on the five. Robinson then tackled his former LSU teammate Taylor on a sweep inches from the goal. Pitts slid into the end zone over the left side to make it 35–10 after Chandler's fifth extra point.

Both teams started substituting freely, including backup quarterbacks Pete Beathard and Zeke Bratkowski. The most interesting play the rest of the way came on the Packers' next possession. As Donny Anderson took a handoff, Williamson came in low. As Fred admitted later, "I was trying to break Donny Anderson's leg, only I went too low and he hit me with his knee in the head."[30] The Hammer stayed down. On the Packers sideline, Wood exclaimed, "That's the Hammer. They just nailed The Hammer!"[31] The victim recalled: "I just laid there. I was too embarrassed to get up. I said, 'I refuse. You want me to get off the field, you carry me off.'"[32] Polite applause accompanied the stretcher taking Williamson to the locker room.

McGee, whose playboy ways Lombardi had tolerated for years because the veteran could make plays, rewarded his boss' faith with seven receptions, all against Mitchell. But Max, who prematurely announced his retirement after the game ("It's a great game to quit on, and I quit!"[33]), didn't win the MVP award as he had hoped. Instead, the Corvette went to Starr. Bart completed 16 of 23 for 250 yards and two touchdowns.

In the relatively quiet Green Bay locker room, Lombardi started his press conference with a football in his hands. "I might say they gave me the game ball, which was very nice." Asked about halftime adjustments, the Packers mentor explained, "We made very little of an adjustment. Our game was good all along. We were just a little more aggressive in the second half. I just told 'em to be more aggressive, to stop grabbing and start tackling." Asked about the loss of Dowler, Vince explained, "We had planned to hit our weak side end, regardless of who was playing. You notice we hit Dale, too, when he played that side." Pressed for an assessment of the Chiefs, the Packers head man tried to be gracious. "The Chiefs are a good team with fine speed, but we wore 'em down. We had a little more personnel than they did." When reporters pressed him on the issue, Vince added, "Dallas is a better team. The Chiefs are good, but not as good as the top teams in our league. That's what you wanted me to say—now I've said it."[34] Lombardi regretted the remark. He later told a friend, "I came off as an ungracious winner, and it was lousy."[35]

The Chiefs were impressed with the Packers and particularly their quarterback. Coach Stram: "I thought Starr did a fabulous job of coming up with the third down play. I think he made seven out of nine in the first half and five out of seven in the second, which is an unbelievable average."[36] One defensive back said, "Bart picks a weak spot and hits it better than any quarterback I ever saw. He really picked our pass defense to pieces. Every time they had third and long yardage, he made it. You can't beat that."[37]

NOTES

1. *Appleton* (WI) *Post-Crescent*, January 15, 1967.
2. David Maraniss, *When Pride Still Mattered: A Life of Vince Lombardi* (New York: Touchstone, 1999), 392.
3. Hank Stram with Lou Sahadi, *They're Playing My Game* (Chicago: Triumph Books, 1986), 130.
4. Edward Gruver, *Nitschke* (Lanham, MD: Taylor Trade, 2002), 159.
5. *Ibid.*, 158.
6. Stram, 129.
7. Gruver, 160.
8. Maraniss, 395.
9. Stram, 130–131.
10. Maraniss, 394.
11. Jim Taylor with Kristine Setting Clark, *The Fire Within* (Chicago: Triumph Books, 2010), 123.
12. Gruver, 160.
13. Maraniss, 394.
14. Paul Hornung as told to William F. Reed, *Golden Boy* (Lincoln: University of Nebraska Press, 2004), 179.
15. Gruver, 160.
16. *Ibid.*, 161.
17. *Ibid.*, 158.
18. Bob McGinn, *The Ultimate Super Bowl Book* (Minneapolis: MVP Books, 2009), 18.
19. *Ibid.*, 17.
20. David Claerbaut, *Bart Starr: When Leadership Mattered* (Lanham, MD: Taylor Trade, 2004), 167.
21. *Ibid.*, 167.
22. Stram, 132.
23. McGinn, 15.
24. Maraniss, 395.
25. Gruver, 163.
26. McGinn, 15.
27. Gruver, 163.
28. *Ibid.*, 164.
29. McGinn, 15.
30. Ken Rappaport, *The Little League That Could: A History of the American Football League* (Lanham, MD: Taylor Trade, 2004), 180.
31. Maraniss, 395–396.
32. Rappaport, 180.
33. Taylor, 125.
34. *Appleton* (WI) *Post-Crescent*, January 16, 1967.
35. Gruver, 164.
36. *Appleton* (WI) *Post-Crescent*, January 16, 1967.
37. Claerbaut, 169.

Statistics

RUPERT PATRICK

Rushing	No.	Yards	Ave	Long	TDs
Jim Taylor	204	705	3.5	19	4
Elijah Pitts	115	393	3.4	20	7
Paul Hornung	76	200	2.6	9	2
Jim Grabowski	29	127	4.4	36	1
Donny Anderson	25	104	4.2	15	2

Rushing	No.	Yards	Ave	Long	TDs
Bart Starr	21	104	5.0	21	2
Zeke Bratkowski	4	7	1.8	4	0
Don Chandler	1	33	33.0	33	0

Passing	Att	Cmp	% Cmp	Yds gained	TDs	Long	Int	% Int	Yds/Attempt
Bart Starr	251	156	62.2	2257	14	83	3	1.2	8.99
Zeke Bratkowski	64	36	56.3	569	4	74	2	3.1	8.89
Elijah Pitts	2	0	0.0	0	0	0	0	0.0	0.00
Paul Hornung	1	1	100.0	5	0	5	0	0.0	5.00

Receiving	No.	Yards	Ave	Long	TDs
Jim Taylor	41	331	8.1	21	2
Carroll Dale	37	876	23.7	83	7
Marv Fleming	31	361	11.6	53	2
Boyd Dowler	29	392	13.5	40	0
Elijah Pitts	26	460	17.7	80	3
Paul Hornung	14	192	13.7	44	3
Max McGee	4	91	22.8	39	1
Jim Grabowski	4	13	3.3	7	0
Bob Long	3	68	22.7	42	0
Donny Anderson	2	33	16.5	22	0
Bill Anderson	2	14	7.0	8	0

Interceptions	No.	Yards	Ave	Long	TDs
Bob Jeter	5	142	28.4	75	2
Dave Robinson	5	60	12.0	23	0
Herb Adderley	4	125	31.3	68	1
Tom Brown	4	21	5.3	15	0
Lee Roy Caffey	3	62	20.7	52	1
Willie Wood	3	38	12.7	20	1
Ray Nitschke	2	44	22.0	23	0
Doug Hart	1	40	40.0	40	1
Tommy Crutcher	1	15	15.0	15	0

Punting	No.	Yards	Ave	Long	Block
Don Chandler	60	2452	40.9	58	0
Donny Anderson	2	89	44.5	49	0

Punt Returns	No.	FC	Yards	Ave	Long	TDs
Willie Wood	22	9	82	3.7	13	0
Elijah Pitts	7	4	9	1.3	6	0
Donny Anderson	6	1	124	20.7	77	1
Tom Brown	2	1	0	0.0	0	0

Kickoff Returns	No.	Yards	Ave	Long	TDs
Donny Anderson	23	533	23.2	61	0
Herb Adderley	14	320	22.9	65	0
Phil Vandersea	3	50	16.7	21	0
Willie Wood	1	0	0.0	0	0
Elijah Pitts	1	0	0.0	0	0

Scoring	TDs All-Rush-Rec-Ret	XPA-XPM	FGA-FGM	Saf	Points
Don Chandler	0-0-0-0	43–41	28–12	0	77
Elijah Pitts	10-7-3-0	0–0	0–0	0	60
Carroll Dale	7-0-7-0	0–0	0–0	0	42

Scoring	TDs All-Rush-Rec-Ret	XPA-XPM	FGA-FGM	Saf	Points
Jim Taylor	6–4–2–0	0–0	0–0	0	36
Paul Hornung	5–2–3–0	0–0	0–0	0	30
Donny Anderson	3–2–0–1	0–0	0–0	0	18
Marv Fleming	2–0–2–0	0–0	0–0	0	12
Bob Jeter	2–0–0–2	0–0	0–0	0	12
Bart Starr	2–2–0–0	0–0	0–0	0	12
Herb Adderley	1–0–0–1	0–0	0–0	0	6
Lee Roy Caffey	1–0–0–1	0–0	0–0	0	6
Jim Grabowski	1–1–0–0	0–0	0–0	0	6
Doug Hart	1–0–0–1	0–0	0–0	0	6
Max McGee	1–0–1–0	0–0	0–0	0	6
Willie Wood	1–0–0–1	0–0	0–0	0	6

Goals Field	1–19 Yds	20–29	30–39	40–49	Over 50	Total	Ave Att	Ave Make	Ave Miss	Long
Don Chandler	6–7	2–4	2–9	2–7	0–1	12–28	31.4	29.8	37.8	47

Statistics from 1967 NFL Record Manual and www.pro-football-reference.com.

Superlatives

Rupert Patrick

Team

The Packers were fourth in most points scored with 335, and led the NFL in fewest points allowed with 163. Their point differential of 172 was second in the league to Dallas, who had a differential of 206. Green Bay finished eighth of 15 teams in yards gained on offense, but wound up the season third in fewest yards allowed.

One usually has an image of the Lombardi Packers being a ball control team, but the 1966 team finished tied with Atlanta for the fewest offensive plays in the league with 824. Despite the fact that Bart Starr had a career year, the Packers only threw the ball 318 times, the least in the NFL. Starr only threw three interceptions in the regular season, and as a result the Packers tied the Cowboys for fewest turnovers with 24.

Individual

Bart Starr was the consensus All-Pro quarterback, leading the league in Passing in 1966. At this time, Passers were rated on an inverse ranking of yards per attempt, completion percentage, interception percentage and number of TD passes. Starr led in completion percentage (62.2), yards per attempt (9.0) and lowest interception percentage (1.2) and was seventh in TD passes thrown (14) for a total of ten points, one plus one plus one plus seven.

Although Passer Rating was not used until 1972, when retroactively applied, Starr's

Rating of 105.0 was easily the highest in the NFL. He was also voted League MVP by both the AP and UPI along with the Newspaper Enterprises Association. 1966 was the only season Starr was first team All-Pro.

In his final season as a Packer, Jim Taylor finished tenth in rushing with 705 yards. Taylor was voted to both the *Sporting News* and UPI postseason teams.

Carroll Dale only caught 37 passes, but his 876 receiving yards finished eighth in the league. His eight TD catches were fifth among receivers in the NFL. His yards-per-reception of 23.7 were good for second-best, only finishing behind Roy Jefferson's average of 24.1.

Elijah Pitts scored ten TDs in 1966 (seven rushing and three on passes), tied for seventh in the NFL in 1966. His seven rushing TDs were also good for sixth in the league.

Three members of the Packers' legendary offensive line showed up in the various postseason all-star lists as chosen by the leading newspapers. Forrest Gregg and Jerry Kramer were both named to numerous All-NFL and All-Conference teams, and the *New York Daily News* named Fuzzy Thurston second team All-NFL. Bob Skoronski made his only Pro Bowl appearance in 1966.

On the defensive side of the line, future Hall of Famers Henry Jordan and Willie Davis were All-Pros, Jordan was voted second team All-NFL by the AP and UPI and *New York Daily News* and Davis was on at least a half dozen different All-Pro teams. Davis also played in his fourth consecutive Pro Bowl.

Ray Nitschke was also named to all the All-Pro teams, being voted first team All-Pro for the second and final time in his career. Fellow linebackers Dave Robinson and Lee Roy Caffey were also named to some postseason teams, Robinson by the *Sporting News* and Caffey by the AP, UPI and *New York Daily News*. Caffey was named to the Pro Bowl team for the only time in 1966.

The Packers returned six interceptions for touchdowns in 1966, with Bob Jeter getting two, and Herb Adderley, Lee Roy Caffey, Willie Wood and Doug Hart also getting a pick six. Jeter and Dave Robinson tied for ninth in the NFL with five interceptions each. Adderley was a consensus All-Pro at Cornerback, while Willie Wood was also All-Pro at Safety.

Rookie Donny Anderson tied for sixth in the NFL with 23 kickoff returns, and his 533 yards were ninth best. Anderson did return a punt 77 yards for a touchdown, one of six players to return a punt for a score in 1966. Willie Wood was fourth in the NFL with 22 punt returns.

Don Chandler finished third in the league with 41 extra points made, and his average of 40.9 yards per punt was tenth-best in the NFL.

Statistics from 1967 NFL Record Manual and www.pro-football-reference.com.

PART 3

The Team

Herb Adderley

Joe Zagorski

Herbert Allen Adderley was born June 8, 1939, in Philadelphia, Pennsylvania, to Charles and Rene Adderley, bound to achieve success. A prep star at Northeast High, he was All-City in football, basketball and baseball. In 1957, the 6–0, 205-pound halfback enrolled at Michigan State where he would win All-Big Ten Honors before becoming the first round draft pick of the Packers in 1961. When his career in the NFL was over, Adderley would own six world championship rings. He would also be awarded the ultimate individual honor in 1980 when he was inducted into the Pro Football Hall of Fame in Canton, Ohio. And yet, such success almost never happened. Packers head coach Vince Lombardi intended to use Adderley on offense as a running back and sometime flanker during his rookie year. Before that year (1961) was over, however, Lombardi was forced to switch Adderley to cornerback. The results of Lombardi's decision would shore up the left side of the Packers defense for a glory-filled decade.

"I was too stubborn to switch him to defense until I had to," Lombardi later remembered. "Now when I think of what Adderley means to our defense, it scares me to remember how I mishandled him."[1]

Changing positions from the offensive side of the ball to the defensive side of the ball, without any real amount of preparation, training or coaching is not an easy thing to do. Yet when cornerback Hank Gremminger was hurt for the Thanksgiving game against the Lions, Adderley took his place with such skill and success that it was clear he was a defensive back. Adderley would become an almost instant success covering receivers tighter and better than anyone else in pro football in the 1960s. Herb was a "shut down corner" before the term was coined, and whether he was defending against the pass or the run, opposing offenses were usually unable to find much success against him.

Adderley's success coincided with the fortunes of the Green Bay Packers, who won their first championship in the Lombardi years in 1961, the same year that Adderley joined the Pack. Late in his rookie season after his switch to defense, Adderley contributed only one interception. He did, however, make his mark on special teams that year, returning 18 kickoffs for 478 yards (a 26.6-yard average).

During the offseason, Lombardi offered the starting left cornerback position to Adderley, who gleefully took it. "So when this opportunity came, I grabbed it," Adderley recalled.[2] Gremminger moved to strong safety and safety John Symank to the bench. Adderley responded by intercepting seven passes in 1962, the highest mark in his career. One of those interceptions came in the third week of the season against the rival Chicago Bears, as Adderley went for a 50-yard touchdown in a 49–0 Packer rout. His most important pick came a week later against the Lions. With Green Bay trailing 7–6 in the final minute, Herb nabbed a Milt Plum pass at midfield and returned it 40 yards to set up a game-winning field goal from Paul Hornung. Later in the season, Adderley returned a kickoff 103 yards in a 17–13 win over Baltimore.

During their 1962 championship season, the Green Bay defense allowed a league-low 148 points. Adderley contributed to that stinginess with his hard-hitting play as much as with his interceptions. The measuring stick of all good defensive backs is the interception statistic, but it is a misleading statistic. After 1962, everyone knew who Adderley was. Few quarterbacks ventured a throw in Adderley's neighborhood, hence bringing about a lower interception total for the consensus All-Pro cornerback. But individual honors were never a focus in Green Bay, and nor were they Herb's main goal.

Winning titles was now becoming an expected annual tradition in Green Bay, but that tradition was derailed during 1963 and 1964, as the Packers dropped to second place both seasons. However, Adderley's level of play remained superior. He intercepted five opposing passes in 1963, and four more in 1964. He also averaged 29.9 yards per kickoff return in 1963, and 26.7 yards per kickoff return in 1964.

In 1965, the Packers and Adderley were determined to get back to the championship game and win another league title. Adderley pulled down six more interceptions that year, returned three of them for touchdowns, and did not allow a single touchdown pass by the opposition. At Pittsburgh in the opening game, Adderley's 34-yard interception and touchdown got the Packers rolling to a 41–9 triumph. The following week his 44-yard interception and touchdown helped Green Bay defeat the Colts, 20–17, in Milwaukee. And in the final regular season game, his 13-yard score at Kezar Stadium against the 49ers preserved a 24–24 tie.

The Packers survived a tough Western Conference playoff game the following week against the visiting and vengeful-minded Baltimore Colts, to gain a berth into the 1965 NFL championship game against the defending NFL champion Cleveland Browns. The game was played at Lambeau Field, where snow, mud, and frigid temperatures combined to make the footing treacherous for both teams. Cleveland wide receiver Gary Collins, who gave Adderley trouble, wasted no time as he beat Herb on an out pattern in the first quarter for a 17-yard touchdown reception.

"The big thing to remember," said Adderley, "is you're going to get beat. The question is, when you get beat, can you recover? They're going to fake you out and beat you, but you've got to retain the right attitude. So someone scores a touchdown on you. You should never think about the play that's past, except briefly, and then only how you're going to keep your man from doing that again."[3]

Adderley rebounded to limit Collins to only two more receptions for the remainder of the game, neither of which was harmful to the Packers as Green Bay won 23–12, for its third world championship in the past five years.

By 1966, Adderley was a seasoned pro, a sharp defender whom the Packers relied greatly upon to take an opposition's best wide receiver and limit his suc-

Herb Adderley.

cess. Adderley was very adept at shutting down pass catchers across the league, and so were the rest of his defensive backfield teammates. "We played 99 percent man-to-man [coverages]," Adderley recalled. "We didn't play zone. Playing zone, you're playing an area. We didn't play anything other than four, five basic defenses."[4] The Packers gave up only seven touchdown passes all year, a Packer record that still stands (it was tied in 1972).

Adderley also made his mark in tackling and forcing on running plays. His tough upper body strength, quick speed and fast reactions to plays made it almost like having another linebacker making open field tackles. Herb was noted particularly for his violent, neck-high takedowns of ball carriers and receivers.

As defending champions, the 1966 Packers had to deal with avoiding complacency to repeat as champions. Their determination to defend their title was visible throughout the 1966 regular season. Adderley contributed four of his team's 28 interceptions, and scored on a 68-yard interception return in a 56–3 win over the Atlanta Falcons in the seventh week of the season. Green Bay would lose only two games in 1966, by a total of just four points. They would win their conference, defeat the up and coming Dallas Cowboys in the NFL Title game, and win the first world championship of professional football between AFL and NFL teams over the AFL champion Kansas City Chiefs.

Adderley would play for three more seasons with the Packers, highlighted by a 60-yard interception return for a touchdown during the Packers' 33–14 victory over the Raiders in Super Bowl II.

Angered that the coaching staff had supported cornerback Bob Jeter for All-Pro but not Herb, he demanded a trade and was dealt to the Cowboys in 1970, convinced that he could still excel at the cornerback position in the NFL. Adderley brought to the Cowboys his invaluable experience from his Packer years, and that experience helped Dallas become a champion in two short seasons. After losing Super Bowl V to the Colts 16–13, Dallas defeated the Dolphins in Super Bowl VI, 24–3. The future Hall of Fame cornerback would make history as the only man to play in four of the first six Super Bowl games.

Despite his success in Dallas, Adderley was in constant conflict with head coach Tom Landry. The system-oriented Landry demanded his players do exactly as they were told and never deviate from their assignments. He berated Adderley for "clueing," or guessing, in coverage because Herb was more comfortable in the Green Bay style that allowed playing hunches. In 1972, Adderley played one final NFL season with the Cowboys, but he did not manage to intercept a pass that year. Dallas failed to defend their world championship when they lost the 1972 NFC Title Game to the Washington Redskins, 26–3.

In Adderley's 12 NFL seasons, he was named All-Pro five years (1962, 1963, 1965, 1966, and 1969), nabbed 48 interceptions for 1,046 return yards (a 21.8-yard average), and returned seven for touchdowns in the regular season. His success mirrored that of the 1960s Packers. "Nine years and five championship teams," Adderley said of those legendary Lombardi teams. "We truly accomplished something special."[5] After retiring, Herb formed his own construction business and helped raise his daughter.

Notes

1. Steve Bisheff, "Class of '80," *Pro!* (August 16, 1980): 3C-8C.
2. *Ibid.*
3. *Ibid.*
4. Cliff Christl, "Herb Adderley Sounds Off on Lombardi-Era Packers," Packers.com, May 15, 2014, www.packers.com.

5. Clifton Brown, "Herb Adderley's Book Shines Negative Light on Tom Landry," Sportingnews.com, October 13, 2012, www.sportingnews.com.

References

Bisheff, Steve. "Class of '80." *Pro!* August 16, 1980.

Brown, Clifton. "Herb Adderley's Book Shines Negative Light on Tom Landry." SportingNews.com. October 13, 2012. www.sportingnews.com.

Christl, Cliff. "Herb Adderley Sounds Off on Lombardi-Era Packers." Packers.com. May 15, 2014. www.packers.com.

Hall of Famer. "Herb Adderley—Class of 1980." Packers.com. July 8, 2014. www.packers.com.

Pro Football Hall of Fame. "Hall of Famers, Herb Adderley." ProFootballHOF.com. July 4, 2014. www. profootballhof.com.

Wiebusch, John, editor-in-chief. *The Super Bowl Celebrating a Quarter-Century of America's Greatest Game.* National Football League Properties. New York: Simon & Schuster, 1990.

Lionel Aldridge

John Grasso

Lionel Aldridge had a successful professional career from 1963 to 1973 with the Green Bay Packers and San Diego Chargers and was twice a member of the Super Bowl champions.[1] His greatest accomplishment, however, occurred after his football career ended—he successfully overcame severe mental illness.

After his National Football League career ended following the 1973 season mental illness set in and Aldridge manifested symptoms of paranoid schizophrenia. In 1974 he began hearing voices. In an article he wrote in *Guideposts* he said, "The voices were very scary and confusing. I didn't know what to do. I didn't want anyone to find out the terrible things happening inside my head. As an athlete I'd been trained to be tough; it was not my nature to seek help. I wanted to be strong. At first I tried to ignore them. *I was just going through a bad period,* I thought. But the voices grew more belittling and threatening, more real. I'd be standing in front of the mirror shaving when I'd hear from the next room, *You don't take very good care of your family.* 'That's bull!' I'd shout. I'd search the house for my tormentor. 'How'd he get in here?' I'd mutter, as my wife, Vicki, shook her head in dismay. There never was any intruder. If a co-worker at the station didn't smile at me in the morning, a voice would hiss, *See? He doesn't think much of you either. He knows you don't deserve your job.* I became hard to get along with. I started talking back to the voices, bickering and pleading and cursing. I am a large and imposing man; it must have scared folks half out of their wits to see me shouting at people who weren't there."[2]

His problems were compounded by a divorce in 1982. One night he got in his car and just drove off from his home in Milwaukee. He spent the next couple of years driving all over the country. He exhausted his funds, had his credit cards cancelled and began sleeping in his car. In his travels while sleeping outdoors he awoke to find his Super Bowl ring missing. He wound up in Florida where he sold his car and wandered the streets homeless. Eventually he returned to Milwaukee where his friends were able to hospitalize him against his wishes. Fortunately doctors were able to cure him. In January 1985 his

Packers teammates got together and had a copy of his Super Bowl ring made for him. He was selected to the Packers Hall of Fame in 1988.[3]

In an article by Scott Schalin in 2011, Aldridge was quoted as saying, "I did recover. Not without setbacks and relapses, not without moments when I thought I could never again face life, but I did get well with the help of friends, doctors who found the right medication to help me and the voice of a loving God." He discovered new strategies to cope with the world, including turning the voices around and convincing himself that, instead of negative things, the voices were actually preaching positive attributes about him. In time, the voices went away thanks to medication and his faith in God's master plan. He then became an advocate of mental health awareness and a board member for the Mental Health Association of Milwaukee and traveled the country giving talks for the National Alliance on Mental Illness. He eventually also landed a job working for the post office in Milwaukee where he remained until his death in 1998.[4]

LIONEL ALDRIDGE   DE   GREEN BAY PACKERS

Lionel Aldridge.

Lionel Aldridge was born February 14, 1941, in Evergreen, Louisiana, a small town in Avoyelles Parish near the geographic center of the state with a population of 310 in 2010. The town's makeup is roughly three-fourths white, one-fourth black.[5] After his parents moved to the Midwest, Lionel was raised by his grandparents in a family of 11 children, eight girls and three boys.

When Lionel was 15 his grandfather died and Aldridge was sent to live with his aunt in Pittsburg, California.[6] He attended Pittsburg High School in Pittsburg, and is one of 13 Pittsburg alumni to play in the NFL with the best known being fullback John Henry Johnson.[7] After the Pittsburg high school coach, Tony Knap, transferred to Utah State University he recruited Lionel to follow him to Logan, Utah.[8]

At Utah State Lionel played football as a wide receiver in 1960 and 1961 with 11 receptions for 179 yards and no touchdowns in 20 games. After defensive tackle and future Hall of Famer Merlin Olsen graduated in 1962, Aldridge was moved to defense. Utah State had excellent teams while Aldridge was there, winning two Skyline Conference co-championships. During Aldridge's years at Utah State he was selected to play in three post season all-star games, the Hula Bowl, All-American Bowl and East-West Shrine Classic.[9] In 1993, he was named to the Utah State All Century Football Team.

In 1963 Aldridge was drafted in the fourth round as the 54th overall selection by the Packers in the NFL draft and by the Houston Oilers in the sixth round as the 47th overall choice in the AFL draft.[10]

In Utah in 1960 there were few blacks. Lionel began dating a white Mormon girl named Vicki Wankier. After he was drafted by the NFL and was engaged to her the NFL tried to block their wedding, according to an October 27, 1987, *Los Angeles Times* article by Bob Oates.[11] It was only through the intervention of Green Bay's color-blind coach, Vince Lombardi, that the Aldridges were able to get married.

The six-feet-three, 254-pound Aldridge started at defensive end for the 1963 Packers, the only rookie to earn a starting position on the two time defending NFL champions. In fact, he was one of only five rookies ever to earn a starting role on a Vince Lombardi-coached NFL team. Aldridge's only recorded statistic for the year was one recovered fumble. Although the Packers in 1963 had an outstanding team they were nosed out of first place by the Chicago Bears. The Packers' post-season activity that year was limited to the Playoff Bowl which matched the second-place Western Conference Packers with the second-place Eastern Conference Cleveland Browns.[12] Although Green Bay easily won the game, 40–23, Lombardi called it "a losers' bowl for losers."[13]

In 1964, Aldridge had his best year statistically for the second place Packers with a league-leading five fumble recoveries including one on November 29, 1964, which he returned 29 yards for a touchdown in the fourth quarter against the Dallas Cowboys to cement a 45–21 victory for Green Bay. This would prove to be the only points he scored in his 11-year NFL career. At seasons-end he was selected for *The Sporting News* All-Conference first team—the only time in his career that he received that accolade.[14]

In 1965, Aldridge played in all 14 regular season games and two postseason games, and had two fumble recoveries for the season as the Packers regained the NFL championship.[15]

In 1966, Aldridge missed one game for the first time in his professional career and only played in 13 regular season games but continued his string of at least one fumble recovery each season with two for three yards. In the NFL championship game victory over Dallas, Aldridge was credited with one of Green Bay's two sacks.[16] In Green Bay's decisive win over the Chiefs in the first AFL-NFL world championship game, the Packers had six sacks of the Chiefs' quarterbacks. Aldridge was credited with half a sack.[17]

During the summer before the 1967 season, Aldridge broke his leg in a preseason game and as a result only played in 12 of Green Bay's 14 regular season games but continued his fumble recovery success with one more. He also was a member of the defensive line for all three of Green Bay's postseason games.[18]

Vince Lombardi's resignation as head coach following the 1967 season fostered a return to mediocrity for the Packers. The nucleus which had been together for the championship years (1960–67) began to age and although Aldridge was still only 27 years old, 13 of Green Bay's key players were 30 years of age or older. Aldridge continued to be a defensive starter for coaches Phil Bengtson and Dan Devine from 1968 to 1971.[19]

On April 18, 1972, Aldridge was traded to the San Diego Chargers for free safety Jim Hill and a 1974 draft choice.[20] The Chargers' assistant coaches included Aldridge's former Green Bay teammates Willie Wood and Forrest Gregg. Former Green Bay head coach Phil Bengtson was a special assistant with San Diego.

While Aldridge was an active player he also worked as a sportscaster for Milwaukee radio station WTMJ and in 1973 became part of NBC television's announcing team for Super Bowl VII.[21]

After suffering through two losing seasons in San Diego Aldridge announced his retirement from professional football on April 3, 1974.[22] Since he had been working part-time as a sportscaster Aldridge decided to pursue that as a full-time career after his retirement.

Lionel Aldridge died on February 12, 1998, in Shorewood, Wisconsin, of congestive heart failure two days shy of his 57th birthday and was found dead in his suburban Milwaukee apartment by his daughter. His weight had ballooned from his playing weight of 254 pounds to over 400 pounds, although he claimed that much of the weight gain came from giving up smoking. He was survived by his two daughters and one grand-daughter.[23]

Dan Devine once said of the man known as the "Big Train," "Willie Davis may have been flashier, but no one was steadier than Lionel Aldridge."[24]

NOTES

1. www.pro-football-reference.com.

2. www.guideposts.org/celebrities/gods-voice-helps-lionel-aldridge-through-mental-illness.

3. www.latimes.com/1987–10-27/sports/sp-16847_1_lionel-aldridge; www.schizophrenia.com/stories/aldridge.htm.

4. www.lombardiave.com/2012/06/17/lionel-aldridge-great-man-great-career-troubled-life/.

5. en.wikipedia.org/wiki/Lionel_Aldridge; en.wikipedia.org/wiki/Evergreen,_Louisiana.

6. www.latimes.com/1987–10-27/sports/sp-16847_1_lionel-aldridge.

7. en.wikipedia.org/wiki/Pittsburg_High_School; www.pro-football-reference.com/schools/high_schools.cgi?id=93b84720.

8. en.wikipedia.org/wiki/Tony_Knap.

9. www.cfbdatawarehouse.com/data/active/u/utah_state/index.php; www.utahstateaggies.com/sports/m-footbl/spec-rel/100611aab.html; www.sports-reference.com/cfb/players/lionel-aldridge-1.html.

10. www.pro-football-reference.com/years/1963/draft.htm.

11. www.latimes.com/1987–10-27/sports/sp-16847_1_lionel-aldridge.

12. www.pro-football-reference.com/teams/gnb/1963_roster.htm.

13. en.wikipedia.org/wiki/Playoff_Bowl.

14. www.pro-football-reference.com; www.pro-football-reference.com/teams/gnb/1964.htm.

15. www.pro-football-reference.com; www.pro-football-reference.com/teams/gnb/1965.htm.

16. www.pro-football-reference.com; www.pro-football-reference.com/teams/gnb/1966.htm.

17. www.pro-football-reference.com; en.wikipedia.org/wiki/Super_Bowl_I.

18. www.pro-football-reference.com; *Milwaukee Journal*, August 21, 1967; www.pro-football-reference.com/teams/gnb/1967.htm.

19. www.pro-football-reference.com/teams/gnb/1968.htm; www.pro-football-reference.com/teams/gnb/1969.htm; www.pro-football-reference.com/teams/gnb/1970.htm; www.pro-football-reference.com/teams/gnb/1971.htm.

20. www.pro-football-reference.com/teams/gnb/1968.htm; www.ultimate70s.com/nfl_roster/GB/1972/N/19760418.

21. www.schizophrenia.com/stories/aldridge.htm.

22. www.pro-football-reference.com/teams/sdg/1972.htm; http://www.pro-football-reference.com/teams/sdg/1973.htm; www.ultimate70s.com/seventies_history/19740403/football.

23. www.nytimes.com/1998/02/14/sports/lionel-aldridge-56-stalwart-on-defense-for-packer-teams.html.

24. John Maxymuk, *Packers by the Numbers* (Black Earth, WI: Prairie Oak Press, 2003), 326–327.

Bill Anderson

JOHN MAXYMUK

Three members of the 1966 Green Bay Packers never appeared in the NFL again after Super Bowl I. Paul Hornung, once the team's biggest star, was the only player not to play that day for Green Bay. However, little-used veteran journeyman ends Bill Anderson and Red Mack ended their pro football careers that day by playing on the sport's biggest stage. For Anderson, it was his second straight championship, which was a long way from how his pro career began.

Walter William Anderson was born July 16, 1936, in Hendersonville, North Carolina. He grew up in Onoco, Florida, near Sarasota, and attended Manatee High School where the football team was the South Florida Conference champion in Bill's senior year of 1953. As an All-Conference player, he was recruited heavily by Coach Bob Woodruff for the University of Florida, but instead chose to enroll in the University of Tennessee, where he would play three varsity seasons under Coach Bowden Wyatt. The Volunteers went 24–7–1 from 1955 to 1957, going to the Sugar Bowl (a 13–7 upset loss to Baylor) after the 1956 season and winning the Gator Bowl following 1957. Anderson was the team's starting wingback in the single wing offense, averaging 11.4 yards per rush on 29 carries and 23.1 yards per catch on 20 receptions. As a senior, the respected team leader and celebrated defensive back was also co-captain of the squad.

The Washington Redskins selected Bill in the third round of the 1958 NFL draft. He would be one of only five of their 30 picks that year who would ever play for the team and the only one who would play more than one full season in Washington. The self-deprecating Anderson claims he enlisted the help of another Tennessee alumnus to make his reputation in the preseason. Playing against the Bears, Bill ran up against massive future Hall of Fame defensive end Doug Atkins. When he tried to block Atkins, Doug "knocked me back three steps and pitched the runner on top of me." After Bill explained his predicament to his Volunteer brother, though, "he gave me a break, and all of a sudden I became the Redskins' best blocker."[1]

During the 1958 training camp, Joe Tereshinski, the Redskins' end coach, told the *Washington Post*, "He showed me that he is a fierce competitor. He is not afraid to stick his nose in there." The coach added, "I think he was the best defensive back on the Tennessee team last season." Anderson commented, "I still feel a little awkward on defense. It's more involved than the 6–2–2–1 we used mostly at Tennessee."[2]

The 6'3", 211-pound Anderson began the year in the Redskins defensive secondary, but when starting end John Carson got hurt early in the season, Bill replaced him at split end. In six years in Washington, Anderson played for three coaches that finished a collective 17–55–6, although his 168 catches in that period, at split end and later tight end, were second only to Bones Taylor in team history. Bill was named to the Pro Bowl in 1959 and 1960, and shared the "Outstanding Redskin" award with defensive lineman Bob Toneff in 1959. Anderson later told Jerry Kramer, "We changed coaches every time you looked around. We had only 18–20 people who could play, and the others shouldn't have been there. We were whipping boys."[3]

When former Florida coach Bob Woodruff came calling again, a discouraged Anderson was receptive. In 1963, Woodruff was the new athletic director at Tennessee and hired his former Gator quarterback Doug Dickey as head coach. Dickey offered Anderson a position as end coach with the Volunteers, and Bill accepted. Redskins coach Bill McPeak wished him well. "He helped out at Tennessee last spring and has the bug I suppose.

Bill Anderson.

With a new coach and young staff, he feels it's a fine opportunity."[4] Also added to the staff was Forrest Gregg who retired for the first time from the Packers. Gregg had played under Dickey in service ball, but was talked into returning to Green Bay just two months later by Vince Lombardi.

After one season as a coach, though, Anderson returned to Washington to restart his playing career. He retired because "I was tired of getting banged around every Sunday." After a year on the sidelines, his feelings changed. "I really want to play now. I didn't know I had it so good. Coaching makes you appreciate being able to play."[5] Returning to the Redskins, he found a logjam at tight end with veterans Preston Carpenter and Bob Jencks as well as dynamic rookie Jerry Smith competing with Bill for playing time. Since Green Bay had lost starting tight end Ron Kramer to the Lions, Vince Lombardi was looking for veteran insurance behind new starter Marv Fleming, so he gave Washington a sixth round pick for Anderson on August 18, 1965. Bill later told the *St. Petersburg Times*, "My first reaction was one of disappointment at being traded. After all, I had made quite a few friends in Washington, and here I had to almost start over again. Yet, I had an idea I might be traded. As it turned out, it was the greatest thing that could have happened to me."[6] He also wondered, "I wasn't fast enough anymore to be a wide receiver, and I wasn't a good enough blocker to be a tight end. What does he want me for?"[7]

Anderson was brought in as a backup and as the edge man on kickoff coverage. He spent most of the 1965 season in that capacity, catching just eight passes all year. As a veteran, he was able to fit in easily. "The Packers don't have many plays to learn. The thing that takes the most time is learning to react automatically to game situations, such as the blitz, changed defenses and things like that. You react fast in the NFL or you don't last."[8]

His seasonal highlight came in Week 12 when Bill caught a 27-yard touchdown for the winning score in a 24–19 triumph over the Vikings. Although having some back problems, Anderson began to be used more late in the year due to Fleming's sore ankle and lackadaisical play. After the Minnesota game, Lombardi beamed, "Anderson was worth his whole year's salary in that one game last week."[9]

The 1965 season concluded with the Packers and Colts tied for the lead of the Western Conference, necessitating a playoff game between the two on December 26, 1965, in Lambeau Field. The Colts were under the handicap of having lost both starting quarterback Johnny Unitas and backup Gary Cuozzo to injuries and were relying on halfback Tom Matte to run the offense. The first play from scrimmage evened things up a bit between the two clubs. Bart Starr connected with Anderson on a pass play, but when rocked by defensive back Lenny Lyles, Bill fumbled. Colt linebacker Don Shinnick scooped up the ball and returned it for a touchdown, with Starr cracking his ribs in the melee at the goal line. "What happened was that the ball hit me in the shoulder, instead of the stomach. Out of the corner of my eye, I saw a defender coming in to hit me, and I was trying to get the ball down into my stomach in time. I didn't quite make it," Bill recalled and added, "If there was a tunnel handy, I'd have crawled into it and run out of the stadium and kept on running."[10]

Ironically, had the play occurred today, it most likely would have been ruled incomplete since Anderson was unable to complete a "football move" after grabbing the ball. In addition, during the scramble for the loose ball, Anderson was hit in the head and suffered a concussion. "It was all a little hazy the rest of the way," he later noted.[11]

Hazy or not, Anderson proceeded to have the game of his life, catching seven more passes from backup quarterback Zeke Bratkowski. Bill's last catch came late in the over-time period and went for 18 yards to move the ball close to midfield; eight plays later, Don Chandler kicked the game-winning field goal. Chandler's first field goal had tied the game in the last two minutes and remains controversial to this day. Whenever anyone questioned Anderson whether that field goal went through the uprights, though, Bill would hold up his hand and reply matter-of-factly, "I'm wearing a dang ring."[12]

One week later, a bruised Starr returned for the NFL championship against the defending champion Browns, held again in Lambeau. Bill again started, but served primarily as a blocker. Starr said, "Early in the game, I was trying to hit Anderson but in the pass coverage Cleveland was using, it was awfully tough to throw to the tight end. They were holding up Anderson at the line of scrimmage."[13] Bill caught no passes that day, but Green Bay won handily 23–12 for Lombardi's third title and Anderson's "dang ring."

At the time, Bill compared the two quarterbacks. "Starr throws a soft ball that is easy to catch. Bratkowski throws a harder ball. Lombardi's passing game is very simple. We have only ten pass patterns, which we switch around every few weeks. Bart does a great job of picking up his number two and number three receivers when his prime target is covered."[14]

In the offseason, Arkansas coach Frank Broyles offered Anderson a spot on his staff, but Bill returned to the Packers for 1966. By opening day, though, he was again backing up Fleming. Anderson got into ten games in 1966 and caught just two passes, including one during the game-winning drive in game two. Despite his diminished role on the Super Bowl-winning Packers, Bill was invited back by Vince Lombardi for 1967. Anderson told Jerry Kramer, "I was committed to getting married, but I told Coach Lombardi that I'd come back if he'd give me a no-cut, no-trade contract. He promised he wouldn't trade me, but he said he couldn't promise not to cut me. I decided to give up football and get married."[15] Bill married Elizabeth Blanchard of Atlanta and had a son while he organized his own insurance agency over the next few years. The marriage eventually ended in divorce, and Anderson remarked to Kramer, "I guess if I had it to do all over again, I'd go back and play the 1967 season and forget about getting married."[16]

A year later, Bob Woodruff intervened in Anderson's life again, pairing him with play-by-play announcer John Ward to broadcast Tennessee football games. Bill would be Ward's color analyst for the next 31 years, and the two would retire together following the 1998 season; their final broadcast was the Fiesta Bowl on January 4, 1999, when Tennessee beat Florida State 23–16 to win the national championship, a fitting conclusion to the longest running broadcasting partnership in college football.

Anderson welcomed retirement as an opportunity to continue to run his insurance agency, play more golf and spend more time with his wife, Jerrie.

NOTES

1. Randy Moore, *Tennessee Volunteers: Colorful Tales of the Orange and White* (Guilford, CT: Globe Pequot, 2004), 60.

2. Dave Brady, "'Skins Like Anderson's Schooling and He May Play End, Halfback," *Washington Post*, August 5, 1958.

3. Jerry Kramer and Dick Schaap, *Distant Replay* (New York: G. P. Putnam's Sons, 1985), 183.

4. Jack Walsh, "Redskin End Anderson Quits Team," *Washington Post*, February 4, 1964.

5. William Gildea, "Bill Anderson Eager in Comeback," *Washington Post*, July 21, 1965.

6. Bob Bender, "Grid Titles Not New to Anderson," *St. Petersburg Times*, January 19, 1966.

7. Kramer, 184.

8. Bender.

9. Bob Addie, "Packers Want Privacy," *Washington Post*, December 9, 1965.

10. Bender.

11. "Dazed Bill Dimly Recalls Game," *St. Petersburg Times*, December 28, 1965.

12. "You Can Learn a Lot by Listening," *Tom Mattingly's the Vol Historian*, accessed February 10, 2015, www.knoxblogs.com/volhistorian/2007/10/30/you_can_hear_a_lot_by_listenin/.

13. Mike Christopulos, "Stuck to Basics, Says Happy Vince," *Milwaukee Sentinel*, January 3, 1966.

14. Bender.

15. Kramer, 185.

16. *Ibid.*

References

Addie, Bob. "Packers Want Privacy." *Washington Post*, December 9, 1965.

Bender, Bob. "Grid Titles Not New to Anderson." *St. Petersburg Times*, January 19, 1966.

Brady, Dave. "'Skins Like Anderson's Schooling and He May Play End, Halfback." *Washington Post*, August 5, 1958.

Christopulos, Mike. "Stuck to Basics, Says Happy Vince." *Milwaukee Sentinel*, January 3, 1966.

"Dazed Bill Dimly Recalls Game." *St. Petersburg Times*, December 28, 1965.

Gildea, William. "Bill Anderson Eager in Comeback." *Washington Post*, July 21, 1965.

Kramer, Jerry, and Dick Schaap. *Distant Replay*. New York: G. P. Putnam's Sons, 1985.

Moore, Randy. *Tennessee Volunteers: Colorful Tales of the Orange and White*. Guilford, CT: Globe Pequot, 2004.

Tom Mattingly's the Vol Historian. Accessed February 10, 2015. www.knoxblogs.com/volhistorian/2007/10/30/you_can_hear_a_lot_by_listenin/.

Walsh, Jack. "Redskin End Anderson Quits Team." *Washington Post*, February 4, 1964.

Donny Anderson

Jay Zahn

Nicknamed "The Golden Palomino," Donny Anderson seemed the ideal successor to Paul Hornung as Green Bay Packer halfback. Both players were multiple threats that excelled at running, receiving, and passing. Both participated in the kicking game on a regular basis; Hornung on placements, and Anderson punting. Both even shared blond hair and reputations as ladies' men.

The reality of Anderson's career proved to be a mixed bag. While Anderson actually outgained Hornung from scrimmage in both rushing and receiving, he scored fewer touchdowns and fumbled more often. Much of Anderson's best work came for losing teams, but he still had a colorful, nine-year NFL career and earned two Super Bowl rings as a reward.

Garry Don Anderson was born in the Texas panhandle city of Borger on May 16, 1943. He grew up in nearby Stinnett, a town of about 2,500 also in the panhandle. The son of John W. Anderson, who'd been an all-district end at Shamrock High School, Anderson excelled in several sports at Stinnett High. In football he was All-State, and Stinnett made it to the state semi-finals in his senior year. Since Stinnett was more than 3,000 feet above sea level in northernmost Texas, Anderson played several games in subfreezing weather, including snow and ice. This experience would prove valuable in years to come.

Though recruited by more than 30 universities, Anderson chose relative upstart Texas Tech, partly because the Red Raiders also accepted Anderson's brother Larry (Bo) into the school to play baseball—Donny also played baseball at Tech. However, Anderson's college football experience was almost derailed by academics—he flunked out his freshman year. But after improving his grades, Anderson stepped right into the Texas Tech lineup as a sophomore, leading the team in rushing. As a junior in 1964 he did even better, leading the entire Southwest Conference in rushing with 966 yards; he also made consensus All-American that year, sharing the backfield with Larry Elkins and Gale Sayers.

At this point Anderson's academic record came into play. Due to flunking out as a freshman, Anderson had spent four years at Tech, but had an additional year of eligibility remaining. His four years of college, though, made him eligible for the NFL draft. NFL frequently drafted such "junior eligible" players, but no team had drafted one in the first round since the Rams selected Dick Bass in 1959. With Vince Lombardi seeing a versatile halfback similar to Paul Hornung and to Frank Gifford from Lombardi's Giant days, the Packers took Anderson with the seventh pick in the first round. On the same day (November 28, 1964) the Houston Oilers selected Anderson first overall in a special "redshirt" draft.

Upon Anderson's drafting, Packers personnel director Pat Peppler said, "All our reports indicate that he is the kind of running back any pro team needs. He's got size [6'3", 215 pounds], speed [4.6 40-yard dash in football gear] and great hands. He has done everything they've asked of him. He could be a runner or flanker for us."[1]

Anderson opted to stay in school in 1965 and had another banner year. Used partly as a flanker/slotback, he got fewer carries, but still gained 705 yards on the ground for ten TDs. As a receiver, he caught 60 passes (tied for the conference lead) for 797 yards and seven more touchdowns. Again he made consensus All-American, this time accompanied in the backfield with USC's Mike Garrett and Illinois' Jim Grabowski.

Meanwhile, the Packers and Oilers bid handsomely for his services as a pro. Though the Oilers reportedly offered an $887,000 contract that included a home complete with swimming pool and furniture, as well as a job with the Oilers for his father, Anderson signed with the Packers for a reported $600,000 following the Raiders' Gator Bowl loss to Georgia Tech on New Years' Eve, 1965.

At the time, Anderson said of his signing, "I understand I'm to be used as a running back, and I'm really looking forward to it. I also plan to keep working on my punting. With Don Chandler around, I don't expect to get that assignment—but I'm confident I can improve as a punter. For the last two years I've worked to add height to my kicks to insure good coverage. Now I'll try to add more distance. I've never done much throwing, but I'm ready to work on that, too. I know the Packers use the run-pass option play, so I'll need to be able to throw."[2]

As was common for top draft picks at the time, Anderson reported late to his first Packers training camp due to his participation in the College All-Star game. After reporting to camp, Coach Lombardi did work Anderson into the mix in the remaining preseason games. The Packers had traded long time backup running back Tom Moore in the offseason. But Paul Hornung, as well as special teams ace Elijah Pitts, remained to compete with Anderson for playing time. Given Lombardi's usual reluctance to play rookies, Anderson would need to wait for his chance.

As he waited, Anderson got a chance to see the attitude that years of winning ways produced. He recently said, "I remember playing Cleveland in Cleveland and we were behind and Fuzzy Thurston made a comment on the sideline … the defense was in, Cleveland had the ball and they were ahead 20–14. And I said, 'Well, this doesn't look too good' and Fuzzy said, 'No, we've got this one won, we got it won.' He said, 'We're going to stop them right here, they're going to punt, we're going to drive down, we're going to score, kick the extra point, get on the plane and go home. I said, 'Man, what a positive attitude that is!' Well, we held them, drove down; Jimmy Taylor ran about 14 yards or something like that [actually a nine-yard pass reception from Bart Starr], scored the touchdown, kicked the extra point, got in the shower, got on the plane and went home, 21–20. That was a big story for me because that is kind of the way the Packers' history is. You teach the young kids all the positive attitude that you can."[3]

Donny Anderson.

Lombardi was willing to sprinkle Anderson and fellow "Gold Dust Twin" Jim Grabowski into the mix when the Packers had established a lead. When the Packers met the winless first year expansion Atlanta Falcons on October 23, Anderson got his chance. Entering in the second quarter of a game the Packers would ultimately win 56–3; Anderson scored his first two regular season touchdowns on a second quarter five-yard run and a fourth quarter 77-yard punt return. "The first one was an off-tackle play and I took one more step to the outside to take advantage of a block by Jerry Kramer and go in … on the second one, it was a long punt and they hadn't got down to cover it," Anderson said at the time.[4]

Anderson continued to attract some notice despite his brief opportunities from scrimmage. After Anderson carried twice for 15 yards in a 31–7 victory at Detroit, Wayne Walker of the Lions said, "That Donny Anderson, he's a lot faster than he looks. If he's going to be a great back in this league—and I suppose he is—one of the things that will be in his favor is that he doesn't look like he's moving as fast as he is. I thought I had him cut off on that one sweep and the next thing I knew I was chasing him. I'd lost the angle because he was faster than I thought."[5]

One regular job Anderson did secure during the 1966 season was kick returner. Anderson's 61-yard kickoff return against the Vikings November 6 was the Packers' biggest play in a 20–17 loss, their last of the 1966 season.

By the final game of the regular season, the Packers had clinched the Western Conference championship. This gave Coach Lombardi a chance to rest his regulars and look at his backups. Anderson took advantage by rushing 11 times for 58 yards and a touchdown in a 27–23 Packer victory at Los Angeles.

For the postseason though, Anderson still found himself confined to the return units. However, when the Packers broke open the first Super Bowl, Anderson and Grabowski got some late-game carries. Anderson made his count, not only gaining 30 yards in four carries, but knocking out Chiefs cornerback Fred "The Hammer" Williamson, who'd threatened mayhem against the Packers in pre-game interviews, with an accidental knee to Williamson's helmet.

By 1967, Paul Hornung had been lost to the New Orleans Saints in the expansion draft, but Elijah Pitts remained the starter at halfback in front of Anderson. Coach Lombardi did plan to use two sets of running backs, with Pitts and Grabowski (who had replaced the departed Jim Taylor) alternating with Anderson and new acquisition Ben Wilson.

Though Chandler remained as placekicker, Anderson did manage to win the regular punting job for the 1967 season. Anderson usually ranked no better than average in terms of gross average as a punter, and in 1967 was second from last in all of pro football to Cleveland's Gary Collins. But Anderson's style was intentional. "I'm not supposed to be a tremendous punter," he said in 1969. "I'm supposed to kick the ball high. I don't particularly care to see anybody run it back. And I'm not a particularly great open field tackler."[6] In addition, Anderson was a rare left-footed kicker. "Being left-footed, I had this high, hanging, backwards spiral going. Most guys weren't used to it. I was a punt returner too, so I knew it was a backwards ball," he said.[7] The Packers set a record in 1967 that still stands, allowing only 22 yards on 13 returns. They led the NFL again in 1969 in this category. Anderson said recently, "If I can say this humbly, I invented hang time…. Lombardi liked the fact that there were no runbacks."[8]

On the field more often in 1967 backing up Pitts, Anderson's explosiveness and versatility started to become evident. Then on November 5, he got a break. Pitts tore his Achilles tendon against the undefeated Colts, and Anderson replaced him at halfback. Though the Packers would lose the game 13–10, blowing a ten-point fourth quarter lead, Anderson stepped forward with 68 yards rushing and 54 yards receiving, including a 31-yard touchdown from Bart Starr. The day wasn't all highlights for Anderson, though, as he was replaced as punter by Chandler after struggling with Memorial Stadium crosswinds.

The next week Anderson got his first career start at halfback against the Century Division leading Cleveland Browns. Though arguably overshadowed by rookie Travis Williams' two kickoff returns for touchdowns, Anderson scored four of his own, three on the ground and one through the air in a 55–7 rout. Anderson also marked the first 100-yard effort of his career, though it was 100 yards receiving, with five receptions for 103 yards to go with 56 yards rushing.

Anderson continued as the regular halfback for the rest of the 1967 season with relief from the speedy Williams. For the season he rushed for 402 yards, caught 22 passes for 331 yards (an impressive 15 yard average) and scored nine touchdowns, tops on the team.

Anderson ran for 52 yards in the Packers' 28–7 playoff victory over the Rams, though he was overshadowed by Travis Williams' 88 yards and two touchdowns. Anderson would play a bigger role the next week against Dallas.

Lombardi persisted in platooning his running backs, alternating Anderson and mid-season acquisition Chuck Mercein (replacing the injured Grabowski) with Travis Williams and Ben Wilson. However, Anderson and Mercein got most of the work, and Anderson and Mercein were major contributors to the Packers' famous final drive in the Ice Bowl.

After being tackled by Willie Townes for a nine yard loss (due in part to a missed block by Mercein) on a first down play, Anderson gained the first down with nifty footwork on two passes in the flat by Starr. Sidestepping Cowboys linebacker Chuck Howley each time, the plays gained 21 yards to the Dallas 30. After a Mercein reception and running play advanced the ball to the three, Anderson narrowly missed a chance at immortality.

An off-right tackle run by Anderson did get the Packers a first down at the Dallas one, but players on both the Cowboys and Packers believed he scored on the play. "He scored! He scored! Why aren't they raising their hands up? My God, they're not going to give it to him!" Dallas' Cornell Green later recalled saying.[9] Anderson himself was content with how things turned out. "Bart Starr's the Super Star of the Green Bay Packers, so I think it turned out correctly. Would it be as big a deal to see Donny Anderson score the winning touchdown every year in the Ice Bowl? I don't think so."[10] After the first down, Anderson's footing failed him on two subsequent dive plays, setting the stage for Starr's famous sneak.

Anderson finally reached playoff paydirt in Super Bowl II. On the Packers' second drive of the second half, they went 82 yards in 11 plays. A 12-yard pass from Starr to Anderson set up the Packers first-and-goal at the one, and two plays later Anderson crashed over the right side untouched for a two-yard touchdown to put the Packers up 22–7 in a game they would win 33–14.

By 1968 Anderson had established himself as a starter. With the Packers' role as three-time defending champions, and memories of the Gold Dust Twins still fresh enough, Anderson's image started appearing on national magazine covers.

Unfortunately, as Anderson entered the most productive phase of his career, the fortunes of his teams took a turn for the worse. Anderson's five most productive seasons would all come with losing squads.

For the 1968 season Anderson rushed for 761 yards in 170 carries for what would be a career high 4.5 yards per attempt. Again, his receiving numbers were also impressive, averaging 13.3 yards per reception on 25 catches. However, the Packers suffered through an inconsistent season under new coach Phil Bengtson, and missed the playoffs.

Anderson did manage to score a berth in the 1969 Pro Bowl, his only such appearance. Anderson played a key role in the game, going off tackle for 22 yards to the one-yard line and setting up Bill Brown's fourth quarter touchdown in a 10–7 victory for the West.

Anderson seemingly had done enough to secure his place in the Packers' lineup. His picture on the cover of the 1969 Packers Yearbook would seem to bear that out. But the Packers were coming off of their first losing season in ten years, which may have made Coach Bengtson more likely to shake things up.

Anderson broke his ribs in the Packers' third preseason game of 1969. Two weeks later he pulled a muscle leaping for a high snap on a punt. When Anderson returned to active duty, he had not only lost his starting spot to Travis Williams but was third on the depth chart behind rookie Dave Hampton.

Eventually fate turned Anderson's way on October 26, when again the Falcons were victims of one of Anderson's biggest games. With Williams out of the lineup with an eye injury, Anderson had the biggest yardage total on the ground yet, gaining 114 yards on 18 carries in a 28–10 Packer win. Though Anderson played more regularly the rest of the year, he finished the season with only 288 yards in 87 carries for a 3.3 yard average, the worst of his career. Again, though, his receiving statistics were impressive, with 308 yards on only 14 receptions.

In 1970 Anderson experienced a reversal of fortune. Williams, Grabowski, and Hampton all missed significant time with injuries, allowing Anderson to get the most carries of his career, 222. Anderson wound up with 853 yards, seventh in the new 26 team NFL. He also had a career high 414 yards receiving.

Others took notice of Anderson's expanded role. George Allen said, "Donny Anderson is running the way we all thought he would. He's such a great football player."[11] Ken Bowman added, "I don't think Donny Anderson has ever run harder. He should make all-pro."[12]

Despite expanded usage of Anderson, coach Bengtson's Packers finished 1970 with a losing record of 6–8, including embarrassing season opening and closing shutout losses to division rival Detroit. Bengtson resigned following the season. Despite his own difficulties with Bengtson, who Anderson said "could not talk football," new coach Dan Devine would provide a fresh set of challenges for Anderson.[13]

Early in the 1971 season, Devine said that "Anderson [and teammate Dave Hampton] aren't what you would call real physical running backs. They are tough runners but not the Jimmy Brown type."[14]

Anderson had another fine season with 757 yards rushing, but was overshadowed by backfield mate John Brockington, who set a pro football record of 1,105 yards rushing for a rookie. Anderson also developed his own communication difficulties with Devine and his teammates, culminating in him walking off the practice field before the season's final game against Miami due to a dispute about his duties as a holder for field goals and extra points.

Devine opted to trade Anderson on February 22, 1972, to the Cardinals for fellow back MacArthur Lane. He took a parting shot at Anderson, saying he was disappointed by Anderson's blocking and preferred Hampton in that role (ironically, Devine would also trade Hampton before the 1972 season got underway). For his part, Anderson predicted that it would take the Packers 25 years to return to the Super Bowl under Devine's leadership. Anderson's prediction became surprisingly accurate, as the Packers indeed did not return to the Super Bowl until 25 years after Anderson's last season with the team, though Devine had long left the organization by then.

Anderson had two productive seasons for Cardinal coaches Bob Holloway and Don Coryell in 1972 and 1973, leading St Louis in rushing in both 4–9–1 seasons, but in 1974 Coryell's decision to go with traditional fullbacks Jim Otis and Ken Willard in the starting lineup meant that Anderson found himself as a backup (to Terry Metcalf) for the first time in five years.

On May 6, 1975, Anderson was traded to the Miami Dolphins. Miami saw Anderson as a replacement for WFL bound Jim Kiick in a receiving heavy backup role. But after playing in just one preseason game, Anderson retired on August 14, 1975. He cited family (his wife Karen was expecting their second child), the injury factor ("I don't want to be 50 and crippled") and that he felt he no longer had the speed to get outside on sweeps.[15]

After his retirement, Anderson took up golf and excelled, eventually joining the Celebrity Golf Tour. He remained active on the tour for 18 years, eventually becoming one of the board members of the tour.

Anderson has also been active in charitable endeavors. With retired teacher Linkie Seltzer Cohn, he wrote the book *Winners for Life*, designed to teach teens the importance of goal setting to achieve dreams. The Winners for Life foundation also issues 50 scholarships a year to at-risk youth.

Anderson now spends time in Texas with his daughter Kesh, son Blake (who played minor league baseball for the Colorado Rockies), and his eight grandsons. In 2011, he reflected back on his football career. "In a very humble way, maybe by playing running back, catching the ball, returning punts and kicks and punting, I would represent five players," Anderson said. "Really that was just the time, though, in the NFL, and the way you used players. I even asked Vince if I could play baseball in the offseason. Baseball was my first love. He asked me if I was out of my mind."[16]

NOTES

1. Chuck Johnson, "1st Round Future a Packer 1st," *Milwaukee Journal*, November 29, 1964.
2. Bud Lea, "The Donny Anderson Story: 'Packers Biggest Challenge,'" *Milwaukee Sentinel*, February 5, 1966.
3. Donny Anderson interview with Ken Crippen, June 27, 2014.
4. Lee Remmel, "Passing to 'Open' Ends Triggered Victory—Starr," *Green Bay Press-Gazette*, October 24, 1966.
5. Chuck Johnson, "Fuzzy Saw Brown, Sank Same," *Milwaukee Journal*, November 1, 1966.
6. Lee Remmel, "Anderson Humble, Content After Finest Performance," *Green Bay Press-Gazette*, October 27, 1969.
7. Ricky Zeller, "Where Are They Now? Donny Anderson Is on the Golf Course," Packers.com, April 14, 2011, www.packers.com.
8. Donny Anderson interview with Ken Crippen, June 27, 2014.
9. Tom Andrews, "New Twist on Icy Thriller," *Packer Report*, May 25, 2009.
10. *Ibid.*
11. Chuck Johnson, "Packers Believe Talbert Was Offside on Key Play," *Milwaukee Sentinel*, October 19, 1970.
12. Bud Lea, "Pack Find It's Tough," *Milwaukee Sentinel*, December 1, 1970.
13. Jim Slocum, "Packer Veterans Say Change Inevitable," *Milwaukee Sentinel*, December 23, 1970.
14. Bud Lea, "Packers' Scoring Ability Stuns NFL Foes ... So Far," *Milwaukee Sentinel*, September 30, 1971.
15. "Donny Anderson Quits Football," *Associated Press*, August 15, 1975.
16. Zeller.

Ken Bowman

RICK SCHABOWSKI

Ken Bowman played 123 games at center for the Green Bay Packers from 1964 to 1973 and was the man who snapped the ball to Bart Starr for his famous quarterback sneak against the Dallas Cowboys, giving the Packers a 21–17 victory in the Ice Bowl.

Bowman's parents grew up in the south side of Chicago but when the neighborhood got so bad that his Dad had to run from the bus stop or risk losing his paycheck, they used all their savings to move and open a gas station in Milan, Illinois, a suburb of Rock Island. There, Kenneth Brian Bowman was born on December 15, 1942.

While the gas station provided employment for Bowman and his brother, Ken always had dreams of going to college. His father stressed, "I'm never going to have the money to send you, but if you can get good enough at a sport, they'll pay you to go to college."[1] Bowman thought a lot about his father's comments, recalling, "That made a hell of an impression on me."[2]

At Rock Island High School, Bowman served as captain of the football team coached by H.V. "Shorty" Almquist, and was named to the Illinois All-State team in 1959. He attracted many scholarship offers but chose the University of Wisconsin–Madison. Ken had dreams of going to law school and entering the legal profession after a football career. "My father used to talk about Rick Casares and Bill George and the Chicago Bears, but I didn't pay much attention. I wanted to be a good football player, as good as I could possibly be, but I was more interested in getting an education."[3]

As a freshman at Wisconsin in 1960, Bowman earned his numerals. He played 173.5 minutes as a sophomore and started at center in his junior and senior years.

Intense competition took place in the early sixties between the NFL and AFL to sign graduating seniors. Bowman, however, received little if any attention. "Before I was drafted, I'm gonna say none. After I was drafted, Verne Lewellen [Packers executive] came down to Madison and talked with me and basically tried to get me to sign a contract. I had been drafted by the Jets, actually the round earlier, [sic] so I got drafted in the seventh round [sic] and by the Packers in the eighth round. Back then, the game was to try to get them to work against each other to your benefit. But the Jets never contacted me. It was kind of funny. I got a hold of Weeb Ewbank years later—he was the general manager and coach of the New York Jets at the time—and said, 'Weeb, what's wrong with you? Seventh round draft choice and you didn't even contact me, didn't even call me?' He said, 'We saw who drafted you in the NFL. You were a University of Wisconsin boy, and at that time the Packers were the team of the decade. So we figured we were not going to be able to compete with 'em.' I said, 'If you only knew, back then I didn't follow the Packers. I came from Chicago originally. If the Bears would have drafted me, you'd have had a problem.'"[4]

Bowman ended up signing with the Packers for a $6,000 signing bonus and received $12,000 for his first season.

Ken Bowman.

After playing in the 1964 College All-Star game, Bowman arrived at training camp. He was very familiar with the Packers offense because Wisconsin football coach Milt Bruhn had implemented a large portion of the Packers offense. "He [Bruhn] went to Green Bay and learned a lot about their offense. We basically ran the Green Bay offense. He transposed the left and right. In Green Bay, the 49 sweep was the sweep around the right end. For me, as a rookie in Green Bay, it sometimes caused a little bit of trouble. Bart would get up there and audibilize on the line of scrimmage. We didn't have a lot of time to think. 'Thirty-two, that's not to my right, that's to my left.' It did create a little bit of confusion for me the first year.'"[5]

The biggest adjustment, however, would be playing under Vince Lombardi. When Bowman was inducted into the Packers Hall of Fame in February, 1981, he called his stay in

Green Bay the best years of his life, especially the winning years under Lombardi. "I remember when I joined the Packers in 1964, my brother asked me if I ever called Coach Lombardi 'Vinnie'? I told him, 'Can you imagine anyone calling Attila the Hun 'Tillie?' When I came here, I knew I had to make a name for myself. I knew the only place I could do it was in the john. So I etched my name in the john. For posterity."[6]

Another great memory of that rookie training camp was an unexpected encounter with Lombardi. "We were staying at Sensenbrenner Hall and it was before supper, and Bob [Skoronski] and I walked down to the Dairy Bar and got an ice cream cone, a big double-dipper ice cream cone. We were walking back and we were shooting the breeze and, lo and behold, here comes Lombardi from Sensenbrenner to the chow hall. I'm walking along eating my ice cream cone and all of a sudden I look at Skoronski and he doesn't have one. I said, 'Bob, where the hell's your ice cream cone?' He said, 'Oh, I threw it in the bush back there.' He didn't want Lombardi to see him."[7]

Although Jim Ringo was the Packers' starting center and had been an All-Pro for seven straight seasons, it didn't faze Bowman at all. "I was twenty-one years old and you know, I thought the Good Lord broke the mold after he made me. I was going to last forever. I wasn't worried about Ringo."[8] Pat Peppler, Green Bay's personnel director from 1963 to 1971, recalled, "Bowman did a great job on really short notice. Ringo was traded and Bowman basically took over. Not much of a drop-off in performance either."[9]

During the last three championship seasons under Lombardi at Green Bay, Bowman didn't always start, sometimes due to his bad shoulder, but he was the primary starter. In 1966, Bill Curry was the starting center, but Curry sprained an ankle early in the Super Bowl. Bowman recalled, "You had to know Coach Lombardi and how he thought about sprained ankles. He didn't care. He wanted us to play. Just tape it up and go. So he came to me and said, 'Curry said he can't go. You go.' I said, 'I'll give you what I got until the shoulder goes.' As luck would have it, I stayed in and played a pretty good game."[10]

Curry was lost to the Saints in the expansion draft, but in the first round of the 1967 NFL Draft, with the ninth overall pick, Green Bay selected center Bob Hyland out of Boston College. Bowman's competitive nature and ability enabled him to keep the starter's job, and Hyland was eventually traded to the Bears. Bowman took things in stride. "I didn't look at either incident as an attempt by the coaches to get rid of me or put me on the bench. Bill took over for me when I injured my shoulder in 1966, and Bob was a No. 1 draft choice and they were just looking for a place to play him. It was a necessary thing."[11]

Bowman's biggest chance at fame was the Ice Bowl. Bowman still is somewhat annoyed about Jerry Kramer gaining almost all the accolades given for that winning touchdown. "It still bothers me a little bit when I hear how Kramer threw the big block. You'd be surprised how many people think he did it alone."[12] Jerry Kramer, Bowman recalled, hit the Cowboys' Jethro Pugh first, "straightening him up."[13] After snapping the ball, Bowman came in a second later and "hit Pugh just below the rib cage with my helmet, driving him back."[14]

After the game, Bowman remembered, "The television people were clamoring for Jerry. I kiddingly grabbed him and said, 'Damn it, Jerry, I hope you tell them the truth—that I helped out on that block.' And he smiled and said, 'C'mon, Ken, let an old man have his day in the sun. You've got 10 or 11 years left to make another block like that.' And then that son of a gun goes on TV and takes full credit for the block. I couldn't believe it."[15]

Bowman said he didn't realize how important that block or the Ice Bowl would become, putting it among the NFL's most historic games. "I was so young and dumb. I let Jerry go up and have the microphone and receive all the credit."[16] Former Packers team historian Lee Remmel offered this perspective in a 2007 interview with *Packer Plus* on the famous block. "Looking back from 40 years' perspective, I think there's quite enough for both of them to share. I don't think there's any reason to diminish one's role or the other's. They both contributed to the end result, which was a victory in what was voted the greatest game of all time."[17]

After Kramer wrote his book *Instant Replay*, Bowman gave Kramer credit for attempting to correct the situation. "Jerry tried to rectify that in his book. He gave the credit to a dual effort on his part and mine. But that didn't quite make up for the fact that he went to places like Miami and New Orleans for speaking engagements and I went to Onalaska and Omro [two small Wisconsin towns]."[18]

During the 1968 season, the first under new coach Phil Bengtson, Bowman played in great pain. "I broke my right thumb and I had to play more with my left hand. There was a photo by Vern Biever that shows my left hand just eaten to bits. The knuckles are almost bare. It shows the cast on my thumb, between that bone from your wrist on up to the first digit. That's where it busted. I couldn't really hit anybody with it. I tried, but my hand would get all swelled up. But, you know, you adapt. That's what playing football is all about, especially at that level."[19]

Fellow offensive lineman guard Bill Lueck was amazed about Bowman's courage. "How much pain that man could tolerate was incredible. You have to be able to play in pain in the NFL, but he was something else. I almost passed out one time watching the doc pull on his arm and put his shoulder back in on the sideline at Milwaukee County Stadium. They taped it up and he went back out there and played."[20]

While playing for the Packers, Bowman went to law school and earned his law degree. Armed with his legal knowledge, Bowman became passionately involved in another battle—serving as union player representative for his Packer teammates. The labor situation flared up to such an extent in 1974 that the players went on strike during the preseason.[21] Bowman recalled, "I wasn't too popular. I guess I antagonized some people around here with my outward appearance. I had long hair. I was the visual strike leader."[22]

On September 10, 1974, Bowman was removed from the active roster and put on the injured reserve list. "I think I was getting a little paranoid about it. I knew it was coming, but I didn't know how and I didn't know when. They'll be subsidizing my legal career now I guess. I get my full salary and they pay the medical expenses, but I'm not allowed to practice or play with the team, and I can't attend team meetings. There are some things I'd like to say, but I'm not going to. They could waive me at any time."[23]

After the Packers' new head coach Bart Starr cut Bowman from the 1975 roster, Bowman filed a workman's compensation claim against the Packers, but he ended up playing for the World Football League Hawaii Islanders.

After returning to Wisconsin in November 1975 at the conclusion of the WFL season, Bowman started a federal lawsuit against the NFL in Minneapolis for his release from the Hawaiians. Bowman won the lawsuit, one of two he won against the NFL. "You don't make a lot of friends when you sue the NFL, but it was a restraint of trade issue to blackball the WFL players from playing in the NFL."[24]

But in the end, Bowman would always be proudest of one thing: "Winning three NFL championships in a row has been my biggest thrill. How many other teams have done it? Winning the second Super Bowl was the real clincher."[25]

Notes

1. Jerry Kramer and Dick Schaap, *Distant Replay* (New York: G. P. Putnam's Sons, 1985), 136.

2. *Ibid.*

3. *Ibid.*

4. Dave Robinson and Royce Boyles, *The Lombardi Legacy: Thirty People Who Were Touched by Greatness* (Louisville, KY: Goose Creek Publishers, 2009), 250–251.

5. Jay Sorgi, "Former Center Bowman Stands in the Shadows of Lombardi-Era Lore," *620wtmj.com*, www.620wtmj.com.

6. Bud Lea, "Bowman Finally Gets Acclaim After Toiling in Anonymity," *Milwaukee Sentinel*, February 9, 1981.

7. Tom Oates, "Lombardi Memories: Ken Bowman," Madison.com, September 8, 2009, www.madison.com.

8. Kramer, 137.

9. Martin Hendricks, "Bowman Didn't Get the Glory for the Ice Bowl Block," *Packer Plus*, January 26, 2012.

10. Sorgi.

11. Mike Christopulos, "Ken Bowman: The Offensive Line's Elder Statesman," *Green Bay Packers 1970 Yearbook*.

12. Rob Zaleski, "Ken Bowman Still Talks of 'That Block," *The Sporting News*, November 24, 1979.

13. *Ibid.*

14. *Ibid.*

15. *Ibid.*

16. Hendricks.

17. *Ibid.*

18. Christopulos.

19. Bill Huber, "Packers Hall Q & A: Ken Bowman," Packer Report, Gnbscout.com, www.gnb.scout.com/story/854088-packers-hall-q-a-ken-bowman.

20. Hendricks.

21. Mike O'Brien, "Say Arrests Result of 'Threat' Made by Packers Bowman," *Lewiston Evening Journal*, July 27, 1974; Mike Kupper, "Arrests Break Peace in Green Bay," *Milwaukee Journal*, July 26, 1974.

22. Kupper.

23. Mike Kupper, "Bowman Knew the End Was Near," *Milwaukee Journal*, September 11, 1974.

24. Hendricks.

25. Christopulos.

Zeke Bratkowski

George Bozeka

Zeke Bratkowski was a relief quarterback extraordinaire during the Packer glory days of the 1960s, who exemplified Coach Vince Lombardi's tenets of loyalty, unselfish team play and intense preparation.

Edmund Raymond Bratkowski was born in Danville, Illinois, on October 20, 1931, the grandson of Polish immigrants. Bratkowski's father Kasmer worked for the state during the Roosevelt administration as a road worker and as a zinc factory worker, and his mother Elizabeth worked in a jacket company as a presser. Bratkowski recalled that "they both worked very, very hard" without a car, catching a bus or walking to work.[1] His father was an outstanding baseball player who played semipro ball. When Bratkowski was eight years old he was the bat boy for his father's team. His father bought him a baseball uniform with the name and image of Chicago White Sox first baseman Zeke Bonura on it. As a result Bratkowski's nickname of Zeke was born. To this day, he is Zeke to everyone except his sister Pat, who still calls him by his given name.[2]

Zeke was a good athlete, and loved playing baseball and football. Every Sunday, he played baseball that was organized by Happy Youhaus, a local barber, using second hand equipment. He also played American Legion baseball and in a number of local baseball leagues. Bratkowski normally played in the outfield or pitched.[3]

Bratkowski started playing football as a 135 pound right guard in high school at Schlarman High School, a new parochial school. The school had no stadium or gym. He also played basketball and baseball in high school. By his senior year, he was a 180 pound back in Coach Paul Shebby's double wing offense. Bratkowski fondly said of his high school coach, "I credit Coach Shebby for not only teaching me football, but also preparing me for life."[4]

Shebby recommended Bratkowski to University of Georgia coach Wally Butts. When Shebby coached at Pittston High School in Pennsylvania he had recommended one of his star players—Charlie Trippi—to Butts and Georgia. Trippi went on to be a two-time All-American, so Shebby's word was golden. Zeke worked out for the University of Georgia, and was offered a football scholarship. He had a chance to play pro baseball with the Brooklyn Dodgers, but his father demanded that he go to college.[5]

Bratkowski played quarterback at Georgia from 1951 to 1953, and established a number of Southeastern Conference and Georgia passing records. During his three seasons, he completed 360 of 734 passes for 4863 yards, 24 touchdowns and 68 interceptions. He was a two time All-American in 1952 and 1953. Zeke was the nation's leading college passer in 1952, and a two-time Southeastern Conference passing champion in 1952 (1824 yards) and 1953 (1461 yards). Bratkowski was also a great collegiate punter, leading the nation with a 42.6 yard average in 1953, beating out future Packer teammate and best friend Bart Starr of Alabama.[6] Zeke stated of his Georgia football experience, "Butts was of the old school, the Bear Bryant school. Very seldom did we not have pads on. He made me a passer. Just through sheer repetition I got better and better. They called him a taskmaster and I guess that's probably the best definition I can give of him."[7]

On January 22, 1953, George Halas and the Chicago Bears took Bratkowski in the second round of the NFL draft with the 17th selection overall as a futures pick. Bratkowski played his senior season at Georgia and after playing in the 1954 College All-Star Game reported to Bears training camp in 1954. George Blanda began the season as the Bears' number one signal caller, but after injuries forced Blanda out, Bratkowski took over as the starter and led the Bears to four consecutive season ending victories and an 8–4 mark overall. For the season, Zeke completed 67 of 130 passes for 1087 yards, with eight touchdowns and 17 interceptions. Bratkowski remembered Coach Halas as "very methodical just like Coach Lombardi, a great teacher, very emotional, very demanding, a great person, both (Halas and Lombardi) were sensational Christians."[8]

Just as Bratkowski was coming into his own as a pro, he was inducted into the Air Force and served for two years as a pilot, missing the 1955 and 1956 seasons. During his Air Force duty, he played service football at Goodfellow Air Force Base in San Angelo, Texas, with fellow NFL players Max McGee and Jim Dooley.[9]

Bratkowski rejoined the Bears for the 1957 season. Halas had him view films and chart plays from the two seasons he missed to rejuvenate his football mind. He played with the Bears through the 1960 season and was traded to the Rams for the 1961 season, playing for the Rams for two and a half seasons before being traded to the Packers during

Zeke Bratkowski.

the 1963 season. During most of his seasons in Chicago and Los Angeles, Zeke was fighting for starting assignments with one or two other quarterbacks. According to Bratkowski, "it was chaotic. The continuity was broken quite a bit. I don't think that's the best situation now that I've coached all these years. You have to have one guy."[10] Zeke's time with the Rams was particularly painful. He suffered through a 3–21 record as a starter as the Rams lost with regularity during a rebuilding phase.

When Zeke was traded to the Packers one of the first people to contact him was Bart Starr. Starr was studying film and asked Bratkowski if he wanted to join him. This fostered a close friendship that has never waned. To Bratkowski, "Bart and I are like brothers. He is the ultimate gentleman. It was a great honor playing with him and on the Packers. I enjoyed my role. I just knew the opportunity was going to turn into something good."[11]

Bratkowski did not see much action during the 1963 or 1964 seasons, but beginning in 1965 his worth to the Packers became apparent. Three times during the 1965 regular season, Bratkowski relieved Starr and led the Packers to victory.

In Week 2 against the Colts, Starr went down with an injury in the third quarter with the score tied 10–10. The Packers added a 41-yard Don Chandler field goal to go ahead 13–10 in the fourth quarter. The Colts responded with a John Unitas to Raymond Berry touchdown pass to take a 17–13 lead. Then with 2:48 left, Bratkowski hit Max McGee for the winning touchdown on a 37-yard zigout pattern, giving the Packers a 20–17 victory.

In Week 9 against the Rams, Zeke relieved Starr in the third quarter with the game tied 3–3. With two minutes to go, Lionel Aldridge recovered a Rams fumble on the Ram 20. Bratkowski led the Packers to one first down to set up a seven-yard game winning field goal by Chandler, as the Packers prevailed 6–3.

Finally, in Week 12 against the Vikings, Starr suffered a finger injury in the first quarter. Down 16–7 in the second quarter, the Packers slowly fought their way back into the game with Zeke at the helm, taking a 21–19 lead on a 27-yard third quarter touchdown pass from Bratkowski to Bill Anderson. Chandler added a 25-yard field goal in the fourth quarter to give the Packers a 24–19 victory.

To top off his extraordinary 1965 season, in the pivotal game of the year, the Western Conference playoff game against the Colts to determine who would play the Browns in the NFL championship game, Bratkowski again came to the rescue after Starr got hurt on the first play of the game. Zeke completed 22 of 39 passes for 248 yards to lead the Packers to a hard fought 13–10 overtime victory. A week later, the Packers defeated the Browns 23–12, to regain the NFL championship after a two year drought.

Zeke was quickly becoming known as the premier backup quarterback in the NFL. Bratkowski explained that the keys to his success were selflessness, team intelligence and preparation. "I try to pattern myself off him [Starr] although all of us call our games differently. Coach Lombardi can't afford to substitute. It's a matter of having one quarterback. I've played under a two quarterback system and I know what it is … it's impossible. Bart and I see a lot of movies and talk together on the sidelines frequently. I'm also on the phone on the sidelines and try to keep close to the game. In fact, I give plays to Bart all the time that come down from upstairs, so I am pretty familiar with the game plan."[12] "Part of my job was to make sure nothing changed. Bart and I could play off each other. It was like one single mind. It became sophisticated because of the simplicity."[13] Starr added, "Zeke and I are only interested in one thing—the best means of winning. He is so unselfish and such a student of the game that we are extremely fortunate to have him. Many clubs don't have a quarterback of his caliber and experience to play."[14]

Bratkowski was again outstanding in 1966. In Week 11 against the Bears, Starr suffered a pulled hamstring early in the game. Bart tried to gut it out, but Zeke eventually replaced him, and led the Packers to a hard fought 13–6 victory throwing for 190 yards and two touchdowns, both to Carroll Dale.

In Week 14 against the Colts, Starr went down with bruised ribs late in the second quarter with the Packers trailing 10–7. Bratkowski replaced Starr and led the Packers to a game winning drive in the fourth quarter as Green Bay pulled out a 14–10 victory.

In the final game of the 1966 season, Bratkowski got his first starting assignment since the 1963 season as Lombardi rested the ailing Starr for the post season. Zeke completed 13 of 23 passes for 245 yards and a touchdown as the Pack defeated the Rams 27–23.

The Packers repeated as NFL champions defeating Dallas in the 1966 NFL championship game and headed into the first AFL-NFL World Championship Game. Bratkowski recalled the buildup and the game, "It wasn't as big as it is now. The entire week was all work. That was the atmosphere. It was very gratifying to be there. I was living in LA then. After the game I went straight home."[15] Zeke played briefly in the first Super Bowl as the Packers defeated the Chiefs.

After their Super Bowl I victory over the Chiefs, the Packers came into the 1967 season determined to win their third straight title. In Week 3 against the Falcons, Starr had to leave the game early, injuring his shoulder after colliding with Atlanta defenders Tommy Nobis and Bob Riggle. Zeke came in and continued his relief mastery leading the Packers to a 23–0 victory, completing 15 of 26 passes for 214 yards and two touchdowns. Bratkowski started the next two games, leading the Pack to a 27–17 victory over the Lions in Week 4 while completing 12 of 19 passes for 154 yards and two more touchdowns, and suffering a tough 10–7 loss to the Vikings in Week 5. Zeke threw his fifth touchdown pass of the season against Minnesota, but was also picked off three times. Bratkowski would see significant action in one more regular season game in 1967, a 13–0 Week 10 victory over the Niners, completing nine of 18 passes for 103 yards. He also saw limited action in a 24–17 Week 14 loss to the Steelers. In the post season, Zeke again saw brief action in the Packers 33–14 Super Bowl II victory over the Raiders.

Under new coach Phil Bengtson in 1968, Zeke with Starr and Don Horn was again part of a threesome at quarterback. He saw action in nine games with five starts. In his starts the Packers went 2–2–1, although he saw very limited action in one of the victories.

Zeke retired at the end of the 1968 season and became an assistant coach with the Packers. The Packers hoped to use Zeke as an emergency quarterback during the 1969 season, but the Vikings blocked the move by claiming Bratkowski on waivers.[16]

In 1971, after the Packers worked out a deal with the Vikings, who still owned his playing rights, Bratkowski came out of retirement to again serve as Starr's backup under new Packer coach Dan Devine. Zeke saw action in six games including one start in Week One, a 42–40 shootout loss to the Giants.

At the close of the 1971 season, Bratkowski again retired and became an assistant coach with the Bears. The Bears actually activated Zeke at quarterback but he did not see any regular season action, officially ending his playing career.

For his career, Bratkowski completed 762 of 1484 passes for 10,345 yards, 65 touchdowns and 122 interceptions. He also rushed for 308 yards and five touchdowns.

With his long playing career was over, Bratkowski spent many years as a successful and respected NFL assistant coach. Zeke has been happily married for over 60 years to his wife Mary Elizabeth. They have two children, Kassie, an estate manager in Wisconsin, and Bob, a football coach. A third child, Steve, was killed in a jet ski accident.

Bratkowski summed up the Packer experience. "Lombardi always talked about the love of each other as players and teammates. Our team was made up of people that somebody, someway, somehow made a big play. No one knew who it was or who it would be but somebody did that. He was a great motivator. He said we don't have the best players but we have the best team, which I've always remembered. People rose to the occasion. Lombardi left an indelible mark on our character and our makeup. If you look at the players that played on that team and how successful they have been, you know when he was talking to us he was thinking after we got out of football. The rings are not tarnished that much, and the money is gone, but the memories they will never be able to take away from us."[17]

NOTES

1. Zeke Bratkowski interview with author, September 29, 2014.
2. *Ibid.*; Furman Bisher, "Georgia Brat," *Sport Magazine*, December 1953, 86.
3. Zeke Bratkowski interview with author, September 29, 2014.
4. *Ibid.*; Mary Kay Sweikar, "Hometown Heart," *Danville Commercial News*, September 6, 2012.
5. Zeke Bratkowski interview with author, September 29, 2014.
6. University of Georgia Football, Georgiadogs.com, www.georgiadogs.com.
7. Zeke Bratkowski interview with author, September 29, 2014.
8. *Ibid.*
9. *Ibid.*
10. *Ibid.*
11. *Ibid.*
12. Len Wagner, "Zeke to the Rescue," *1965 Packers Yearbook*, 41–43.
13. Zeke Bratkowski interview with author, September 29, 2014.
14. "Bratkowski an Able Understudy for Bart Starr," *Chicago's American*, December 8.1965.
15. Zeke Bratkowski interview with author, September 29, 2014.
16. "Vikings Block Brat Waivers," *Milwaukee Sentinel*, September 5, 1969.
17. Zeke Bratkowski interview with author, September 29, 2014.

Allen Brown

MATT REASER

Allen Brown had the distinction of playing for two legendary football coaches during his football career. Brown was born March 2, 1943. A native of Natchez, Mississippi, and one of 11 children, Brown was a star on the gridiron for his hometown Natchez High School. He won nine letters in high school, where he lettered in football, basketball and track. It was football where he made his name when he earned second-team All-Conference recognition as a junior before being selected as first-team All-Conference end his senior season. Ready to continue his football career at the collegiate level, Brown strongly considered LSU, but ultimately was convinced by his brothers and the Ole Miss coaching staff—specifically assistant coach Ray Poole—to attend the University of Mississippi.[1]

As a Rebel, Brown played for legendary Ole Miss coach Johnny Vaught—who was inducted into the College Football Hall of Fame in 1979.[2] Brown earned three letters (1962–1964) while contributing to and continuing one of the most successful runs in Ole Miss football history: a three-season span that included championships, bowl games, an undefeated season and a cumulative overall record of 22–6–3.[3]

Allen Brown made an immediate impact as a sophomore. He was named to the All-SEC Sophomore team while contributing to a historic season for his school.[4] An undefeated 6–0 record in the conference earned Mississippi the SEC championship and an invitation to the Sugar Bowl. With a 9–0 overall record, Ole Miss went on to beat Arkansas 17–13 in the Sugar Bowl to finish the year 10–0 and complete the undefeated season. Ole Miss was named national champions by a number of polling organizations.

His junior season began with a 0–0 tie against Memphis before Ole Miss won seven games in a row. A 10–10 tie against arch-rival Mississippi State ended the win streak, but kept the Rebels undefeated at 7–0–2. Their 5–0–1 conference record earned them a second straight Southeastern Conference championship. It also earned them a repeat trip to the Sugar Bowl where Ole Miss lost to Alabama 12–7. Brown was recognized with multiple All-Conference honors including being named first-team All-SEC by the Associated Press.[5]

The 1964 Rebels season did not go as well as the previous two years, but that did not stop Brown from taking advantage of his final season at Ole Miss. A 5–4–1 record and a losing record in the conference didn't meet expectations, although Ole Miss was still chosen to play in the Bluebonnet Bowl, where they lost to Tulsa 14–7. Individually it was a great season for the 1964 Rebel co-captain. Brown was selected first-team All-SEC, both by the Associated Press and United Press International. He was also recognized nationally for his defensive skills with first-team All-America honors coming by way of the Associated Press, *Time* Magazine and *The Sporting News*. Brown capped off his college career by being selected to play in both the Blue-Gray Game and the Senior Bowl and his hometown of Natchez, Mississippi, honored him with Allen Brown Day.[6]

For his contributions to Ole Miss football he was inducted into the Ole Miss Athletic Hall of Fame in 1989. The Southeastern Conference selected Brown as a SEC Football Legend in 2004. In 2010 he was enshrined

Allen Brown.

into the Mississippi Sports Hall of Fame and in 2012 he was honored by the Ole Miss M-Club Alumni Chapter with the Service Award.[7] Two of Brown's sons also went on to play football at Ole Miss. His son Tim, a guard, was co-captain of the 1989 team, while his son Burkes was an offensive tackle for the Rebels, lettering in 1991 and 1992.[8]

Brown was drafted in both the third round of the 1965 NFL draft by the Packers, and the third round of the 1965 AFL draft by the San Diego Chargers. Given the two options the 6'5", 230-pound tight end from Mississippi chose the Packers, signing with Green Bay on December 21, 1964.[9] Amidst the beginnings of his professional football career Brown married his high school and college sweetheart Margaret Burkes in 1965.[10]

The transition from the college game to the pros included participation in the College All-Star Game for Brown. Unfortunately, during a camp practice with the All-Stars he suffered a dislocated left shoulder. "I hurt my shoulder in a pass scrimmage in practice with the All-Stars," Brown described. "I collided with Dick Butkus [University of Illinois]. He hit me as I was catching the ball."[11] Brown underwent emergency surgery and missed the entire 1965 NFL season.

Going into 1966 the Packers coaches were excited to see what Brown could do, considering him one of the most promising tight end prospects to ever come into the NFL. Brown himself was ready to get back on the field and make his Packers debut. "It's been about a year and a half," he noted at the time, while adding, "I sure am anxious to play in a game." He spent the previous year on the taxi squad while he recovered from the shoulder surgery and he used that experience to familiarize himself with the playbook. "You learn a lot by playing," Brown said in a 1966 interview, "but I was able to study the plays a lot. It takes a long time to learn 'em, so in that way it's helped me a lot. I ran through a lot of plays last year, too, but didn't have any contact." He also detailed the difference between the Packers passing game and what he was used to at Ole Miss. "[It's] a lot different than we ran in college. We always ran a rollout series at Ole Miss," Brown explained. "Here it's dropback—it's a bit different."[12]

Ironically, his first game action as a pro was in the College All-Star Game. This time, though, he was on the roster of the defending NFL champions. In the third quarter he had his first reception as a Packer, going for 23 yards on a pass from Bart Starr. Two weeks later in a preseason game against the Cowboys, Brown led the Packers in receiving with three receptions for 28 yards. As a young player full of potential, Brown showed glimpses of the tight end he could be.

After the regular season began, he was given his first extended playing time at tight end in the Packers' 56–3 win over the Falcons. Unfortunately, injury struck again in practice the following week when he injured his knee. It required surgery and Brown was put on the injured reserve list November 1, 1966, ending his 1966 season.[13]

Brown was back on the field for the 1967 season. During a preseason game against the Steelers, Brown scored his first touchdown as a Packer on a six-yard pass from Zeke Bratkowski. "It's a good feeling, I'll tell you, getting that first one," Brown said after the game. He added, "Claudis James ran a real good route on the play and cleared it out for me. So it was pretty well open." When asked about how his surgically repaired knee was holding up, he replied, "[It] feels good. It feels stronger since those two-a-day workouts are over. I feel I'm at full strength for the first time since I came here in '65." In regard to his history with injuries Brown said, "If you start thinking about it, you're going to get hurt. There's only one way to play this game—all the way." The soft-spoken Brown gave his outlook for the 1967 Packers, "I think the team looks a lot better than it did last year," he said. "We have a lot more speed this year—we're a lot quicker." Asked about a personal goal Brown replied, "I just want to play."[14]

When the regular season started, Brown contributed at tight end and on special teams. He had his first official (regular season) reception in the Packers' 55–7 victory over the Cleveland Browns. Two weeks later, he added two more receptions in Chicago in a 17–13 win over the Bears. On December 17, 1967, the Packers hosted the Pittsburgh Steelers in the regular season finale. While covering a kickoff, Brown was seriously injured—he suffered a ruptured kidney—and he was rushed to St. Vincent hospital at halftime.[15] The injury ended his season a week before the playoffs.

Citing injuries, Allen Brown retired from professional football June 13, 1968.[16]

Notes

1. Mississippi Sports Hall of Fame & Museum, Msfame.com, www.msfame.com/hall-of-fame/inductees/allen-brown.

2. National Football Foundation, Footballfoundation.com, www.footballfoundation.org/Programs/CollegeFootballHallofFame/SearchDetail.aspx?id=50062.

3. "Brown Headed to Mississippi Sports Hall of Fame," OleMissSports.com, July 30, 2010, www.olemisssports.com/sports/m-footbl/spec-rel/073010aac.html.

4. Mississippi Sports Hall of Fame & Museum, Msfame.com, www.msfame.com/hall-of-fame/inductees/allen-brown.

5. *Sarasota Herald-Tribune*, December 3, 1963.

6. Mississippi Sports Hall of Fame & Museum, Msfame.com, www.msfame.com/hall-of-fame/inductees/allen-brown.

7. Justin Whitemore, "Allen Brown to Be Recognized at Ole Miss Game Today," *The Natchez Democrat*, September 1, 2012, www.natchezdemocrat.com/2012/09/01/allen-brown-to-be-recognized-at-ole-miss-game-today.

8. "Brown Headed to Mississippi Sports Hall of Fame," OleMissSports.com, July 30, 2010, www.olemisssports.com/sports/m-footbl/spec-rel/073010aac.html.

9. "Mississippi's Brown Signs with Packers," *The Victoria Advocate,* December 22, 1964.

10. Lee Remmel, "Allen Brown Eager for Action in Friday's Game. Tight End Prospect Has Waited Year-And-A-Half for Taste of Combat," *Appleton* (WI) *Post Crescent*, August 2, 1966.

11. Lee Remmel, "Allen Brown Anxious for Combat," *Green Bay Press-Gazette*, August 2, 1966.

12. *Ibid.*

13. "Allen Brown Has Knee Operation," *Appleton* (WI) *Post Crescent*, November 2, 1966.

14. Lee Remmel, "'It's a Good Feeling,' Says Allen Brown of First TD as Packer," *Appleton* (WI) *Post Crescent,* August 16, 1967.

15. Bud Lea, "More Injuries ... but Packers Confident," *Milwaukee Sentinel*, December 19, 1967.

16. "Pitts Is Signed; Brown Retires," *Milwaukee Journal*, June 13, 1968.

Robert Brown

Michael D. Benter

"We called Bob 'Hock' or the 'Hocker'—from ham hocks—because of the size of his hands. They were enormous. His feet weren't exactly delicate, either. He wore a size 15 shoe. He made his own shower sandals from a used car tire."

—Jerry Kramer, *Distant Replay*[1]

When he made his first start for the Green Bay Packers in the fourth game of the 1966 season against the Detroit Lions, defensive end and tackle Bob Brown was technically a rookie. However, Brown wasn't the typical rookie, just out of college and naïve to the brutally honest and cutthroat environs of professional football. He had been around.

Robert Eddie Brown was a countrified 27-year-old from Bonita, Louisiana, in Morehouse Parish on the Louisiana side of the Arkansas-Louisiana border. He was born there on February 23, 1939. His parents were sharecroppers and he was one of 12 children. Life was tough and work on the farm was hot, hard and redundant.[2]

Brown played high school football in Bastrop, roughly 20 miles southwest of Bonita, at Morehouse High. There he played well enough to receive a scholarship to play college ball at Arkansas A.M. & N., now called the University of Arkansas–Pine Bluff. Future NFL stars Manny Sistrunk and L.C. Greenwood were former A.M. & N. players, as well.[3]

At A.M. & N. Brown savored one moment in particular, a game against the Grambling Tigers in 1962. "I played on Buck Buchanan, and we scored two TDs over Buck, which stands as a great day." Ironic, because the two antagonists soon would be linked to the NFL's Green Bay Packers. Buchanan was a 17th-round Packers draft choice in 1962—although he never signed with the team—and most of Brown's NFL career was spent in Green Bay.[4]

Despite his small college background, Brown made the *Pittsburgh Courier*'s Honorable Mention All-American team in 1963. He stood 6'5" and weighed around 270 when in condition and 320 when out, and the 49ers selected him in the 13th round of the 1964 NFL draft. Even though he played on both sides of the ball in college, Brown's pro positions were at defensive end and defensive tackle. However, the 49ers cut him before the 1964 season began, so he latched on with a United Football League team in Wheeling, West Virginia—the Wheeling Ironmen.

Wheeling was a far cry from the big city action of the NFL in competition as well as pay. It was a place for former NFL players barely hanging on to their professional careers in hopes of getting one last call from the NFL, or guys like Brown—young, scrappy and hopeful for that first chance with a big league club. For that chance, Brown played in Wheeling for $150 a game.[5]

Brown played well enough in Wheeling to earn himself a second tryout with the 49ers prior to the 1965 season. Again, though, Brown was cut by the 49ers, and as a result he signed with the Toronto Argonauts of the Canadian Football League, for whom he appeared in five games that year.[6]

Because of a positive scouting report filed by personnel man Pat Peppler based on a Wheeling game film, the Packers gave Brown a tryout in 1966, and he made the champions' roster.[7] He and another rookie, Jim Weather-

Robert Brown.

wax, were new additions to the Packers' defensive line that fall, a notable achievement for each given the veteran nature of the Packers' squads throughout the mid to late '60s.

When Lionel Aldridge, a starting defensive end for the Packers, was unable to go against Detroit in the fourth game of the 1966 season, Brown got the call from Coach Lombardi to take Aldridge's spot. Even though Detroit had success running against him early, Brown resolutely stood his ground and played fairly well thereafter. He sacked Detroit quarterback Milt Plum on one occasion. He batted down a pass at the line of scrimmage. Lombardi noted after the game that Brown had held his own against Lions tackle Darryl Sanders, "a helluva tackle," and had "knocked him down more than once."[8]

Brown himself was evenhanded in his assessment of his rookie debut: "I was green as grass. I made a few mistakes … but I learned a whole lot. I blocked one pass—and just missed another one."[9]

Brown didn't see much action the rest of the 1966 regular season, playing extensively only in a 56–3 blowout victory over Atlanta on October 23, and against the Los Angeles Rams in December after the Packers had clinched the Western Conference title.[10] However, he was active for all 14 regular season games in 1966 and 1967, seasons that ended in Super Bowl wins for the Packers. As a member of the special teams, he jarred the ball loose from Dallas' Mel Renfro on a kickoff return in the 1967 NFL Title game that Jim Grabowski scooped up and returned for the second Packers touchdown. He also had one of Green Bay's six sacks in Super Bowl I. Though he played at end and tackle for the Packers' defense in 1966, he was solely an end in 1967.

In *Instant Replay*, All-Pro guard Jerry Kramer noted how difficult it was to go up against Brown and one of his linemates in practice, specifically in the "nutcracker drill" (which pitted an offensive man leading a ball carrier against a defensive man in a "chute" between two padded dummies): "We had another lovely nutcracker drill, and I jumped in against Kostelnik … then against Bob Brown, who's close to 280. With pads on, they've got to weigh at least 290 apiece. By the time we finished the nutcracker, I had two scratches on my forehead and the blood was trickling down between my pretty blue eyes and my tongue was bleeding."[11]

Not bad for a young guy Kramer once described as "a shy boy with a high, squeaky laugh, as though he isn't used to laughing."[12]

Brown wasn't laughing when he was playing on the other side of the line from Kramer in practice. The no-nonsense approach he took to his craft stayed with Kramer even 15 years later, "There was nothing cute about the way he played. He was just bull strength coming straight ahead with all he had. He wasn't going to go around you. He wasn't going to lull you … play games with you. He was just going to run the hell over you."[13]

In 1968 Brown appeared with teammate Forrest Gregg on the cover of *Sports Illustrated*, with a headline warning, "The Packers Are Not Dead." The team was on the decline, though, and Brown could do little about it. He'd play in only six games due to injury. He suffered a broken arm in one game and played courageously on what was later determined a broken leg in another. It was the last time he'd miss any games in what would become an 11-year NFL career.[14]

By 1969, a season in which he filled in for an injured Henry Jordan, Brown played well enough to be chosen Green Bay's most valuable defensive player by the Wisconsin Pro Football Writers. When Jordan retired after the 1969 season, Brown ably took his spot in the starting lineup.

Brown was a veteran presence with the Packers through the descending years of Coach Phil Bengtson's tenure, and was with the team in 1972 when the strength of then-coach Dan Devine's team was its defense.

In March 1972, Brown was "shot in the neck by a passenger in his car" in West Memphis, Arkansas. "An electrician from West Memphis," whom Brown knew and with whom he had been playing cards, asked him for a ride home and then shot him from the backseat. The shooting was a mystery to Brown and another passenger in Brown's car, W. C, McMiller, because it was unprovoked. "They weren't even mad at each other," Bob's wife Shirley said.[15] Bob spent about a week in the hospital before he was released. The bullet had "entered the back of his neck and emerged through his lower jaw."[16]

That November, Brown again made the news in Wisconsin when his car was stolen from the Packers' parking lot at Lambeau Field and later located in Manistique, Michigan, in Michigan's Upper Peninsula. Oddly, one of Brown's Super Bowl rings was still in the car when it was found "out of gas but otherwise undamaged."[17]

What had started out for Brown as a terrible year by getting shot in early spring and having his car stolen in late fall ended well, however. The Packers made the playoffs and Brown was named second team all-pro at defensive tackle by UPI after the 1972 season. In fact, it was postulated that Brown having his jaw wired shut from the shooting ensured that he ate less and therefore came into the 1972 season in possibly the best shape of his career.[18]

Brown did indeed like to eat. He was a great cook, a wonderful and cheery guy with whom to socialize, a man with a voracious appetite and thirst for down-home food and drink.

Larry McCarren, a Packer center from 1973 to 1984, remembered a more serious side of Brown. A veteran, who had been around the block with the Packers and expected youngsters to be aware of the Packers way of doing things, Bob made McCarren and other newcomers to the team aware of what was expected of them when the Packers were scheduled to meet the rival Bears: "When I first got here, Bob Brown gathered all the young guys together and explained to them, 'This is Bear week' ... I was expecting something mystical to come down from up high, but he explained, 'This is Bear week, so there is no bullshitting this week. You really get wired for this one.'"[19]

Unfortunately, the Packers' 1972 season was not followed by a successful campaign in 1973. The team tried to re-tool, and one way they saw to do that was to send Brown, who was involved in a contract dispute, to Tommy Prothro's San Diego Chargers in exchange for a third-round draft choice.

Because of Brown's epicurean proclivities, Bob was overweight in Prothro's estimation and was put on a diet to lose 40 pounds. The weight loss helped Brown earn a starting spot at right defensive tackle for the Chargers, but the following season he "got lost in a youth movement" and became a free agent, signing with the Cincinnati Bengals for whom he played the final two years of his NFL career, 1975–1976.[20]

Out of football for one season, he tried to make a comeback with Bart Starr's 1978 Packers, signing a contract in the spring of that year. Unfortunately, he was unable to make the team and retired from football.

After football Brown returned to West Memphis, Arkansas. He and Shirley had seven children. She was a school teacher and Bob was, for all intents and purposes, retired; he enjoyed fishing and betting on dogs at the track.[21]

Brown died "of heart failure" in Memphis, Tennessee, on January 10, 1998. He was 58 years old. He is buried in Paradise Gardens Cemetery in Edmonson, Arkansas.[22]

NOTES

1. Jerry Kramer and Dick Schaap, *Distant Replay* (New York: G.P. Putnam's Sons, 1985), 208.
2. *Ibid.*, 207.
3. Vintage Football Card Gallery, Footballcardgallery.com, accessed October 9, 2014, www.footballcardgallery.com/college/Arkansas_AM_and_N/.
4. E-mail biographical information on Brown from Cliff Christl, Packers team historian, September 18, 2014.
5. Ohio Valley Athletics, "Remembering the Wheeling Ironmen of the Continental Football League," Ohiovalleyathletics.com, accessed October 8, 2014, www.ovathletics.com/home/remembering-the-wheeling-ironmen-of-the-continental-football-league/3581, originally published in *Sports Illustrated*, December 16, 1968. "We Look at the Super Bowl Last Year and Find Two of Ours Who Used to Play for $150, Bob Brown of Green Bay and Andy Rice of Kansas City," said Lou Blumling, coach, Wheeling Ironmen.
6. Martin Hendricks, "Brown Threw His Weight Around," *Milwaukee Journal Sentinel*, Jsonline.com, accessed October 7, 2014, www.jsonline.com; John Maxymuk, *Packers by the Number: Jersey Numbers and the Players Who Wore Them* (Black Earth, WI: Prairie Oak Press, 2003), 313; Christl e-mail.
7. Hendricks.
8. *Chicago Defender*, October 8, 1966.
9. *Ibid.*
10. *Milwaukee Journal*, October 24, 1966, December 19, 1966.
11. Jerry Kramer, *Instant Replay*, ed. by Dick Schaap (New York: New American Library, 1968), 10, 21.
12. *Ibid.*, 84.
13. *Ibid.*, 207–208.
14. *Sports Illustrated*, October 26, 1968.
15. *Milwaukee Journal*, March 3, 1972.
16. Maxymuk, 313.
17. *Milwaukee Journal*, November 15, 1972.
18. Hendricks.
19. Gary D'Amato and Cliff Christl, *Mudbaths and Bloodbaths: The Inside Story of the Packers-Bears Rivalry* (Black Earth, WI: Prairie Oak Press, 1997), 10.
20. *Milwaukee Sentinel*, September 24, 1976.
21. Kramer, 209–210.
22. Robert Eddie Brown obituary, *Memphis Commercial Appeal*, January 15, 1998.

Tom Brown

John Maxymuk

Tom Brown's entrance to professional sports was contingent upon the vagaries and tensions of international politics. Although Rogelio Alvarez was slated to be the first baseman for the Washington Senators in 1963, Fidel Castro would not allow any Cuban baseball players off the island in the spring following the recent Cuban Missile Crisis. Hence Bonus Baby Brown was rushed to the major leagues that spring with a further boost from inside the Beltway. When the Senators delivered their annual invitation to President John F. Kennedy for the opening day game, Kennedy joked, "I'll come to the game if you start that boy from Maryland."[1] Thus, the raw 22-year-old Brown was the Nats' starting first basemen on opening day.

Thomas William Brown was born into an athletic family in Laureldale, Pennsylvania, on December 12, 1940. A celebrated schoolboy star in both baseball and football, Brown chose the University of Maryland because they agreed to let him play both sports. In baseball, the Terrapin star batted .449 and was an All-American; in football, he played running back, receiver and defensive back. As a senior, Tom caught 47 passes on offense and intercepted 12 passes on defense.

Brown was drafted in the second round of the 1963 NFL draft by the Packers, and by Buffalo in the third round of the AFL draft. Three and a half weeks later, he attended the 1962 NFL championship game as Vince Lombardi's guest. That windy day in Yankee Stadium the wind chill was eight degrees and the ground was rock hard. Tom later told the *Baltimore Sun*, "I took one look at the frozen field and the size of the players and said, 'I'm going to play baseball.'"[2]

Brown played well in spring training for the Senators at first base and at all three outfield positions, too. However, after going 0 for 2 on opening day, Tom's fortunes did not improve. Batting just .100 at the end of June, he was sent to the minors. Recalled in September, he raised his rookie batting average slightly to .147 with 45 strikeouts in 116 at bats for the last place Senators.

Lombardi called Tom during the offseason and joked, "Listen Brown, we've seen your batting average and we think you might be interested in playing football."[3] Tom told Vince he'd like to try baseball one more year. He played another season for the York White Roses of the Eastern League, but did not improve his hitting, so he reported to Packers training camp in July 1964. Still, Brown maintains, "I think he always appreciated the fact that I played baseball. He always liked baseball, Lombardi did. He liked to watch it."[4]

Brown quickly adapted to pro football. "I think I'm a better prospect in football. And football is a better game to play.... You play football once a week, and you prepare for just one game a week. Your family life is better, too."[5]

Lombardi made Brown a full-time defensive back in Green Bay. As a rookie, Tom backed up cornerbacks Herb Adderley and Jesse Whittenton as well as safeties Willie Wood and Hank Gremminger. Brown replaced Gremminger as the starting strong safety in 1965, with Bob Jeter and Doug Hart replacing Whittenton the same year. From 1965 to 1968, this four-man secondary with Hart as the top reserve formed a no-passing zone on the gridiron, allowing the fewest passing yards in the league each season. This group played a big part in the Packers winning three consecutive championships. "Lombardi said no team would ever win three consecutive world championships again." Tom remembered, "He said the teams are too well balanced now."[6]

Brown attributes most of the team's success to Coach Lombardi in cultivating the attitudes of the players. "Most professional football players are basically lazy guys. We want to take the easy way out. We are so far superior. We've always been better. As nine-year olds. Ten year olds. We were always the best athletes on the field. We probably got preferential treatment from youth coaches and all the way up. So we never really had to give 100 percent effort. Because if we gave 75 percent we were better than the other kids."[7] Slacking off wasn't possible with Lombardi. "He would holler at you and harass you so much that you would say to yourself: You'd better not blow it or it's all over for you. He instilled that in you and I can't explain why. I've tried lots of times, at banquets and things, but you really had to have been there and played for him." Brown continued, "I depended on him to motivate me, to get me to play. When he wasn't there, Bill Austin [Lombardi's successor in Washington] or anyone else just couldn't do that."[8]

Tom was a humble player who played in every game during his five years with the Packers. In that time, he intercepted 13 passes and recovered six fumbles. Willie Wood said, "Tom was a self-made ballplayer. He didn't have blazing speed. But he was very astute. He was never out of position."[9] He also returned seven kickoffs in 1964, but was switched to punt returner in 1966.

Tom Browns' most famous interception occurred in the 1966 NFL championship game with Dallas. Brown had given up a long touchdown pass to Frank Clarke earlier and had just been called for pass interference in the end zone, which set up the Cowboys on the Packers two-yard line. With less than a minute to play, linebacker David Robinson forced Cowboys quarterback Don Meredith to throw a bad pass on fourth down that Brown intercepted to clinch the game.

According to Brown, "Well, I guess it's no secret that a lot of people had the feeling I was the weak link in the Packers secondary. I don't think that's true, but I am aware of the charge."[10] Lombardi was comfortable with Brown, though. During a 1967 game in St. Louis, Brown played with a dislocated shoulder. After the game, the coach told Brown, "Some people say you're not very tough, but I want to tell you, you're tough enough for me."[11]

Lombardi retired as Packers coach after that season, but remained as General Manager in 1968. That year, Brown scored the only two touchdowns of his NFL career, one on a fumble return in a victory over the Saints and one on a 52-yard punt return in a losing effort against the Rams.

After one season, Lombardi could not sit on the sidelines any longer, and he signed on as the Head Coach for the Washington Redskins. His first trade on February 27, 1969, was to send Green Bay a fourth round draft pick for Tom Brown. Lombardi planned on switching Brown to free safety in his overhaul of Washington.

Tom Brown.

Lombardi replaced 19 players from the 40-man roster in 1968. Unfortunately, Tom separated his shoulder again in a preseason game with Detroit. "Here I've been switched from strong to free safety, and I want to prove that I can play another position and show everybody I'm no weakling. It's a hell of a challenge, and now I've got this shoulder that's popping out when I grab at people. As far as the shoulder goes, I am going to have to learn to tackle all over again. I've always been an arm tackler, and now I'm going to have to hit with my shoulder. And I'm going to have to learn to live with the pain. I think about it all the time. I think to myself, I am going to have to be tough. But I've got something to prove and I figure I'll be tough enough to do it. I played four years in the starting backfield of a championship team and at the end of that to be known as a weak link—well that's worth some pain to prove wrong."[12]

Brown then reinjured that shoulder during the first regular season game and his season was over as Lombardi lifted the Redskins from a 5–9–0 record in 1968 to a 7–5–2 mark in 1969.

Tragedy struck following that promising season. Lombardi was brought down by an aggressive case of colon cancer. "When I went to sign my contract in the spring he called me in and said, 'We're really counting on you. We have a shot at winning this thing.' So of course I got excited about that and I really went out and worked hard. And then, when I saw him in the hospital bed, I knew there was no way he would ever coach again. Or maybe even get out of bed again. My whole desire, my whole attitude to play just went boom … down."[13]

Cut by the Redskins, Tom Brown was in Minnesota trying to make the team when he woke up suddenly at 6:30 a.m. on September 3, 1970. He knew Lombardi was gone. "Every player that played for him has a lasting memory and does something that Coach Lombardi taught them about life. He was not only a coach, he was a teacher of life. He said you guys aren't going to be playing very long, your careers aren't going to last that long, so pick something that you like to do and do it for life. If you're doing something you like, you'll never have to work another day in your life."[14]

Brown did not make the Vikings and retired. He began working for Maryland's Parks and Recreation Department, and then in 1974 he followed his old coach's advice: "Lombardi always would say, 'When you retire, no matter where you live, give something back to the community.'"[15]

That year, Tom opened the Tom Brown Rookie League in Salisbury, Maryland. For the past 40 years, Brown's sports camp has welcomed children between five and 12 to learn the fundamentals of baseball, basketball and football. While some may find it surprising, Brown puts no emphasis on winning, just the fundamentals, because he is dealing with kids, not professional athletes. "So many people have a misconception about Lombardi. They act crazy with kids and use Lombardi as an excuse. I hate it when people misuse him."[16] There is no doubt that his old coach would be proud of what Tom Brown has done with his life.

NOTES

1. Ryan Marshall, "Legend Tom Brown, Now a Hall of Famer, Reflects," *Delmarva Now*, November 15, 2014.

2. Mike Klingaman, "Catching Up with … Former Terp/Packers Safety Tom Brown," *Baltimore Sun*, October 10, 2013.

3. Marshall.

4. John Wiebusch, *Lombardi* (Chicago: Triumph Books, 1997), 178.

5. "Tom Brown Happy He Gave Up Career in Baseball," *Toledo Blade*, August 22, 1965.

6. Wiebusch, 94.

7. David Maraniss, *When Pride Still Mattered* (New York: Simon & Schuster, 1999), 372.

8. Wiebusch, 178.

9. Jerry Kramer and Dick Schaap, *Distant Replay* (New York: G. P. Putnam's Sons, 1985), 170.

10. Tom Dowling, *Coach* (New York: Norton, 1970), 72.

11. Michael O'Brien, *Vince* (New York: William Morrow, 1987), 295.

12. Dowling, 72–73.

13. Wiebusch, 202.

14. Stephen Waldron and Aimee Rodriguez, *Tom Brown: Backup Plan*. YouTube video for journalism class at the University of Maryland uploaded December 13, 2012, Youtube.com, www.youtube.com/watch?v=3ldQDsQ2oi4.

15. Waldron.

16. O'Brien, 383.

Lee Roy Caffey

Greg Selber

In retrospect, Lee Roy Caffey always seemed destined for the big time. As a ten-year-old, the native of Thorndale, Texas, participated in the Milk Bowl, an annual collision between youth grid champs from Oklahoma and Texas. The ball game, played in Marlin in 1951, gave young Caffey the thrill of a lifetime when he was able to meet the legendary Jim Thorpe, who had come in for the day.

Caffey always said that the chance to shake hands with the World's Greatest Athlete convinced him that football was his passion, saying that "he was an idol ... a champion.... I'll never forget meeting him."[1]

He then pursued the passion for football with zest. At Thorndale High School he also excelled at basketball and track, showing his budding ability by winning a gold medal in the high jump at the state track meet.

The rangy fullback-linebacker broke a collarbone early in his senior season of high school, playing only three football games that campaign. But news of his size, speed and all-around skills traveled throughout the state, and Caffey earned a ride south to College Station, where he became a three-year starter for Texas A&M.

The squad won only eight games total during the stretch but Caffey was a standout; the 6–4 bruiser punted, ran a ten-flat 100-yard dash, led the team in rushing in 1963, and was invited to the College All-Star Game where he played alongside another future Packer linebacker—Dave Robinson of Penn State.[2] Down the road he would be named to the university's Athletics Hall of Fame and earn a spot on the Southwest Conference All-Decade Team for the 1960s.

It seemed that Caffey, whose combination of speed and size made him a hot professional commodity, was doomed to play for another losing entity when the Philadelphia Eagles picked him in the 7th round of the 1963 draft. Indeed, the Eagles were to go just 2–10–2 in 1963 under Coach Nick Skorich, but Caffey was a difference-maker as a rookie, recovering five fumbles and returning an interception 87 yards for a score—against the New York Giants in a 42–14 loss on November 10. Later in the season the rookie helped the Eagles tie the Steelers 20–20 by recovering a fumble on a kickoff cover to set the Eagles up for a touchdown and 14–3 lead.

Fresh off an All-Rookie season, Caffey received a jolt when the Eagles packaged him in May 1964 to Green Bay in a deal which brought disgruntled veteran Jim Ringo to the City of Brotherly Love. But in reality, Caffey always said that moving from Philly to the Midwest was fine for him, as Green Bay was more in tune with his small-town origins.

Caffey's new team was definitely a better fit, in terms of success as well, as Green Bay was in the midst of the glory years. For the 1964 season Caffey was plugged in at linebacker behind starter Dan Currie.

The new addition showed his versatility when he was tabbed to handle kickoff duties for the Packers after Jerry Kramer had surgery and Paul Hornung became unavailable, and in November he boomed a couple of touchbacks against the Cleveland Browns.

Caffey also fit right in with his freewheeling style on defense, showing a knack for the big play, belting Dallas quarterback John Roach on November 29 and making him cough up a fumble that Henry Jordan snagged and ran back for a six-pointer in a 45–21 victory. In the Playoff Bowl opportunity knocked and Caffey answered again, blasting a St. Louis Cardinal runner and causing a turnover in a 24–17 loss.

Athletic and into weightlifting and later racquetball, the big-play linebacker was always able to parlay his versatile skill set into important plusses for the Pack.

He contributed touchdowns against the Bears in 1965 and Colts in 1966, both on interception runbacks and each aiding a Green Bay victory. It hadn't taken him long to make the starting lineup after Currie was shipped to the Rams following the 1964 season. Soon the tall, agile Texas was paired with two real stars, bone-crushing Ray Nitschke and Dave Robinson, who became a starter in 1964 after caddying for Bill Forrester in 1963.[3] The linebacking crew became a definite Green Bay strength, eventually becoming known as one of the top outfits in the NFL. Caffey started at left linebacker before moving to the right side, but wherever he played, good things generally happened at his point of attack. Adept at using his speed on the blitz, often getting into the backfield just as the play was developing, Caffey continually gummed up the works for the opposing offense.

In his 2012 book, *Closing the Gap*, former Packer great Willie Davis suggested that Caffey's athleticism was formidable, making up for an occasional tendency to lose focus.[4]

Davis wrote that Caffey lived off tremendous instincts, never quite getting the playbook memorized, so to speak. With Nitschke wreaking havoc in the middle, the outside 'backers could run and hit, and Davis laughed when recalling that both Caffey and Robinson were "big talkers" on the field.[5]

And it was thus not just on the field, as legend is replete with anecdotes of Caffey's amazing success in negotiating contracts with the no-nonsense Lombardi, a tough sell to say the least.

His drawl of a line was always: "Vince, I'm just a country boy from Texas and I'm buying land, and I need all the help I can get." Most times, it was sufficient to help him receive the numbers he'd gone to Lombardi looking for.[6]

With the ability to either blitz with force or to wait, read, and react, Caffey—now with a full 240 pounds hanging well on a long 6–4 frame—reached the pinnacle with a selection as All-Pro in 1966, having made the Pro Bowl the previous season. In January 1967, Caffey became the first Aggie to play in a Super Bowl and came up with seven tackles—including a sack of QB Len Dawson—as the Pack shut down the Chiefs.

During the 1967 season, Caffey once again showed his bona fides in the clutch, against Dallas in the NFL title game on New Year's Eve. In the third quarter of that famous Ice Bowl Game at Lambeau Field, he forced a fumble that was snagged by Herb Adderley, stopping a Dallas drive at the Pack 13-yard line. Later, the strapping Texan turned in a key sack of quarterback Dan Meredith, good for a loss of nine yards and the end of another Cowboy march.

Lee Roy Caffey.

With temperatures well below freezing, the game became as much about survival as anything else.

"That is the coldest I've ever been in my life," Caffey told the *Wisconsin State Journal.* "I've never experienced anything like that. I got to the point where I couldn't feel at all—I was numb. I can't speak for anybody else, but I know every time I fell down it killed me."

The Texas boy then admitted that the pounding he had taken in the Ice Bowl, from weather and foe, was off the charts.

"As far as I'm concerned," he sighed. "I'm beat up worse than in any game I've played all year."[7]

ESPN later voted the Robinson-Nitschke-Caffey crew onto its list of top ten defensive trios of all time, with two of the three eventually making the Hall. While Caffey did not, he was always a valuable if at times unpredictable defender, picking off 11 passes during his career. And he collected a third Super Bowl ring after his Green Bay days were over in 1969, going from the Bears in 1970—where he played alongside the fearsome Dick Butkus—to a spot with his home state Dallas Cowboys in 1971, in time to take part in that franchise's first Super Bowl triumph, over Miami.

Caffey's run through the league ended after one season with San Diego in 1972, and he retired, leaving a legacy of productive snaps behind. His worth to the Green Bay defenses of the mid–1960s was solidified for history's sake when he scored a spot on the franchise's 75th Anniversary All-Time Team, in the 1990s.

But those who had seen the raw-boned speedster bring it back in the day needed no reminders. Caffey was an awesome physical specimen, somewhat like his old hero Jim Thorpe, and carved out a fine niche in NFL history. He expressed no regrets about giving up the game he had always loved.

"Football was great to me. I had ten good years, a good career and no serious injuries like torn knees or shoulders," he noted in a 1973 interview back home in Texas. "There were a lot of bruises, of course, but in all I was very fortunate. Now I'm 31 and ready to let my wife and children settle into a real home life. And it's time for me to get involved in business."[8]

At this point in life, he indeed established a successful car dealership back home in Central Texas, returning to his rural roots and settling into another winning groove as a businessman. Caffey died in Houston in 1994 at the age of 52 of colon cancer.

NOTES

1. "From Milk Bowl to NFL and Back," *Matchless Milam* (Milam County Heritage Preservation Society, 1986), 283.

2. John Maxymuk, *Packers by the Numbers* (Black Earth, WI: Prairie Oak Press, 2003).

3. *Ibid.*

4. Willie Davis with Jim Martyka and Andrea Erickson Davis, *Closing the Gap: Lombardi, the Packers Dynasty, And the Pursuit of Excellence* (Chicago: Triumph Books, 2012).

5. *Ibid.*

6. Jerry Kramer and Dick Schaap, "Nitschke Made His Mark on and Off the Playing Field," *Wisconsin State Journal*, December 28, 1985, 21.

7. Lee Remmel, "Packer Defense Held Hot Hand," *Wisconsin State Journal*, January 3, 1968.

8. *Matchless Milam.*

Don Chandler

George Bozeka

Don "Babe" Chandler played on four championship teams during his 12 year NFL career with the New York Giants and Green Bay Packers. He was considered one the finest kicking and punting specialists of his generation. Packer roommate Jerry Kramer said of Chandler, "Don was a winner, and he associated with winners … he was solid, honest, consistent, a hell of a human being. I respected him. I admired him. I loved him."[1]

Donald Gene Chandler was born in Council Bluffs, Iowa, on September 5, 1934, but he grew up in Tulsa, Oklahoma, the son of Ben Chandler, a former semi-pro fullback and a Western Union maintenance worker. He attended Will Rogers High School. Chandler initially attended Bacone Indian College in Muskogee, Oklahoma, before transferring as a junior to the University of Florida in 1954. Chandler played halfback, placekicker and punter for Coach Bob Woodruff in 1954 and 1955, leading major college football in punting with a 44.3 yard during his senior season. After graduating from Florida in 1956, Chandler was drafted by the New York Giants in the fifth round of the 1956 NFL Draft with the 57th pick overall.[2]

Chandler and fellow rookie Sam Huff were initially uneasy about their chances of making the Giants as they constantly took hell from "bellering" head coach Jim Lee Howell.[3] Twice the homesick Chandler tried to leave training camp.[4] On both occasions, Vince Lombardi, then the Giants offensive coordinator, forced him to stay, stating, "Listen, you may not make this ballclub but you're sure as hell not going to run out on me."[5] A shoulder injury precluded Chandler from being a heavy duty performer, but he eventually made the team by becoming the Giants' regular punter and averaging 41.9 yards per punt for the 1956 season. The Giants, with the nucleus in place for a sustained run of excellence that would last during Chandler's nine seasons with the club and include six Eastern Conference Championships, capped the 1956 season by winning the NFL Championship with a dominating 47–7 victory over the Chicago Bears.[6]

The 1957 Giants failed to repeat, finishing second to the rival Cleveland Browns, but Chandler again was the team's leading punter, averaging 44.6 yards per punt.

In 1958, Chandler averaged 44 yards per punt with a league high 65 total punts and an NFL long punt of 67 yards, as the Giants won the Eastern Conference crown in a pivotal playoff game with the Browns 10–0 after both tied with regular season records of 9–3. This set the stage for the Giants' historic 23–17 sudden death loss at Yankee Stadium to the Baltimore Colts in the 1958 NFL Championship game.

Chandler again led the Giants in punting in 1959, averaging a career high 46.6 yards per punt and finishing second league wide to Yale Lary's 47.1 average for the Lions. Babe was particularly effective in a key Week Three 10–6 victory over the Browns averaging 54 yards on 8 punts with three amazing coffin corner punts that went out of bounds on the 4, 5, and 6 yard lines.[7] The Giants again won the Eastern Conference setting up a Championship game rematch with the Colts in Baltimore. The Colts blew open a close game in the fourth quarter winning their second consecutive NFL Championship 31–16.

The 1960 season was a disappointment for both Chandler and the Giants. Chandler punted in only eight games because of injuries with a 40.5 yard average and the Giants finished in third place behind the Browns and eventual NFL Champion Eagles with a 6–4–2 record.

A healthy Chandler was back on the top of his punting game in 1961 with a 43.9 yard average, as the Giants finished atop the Eastern Conference with a 10–3–1 record. Chandler was involved in two key plays late in the season that cemented the Giants' trip to the championship game. One came in Week Thirteen against the Eagles. The Giants and Eagles were tied for first in the East at 9–3. Chandler drew a controversial roughing the kicker penalty, allowing the Giants to keep a drive alive and score their final touchdown in a 28–24 victory which put the Giants in first all alone. In Week Fourteen, the Giants were tied with the Browns 7–7 late in the game. The Eagles had already won their final game to finish 10–4. A tie would give the Giants the Eastern crown, a loss would mean a playoff rematch with the Eagles. With a little under two minutes to go the Giants had to turn the ball over to the Browns. Chandler, who had already had two punts downed on the three yard line in the first half, proceeded to hit a punt that coach Allie Sherman called the greatest he had ever seen. The ball traveled 80 yards from the point of contact, 64 yards from the line of scrimmage, and buried the Browns and their hopes on their own seven yard line. The tie held up and the Giants were conference champs.[8] In the NFL Championship game the Giants met Lombardi's Packers and were beaten decisively 37–0.

With the retirement of Pat Summerall in 1962, Chandler took on the added duties of placekicker for the 1962 season. Chandler led the Giants in scoring with 104 points (breaking Gene "Choo Choo" Roberts's club record of 102 set in 1949), converting 19 of 28 field goals (for a league leading percentage of 67.9%) with a long of 48 yards, and converting 47 of 48 extra points. Chandler also set a Giants record for most field goals in a game with four on two occasions, in a 19–14 Week Ten victory over the Eagles, and in a 26–24 Week Twelve victory over the Bears. In addition he averaged 40.6 yards per punt. The Giants again led the Eastern Conference with a 12–2 record, but again lost to the Packers in the Championship game 16–7.

Babe experienced one of his greatest all around seasons in 1963. Chandler led the Giants and the NFL in scoring (106 points, breaking his club mark of 104 set in 1962), points after touchdown attempted (56), points after touchdown made (52), and tied for long field goal (53 yards, also a Giants club mark) with the Cowboys' Sam Baker. The 53 yarder in a 34–27 week 12 victory over the Cowboys was also the longest of Chandler's career. Chandler converted 18 of 29 field goals for the season and averaged 44.9 yards per punt. The Giants won their third straight Eastern conference crown with an 11–3 record but lost to the Bears in the NFL Championship game in a 14–10 defensive struggle.

The 1964 season was a turning point for

Don Chandler.

the fortunes of the Giants and Chandler. Chandler retired and unretired before the start of the season as a result of a dispute with Coach Allie Sherman. Chandler wanted to commute to games from Tulsa because of job commitments, but Sherman would have none of it, stating, "You are either a full time professional football player or you are something else. Maybe it was okay in the past, but the game has grown to where no one can do their best with a part-time effort."[9] The aging Giants finished a dismal 2–10–2, the worst record in the NFL, and last in the Eastern Conference. Chandler maintained his prowess as a punter averaging 45.6 yards but his placekicking statistics took a nosedive. He scored only 54 points, converting only 9 of 20 field goal attempts and 27 of 29 extra points.

After the 1964 season, Chandler was traded to the Packers, reuniting the specialist with Vince Lombardi. Chandler later claimed, "The Giants did me a big favor. With Green Bay you always have a chance to win that championship. Winning is the big thing."[10] Lombardi was attempting to strengthen a perceived Packer weakness. Paul Hornung had lost his place kicking touch in 1964 after serving his one year gambling suspension in 1963, and Jerry Kramer, who handled the placekicking job in 1963, was hampered by injuries.[11]

Babe immediately solidified both the kicking and punting positions for Green Bay, scoring a team high 88 points as he converted 17 of 26 field goals and 37 of 38 extra points. His punting average was 42.9 yards with an amazing league season long punt of 90 yards in Week Four on October 10 against the Niners. The punt actually traveled 113 yards, as Chandler hit the punt from his own goal line and it rolled three yards out of the Niners end zone; 90 yards officially since the Packer line of scrimmage was their own 10. The booming punt was the longest since Fats Henry's 94 yarder in 1923 for the Canton Bulldogs and Joe Lintzenich's 94 yarder for the Bears in 1931. Legend has it that during an exhibition game with the Giants in 1961, Chandler hit a punt that traveled 107 yards in the air against the Packers.[12] The 90 yard punt earned Chandler the AP Defensive Player of the Week honors.[13]

The Packers finished the season tied for first place in the Western Conference with the Baltimore Colts with identical 10–3–1 marks. This set up a playoff game with the Colts on December 26, 1965. Chandler would prove to be the hero of the game. Babe hit a controversial 27 yard field goal with two minutes left to tie the game 10–10, and hit a 25 yard game winner 13 minutes into overtime to give the Packers a 13–10 victory. A week later Chandler scored 11 points (3 field goals, tying the playoff record, and two extra points) as the Packers won the NFL Championship game 23–12 over the defending champion Browns on a cold, wet day at Lambeau Field.[14]

The 1966 season proved inconsistent for Chandler. Though the Packers again captured the Western Conference crown and went on to win the NFL Championship and the First AFL-NFL World Championship Game (Super Bowl I) Chandler struggled, converting only 12 of 28 field goals and 41 of 43 extra points for 77 points which was still a team high. His punting average dropped to 40.9 yards. The NFL had raised the uprights from 10 feet to 20 feet above the crossbar in 1966 after Chandler's controversial field goal against the Colts, and Chandler admitted that it affected his performance. "I found when the posts were raised, the range got more narrow, especially on longer field goal attempts…. It bothered me all year. I wasn't pleased with my performance…."[15]

Much as he had in 1965, Chandler would follow up his less than stellar 1966 season with a great season in 1967, his last in the NFL. Rookie Donny Anderson took over the

Packers' punting duties which allowed Babe to concentrate entirely on his place kicking duties. Chandler converted 19 of 29 field goals and was a perfect 39 for 39 on extra points. He again led the team in scoring with 96 points. Chandler had one of his greatest single game performances in the Green Bay's Super Bowl II victory. Babe converted on 4 field goals and all 3 of his extra point tries to score 15 points for the Packers. Chandler later put the game in perspective, "I've always been driven by the fear of failing or reaching the point where they would ask me to retire. To have one of my best kicking games of my life in my last game made it my biggest thrill."[16] For his efforts Chandler was named to the Pro Bowl.

In July of 1968, Chandler announced his retirement to pursue his successful real estate business in Tulsa. The Packers would miss Chandler in 1968 and attempted to talk him out of retirement but he was steadfast.

Chandler finished his career with a punting average of 43.5 yards and 530 total points converting 94 of 161 field goal attempts and 248 of 258 extra points.

In retirement, several accolades came Chandler's way. He was named to the NFL's All Decade Team of the 1960's, the Packers Hall of Fame, the Giants Wall of Fame, the University of Florida Hall of Fame, and the Oklahoma Sports Hall of Fame.

On August 11, 2011, Chandler died of cancer at the age of 76 in Tulsa. He was survived by his wife Pat, four children, and several grandchildren and great grandchildren. Upon his death, son Bret spoke proudly about his father. "He was really a very humble man … he was a good father. Football was an important part of his life, but it's not what defined him…. He was the best man at my wedding. That kind of sums up our relationship. We were fortunate to spend a lot of time together. "[17]

Chandler eloquently characterized his time with Lombardi and the Packers. "He was hypnotic when he wanted to be. I remember the first time I sat in when he delivered one of those pregame speeches. When it was over, I was afraid to miss a field goal, not because we might lose, but because I'd have to face him afterward."[18]

NOTES

1. Jerry Kramer with Dick Schaap, *Distant Replay* (New York: G. P. Putnam's Sons, 1985), 200.
2. Don Smith, "New York Giants Press Release," 1964.
3. Gerald Eskenazi, *There Were Giants in Those Days* (New York: Grossett & Dunlap, 1976), 80.
4. David Maraniss, *When Pride Still Mattered* (New York: Simon & Shuster, 1999), 168.
5. Joe Falls, "Don Chandler, Kicker," *Sport Magazine*, January 1966, 75.
6. Richard Goldstein, "Don Chandler, Standout Kicker in NFL, Dies at 76," *New York Times*, August 12, 2011.
7. Eskenazi, 152.
8. Norman Miller, "Giants Sneak Into NFL Playoff," *Clovis News Journal*, December 18, 1961; Jerry Izenberg, "Chandler Kicked All the Way to Green Bay," *New York Herald Tribune*, December 18, 1961.
9. Jim McCulley, "Chandler Says He'll Play," *New York Daily News*, July 22, 1964.
10. Seymour Smith, "Famine Ends for Kicker," *The Baltimore Sun*, December 20, 1966.
11. Bud Lea, "Packers Get Kicking Star Chandler," *Milwaukee Sentinel*, January 13, 1965.
12. Joe Falls, "Don Chandler, Kicker," *Sport Magazine*, January 1966, 74; Gerald Eskenazi, *There Were Giants in Those Days* (New York: Grossett & Dunlap, 1976), 193.
13. Ken Hartnett, "Chandler Punt Wins NFL Honor," *St Paul Dispatch*, October 13. 1965.
14. John Maxymuk, *Packers by the Numbers* (Black Earth, Wisconsin: Prairie Oak Press, 2005), 150–151.
15. Bud Lea, "Packers Test Sling-Shot," *Milwaukee Sentinel*, July 20, 1967.
16. Rhett Morgan, "Former NFL Kicker and Tulsan Don Chandler dies," Tulsaworld.com, August 12, 2011.

17. Ibid.

18. Bud Lea, *Magnificent Seven: The Championship Games That Built the Lombardi Dynasty* (Chicago: Triumph Books, 2004), 57.

Tommy Joe Crutcher

GREG SELBER

If there was a fella who lived up the old Texan stereotype of brash, tough, and full of fun, it had to be Tommy Joe Crutcher, a linebacker who rolled into the National Football League like a twister and produced a trail of success and no small number of hilarious stories in his wake.

Crutcher, who played for the Packers from 1964 to 1967 and also toiled with two other clubs before returning to Green Bay in 1971 for a two-year stint ending in 1972, was another of those gifted physical specimens from the Lone Star State. Like teammate Lee Roy Caffey, he was tall (six-feet-four) and raw-boned, a 230-pounder with excellent wheels. Crutcher loved the high life, such as it was in the small Midwestern town, and though he never managed to crack the starting lineup, was a valuable backup linebacker for three championship seasons.

He came into the world in 1941 and later emerged as a super asset for the McKinney High School football team playing both fullback and linebacker, and helping the Lions reach the 1958 state semifinals, where they were derailed by Breckenridge, the eventual AAA state champions.

At six-feet-three, 192 pounds in high school, with 10.5 speed, Crutcher rushed for 1,070 yards as a junior during the 1958 season, a very high total for the time period. Selected Co-Captain and All-State as a senior in 1959, the hard-charging two-way standout gained 850 yards on 143 carries while playing in only seven games because of injuries. After graduating from McKinney, Crutcher enrolled at TCU to play football under Coach Abe Martin.

The parallels to Caffey were uncanny, as Crutcher toiled in relative obscurity for a Horned Frog group that played sub-.500 ball (13–14–3) during his three varsity seasons, just as Caffey starred for an average Texas A&M bunch concurrently. They were both born in 1941 and were angular and speedy.

At TCU, Crutcher continued to go both ways. He led the Horned Frogs in rushing for three consecutive seasons. In 1961 he led the team to a stunning 6–0 upset of Texas, which came into the November 18 game at Memorial Stadium in Austin ranked number one in the nation. As a result, Alabama won the 1961 AP and UPI poll titles. Legendary Texas coach Darrell Royal famously likened TCU "to a bunch of cockroaches." Royal continued, "It's not what they eat and tote off. It's what they fall into and mess up that hurts."[1] Earlier in the 1961 season, the Frogs tied Woody Hayes and his Ohio State Buckeyes 7–7 in Columbus. The 8–0–1 Buckeyes were named national champions by the Football Writers Association of America.[2]

Crutcher was further honored as an All Southwest Conference and All-American running back in 1963 and was named to the *Fort Worth Star-Telegram's* All-Time TCU Team in 1995. These college accomplishments prompted the Packers to tab him in the third round of the 1964 draft, at No. 41.

Leland "Lee" Remmel, legendary sports writer for the *Green Bay Press-Gazette*, once described Crutcher as a "a tough hard-nosed football player in the Texas tradition," adding that the good-natured ballplayer "played with great love for the game and always had a smile on his face."[3]

Bulked up to 230 pounds by now, he was athletic enough to spend some time on the return team, averaging 19.4 yards on eight kickoff runbacks. But he was behind the eight ball with Green Bay, as Caffey, Robinson, and Nitschke were firmly entrenched as starters at linebacker.

After the 1967 season, the TCU grad latched on with the New York Giants, playing two seasons for Allie Sherman's club.

He spent the 1970 season on injured reserve with the Rams and then returned for another stint with Green Bay.

Despite his athletic ability and promise, Crutcher never really lived up to his own expectations as a professional, though he did earn three championship rings. Years later, Bud Lea of the *Milwaukee Sentinel* noted as much in a column discussing a mid–1960s Packer reunion, in 1984.[4] In it, Crutcher described himself as "a cocky little devil back then," and laughed with Lea over all the terrific yarns from the old days. It seemed that everyone had a favorite "Tommy Joe story," usually revolving around the fun-loving linebacker's zest for the party scene or his unique personality.

There was the time he waltzed into a local Green Bay eatery hankering for a fine cut of meat. Crutcher informed the gal waiting on him that he wanted a "stahhk" and was surprised when presented with a plate of pancakes. Seems ol' Tommy Joe was after a "steak," but his thick Texan drawl betrayed him.

He was famed for an inability to remember the names of his teammates, taking care of the communication problem by giving them all nicknames. To Crutcher, end Ron Kramer became "Spanky" and Caffey "Buckwheat." Completing the humorous play on characters from the child-based Our Gang comedy series of yesteryear, the zany linebacker called himself "Alfalfa," Lea recalled in the column.

Teammate Jerry Kramer speculated that like many good ol' boys, Crutcher may not have been as naïve as all that. In *Instant Replay*, the Packer guard suggested that Crutcher deliberately played the role, but that nonetheless, it was hilarious.[5]

"He wears a pair of boots that have to be 40 years old—I don't know what holds them together. And he loves to use country sayings," Kramer wrote. "Today when he was playing Lee Roy, Lee Roy said, 'If I could only get a cut,' and Tommy Joe snapped back, 'If a frog had wings, he wouldn't whomp his ass every time he jumped.'"

Kramer finished the anecdote, illustrating his amusement at the back-and-forth between the Texan friends. "When he lost to

Tommy Joe Crutcher.

Lee Roy, Tommy Joe allowed, 'I ain't seen nothin' like that since Cecil Barlow's cow got caught by the brush.' He's beautiful."

But perhaps the wildest Crutcher tale concerns a Super Bowl ring, and was recounted by Bob Greene of the *Chicago Tribune* in 1987.[6] After a night of good times at the Tropics Bar—it was Crutcher's favorite watering hole in town—Crutcher went back to his hotel room with no fewer than three young ladies. In 1987, he told Greene that when he woke up the next morning, the guests were gone, along with his ring from the first Super Bowl.

Thinking it was gone forever, Crutcher ordered another ring for around $700 and never gave the mishap much thought after that. Years later, through a circuitous route, the ring turned up, apparently after having been left in the bathroom at the Tropics, to be found by a cleaning woman.

The Colorado man who ended up with the prize—emblazoned with Crutcher's jersey number of 56—had been trying to sell it, asking upward of $18,000. Upon being contacted by reporter Greene and told of the availability of the priceless memento, Crutcher was iffy.

"I said the top offer so far was $18,000," Greene wrote.

Whereupon Crutcher laughed.

"Hell…. I'm nostalgic, but I ain't $18,000 worth of nostalgic," he quipped with a chuckle. "Tell him I'm not a buyer, but good luck in selling it."

He had his run in the pros, did Tommy Joe Crutcher, and at times some folks felt he was smarter than he seemed, playing the Country Boy role for laughs. Makes sense, considering the TCU ex sank some of his pro salary into the grain business back home in Texas, becoming a successful dealer with the Southwest Grain Co. and its 24,000-acre spread in South Texas, and remaining in that mode until shortly before his 2002 death in the small coastal village of Port Isabel.

He lived 60 years of unfettered action—in football, business, and otherwise—and Crutcher will be recalled as a loveable free spirit who did his own thing with style, and was a pretty damn good ballplayer to boot.

NOTES

1. "November 18, 1961: The Day TCU Cost the Horns a Shot at Their First National Title," Statesman.com, November 17, 2011, www.statesman.com.

2. Jack Park, *The Official Ohio State Football Encyclopedia* (New York: Sports Publishing, 2001).

3. "Former Packers LB Crutcher Dead at 60," Packers.com, Associated Press, February 18, 2002, www.packers.com.

4. Bud Lea, "Tommy Joe Crutcher Recalls What It Was Like in Glory Days," *Milwaukee Sentinel*, October 12, 1984.

5. Jerry Kramer, *Instant Replay: The Green Bay Diary of Jerry Kramer*, ed. Dick Schaap (New York: Anchor Books, 1968).

6. Bob Greene, "Super Bowl Story Has a Familiar Ring," *Chicago Tribune*, August 9, 1987.

Bill Curry

JOHN MAXYMUK

The starting center for the Packers in the first Super Bowl had a short career in Green Bay, but that brief time left a lifetime of influence on the man. An articulate speaker and the author of two thoughtful memoirs, Bill Curry spent more seasons, 20, as a head coach than any of Lombardi's former Packers, although his understanding of the famed coach was much more complicated, questioning, and critical than many of his Green Bay teammates. His coaching success, like that of all his former teammates, was limited.

William Alexander Curry was born on October 21, 1942, in College Park, Georgia, to Willie and Eleanor Curry. His father was an early proponent of bodybuilding, having transformed himself from a sickly 142-pound weakling into a 191-pound junior national light heavyweight champion weightlifter as a young man. Willie served in World War II as an infantry captain and, after the War, taught boxing, weightlifting and gymnastics at the Georgia Military Academy. From him, his son Bill learned persistence and perseverance.

Bill's first love was baseball, and he dreamed of pitching for the New York Yankees as he grew up in the 1950s, but as he came to the realization that he was not good enough for the major leagues he began to take greater interest in football. He remembers the excitement of Johnny Unitas' heroics in the 1958 NFL championship game making a strong impression on him; ten years later, he would be snapping the ball to the legendary Unitas in Baltimore.

After graduating from College Park High School in 1960, Curry enrolled at Georgia Tech, largely because it allowed him to remain close to his high school girlfriend, Carolyn Newton, whom he had known since grade school. That was a fortuitous decision for many reasons. First, he and Carolyn would marry as college students and remain together over 50 years later. Second, at Tech he would encounter Coach Bobby Dodd, a respected, no-nonsense leader who insisted that his players go to church, go to class and refrain from drinking and carousing. Because of Dodd we get to reason number three: Bill would earn his degree in industrial management from Georgia Tech while attracting the attention of pro scouts for his play on the gridiron as a smallish but active center/line-backer.

In the 1964 NFL draft held December 2, 1963, Lombardi went heavy on centers, drafting Jon Morris from Holy Cross in round two, Ken Bowman from Wisconsin in round eight, and Curry in round 20 with the penultimate pick in the draft. Curry, who had red-shirted one year at Georgia Tech, was also selected by the Oakland Raiders in the 23rd round of the AFL draft that year. While Curry played his senior year at Tech, Morris signed with the Boston Patriots and played in the AFL All-Star Game and Bowman eventually won the starting center job with the Packers because Vince Lombardi traded both his centers after the 1963 season: All-Pro starter Jim Ringo went to Philadelphia, and three-year backup Ken Iman was sent to Los Angeles.

Following his final game with the Ramblin' Wreck against Georgia, Bill and wife Carolyn were flown to Dallas to watch the Packers beat the Cowboys 45–21 on November 29, 1964. Curry got to meet Lombardi and Bart Starr on the sidelines and in the locker room, and Bill signed his rookie contract that night without negotiating with the Raiders at all. That summer, Curry was selected for the College All-Star Game and was scheduled to report to Green Bay the day after that game. When the airline could not find his reservation, Bill nearly panicked at the thought of being late for his first practice as a Packer, but had the brilliant thought to invoke the threat of Lombardi's wrath on the man at the North Central Airlines counter in Chicago should it be his fault that a Packer missed practice. With that, the man chartered a Piper Cub plane to get Curry to Green Bay on time.

Once there, Curry had a personal session with the coach in which Lombardi drew up all of the Packers' plays on a yellow legal pad and succinctly explained them. Later Bowman would add details and help Curry learn the basics of the position and its responsibilities. In August, he told the *Milwaukee Sentinel*, "I'm just keeping my stuff in the suitcase in case I'm leaving. I don't want to leave, of course." He added, "They ought to call it something else besides football. It's not like football like I played before. It's so much quicker. You just don't have time to fiddle around. Everyone moves so fast. And technique is so important here."[1]

In addition to learning the game, Bill was growing up and learning about life. One big change for him was playing on a racially integrated team. Curry had grown up in the Deep South during segregation. Although in his second memoir, he movingly details working for a dignified black supervisor in a manual labor summer job during high school, Bill was fearful and unsure around his black teammates, figuring they would mistrust and resent him for his southern background. He credits defensive end and team captain Willie Davis for helping him overcome his past and begin to see all his teammates in the same light. Davis reached out to Curry during training camp and offered his support and understanding, beginning a lifelong friendship of the two men.

Curry also credits quarterback Bart Starr for welcoming him to the team, with the quarterback even going so far as having Carolyn stay with the Starrs until more permanent arrangements could be made. With both Starr and Lombardi, Bill shared a deep spirituality. His fellow Packers looked on him as something of an authority on religious matters and tagged him with the nickname of Elmer Gantry, a fictional evangelist. One time, roommates Paul Hornung and Max McGee were arguing about whether Hornung going to confession absolved Paul of his sins or just made him a hypocrite by continuing to sin after confession. They called in Curry to adjudicate the dispute. Reluctantly, he tried to strike a middle ground by telling them that their argument was not between themselves but concerned a higher power, to which McGee quipped, "You're not going to bring that damned Lombardi into this."[2]

Not all of Bill's teammates were so hospitable. With linebacker leader Ray Nitschke, Curry formed a bitterly competitive rivalry that only grew over their careers and still flummoxed the southern gentleman 40 years later. However, Bill came through that first training camp unscathed by the Turk and made the team. As a rookie, he was a backup at both center and linebacker, snapped the ball on punts and field goals, and played on other kicking and coverage units, too. He also won a ring as a member of the 1965 NFL champions. Years later, Hornung would assess Curry for the *Lexington Herald-Leader*. "He was very, very quick. And Smart. He would just stop the other guy with his head and with his quickness."[3]

Bill Curry.

Curry returned in 1966 as number two on the depth chart at center, but when Bowman separated his shoulder at the end of the exhibition season, Bill opened the season as starting center. What's more, he remained the starter even when Bowman recovered. In December, offensive line coach Ray Wietecha told the *Milwaukee Journal*, "Curry got his chance because Ken Bowman got hurt. He had to learn all the lessons that Bowman learned the year before. Curry made good progress. But it's tough breaking in. You could notice his improvement between spring training [sic] and up through about the fourth league game. From then on, it depended a lot on who the opposing middle linebacker was, how good a day he had. That's always the way."[4]

Bill started in the NFL championship against the Cowboys and then the very first Super Bowl against the Chiefs. In the Super Bowl, though, he left early in the second half with a leg injury and was replaced by Bowman. It would be his last game as a Packer; 25 days later on February 9, 1967, Vince Lombardi called Curry to tell him that he had been left unprotected in the New Orleans Saints' expansion draft and the new team had picked him. It was a devastating blow emotionally to be rejected by the league's best team and sent to its newest and worst. Less than a month later on March 6, Curry's fortunes were reversed again when Don Shula called Bill to tell him he was now a Baltimore Colt, having been included in the deal that sent the Saints' top draft pick and Curry to the Colts for highly regarded backup quarterback Gary Cuozzo, a second round draft pick and guard Butch Allison. The Colts would select defensive end Bubba Smith with that pick and reap a steal by gaining two future stars for very little.

Bill would spend the next six seasons in Baltimore, going to two Super Bowls and two Pro Bowls as a Colt. In his first year in the Charm City in 1967, Curry was a reserve linebacker who got to start a couple of games when starter Ron Porter was injured. Shifted to center in 1968, Curry won the starting job for the ill-fated Colt team that lost to Joe Namath's Jets in Super Bowl III. Along the way, Bill became the media's go-to-guy for quotes on his former coach. Before a December Colts-Packers game, Curry told the *Washington Post*, "There's a lot of individual encouragement among the players on this team. At Green Bay, there was a fear of humiliation in front of your peers."[5] And then in the January build up to the Super Bowl, Bill contrasted Don Shula's "enthusiasm" with Lombardi's terror to the *New York Times*. "Most of the Packers were afraid of his scoldings and his sarcasm. It's a form of motivation that works for some people. But it didn't work for me."[6]

Curry's brilliant second memoir, *Ten Men You Meet in a Huddle*, has perceptive chapters on what he learned from ten very influential people in his football life. Perhaps the most interesting, though, are the chapters on Lombardi and Shula, written with the benefit of 40 years of hindsight in which he tries to give each man his due. His chapter on Shula, subtitled "Teacher," concludes, "He did it without the distance and aloofness of Bobby Dodd, or the anger and cruelty of Vince Lombardi. To me, Don Shula was the model of what an NFL coach ought to be. He was the best."[7]

His chapter on Lombardi, subtitled "General," retells the final meeting of Curry and Lombardi by the coach's hospital deathbed in which he apologizes for the tone of his remarks to the *Times* and admits Lombardi meant a lot to his life. Lombardi's response was "You can mean a lot to mine if you will pray for me." Despite his distaste for Lombardi's methods, Curry ultimately says, "Coach Lombardi forced me against my will to grow up and be a man. He took me places I simply could not have gone without him. I fought him every step of the way, but he was steadfast and confident that his path was the correct path to victory. He was right."[8]

Johnny Unitas returned from injury in 1969, but the aftermath of the crushing loss to the Jets left the team in a fog all season, and Shula departed for Miami in 1970. Shula was replaced by Don McCafferty, nicknamed "Easy Rider" for his low key demeanor, and the Colts responded with a Super Bowl winning season. After losing to Shula's Dolphins in the 1971 postseason, though, Carroll Rosenbloom traded his Colts ownership for Robert Irsay's Rams ownership and an era ended. With the unstable Irsay came peripatetic general manager Joe Thomas who gleefully dismantled the aging Colts. After Curry's second Pro Bowl appearance in 1972, he found himself traded to the 1–13 Houston Oilers, perhaps as punishment for being the vocal vice president of the NFL Players Association. Bill then served as president of the Association from 1973 to 1975 as his playing career wound down. He appeared in only four games in 1973 before tearing up his knee. Cut by the Oilers in 1974, he played in ten games for the Rams that year.

When Bart Starr was named coach of the Packers for the 1975 season, Curry tried out for the team, but was cut. He did some scouting for Green Bay that year and then returned to his alma mater in 1976 as an assistant coach. Starr brought him back to Green Bay as offensive line coach in 1977, and he served in that capacity for three years. From 1980 to 1996, Bill served as head coach at Georgia Tech, Alabama, and Kentucky.

Over the next decade, Curry primarily worked as a college football analyst for ESPN, while also serving in academic leadership positions and drawing on his broad experiences to develop a second career as a public speaker. In 2008, he left ESPN to return to coaching as the first-ever football coach of the Georgia State Panthers. The Panthers did not play their first game until 2010. Bill coached Georgia State for three years before retiring in 2013, with a 20-year collegiate coaching record of 93–128–4. He continues as a sought-after public speaker, a man with the unique background to discuss the qualities and distinctions of both Starr and Unitas, as well as Lombardi and Shula with passion, humor, and insight.

NOTES

1. "Packer Rookie Hasn't Unpacked," *Milwaukee Journal*, August 25, 1965.
2. Jerry Kramer and Dick Schaap, *Distant Replay* (New York: G. P. Putnam's Sons, 1985), 130.
3. John Clay, "Bill Curry: A Closer Look," *Lexington Herald-Leader*, January 14, 1990.
4. Chuck Johnson, "Packer Linemen Know Their Jobs, Must Do Them," *Milwaukee Journal*, December 30, 1966.
5. William Gildea, "Colts Won't Miss, Bill Curry Vows," *Washington Post*, December 6, 1968,.
6. William N. Wallace, "Lombardi Is Not Curry's Dish," *New York Times*, January 8, 1969, 54.
7. Bill Curry, *Ten Men You Meet in a Huddle: Lessons from a Football Life* (New York: ESPN Books, 2008), 233.
8. *Ibid.*, 103.

REFERENCES

Clay, John. "Bill Curry: A Closer Look." *Lexington Herald-Leader*, January 14, 1990.
Curry, Bill. *Ten Men You Meet in a Huddle: Lessons from a Football Life.* New York: ESPN Books, 2008.
Gildea, William. "Colts Won't Miss, Bill Curry Vows." *Washington Post*, December 6, 1968.
Johnson, Chuck. "Packer Linemen Know Their Jobs, Must Do Them." *Milwaukee Journal*, December 30, 1966.
Kramer, Jerry, and Dick Schaap. *Distant Replay.* New York: G. P. Putnam's Sons, 1985.
Milwaukee Journal, August 25, 1965.
Plimpton, George, and Bill Curry. *One More July: A Football Dialogue with Bill Curry.* New York: Harper & Row, 1977.
Wallace, William N. "Lombardi Is Not Curry's Dish." *New York Times*, January 8, 1969.

Carroll Dale

John Grasso

Although Carroll Dale played professional football for 14 years, from 1960 to 1973, his first five years were relatively uneventful as a member of the Los Angeles Rams. The turning point in Dale's National Football League career occurred on April 13, 1965.[1] On that day, Dale was traded to the Packers for linebacker Dan Currie. Vince Lombardi was looking to replace veteran receiver Max McGee. Packer backup quarterback Zeke Bratkowski had played with Dale in Los Angeles and recommended his acquisition. Rams coach Harland Svare, himself a former linebacker, was looking to add additional strength to his already substantial defense and Currie was thought to be the answer.[2] Unfortunately for the Rams, the Packers got the better of the deal as Currie was only able to play two years for them while Dale became one of the stars of the Packers' Super Bowl teams and played for nine more seasons—eight with the Packers. Dale's greatest successes on the football field, including two Super Bowl victories, came while a member of the Packers.[3]

In one respect, Dale and Lombardi were similar—both had deep religious feelings. Lombardi attended daily Mass at a local Roman Catholic church and Dale was also a Christian, although non–Catholic, and usually led his team in prayer meetings. Dale had been active in college in the Intervarsity Christian Fellowship and became a member of the Fellowship of Christian Athletes in the NFL. One of Dale's pet phrases was "The Bible is my number one playbook."[4]

Carroll Wayne Dale was born April 24, 1938, in Wise, Virginia, a small town of about 3,000 in the mountainous southwest corner of the state. The famous actor George C. Scott was born in Wise 11 years before Dale.[5]

Dale was raised in Wise and attended the then new J.J. Kelly High School in Wise. Dale's grade school was located in the same building as the high school and as an eighth grader he began playing on the high school football team. The team was known as the Indians of Kelly High in the Virginia High School Class A Lonesome Pine District. Players in the 1950s played both offense and defense and Dale played end both ways. Although there was not a state playoff system in the 1950s, the school was declared champion in Dale's senior year.[6]

After graduating from high school in 1956 Dale visited a number of colleges. He initially signed with Tennessee but later changed his mind and attended Virginia Tech. He chose Tech since he was from a small town and felt he would fit in better in Blacksburg, home of Virginia Tech.[7] Dale played wide receiver (wearing #84) for the Hokies from 1956 to 1959. During his four years at Tech he appeared in all 40 games (starting the last 39), and caught 67 passes for 1,195 yards, an average of 17.8 yards per catch, and 15 touchdowns. Dale led the Hokies in pass receiving each of his four seasons. His six touchdown receptions as a junior in 1958 was tied for fourth best in the nation among NCAA teams. In 1959, his senior season, Dale was a captain of the team, caught six touchdown passes and was tied for third best in the nation. As a junior in 1958, he was named the Southern Conference Player of the Year and won the Jacobs Blocking Trophy. In 1959 he earned first-team All-America honors from the Football Writers of America and the Newspaper Enterprise Association. He was named to the Associated Press second-team All-America squad in both 1958 and 1959.[8]

The six-foot, two-inch, 200-pound Dale was selected in the 1960 National Football League draft in the eighth round by the Los Angeles Rams as the 86th overall selection. He signed for $8,000 plus a $500 signing bonus.[9]

Dale's first professional experience occurred on August 7, 1960, when he played with the College All-Stars in the annual College All-Star Game in Chicago. The All-Stars lost to Baltimore, 32–7. Johnny Unitas led the Colts to the one-sided victory while quarterback Don Meredith and receiver Gale Cogdill had good games for the All-Stars.[10]

Dale toiled for the Rams for the next five seasons. Wearing #81 and playing tight end (1960–1962) and flanker (1963–1964) on a series of mediocre teams, Dale caught 149 balls for 2663 yards and 17 touchdowns during his time in Los Angeles. In 1963, Dale experienced his best day as a professional with seven receptions for 207 yards and three touchdowns against Detroit in a 28–21 victory for the Rams on November 17, 1963.[11]

After his trade to the Packers in the spring of 1965, the 1965 season started slowly for Dale at flanker, now wearing #84, as the Packers' primary receiver was split end Boyd Dowler who finished the season with 44 receptions for 610 yards and four touchdowns. Dale caught 20 for 382 and two touchdowns. Quarterback Bart Starr also had future Hall of Famers Paul Hornung and Jim Taylor in the backfield and they were also excellent receivers. Dale's best moments in his first season with Green Bay occurred in the December 26, 1965, conference playoff against the Baltimore Colts. After Starr was hurt in the opening moments of the game, Bratkowski quarterbacked the team. Dale caught three passes for 63 yards including one in overtime and helped lead the Packers to a 13–10 overtime victory. In the NFL championship Game against the Cleveland Browns, Dale scored the first touchdown with a 47-yard reception from Starr. Green Bay went on to win 23–12.[12]

In 1966 Dale was moved to split end. He played in all 14 regular-season games and had a fine season with 37 catches for 876 yards and seven touchdowns. In the 1966 NFL championship game Dale caught five passes for 128 yards and had a 51 yard touchdown reception. Two weeks later the Packers won the first AFL-NFL World Championship Game by defeating the Kansas City Chiefs, 35–10, on January 15, 1967. Dale had four catches for 59 yards in that game.[13]

For the 1967 season Dale played flanker with Marv Fleming at tight end and Boyd Dowler at split end. The Packers again had an excellent season, finishing at 9–4–1 and leading the Central Division of the newly realigned NFL. On December 23 they defeated Dale's former team, the Los Angeles Rams, 28–7 to win the Western Conference championship. Eight days

Carroll Dale.

later the Packers met the Cowboys in the Ice Bowl. In a recent interview, Dale remembered the game. He said, "It was so cold that I did not even attempt to catch the first pass thrown to me. I was afraid that if I reached for the ball my fingers might break off."[14]

Dale's statistics for the season included 14 games, 35 receptions, 738 yards, and five touchdowns including one of 86 yards. In the three postseason games he caught 13 passes for 196 yards which included a touchdown in the Rams game.[15]

On January 28, 1968, two weeks after the Packers' second Super Bowl victory, head coach Vince Lombardi resigned his coaching position although he retained his general manager duties. Although the Packers struggled under new coach Phil Bengtson, Dale had a good year with 42 receptions (his highest to date) good for 818 yards and a career high eight touchdowns. For the first time in his career he was selected for the NFL postseason all-star game, the Pro Bowl.[16]

In 1969 Lombardi left the Packers and became head coach and general manager of the Washington Redskins. Bengtson remained as Packers head coach and also assumed the general manager position. The Packers again had a mediocre season, but Dale, at wide receiver, had another excellent season with 45 catches, good for a career high 879 yards and six touchdowns in 14 games. Dale again was selected for the Pro Bowl.[17]

The 1970 NFL season began with the shocking news that Vince Lombardi died on September 3, 1970, less than two months after he officially was diagnosed with cancer. The Packers continued to play uninspired football for Bengtson, but Dale had another outstanding season as a wide receiver finishing with a career best 49 receptions for 814 yards and two touchdowns. On September 27, 1970, in a 27–24 victory over Atlanta he scored two touchdowns—the second one covering 89 yards, the longest of his career. For the third and final time in his professional career he was selected for the Pro Bowl. In that game he caught a 28-yard pass from Roman Gabriel with 72 seconds left to give the West team a 16–13 victory.[18]

Phil Bengtson was released following his third year with the Packers and replaced with Dan Devine, a successful college coach at Arizona and Missouri, but who possessed no previous coaching experience in professional football. Devine, who had been a college head coach for 16 years and had had just one losing season, finished the 1971 season with a record of 4–8–2, his worst season as a coach. Scott Hunter became Green Bay's primary quarterback with Starr as his mentor and backup. Wide receiver Dale, now 33 years old, was still the Packers' leading receiver with 31 receptions for 598 yards and four touchdowns.[19]

The 1972 season proved to be Dale's last with the Packers. They had their first successful year since 1967. A record of 10–4 was good for first place in the NFC Central Division but in the playoffs they were defeated by the Washington Redskins, 16–3. Dale's played in all 14 games but his production fell to the lowest of his pro career with only 16 catches for 317 yards and one touchdown. He had two more receptions for 28 yards in the playoff game. Prior to the 1973 season, the 35-year-old Dale was released by the Packers and signed by the Minnesota Vikings.[20]

Dale's final NFL season was 1973. He was still good enough to start at wide receiver in 12 of Minnesota's 14 games but only caught 14 passes for 192 yards and for the first season in his pro career did not have a touchdown. The Vikings had a good year under head coach Bud Grant finishing at 12–2, first in the NFC Central Division. In the postseason playoffs they defeated the Washington Redskins, 27–20, and the Dallas Cowboys, 27–10. The Vikings lost to the Miami Dolphins, 24–7 in Super Bowl VIII. Dale caught two passes for 31 yards in the Redskins game and played in the next two post season games but did not catch a pass in either of them.[21]

On April 23, 1974, Dale was released by the Vikings. He was claimed by the Chicago Bears but did not play for them and retired.[22] His NFL regular season career totals are three teams, 14 years, 189 games, 438 receptions, 8,277 yards, 52 touchdowns, four rushing attempts for 30 yards and no touchdowns. In 11 postseason games (three of which were Super Bowls) in five seasons he caught 31 passes for 565 yards and three touchdowns.[23]

After Dale retired he returned to his hometown of Wise and began operating a small coal mining business (Sunshine, Inc.) for the next 17 years. During that time he was elected to four sports halls of fame: 1976, the Virginia Sports Hall of Fame, 1979, Packers Hall of Fame, 1982, Virginia Tech Hall of Fame and in 1987, the College Football Hall of Fame.[24]

In 1991, the University of Virginia–Wise campus began a football program and hired Dale as athletic director. The high school stadium at Dale's alma mater, J.J. Kelly High School was renamed Carroll Dale Stadium and the university used that facility for their football games until 1997. Dale originally also worked as the wide receivers coach in addition to his athletic director duties but realized coaching was not for him and stopped doing it.[25]

He later became the assistant vice chancellor for athletic development. In this new capacity he was primarily a fund-raiser for the university's athletic department. On February 8, 2006, he was officially recognized by the Virginia House of Delegates (House Joint Resolution No. 284) for his "valuable service to Southwest Virginia and the Commonwealth."[26]

NOTES

1. en.wikipedia.org/wiki/Carroll_Dale.

2. www.fs64sports.blogspot.com/2012/04/1965-packers-obtain-carroll-dale-from.html.

3. en.wikipedia.org/wiki/Carroll_Dale; www.pro-football-reference.com/players/C/CurrDa00.htm.

4. en.wikipedia.org/wiki/Vince_Lombardi; *Sarasota Herald-Tribune*, December 25, 1971; www.intervarsity.org/news/intervarsity-alumni-carroll-dale.

5. en.wikipedia.org/wiki/Carroll_Dale; en.wikipedia.org/wiki/Wise,_Virginia; en.wikipedia.org/wiki/George_C._Scott.

6. en.wikipedia.org/wiki/Carroll_Dale; en.wikipedia.org/wiki/J._J._Kelly_High_School.

7. Carroll Dale interview with Gary A. Sarnoff, August 11, 2014.

8. en.wikipedia.org/wiki/Virginia_Tech_Hokies_football; www.sports-reference.com/cfb/schools/virginia-tech/.

9. Carroll Dale interview with Gary A. Sarnoff, August 11, 2014; www.pro-football-reference.com/players/D/DaleCa00.htm.

10. www.mmbolding.com/BSR/The_Chicago_All-Star_Game_1960.htm.

11. www.pro-football-reference.com/players/D/DaleCa00.htm; www.pro-football-reference.com/teams/ram/1960.htm; www.pro-football-reference.com/teams/ram/1961.htm; www.pro-football-reference.com/teams/ram/1962.htm; www.pro-football-reference.com/teams/ram/1963.htm; www.pro-football-reference.com/teams/ram/1964.htm.

12. www.pro-football-reference.com/players/D/DaleCa00.htm; www.pro-football-reference.com/teams/gnb/1965.htm.

13. www.pro-football-reference.com/players/D/DaleCa00.htm; www.pro-football-reference.com/teams/gnb/1966.htm.

14. www.pro-football-reference.com/players/D/DaleCa00.htm; www.pro-football-reference.com/teams/gnb/1967.htm; en.wikipedia.org/wiki/1967_NFL_Championship_Game; Carroll Dale interview with Gary A. Sarnoff, August 11, 2014.

15. www.pro-football-reference.com/players/D/DaleCa00.htm.

16. www.pro-football-reference.com/players/D/DaleCa00.htm; www.timelines.ws/20thcent/1968.HTML;www.pro-football-reference.com/teams/gnb/1968.htm.

17. en.wikipedia.org/wiki/Vince_Lombardi; www.pro-football-reference.com/teams/gnb/1969.htm.

18. www.pro-football-reference.com/players/C/CurrDa00.htm; www.pro-football-reference.com/players/D/DaleCa00.htm; www.pro-football-reference.com/teams/gnb/1970.htm; *Pittsburgh Post-Gazette,* January 19, 1970.

19. www.pro-football-reference.com/players/D/DaleCa00.htm; www.pro-football-reference.com/teams/gnb/1971.htm; en.wikipedia.org/wiki/Dan_Devine.

20. www.pro-football-reference.com/players/D/DaleCa00.htm; www.pro-football-reference.com/teams/gnb/1972.htm; *Tuscaloosa News*, September 14, 1973.

21. www.pro-football-reference.com/players/D/DaleCa00.htm; www.pro-football-reference.com/teams/min/1973.htm.

22. *Milwaukee Sentinel*, April 24, 1974.

23. www.pro-football-reference.com/players/D/DaleCa00.htm.

24. en.wikipedia.org/wiki/Carroll_Dale;www.footballfoundation.org/Programs/CollegeFootballHallofFame/ SearchDetail.aspx?id=50083.

25. www.packers.com/news-and-events/article_zeller/article-1/Packers-deep-threat-still-in-the-fast-lane/886b7ff3-d00d-4678-a676–7dd3160c9503.

26. www.lis.virginia.gov/cgi-bin/legp604.exe?061+ful+HJ284+pdf-Official state recognition.

Willie Davis

George Bozeka

Willie Davis was blessed with the three attributes—speed, agility, and size—that Vince Lombardi considered most important for a successful football lineman. "Give a man any two of those dimensions and he'll do ok," the Green Bay Packers coaching legend summarized. "Give him all three and he'll be a great football player." During his ten seasons with the Packers, Davis became one of the best defensive ends to ever play in the NFL.[1]

Willie Delford Davis was born on July 24, 1934, in Lisbon, Louisiana, the son of sharecroppers Nodie Bell and David Davis. When Willie was three years old, his family escaped from a manipulative and cruel land baron. First, his father left separately, and then the family followed with Willie's mother Nodie bravely leading the escape by the darkness of night. Willie's father David walked out on the family when Willie was eight years old, leaving Willie's mother to raise three children. Davis stated in his autobiography that his mother "was and always will be the strongest and most influential person in my life." She resolutely rallied the family.[2]

Davis grew up in Texarkana, Arkansas, and attended Booker T. Washington High School. He starred in three sports: football, basketball, and baseball. His football career almost never got started. His mother would not let him play organized football because she feared Willie would get hurt. Davis played two varsity games before his mother found out he had disobeyed her. With his third game being played out of town, Davis confessed knowing there was no way he could continue his ruse. With the help of his coach, he was finally able to convince his mother to let him play.[3,4]

His high school coach was Nathan "Tricky" Jones, one of the premier black high school coaches in the state and a science teacher at Booker T. Washington. During both

Willie's junior and senior years Booker T. Washington won state championships, as Davis played tackle on offense and linebacker on defense. He was named All-State his senior year. Packer teammate Jerry Kramer stated that Jones "taught Willie that a man could be big and strong and intelligent at the same time."[5,6]

Davis accepted a full scholarship to play football at Grambling State University for legendary coach Eddie Robinson. Coach Robinson won Davis over after visiting Willie's high school squad. "He called us 'gentlemen' and spoke articulately, honestly, and passionately about the importance of college, especially for young black men. We hung on his every word." Robinson won Willie's mother over during a home visit, promising that Willie would attend church.[7]

Willie played both offense (guard and tackle) and defense (linebacker) at Grambling, but defense was becoming his passion. He was a two time team captain and an NAIA All-American. During his senior season of 1955, Grambling won the mythical black national championship by defeating Florida A&M 28–21 in the Orange Blossom Classic at the Orange Bowl in Miami. Davis was credited with 19 tackles and assisted on 16 more in a great "all-over-the-field performance."[8,9]

His performance caught the eye of pro scouts and he was drafted in the 15th round of the 1956 NFL draft by Paul Brown and the 1955 NFL champion Cleveland Browns. Davis signed with the Browns for $6800 for one year, but was immediately drafted by Uncle Sam upon arrival at his first preseason camp. He played service football, winning all army and all service acclaim. Davis came out of the army bigger, faster and stronger. "I left the military a stronger, more focused and mature man. I learned independence, responsibility, accountability, resolve, and the ability to make tough decisions. I would need all those things when I finally returned to Cleveland."[10]

After serving two years in Missiles and Special Services for the army, Davis was honorably discharged in 1958 and back in camp with the Browns. At 6′3″ and 243 pounds, Davis was the classic tweener, seeing action mostly as a defensive end with Cleveland in 1958 and 1959 as he learned the pro game. In the off season, Davis took graduate courses and served as a substitute teacher. Paul Brown planned to use Davis at left offensive tackle in 1960 as Lou Groza's replacement, but at the end of the 1959 season, Brown traded him to the Packers for A.D. Williams, a young offensive end.[11,12]

Davis was terrified by the trade. A trade to Green Bay was often used by Coach Brown as a motivational threat. "It wasn't just our coaches. Everybody looked at Green Bay as a last resort, a place of desperation, horrible weather, and even worse—bad football. It was dubbed 'Siberia of the North' by players, coaches, owners, and even analysts. It didn't seem like a true NFL team, and more than a decade of losing seasons did little to change that perception."[13,14]

Considering retirement, Packer scout Jack Vainisi convinced Davis to first chat with Packer coach Vince Lombardi. Lombardi outlined his plans to use Willie as a defensive end and his plans to make Green Bay a winner. Despite some remaining doubts, Willie decided to give Green Bay a try.[15]

It proved to be a wise decision. "Coach Lombardi was more than football … [he] was also the single most influential person in my adult life. He was responsible for my success on the football field and throughout the course of my life after football as a successful business leader."[16]

Davis would play for the Packers for the next ten seasons, eight with Lombardi. Kramer stated, "He never missed a game, 138 straight regular season games, six NFL championship games, and two Super Bowls. He hated to sit out even a play. Once, I was standing on the sidelines when Willie came out of the game with a dislocated finger. As he turned his hand palm up for the trainer to examine, I saw a bone sticking through his skin. The trainer grabbed the finger, yanked the bone back in place, then taped the finger to the adjoining fingers. Willie ran back to the game."[17]

Sacks were not kept as an official NFL statistic until 1982. Unofficially, it is estimated that Davis had over 100 sacks during his ten-year Packer career and possibly more than 120 with a minimum of 40 during the 1963–1965 seasons alone. Willie stated in 2005, "I would think I would have to be the team's all-time leader in sacks. I played for ten years and I averaged in the teens for those ten years. I had twenty-five one year. Hornung just reminded me of that the other day."[18] Davis also has the Packer records for the most fumble recoveries (21) and the most safeties (2).[19] Davis was named first team All-Pro five times, in 1962 and from 1964 to 1967, and to the Pro Bowl five consecutive seasons from 1963 to 1967.

Throughout his career, Davis had the respect of his teammates on and off the field. For fellow Packer Bill Curry, who was born and raised in the heart of the South, Willie shattered every stereotype that he'd learned growing up in the South. "I'm walking out of the dorm one night at St. Norbert College and this voice comes out of the darkness, 'Bill.' It was Willie Davis, I thought it was God. I just sat down in the grass terrified. He said, 'I'd like to speak with you,' and I thought he was going to tell me to go home. He said, 'I've been watching you at practice and I think you've got a chance to make our team, and I'm going to help. When [Ray] Nitschke's snapping your facemask and Lom-

bardi is screaming in your face and you don't think you can take another step, you look at me and I'll get you through it.' He didn't just help me to play in the NFL for ten years, he changed my life because I was never able to look at another human being in the same way I had. It was an unexpected, unde-served, unrewarded act of kindness by a great leader and a great man. I've never forgotten that and that is the dif-ference in the outstanding teams and the others. If you've got Willie Davis, nobody can beat you."[20]

In *Vince Lombardi on Football*, Lombardi elaborated on what made Davis great on the field. "For a big man, 6'3" and 240 pounds, he had great abil-ity and terrific strength in the upper torso. It is this quickness and this strength that made him one of the great pass rushers. Very few offensive tackles could handle Willie one-on-one in a passing situation and this was a great help to our pass defense because it

Willie Davis.

meant that they would have to keep a back in to assist that tackle, thereby releasing one of the linebackers to help out in the pass coverage…. In addition to his great pass rush Willie was a superb tackler and always at his best in the big games."[21]

Like many of the Lombardi Packers, Davis was a driven man on the football field. "Every year since I started in football I wanted to know right off what the worst part of my game was…. Back in 1960 we lost the championship game to the Philadelphia Eagles. I lived the whole off season with that game, wondering whether I gave all I could on every play…. I used that game ever since as motivation. Since then every time the ball is snapped if I can be anywhere near the play I think it's my responsibility to be there."[22]

In 1961, the Lombardi Packers would go on to win their first NFL championship, and the victory was very satisfying for Davis. Davis was one of the few Packers to be ignored in the various 1961 All-Pro listings that came out before the championship game. His fierce pride was wounded. Davis was a terror, as the Pack went on to crush the Giants 37–0. After the game, Davis admitted, "I felt I deserved the recognition and I was out to prove it in this game. I want to be recognized as the best, and that's always in my thinking."[23] Davis and his relentless style had the respect of Giants quarterback YA Tittle. "Davis is a great pass rusher. He's strong and aggressive. He's always towering above you, coming, coming all the time."[24]

The Packers repeated in 1962, and Davis was named to his first All-Pro team. Davis and the Packers were thinking three-peat in 1963, but the Packers failed to reach the championship game in either 1963 or 1964.

In 1965, Davis got huge personal satisfaction as the Packers defeated the defending champion Browns in the NFL championship game 23–12. "We were champions again. I had also achieved my personal goal of beating the Browns in an extremely meaningful game, playing as well as I could and frustrating my old friend and nemesis [Jim Brown] … it was the start of the most dominating run in all of football history."[25]

The 1966 season was a special challenge for Davis and the Packers. With the first AFL-NFL World Championship Game looming at the end of the season, "competition just became more fierce. There would be more meetings. There would be open competition for starting roles, including players who had filled those roles for a long time. There would be numerous speeches, from motivating to almost threatening, but all with a singular message—we were the Green Bay Packers, we were the world champions, and we would *stay* world champions."[26]

Going into Week 14 of the season, the Packers were two games ahead of the Colts, their next opponent. Late in the game, with the Packers clinging to a 14–10 lead, Davis forced a Johnny Unitas fumble from the blind side that would be recovered by linebacker Dave Robinson to seal the victory and conference title. The play would go on to be known as the "Million-Dollar Fumble," which Davis found comical. "It's funny they called it the "Million-Dollar Fumble because I was about a $10,000 player and I never saw any of that money!"[27]

After defeating the Rams in Week 15, the Packers faced the Cowboys in the 1966 NFL championship game. The defense came up big, sealing a 34–27 victory with a huge goal line stand. Davis stated, "It was one of the best defensive stands and one of the best games we had played together. It was yet another title, but this one felt incomplete. We didn't admit it but we knew it was true. Our work wasn't done yet."[28]

The Kansas City Chiefs and upholding the pride of the NFL laid ahead. Davis recalled, "By the time we took the field, we had telegrams and phone calls from other players in the NFL telling us that somehow we had to carry the ball for the entire league."[29] After a conservative first half, the Packers put the screws to the Chiefs and won the first Super Bowl 35–10.

In 1967, the Packers and Davis would seal their legacy by defeating the Cowboys in the Ice Bowl, and repeating as Super Bowl II champions over the Raiders 33–14. Regarding the Ice Bowl, despite the bone chilling cold, Davis remembered, "I unwittingly did something that helped a few members of my team calm down before the big game. The captains walked out for the coin toss and despite the freezing cold, I was somehow pouring with sweat, I was so amped for the game. As I walked back, I asked one of our staff for a towel to wipe the sweat off my head. That small gesture showed everyone that Willie Davis wasn't concerned with the cold. I was ready to play."[30] Going into the Super Bowl, Davis recalled that the Packers went into the game determined to win and convinced they would win. The only added challenge was the rumor that it would be Lombardi's last game.[31]

Lombardi would retire after the 1967 season, and Davis suffered through two of his toughest seasons before retiring after the conclusion of the 1969 season.

When Davis heard that Lombardi was very ill in 1970, he like many of his Packer teammates made the pilgrimage and visited their coach. It was difficult for Davis and his teammates to see their indestructible leader felled by the ravages of cancer. Davis recalled, "He caught my attention and told me something that not only moved me but touched my heart for the rest of my life. 'Willie, you are the best deal I ever made.'"[32]

During his playing career, Davis had earned his master's degree in business from the University of Chicago. In retirement, he became a successful businessman, and was interviewed to replace Pete Rozelle when he stepped down as NFL commissioner.[33]

In 1975, Davis was inducted into the Green Bay Packers Hall of Fame, and in 1981, he was inducted into the Pro Football Hall of Fame. He was also named to the NFL 1960s All-Decade Team. As Davis emotionally stated at his Hall of Fame induction in Canton, "It's a long way from Texarkana, and nobody ever said the road would lead here."[34]

Notes

1. Don Smith, "Willie Davis, Enshrinee," *Pro Football Hall of Fame Press Release*, April 1, 1981.
2. Willie Davis with Jim Martyka and Andrea Erickson Davis, *Closing the Gap: Lombardi, the Packers Dynasty, and the Pursuit of Excellence* (Chicago: Triumph Books, 2012), 5–6.
3. *Ibid.*, 15–16.
4. Lee Remmel, "Canton Honor for Davis Culminates a Career," *Packer Report*, March 1981.
5. Jerry Kramer and Dick Schaap, *Distant Replay* (New York: G. P. Putnam's Sons, 1985), 73.
6. Davis, 19–22.
7. *Ibid.*, 23.
8. Smith.
9. Davis, 32–36.
10. *Ibid.*, 40–41.
11. Smith.
12. Davis, 57.
13. Smith.
14. Davis, 58.
15. *Ibid.*, 58–59.
16. *Ibid.*, 63.
17. Kramer, 77.
18. "Letter to Lee Remmel," Packers.com, July 20, 2004, www.packers.com.
19. "Individual Records," Packers.com, www.packers.com.
20. Packers.com, www.packers.com.

21. George L. Flynn, *Vince Lombardi on Football, Volume II* (Greenwich, CT: New York Graphic Society and Wallynn, 1973), 28–29.

22. Ken Hartnett, "Barnes 1960 Run Still Haunts Davis," *St. Paul Dispatch*, November 23, 1965.

23. Ed Stone, "Wounded Pride Spurs Packers' Davis to Heights," *Chicago American*, October 2, 1962.

24. Bud Lea, "Davis Gives Qbs the 'Willies,'" *Milwaukee Sentinel*, October 10, 1963.

25. Davis, 218.

26. *Ibid.*, 220.

27. *Ibid.*, 225–228.

28. *Ibid.*, 233.

29. Frank Derry, "Remember; Hall of Famer Willie Davis Recalls First Super Bowl," *Browns News Illustrated*, January 31, 1983.

30. Davis, 263.

31. Derry.

32. Davis, 287.

33. *Ibid.*, 339.

34. *Ibid.*, 323.

Boyd Dowler

RANDY SNOW

Whether as an offensive end, a flanker, a split end or (the catch-all term now used for all those positions) a wide receiver, Boyd Dowler was always one of the team's top receivers in his 11 seasons with the Packers. He was the NFL's Rookie of the Year in 1959, and a starter for the Packers in the other years. Standing 6'5", Dowler was also one of the tallest players on the team, and a huge target for Bart Starr's passes. He was versatile, handling most of Green Bay's punting in 1961 and 1962, and had played even more positions in college. By 1966, Dowler was in his eighth season and had already helped the Pack win three NFL championships. The 1966 season was an aberration for Dowler, his only one for the Packers where he had less than 400 yards receiving, and the only one in his Green Bay career where he didn't score a touchdown.

Born on October 18, 1937, in Rock Springs, Wyoming, Boyd Hamilton Dowler moved with his family to Cheyenne and was All-State in football, basketball and track. Surprisingly, the future receiver never caught a pass during his high school football career. His play as a quarterback won him a scholarship to the University of Colorado in Boulder. Wearing jersey number 44 for the Buffaloes, he threw, caught and passed the ball in his three varsity seasons. Since the NCAA rules of that era limited colleges to "one-platoon" football, Dowler was a defensive back as well. So versatile was he that, in his senior year in 1958, Dowler was the Buffs' leader in passing (320 yards), receiving (154 yards), punting (43.3 yards on 33 boots) and interceptions (five). Even weighing 220 pounds, Dowler was an accomplished track star at Colorado, running the 100-yard dash in 9.9 seconds and specializing in high hurdles.[1]

Dowler was the Packers' third round selection at draft time, and 25th overall. The Packers, on their way to the NFL's worst record (1–10–1) when they drafted their first picks on December 2, 1958, hadn't yet hired Vince Lombardi, and the two players drafted ahead of Dowler—quarterback Randy Duncan and punt returner Alex Hawkins—would never play for the Packers, going to Canada and Baltimore, respectively. Lombardi signed Dowler on June 10, 1959, and wasn't disappointed. Dowler caught 32 passes for 549 yards and four touchdowns and, as noted, was the NFL Rookie of the Year. As for Lombardi, in his first year as a head coach, he turned the 1–10–1 franchise around to a 7–5–0 record.

Going into the 1965 season, Dowler had amassed 3,935 yards receiving on 245 catches in his first six seasons, with an All-Pro selection in 1962. During that 1965 season, the Packers were 8–3–0 as December began, a game and a half behind 9–1–1 Baltimore with only three chances left in the season. Dowler caught a touchdown pass in all three games, including a 42–27 win at Baltimore to give the Packers the conference lead (10–3–0 to 9–3–1) with one week left. The Colts closed their season at 10–3–1 with a Saturday win over the Rams, and the Packers could not afford to lose their final game, played the next day at San Francisco. Dowler's 43-yard touchdown catch against the Niners helped the Packers gain a 24–24 tie. Since Baltimore and Green Bay both finished at 10–3–1, the conference title had to be decided by a playoff on the day after Christmas. Dowler caught five passes for 50 yards as the Packers won in overtime, 13–10, to go to the NFL championship. In the title game, Dowler caught five passes again, this time for 59 yards, as the Packers beat the Browns, 23–12, for their first championship in three years. Dowler finished the season with 44 catches for 610 yards and four touchdowns. In recognition of a great year, Dowler was selected to his first Pro Bowl after seven seasons in the NFL. The year 1966 looked promising. Instead, it turned out to be the worst of his Packer career.

Even before 1966 started, Dowler found that he was becoming a victim of his own success, as he explained to *Green Bay Press-Gazette* columnist Lee Remmel in a November 16 interview. "I was double covered toward the end of last season," Dowler explained, "and have been more so this year, but the main thing is, teams are getting a lot more action out of their linebackers. I think the defenses are just improving. This makes it necessary to throw to the backs a little more now. A lot of backs are up among the league's leading receivers as a result. I think the backs are improving and the coverage is improving."

It certainly was. Bart Starr wasn't throwing many passes Dowler's way. "I caught ten in our first two games," he told Remmel, but not too many since." Dowler had done very well in the Chicago College All-Star Game at the beginning of the preseason, reeling in six passes for 80 yards, including a touchdown in the first quarter on the way to a 38–0 win over the college boys. It turned out that it would be Dowler's *only* touchdown catch in 1966, and it didn't even count. The Packers' first two opponents of the regular season were their last two of 1965. Dowler had six for 73 yards in the opener against Baltimore, and four for 61 in a title game rematch at Cleveland, "but not too many since" was an understatement—one catch the next week, two apiece in the fourth and fifth games, and a lone reception in the sixth game.[2]

Boyd Dowler.

A few days after his 29th birthday, Dowler snagged only two passes in his seventh game, the season now halfway done. Instead, Starr was throwing more than ever before to halfback Elijah Pitts. Carroll Dale was having his best year yet, and Jim Taylor and Marv Fleming were catching more pigskins than Dowler. While number 86 wasn't quite getting "eighty-sixed," he wasn't the open target that he had been, and he closed the 1966 regular season with 29 receptions for 392 yards—and, unlike Pitts, Dale, Taylor, Fleming, Paul Hornung and Max McGee, no touchdowns.

Dowler was having his worst year ever off the field as well. At home, 1966 had started with great promise for Boyd and Pat Dowler as they learned that their second child was on the way. Kerry Susan Dowler was born on September 19, the day after he returned from Cleveland. Two months later, on November 30, the baby died of pneumonia. Dowler played the next scheduled game on December 4, and even caught a pass for 13 yards in a 20–7 win over the 49ers at Milwaukee, but it was his last reception for the regular season. On December 10, for the first time in four years, Dowler didn't catch a pass in an NFL game, but the Packers clinched the Western Conference crown a week early with a 14–10 win at Baltimore. Dowler didn't catch a pass in the season closer either.

As noted, Boyd Dowler didn't score in any regular season games in 1966. His first touchdown of the season wouldn't come until the first day of 1967, when the Packers went to Dallas for the NFL championship. Dowler caught a 16-yard touchdown pass from Starr to put the Packers ahead 28–20 at the end of the third quarter. The next day, the *Sentinel*'s Bud Lea would comment, "Dallas fans found it hard to believe that this was the first scoring pass Dowler has caught this season." The seven points proved to be the margin of victory, and the Packers were heading to Los Angeles for the first AFL-NFL World Championship Game.

Then, as now, both teams had two weeks to prepare for the big game, and media interest was high in 1967 as both CBS and NBC prepared to broadcast the Super Bowl. The Packers and the Chiefs knew little about each other. In the seven years of the younger league's existence, there had never been a meeting between an NFL team and an AFL team. When the two league champions arrived in California, the Packers stayed in Santa Barbara and the Chiefs lodged in Long Beach, and the nation's sports reporters were interviewing any player who could give them an interesting quote.

They found their man in Kansas City cornerback Fred "The Hammer" Williamson, a powerful defender who had a black belt in karate and taekwondo. In the AFL championship game the week before, Williamson had clobbered Bills wide receiver Glenn Bass with his forearm and forced a fumble.

Williamson had a flair for self-promotion and dressed in style, wearing bright white shoes for every game. *Sentinel* columnist Bud Lea called Williamson "The Cassius Clay of professional football" (Lea, like a lot of sports commentators at the time, wasn't ready to accept that the boxer had changed his name to Muhammad Ali). Williamson, like Ali, liked to taunt his opponents, and the target of Williamson's caustic observations was the man whom he was assigned to cover in the game, Boyd Dowler.

On the Monday before the Super Bowl, Williamson told reporters, "As the best cornerback in football, I find all the criticism of AFL defenses ridiculous…. We'll see what they say after the game, after they compare how Herb Adderley covers Otis Taylor and how I cover Boyd Dowler." Sensing a good story, a reporter asked Williamson what he had to say about Dowler and the rest of the Packers. "Dowler?" Williamson said with a laugh. "Is he a tackle?" (a joke that fell flat, since Williamson had mentioned Dowler by name a moment earlier). Williamson paused. "Boyd Dowler can expect me to drop the hammer on him. He will know I'm there. I want complete respect from the receiver I am covering. When I hit a receiver, it stings…. The hammer is nothing more than a motion perpendicular to the earth's latitude. It is my basic style and Boyd Dowler may as well anticipate it."[3]

The reporters sought Dowler out in Santa Barbara, hoping, perhaps, to get an angry response that would draw an even stronger reaction from Williamson. Instead, Dowler just laughed it off. "He must really be something," he mused. "We've never played against each other, but if I catch the ball, I'm not going to worry about what he does. We've watched him on film. Those white shoes only make his feet look big. He's a pretty good defensive back." Noting that the Chiefs player was shorter (six-feet-three to Dowler's six-feet-five) and not as heavy, Dowler wasn't worried about Williamson dropping a hammer or anything else on him. "He'll have to get up pretty high to smack me in the helmet," Dowler said, then added, "And if he does, he won't be the first to hit me in the head…. I feel that anybody who lets you catch the ball just to hit you isn't playing team football."

Dowler found it somewhat strange that Williamson was focusing on him, since the Chiefs' cornerback would be covering the receivers on the right side of the field, while Dowler would be running his patterns on the left side. "I'm surprised that he singled out me. I won't be on his side that much, but Carroll Dale will. His remarks don't make us angry. We're all more amused than anything else." As it turned out, Dowler and The Hammer would never confront each other, though both would end up as casualties of the first Super Bowl.

Dowler was expecting to have a big day. While his NFL opponents had double-teamed him during the regular season, the AFL's Chiefs were an unknown quantity. It seemed likely that Bart Starr would send several passes in Dowler's direction. It didn't turn out that way. The Packers won the coin toss and took the opening kickoff to their own 25-yard line. Taylor gained four yards on a run, and Pitts another five to make it third-and-one. Taylor was chosen to run the ball, and Dowler moved forward to block Chiefs safety Johnny Robinson, leading with his right shoulder. As the two collided, Dowler became the first player to be injured in a Super Bowl, suffering a shoulder separation. Max McGee took his place and became the first player to score in a Super Bowl. As for Fred Williamson, who had promised a few days earlier to "drop the hammer" on Dowler, he made a couple of tackles, and then, as the *Sentinel* put it, "got the Packers going instead" from his intended victim, Donny Anderson. "The second time Anderson carried the ball," the Milwaukee reporter noted, "he ran over Fred Williamson so hard that the Chiefs' defender had to be taken off the field on a stretcher."

Happily, Dowler's story doesn't end with that 35–10 Super Bowl win. Healed up for the 1967 season, he had the most receptions of his career (54), and his 836 yards receiving were second only to the 901 that he had gained in 1963. Dowler made the first two touchdowns in the Packers' Ice Bowl title game victory over the Cowboys ("I got two of our scores that day," he would say later. "Actually, nobody remembers. It seems they just remember Bart sneaking over for the winning touchdown"). On they went to Super Bowl II and warmer weather in Miami, to face the AFL champion Oakland Raiders. Dowler's Super Bowl legacy wouldn't be limited to being "the guy that Max McGee replaced." Dowler made the first touchdown of the game. The Packers had returned a punt to their own 38 and, on first down, Starr threw a pass that traveled 23 yards. Dowler reeled it in and sprinted the remaining 39 yards, finishing well ahead of his pursuer, Oakland linebacker Dan Conners. Green Bay won, 33–14, and Dowler won another $15,000 and a second Super Bowl ring.

Dowler had a couple more good years with the Packers, with 668 yards receiving in 1968 and 477 in 1969, then retired from playing to take a job with George Allen as an assistant coach for the Los Angeles Rams in 1970. When Allen took the head coaching job for the Washington Redskins in 1971, Dowler followed, and returned to the playing field while continuing as the receivers coach. Since the Packers still had the rights to Dowler as a player, Allen traded a future fifth round choice to Green Bay as compensation. Dowler started seven games, then returned to coaching.

During his 11 seasons with Green Bay, Dowler didn't miss a single game, even after being put into a U.S. Army uniform. During the 1961 season, while Dowler and fellow starter Ray Nitschke were on active duty for the 32nd Infantry Division (their Wisconsin Army National Guard unit had been called up for one year during the Berlin Crisis and assigned to Fort Lewis, Washington), the army let them play NFL ball on the weekends. Appropriately, Dowler and Nitschke were the two players named to the Packers Hall of Fame in 1978. "It's great to be recognized individually," Dowler told a reporter, "but looking back, the thing I value more than anything is the closeness and the relationship we had with the coaches and the whole Packer organization. I think we were a little unique in that." It was all characteristic of a quietly modest NFL star.

NOTES

1. Colorado Buffaloes 2013 Information Guide, Cubuffs.com, www.cubuffs.com/fls/600/football/2013_Info_Guide/376–377_all_time_numbers.pdf?DB_OEM_ID=600.
2. Lee Remmel, "Personality Parade," *Green Bay Press-Gazette*, November 16, 1966.
3. "Williamson 'Well-Suited' for Super Bowl," *Long Beach* (CA) *Press-Telegram*, January 10, 1967.

Marv Fleming

JAY ZAHN

Marv Fleming may be best remembered as the answer to a football trivia question—who was the first player to play in five Super Bowls? Fleming, a man of many interests, occasionally chafed at that role. Beyond the rings, he played 12 years in the NFL, nine of them as a starter. His teams ran up a tidy 121–41–6 record in his 12 seasons, and an even better 15–3 record in playoff games.

Marvin Lawrence Fleming was born January 2, 1942, in Longview, Texas. His mother was a beautician; he did not know his father until later in his life. Fleming and his family later moved to Southern California. He attended Compton High School, which had a long, successful athletic tradition and counted Duke Snider, Don Klosterman, and Pete Rozelle among its alumni. Fleming won nine letters at Compton, in football, basketball, and track, and was all CIF (California Interscholastic Federation) Central Section in basketball as a junior.

The demographics of Compton High underwent a transformation during Fleming's attendance from predominantly Caucasian to African American. While at Compton, Fleming was friends with a Yugoslavian immigrant named Miroslav Kesic who fatally shot teenaged African American Melvin Joe Green in what was viewed a case of justifiable homicide. Fleming publicly defended Kesic against charges that the incident was racially motivated.

After high school, Fleming was recruited to Utah by coach and former UCLA quarterback Ray Nagel. Nagel mined the California prep scene heavily, and at one time nearly half of Utah's roster hailed from California.

Since college football still operated until limited substitution rules, Fleming played end on both offense and defense and contributed both ways. Over his varsity career, he caught 35 passes for 598 yards and six touchdowns at offensive end. On defense, he saved a 1961 victory over Oregon by intercepting a late game pass, and returned an intercepted lateral for a touchdown against the Ducks in 1962. He even booted a kickoff between the uprights and over the crossbar in a 1961 game. Fleming also butted heads with future Packers teammate Lionel Aldridge, who played for rival Utah State. Fleming and Aldridge were the ends on the 1961 All-Skyline Conference first team.

Following his senior year, Fleming took part in the college East-West Shrine game played in Kezar Stadium. Though Fleming's team, the West, lost 25–19, he finally got a chance to team up with Lionel Aldridge, as both played defense for the West in the contest.

The Packers drafted Fleming in the eleventh round of the 1963 NFL draft; he was drafted in the ninth round of the 1963 AFL draft by the Denver Broncos as well. Although the Packers had Fleming rated as one of the top 18 players in the country, they delayed drafting him because they had heard he was talking with scouts from the Canadian Football League, and the Denver Broncos had spread rumors that Fleming had already signed with them. Despite being picked in the eleventh round, Fleming still attracted attention in his first Packer camp for his muscular frame and ability. After getting a look at flanker, Fleming moved to tight end.

With All-Pro tight end Ron Kramer still starting in Green Bay, Fleming would need to be content to compete for a backup position. This wasn't assured either, as 1962 backup Gary Knafelc returned. Knafelc, however, wanted a guarantee from Vince Lombardi that he would play at least three games in the 1963 season in order to secure his pension. When Lombardi refused, Knafelc retired (and later played the 1963 season with the 49ers.)

Knafelc's retirement didn't secure a backup job for Fleming, though; Lombardi tabbed sixth round draft pick Jan Barrett and veteran Lew Carpenter as his immediate replacements. Fleming didn't catch a pass in the 1963 preseason, but he did make an impact. On the opening kickoff of his first exhibition game against Pittsburgh, Fleming not only made the tackle but forced a fumble by Jackie Simpson. Fleming even got a preseason start against Washington when Ron Kramer came down with the flu.

Though Lombardi would later admit that Fleming was on the borderline to be cut, both he and Barrett made the team as backups. By early October Barrett had been released, and Fleming had the backup tight end job to himself. Fleming would get another big break in a game against the Colts later that month.

In the October 27 game in Baltimore, Ron Kramer injured his knee in the second quarter and had to leave the game. Fleming was pressed into service and made an immediate impact. He caught three passes for 51 yards, including an 11-yard touchdown from John Roach, on a second quarter drive that put the Packers ahead 17–3. Green Bay wound up winning the game 34–20.

The next week against Pittsburgh, Fleming got his first regular season start as a pro.

He caught a 33-yard pass from Roach to set up a touchdown in a 33–14 Packer victory. Asked about his adjustment to the starting lineup, he said at the time, "I felt a lot better last week. This time I knew I was going to start and there was a lot of pressure. Last week in Baltimore, it happened so fast I didn't have any time to think about it."[1] Fleming got one more start against Minnesota a week later, and again contributed, scoring the Packers' first touchdown on a 12-yard pass from Roach in a 28–7 win.

Fleming backed up Ron Kramer again in 1964, catching four passes for 36 yards. Kramer played out his option during the 1964 season, and signed with the Detroit Lions in July of 1965. This would seem to have cleared the way for Fleming to start. Lombardi seemed to indicate as much, saying that "Fleming is a fine blocker—better than the man he's succeeding."[2] However, Lombardi hedged his bets by trading with the Redskins for Bill Anderson, a former Pro Bowler who was making a comeback after a year's retirement as a University of Tennessee assistant coach.

Marv Fleming.

Regardless, Fleming was in the starting lineup on Opening Day of 1965 and he paid immediate dividends. He caught four passes for 61 yards in a 41–9 romp over the Steelers, including a 31-yard touchdown pass from Bart Starr that put the Packers ahead to stay.

Fleming injured an ankle against the Cowboys in the season's sixth week, forcing him to sit out the second half of that game and the next week's game against the Bears. Anderson replaced Fleming in the lineup, and even after Fleming returned Lombardi started alternating the two players more. Lombardi started Anderson in the Western Conference playoff game against the Colts. Anderson caught eight passes in that game, while Fleming didn't catch a pass in either that game or the NFL championship game against the Browns.

Based on those results, for the 1966 season Anderson appeared to have the upper hand. However, in preseason it was considered an "open" position, with Fleming, Anderson, and Allen Brown (a 1965 third round draft choice who had missed that year with an injury) getting starts at the spot. Fleming finally won the battle when Anderson injured his ribs in a preseason game against the Giants and couldn't play.

Fleming caught five short passes in the first two games, but hit on the biggest play of his career to date against the Rams in the third week, rumbling 37 yards to the Rams' six-yard line to set up the Packers' first touchdown in a 24–13 victory. The next week against Detroit, it would take Fleming all of four plays to better that mark. Starr hit Fleming with an eight-yard pass, Fleming broke a tackle by Bruce Maher, and went the rest of the way for a 53-yard touchdown, the longest play of his career. "I caught the ball and he hit me and I ran for daylight. How's that?" Fleming said at the time.[3]

Fleming's other touchdown of 1966 came November 27 in Minnesota. A ten-yard reception from Bart Starr put the Packers up 21–3 in the second quarter. The Packers

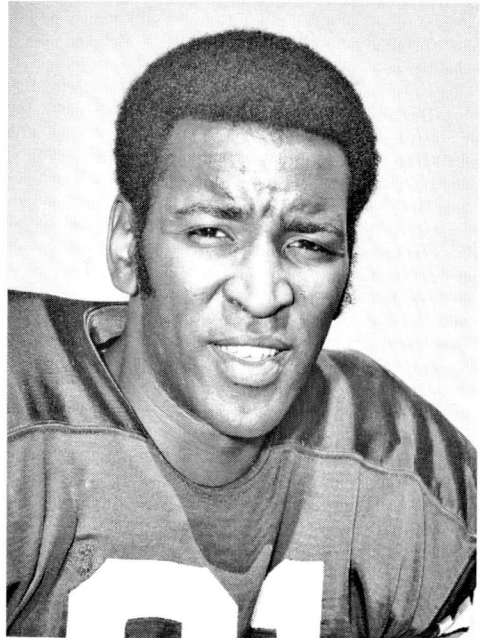

won 28–16 to avenge an earlier loss to the Vikings. Fleming said at the time, "It was about time. It seems whenever I catch it, I catch it in a crowd—so you get used to it. When I leave the line of scrimmage, I'm in a crowd—and I end up in a crowd."[4] Fleming wound up giving Viking safety and former Packer Dale Hackbart an inadvertent piggyback ride into the end zone on the play.

The 1966 season proved to be statistically the best of Fleming's career. Both his 31 receptions and 361 yards gained would be career highs, and he was third on the team in receptions to Jim Taylor and Carroll Dale. Late in the year Fleming reflected upon his improved performance. "The biggest thing was the way things were at the start of the season, when I found myself competing with Bill Anderson, Tony Jeter [1966 third draft choice] and Allen Brown for the job. I believe that was the start of it. It started me doing as well as I could…. Bill Anderson is a great football player—he has a lot of experience. I know if I didn't give my full 100 percent, I wouldn't be in there. So I try to give my full 100 percent each time. Another thing, I'm concentrating a little more on the game during the week. I get myself prepared during the week. I just remind myself I'm in Green Bay to play football—everything else is secondary. Another big thing is when you win the confidence of the other players…. I feel the players have shown more interest in me. That, in turn builds more confidence in me. Another big factor is our end coach, Bob Schnelker. He's chewed me out and he's praised me whenever, I feel, that he thinks I need either one. He's helped me technically, too—he's helped me all around. I feel I've gotten a lot more aggressive in blocking, too. When I go out there, I try to make every play a good block. When I hit guys this year, I hit them to gain respect. I don't want anybody pushing me around. I feel I'm big enough [six-feet-five and 240 pounds] on the field so I don't have to let anybody push me around."[5]

Fleming continued to be a regular receiving target in the 1966 postseason. In the NFL championship game in Dallas, Fleming caught three passes for 50 yards. A 24-yard completion from Bart Starr to Fleming on third-and-19 kept a fourth quarter drive alive that resulted in the Packers' fifth touchdown of the day in the 34–27 victory.

In the Super Bowl, Fleming caught the first pass completed by Bart Starr. An 11-yard gain, it gave the Packers first down on their own 34-yard line. Four plays later Starr would hit Max McGee with a 37-yard touchdown pass for the first points in the Packers' 35–10 victory. Another 11-yard play from Starr to Fleming kept a drive alive that resulted in a 14-yard touchdown run by Jim Taylor.

Fleming was a free spirit who liked to keep his teammates loose. His carefree attitude often drew the ire of Coach Lombardi. Lombardi once threatened to hit Fleming with a chair in a meeting, and called Fleming stupid and lazy at other times. In later years Fleming reflected on their relationship.

"Lombardi pushed me and pushed me and pushed me, and then a lot of times he'd put his hand on my shoulder and say, 'Way to go there.' No one else saw him do it, but I saw it, I felt it, and I said to myself, 'This man likes me, and it's okay for him to push me, it's okay.'"[6]

An offseason Achilles tendon injury, and a preseason shoulder separation, slowed Fleming considerably during the 1967 season. Despite starting the entire season, his numbers were down to only ten catches for 126 yards and a touchdown.

Fleming had better luck in the 1967 postseason, catching three passes for 30 yards in the divisional playoff game against the Rams. Moreover, Lombardi used Fleming in conjunction with Forrest Gregg to neutralize the pass rush of the Rams' Deacon Jones.

Jones didn't get a sack in the game, the Packers gained more than 350 yards on the ground and through the air, and won 28–7.

Fleming didn't catch any passes in the Ice Bowl against the Cowboys, but he later reflected upon his preparation for cold weather games. "You condition yourself to it.... [In the Ice Bowl] all I wore is a thermal, a lined thermal. I made it through the whole game. I got a little bit of frostbite, but what you do is, what I used to do is I set my mental clock, we've got 60 minutes to play this game, they've got 60 minutes too, but I'm going to utilize this 60 minutes because I'm used to this weather and go from there."[7]

Fleming was a busy receiver again in Super Bowl II He caught four passes for 35 yards; three of the catches helped set up three separate Don Chandler field goals.

While the Packers fell back without Vince Lombardi in 1968, Fleming personally bounced back, hauling in 25 catches for 278 yards and three touchdowns.

Reporting to camp in 1969, Fleming said he was ready for "a bigger year than ever."[8] Behind the scenes, though, Fleming was playing out his option during the season, as his predecessor Kramer did. Fleming missed two early games with a bruised shoulder, but caught 18 passes for 226 yards and two touchdowns in the games he did start.

On May 18, 1970, after dickering with half a dozen clubs, Marv Fleming signed with the Miami Dolphins as a free agent. Coach Don Shula, also new to the Dolphins, said that Fleming was "one of the best blocking ends in the NFL and he should be very helpful for the Dolphins in developing a consistent running attack."[9]

Shula's prediction bore out. Though Fleming's pass receiving statistics continued to decline—he would catch only 48 passes in five years with Miami—but the Dolphins and their rushing attack only got better. Miami would appear in three Super Bowls and win two during Fleming's time with the team, and complete a perfect 17–0 season in 1972.

After the 1972 season, Fleming caused a stir among old Packer teammates with some comments. "The Packers were a hungry team, but not like this club. The personnel is better than we had with the Packers. We never accomplished a perfect season at Green Bay and that's why this is a better team."[10] Former Packer Max McGee retorted, "How can Marv Fleming remember back that far? When he played for Green Bay, he couldn't even remember the snap count from the huddle to the line of scrimmage."[11]

On June 23, 1975, the Dolphins traded Fleming to the Washington Redskins for the rights to former Redskins Charley Harraway and a draft choice. But on September 9, the Redskins cut Fleming, ending his pro football career.

Fleming pursued acting during and after his pro football career, appearing in some television commercials. The highlight of his acting career likely was a brief appearance in Warren Beatty's football movie *Heaven Can Wait*. However, acting gigs were sparse enough that in 1976, despite a net worth described as half a million dollars, Fleming opted to collect unemployment checks for being out of work as an actor. Fleming also worked as a player and executive agent.

In 2010, Marv Fleming was elected to the Green Bay Packers Hall of Fame. Former teammates congratulated him on his selection. Dave Robinson said, "Marv had a real tough job. He followed Ron Kramer. Everybody thought that when Ron left and went to Detroit that the offense was going to suffer. The tight end is the key man on the Green Bay power sweep, and Marv stepped up and was excellent on the sweep.... He was as good if not a better blocker than Ron Kramer. He had great hands. He caught the ball for us. We never missed a beat. Ron Kramer was missed, but Marv Fleming was the one who was there for the three consecutive world championships, '65–67."[12]

Fleming's own feelings on his worth as a football player may be best summed up by comments he made in 1975, in his last NFL training camp. He said, "[The Redskins] have a tight end who likes to block. A tight end who dedicates himself to fulfilling his job. It's what Lombardi used to describe as singleness of purpose. My big thing isn't catching the 50-yard pass and running over some guy. It's to be able to block a lineman. I get a thrill out of feeling the footsteps of the ball carrier going past."[13]

NOTES

1. Lee Remmel, "'I'm Getting My Legs Under Me,' Happy Taylor Concedes," *Green Bay Press-Gazette*, November 4, 1963.

2. Art Daley, "Talent Changeover Should End Pack 'Dropoff,' Lombardi," *Green Bay Press-Gazette,* July 20, 1965.

3. Lee Remmel, "Defense Sparks Packers Past Detroit, 23 to 14—Wind Was Baffling, Chandler," *Green Bay Press-Gazette*, October 3, 1966.

4. Lee Remmel, "Adderley Played 'Waiting Game' on Key Interception," *Green Bay Press-Gazette*, November 28, 1966.

5. Lee Remmel, "Personality Parade," *Green Bay Press-Gazette*, November 30, 1966.

6. Jerry Kramer and Dick Schaap, *Distant Replay* (New York: G. P. Putnam's Sons, 1985), 178.

7. Rich Fercey, Packers Hall of Fame Podcast, interview with Marv Fleming, April 27, 2012.

8. Lee Remmel, "First 'T-Day' Gauges Pack's Fitness for NFL Grind, Running Tests Are First 'Drill,'" *Green Bay Press-Gazette*, July 17, 1969.

9. Lee Remmel, "Clancy Returns Home to Packers in Fleming Deal," *Green Bay Press-Gazette*, May 19, 1970.

10. "Miami Dolphins Win Super Bowl VII," United Press International, January 15, 1973.

11. Ron Buckli, "Buckshot," *Eau Claire* (WI) *Leader Telegram*, April 24, 1973.

12. Brian Carniveau, "Fleming Thankful for Hall of Fame Career," Cheeseheadtv.com, July 17, 2010, www.cheeseheadtv.com.

13. Leonard Shapiro, "Tight Ends Put in Jam by Fleming," *Washington Post*, July 26, 1975.

Gale Gillingham

RICK SCHABOWSKI

Fellow guard Jerry Kramer has fond memories of Gale Gillingham: "Gilly went hard in practice and games. You could count on him. He was a very good football player and teammate. Intelligent, athletic, and a good guy."[1]

Gale Herbert Gillingham was born on February 3, 1944, in Madison, Wisconsin, to Verlin and Shirley (Lancaster) Gillingham. His trucker father was on the road most of the time, leaving Gale and his younger brother and mother to run their small dairy farm in Stoughton. They moved to Tomah, Wisconsin, in 1958 and then to Little Falls, Minnesota, 96 miles northwest of Minneapolis, in the fall of 1960.

Gillingham played fullback for Little Falls High School before enrolling at the University of Minnesota. After dropping out of school for a year, he returned to the playing field at his fullback position as a sophomore. Reflecting on his return to the team, Gillingham said, "I weighed 235 pounds that year and the coach wanted me to lose 15 pounds and I tried but I just couldn't do it. I kept trying, but it just didn't work, so finally I asked if I could be moved to tackle. We had a bit of a shortage there that year and so the coaches agreed."[2] Gillingham played both offensive and defensive tackle and was voted to the

1965 All-Big Ten team. While at Minnesota, in August 1964, Gillingham married Jeanne Francis Hoglund, a marriage that produced three sons and a daughter but ended in divorce.

The Green Bay Packers selected Gillingham in the first round of the 1966 draft, the 13th overall selection, but he was pursued by the AFL's New York Jets. "The Jets took me out to New York after our last game with Wisconsin. I probably would have made more money playing in New York, but Green Bay was closer to home, and they were the champs."[3] Gillingham inked a contract with the Packers calling for $17,500 in his rookie year.

Gillingham was selected to the College All-Star team that would face his future employer, the Packers, at Soldier Field on August 5. Unfortunately, he broke a small bone in his hand during a blocking drill on Saturday, July 16. "We were just going one-on-one and I broke it. I was just blocking and caught myself, then fell to the ground. The next thing I knew it was broken."[4] Gillingham didn't report the injury to All-Star coach John Sauer until Monday. "It was hurting all the time, but I didn't want to say anything until I knew it was really hurt. It was turning black, so I figured I'd better do something about it."[5] Lombardi wanted Gillingham at the Packers camp. "Lombardi made no bones about it; he told them, 'He's my property, get him up here.' Away I went."[6]

Recalling his arrival at the 1966 Packers training camp during his induction into the Packers Hall of Fame in 1982, Gillingham said, "When I arrived in Green Bay in 1966, I didn't have these whiskers. I had a crew cut, a healthy body, and a lot of enthusiasm, but I didn't know anything about playing on the offensive line. Forrest Gregg, the dean of the offensive linemen, took me under his wing here. He treated me like a brother and taught me all the techniques. Dave Hanner was the man I could always talk to. He gave me a pat when I needed it and a kick in the pants when I needed it. And Lombardi was the greatest coach ever!"[7]

Lombardi was focused intensely on the 1966 College All-Star Game, having lost the game in 1963. Although injured, Gillingham worked hard at the Packers camp. "I had my right hand in a cast and Lombardi just told me to do what the hell I could do to get ready."[8] Taskmaster Lombardi wanted a big win, and Gillingham recalled, "I told [Jim] Grabowski the night before the game, 'For God's sake, you and Donny [Anderson] need to get hurt warming up because you are going to get massacred.' I had seen both camps and I thought there was a little different approach in Green Bay."[9] Indeed, the Packers destroyed the All-Stars 38–0.

Despite the damaged right hand, Gillingham got a lot of playing time in the preseason as an alternate to Fuzzy Thurston at left guard. Lombardi pointed out that Gillingham has played "as much as the other two [Jerry Kramer and Thurston]"[10] against the Cowboys in the exhibition game on August 21, 1966. A humble Gillingham responded with a smile, saying, "I haven't done very well, but I've played a lot."[11]

On the switch from tackle to guard, Gillingham stated, "I'm too small to play tackle as a pro. I'd rather be taller if I was going to play tackle because these defensive ends are so tall! It helps you on your pass blocking if you're taller."[12]

Gillingham noted there was a big difference between the college game and the pros. "You have to sustain your block so much longer," he said. "That's the hardest part. In college, you drove a guy back three yards and a back would go through for three yards. Here, you may move him a half yard and you turn him or shield him, just stay in his face. Whatever you can do. Here the guy who keeps his feet is the one who's going to win."[13]

Gillingham began the 1966 season on special teams, but on the last play of the third quarter in a game against the 49ers on December 4, Fuzzy Thurston injured his ankle, and Gillingham filled in for the rest of the game, helping to clear the path for two Packers touchdowns. Thurston's injury persisted, giving Gillingham his first start against the Colts on December 10, 1966. He had a superb game against a quality Colts team. Gillingham's opponent across the line of scrimmage, nine-year veteran Billy Ray Smith, said, "The kid did real good. I'm sure he's going to be a good football player."[14] Henry Jordan noted about Gillingham, "He's almost as strong as Jerry Kramer, and I never thought anybody could be that strong."[15] Gillingham praised his teammates, commenting that he got "a lot of help from Jerry [Kramer]. He told me the little things that linemen do and I felt well prepared, and Bart and Zeke called quite a few quick counts. That makes it easier for somebody like me because they don't get as quick a jump."[16]

Gillingham's stepping into the lineup exhibited a trait that kept the Packers successful—unity. Jerry Kramer noted, "We had no fear, no worry about Gilly because we had him ready. Fuzzy was with him at every practice, every meeting and on the sidelines. Without Fuzzy's help, I don't think he would have had the confidence to do the job. But that's the great thing about this club. Unity. A veteran might be fighting for his job, but at the same time he will do anything he can to help his replacement. But everyone with the Packers is dedicated to one thing—winning, and it's this unity that has made this division title possible."[17]

The final judge and jury, however, was Coach Lombardi. Recalling Lombardi's film sessions, Gillingham said, "They were brutal. Jerry Kramer, Fuzzy Thurston, and I sat together during those film sessions. Everyone got the wrath of Lombardi. You can't do everything right every play. He was a hard-driving guy, especially on the offensive linemen. It was his will that drove us."[18] Gillingham anxiously waited to "find out if I was any value out there." Coach Lombardi's evaluation—"He really did a workmanlike job."[19]

One of Gillingham's favorite memories of the 1966 season wasn't after a win but a loss to San Francisco. Gale recalled that Lombardi turned to him at the airport and asked, "What do you think of everybody having a beer?" Gillingham answered, "Coach, I think it's a hell of an idea."[20] The team was shocked. Lombardi had a rule that the team was not allowed to go to bars at the airport or the hotel where they were staying, but the coach felt for his players, who played hard in the loss.

Thurston hurt his knee in the 1967 training camp, and Gillingham became the starter at left guard. Jerry Kramer, in his book *Distant Replay*, wrote about the

Gale Gillingham.

change in the lineup that "Gilly was such a good kid, had such a good attitude that none of us who had been on the offensive line for so long really resented his arrival. It was just the natural progression of life. Fuzzy was aging, slowing down a bit. Gilly was young and swift and strong. Of course, we all envied his youth and his speed and his vigor and hated him for all the things we had lost."[21]

The Packers defeated the Raiders, 33–14, in Super Bowl II, and it was Vince Lombardi's last game as Packers coach. New head coach Phil Bengtson was unable to continue the Packers' winning tradition, but Gillingham maintained his high level of play. He was moved to right guard in 1969 and earned first-team All-Pro honors in 1969 and 1970. He also played in the Pro Bowl in 1969, 1970, 1971, 1973 and 1974, and was named NFL Lineman of the Year in 1971.

Gillingham was always very dedicated and focused about his job. Packers trainer Domenic Gentile has very strong comments about Gillingham. "He was a high-intensity type player. He was such a perfectionist that in his eyes he had to be errorless at every practice. He could not stand mediocrity."[22] Gillingham also was one of the pioneers in using weight lifting in training, observing, "In Green Bay, at first hardly anybody lifted, so you didn't do much of anything during the season. But I always tried to hit it in the offseason. The weight setup in Green Bay was what you could go into most garages and find."[23]

Under new coach Dan Devine, Gillingham played the 1971 season without a contract but made it clear he would never do that again. Gillingham commented, "It's a pretty miserable feeling going through twenty games without a contract. I suffered an ankle injury in training camp, and I hate to think what could have happened had I sustained a serious injury."[24]

Coming off three consecutive Pro Bowl seasons on the offensive line, Gillingham was shifted to defense by Devine for the beginning of the 1972 season. In Week 2 against Oakland on September 24, 1972, Gillingham suffered a serious knee injury and missed the rest of the season. The Packers won the Central Division in 1972 but stalled in the playoffs. Center Ken Bowman grumbled, "They made the rocket science decision to move an All-Pro guard and put him over on defense and have his knee blown out."[25] Running back McArthur Lane added, "I was totally irate because Gilly was the icon of our offense. Wherever Gilly went, we went. For him to be taken from us at that point in time I thought was totally uncalled for, number one. Number two, it ended up backfiring because we lost him for the whole season because of the move. Yet today, I'm still upset with the decision they made."[26]

Gillingham was not happy about the move either, nor was he comfortable playing for Devine. "Devine may have been a good college coach, but he was not a pro football coach. He was simply out of his league in the NFL. It was not a good move. What was really ridiculous about it is that we played six exhibition games back then, but Devine waited until the regular season to put me on defense. I started the game with basically no practice time. I wanted to leave [Green Bay], but I was the team captain. I tore up my knee. Devine comes in and said that he was planning to switch me back to offense. He knew it was a mistake, but it was too late."[27]

Gillingham returned to the Packers in 1973, starting at right guard, and was elected to the Pro Bowl in both 1973 and 1974. The Packers hired Bart Starr for the 1975 season, but Gillingham decided to sit out the season. "Bart Starr was a great quarterback and teammate, but he wasn't ready to be a head coach at that time. We really had no chance to win, and I couldn't take it anymore. I had no faith in the line coach [Leon McLaughlin] and didn't fit into the system. I wanted to be traded."[28]

Following the 1975 season, "Bart called me and asked me if I wanted to play again. I think it was right after the Super Bowl. I said I would." What was the main reason for his return to the playing field? "I missed playing on Sunday afternoons. I saw the Packers play five or six times, and it was hard to watch. Especially when they weren't doing well. I missed the guys."[29] In 1976, Gillingham started every game for the Packers, but the Packers held him out of practice so his knee would be ready for the games.

On March 1, 1977, Gillingham retired for the second and final time, receiving compliments from Starr. "I want to salute him. He was an outstanding achiever and he had an outstanding career. He did all that was expected of him, and with considerable pain the last few years. I've known him both as a teammate and in a coach-player relationship and it was a difficult decision for him and us. He's one of the proudest men around, and I know he would have preferred to play longer. I look at the effort and the sacrifices he made, despite his condition, and I can only marvel."[30] Teammate Ken Bowman also spoke highly about Gillingham, "He's the best guard I ever played with, and that takes in some pretty good people. The guy had everything that you needed to be a great ballplayer. He was big, and he could run like a deer."[31]

Gillingham went back to Little Falls, Minnesota, and owned and operated Goedker Realty until 2010. Gale died of a heart attack while lifting weights, a passion he shared with his sons, on October 20, 2011.

Gillingham once told Jerry Kramer, "I love my kids dearly, but I have never been as close to people as I was every Sunday when I walked through that damn tunnel to the field. I thought so much of those guys walking with me. I didn't want to do anything to let them down. We would kill for each other. We would do anything for each other."[32]

NOTES

1. Martin Hendricks, "Gillingham Survived Some Tough Packers Years," *Milwaukee Journal Interactive,* August 31, 2011.

2. Len Wagner, "Losing Battle of Beltline Helped Gillingham," *Green Bay Press Gazette,* September 9, 1966.

3. Bud Lea, "Gillingham Plays It Cool," *Milwaukee Sentinel,* August 28, 1968.

4. Lee Remmel, "Injured Gillingham Joins Packers," *Green Bay Press-Gazette,* July 30, 1966.

5. *Ibid.*

6. Herb Adderley, Dave Robinson and Royce Boyles, *Lombardi's Left Side* (Olathe, KS: Ascend Books, 2012), 164.

7. Bud Lea, "Former Pack All-Pro Guard Gale Gillingham Paid the Price Before Entering Packer Hall," *Milwaukee Sentinel,* February 15, 1982.

8. Adderley.

9. *Ibid.*

10. Lee Remmel, "Personality Parade," *Green Bay Press Gazette*, August 24, 1966.

11. *Ibid.*

12. *Ibid.*

13. *Ibid.*

14. Bud Lea, "Gillingham Learns of Packers' Unity," *Milwaukee Sentinel,* December 13, 1966.

15. Art Daley, "Packers Won Title with Four-Fifths Normal Strength," *Green Bay Press Gazette,* December 13, 1966.

16. *Ibid.*

17. Lea, "Gillingham Learns."

18. Hendricks.

19. Daley, "Packers Won."

20. Jerry Kramer and Dick Schaap, *Distant Replay* (New York: G. P. Putnam's Sons, 1985), 124.

21. *Ibid.*

22. Dominic Gentile with Gary D'Amato, *The Packer Tapes: My 32 Years with the Green Bay Packers* (Madison: Prairie Oak Press, 1995), 88.

23. Mike Vandermause, "Green Bay Packers G Gale Gillingham Deserves Pro Football Hall of Fame Consideration," *Green Bay Press Gazette,* October 21, 2011.

24. Bud Lea, "Gillingham, Pack Near Agreement on New Contract," *Milwaukee Sentinel,* February 17, 1972.

25. Vandermause.

26. *Ibid.*

27. Hendricks.

28. *Ibid.*

29. Dale Hoffman, "Gillingham to Give It an All Out Go," *Milwaukee Sentinel,* July 13, 1976.

30. Mike Kupper, "Gillingham Retires, Leaving Obvious Hole," *Milwaukee Journal,* March 1, 1977.

31. Hendricks.

32. Kramer.

Jim Grabowski

Jeffrey J. Miller

In Wisconsin lore, he was one of the Green Bay Packers' "Gold Dust Twins" of 1966—one of a pair of number-one draft choices who signed for a then-astounding combined million dollars in salary, creating a blizzard of hype for the time. And though he may not have lived up to the hype that surrounded his entry into the National Football League, Jim Grabowski walked away from the game at 27 with two Super Bowl rings and a permanent spot in the collective memory of fans of one the most historic franchises in all of pro football.

James S. Grabowski was born on September 9, 1944, in Chicago, Illinois, the son of a butcher. He played his high school ball at Taft High on Chicago's northwest side, where he became a local star. He was heavily recruited by both Illinois and Michigan, but ultimately chose to stick with his home state university. He would not regret that decision.

As a sophomore in 1963, Grabowski ran for only 616 yards, but was named Most Valuable Player in the Rose Bowl by rushing for 125 yards in leading the Fighting Illini to a 17–7 win over the Washington Huskies. That performance was merely a preview of what was to come. He received All-America honors a year later, after rushing for 1,004 yards, which included a 239-yard performance versus Wisconsin that stood as an Illini record until 1990. He was even better in his senior season, earning a second-straight All-America selection and placing third in the 1965 Heisman Trophy voting after gaining 1,258 yards on the ground. He also received the *Chicago Tribune* Silver Football Award as the Big Ten Conference's Most Valuable Player. At the end of his college career, he was the all-time leading rusher in Big Ten history with 2,878 yards and had surpassed the legendary Red Grange at Illinois by over 800 yards. Proving that he was no one-dimensional jock, Grabowski also earned Academic All-America honors in both his junior and senior years.

Fortunately for Grabowski, 1966 was the pinnacle of the draft wars between the senior National Football League and the upstart American league. With more than a little thanks to Joe Namath and the New York Jets, college players were perfectly situated to play the two leagues against each other as they sought to score huge contracts that were once unfathomable. When the NFL held its draft on November 27, the Green Bay Packers selected the six-feet-two, 220-pounder with the ninth overall pick. The AFL held its draft that day, too, and Grabowski made history as the first-ever pick of the Miami Dolphins, the league's newest franchise slated to begin play that fall. Miami's decision to pick him first overall was another stroke of good fortune for Grabowski, as it gave him leverage to use in his negotiations with the Packers.

As expected, the Dolphins offered Grabowski a boatload of cash, but he wanted to hear what the Packers were offering before signing. With league prestige at stake, there were rumors that the Dolphins transferred Grabowski's rights to the Jets on Sunday, December 19, and Jets executive Sonny Werblin, the man who signed Namath one year before, worked the phone to try to land Jim. However, Grabowski had always dreamed of playing in the NFL, so he wasn't about to go with the new league until meeting with the legendary Vince Lombardi.

As the fullback recalled: "We're flying up to Green Bay [for contract talks] and Arthur [Morse, Grabowski's attorney] whispers, 'Jim, no matter what Lombardi offers, say you want twenty-four hours to think about it.' And I say, 'Of course, twenty-four hours.' We get to Green Bay and a car picks us up and takes us over to Lombardi's office in the stadium. We walk in there: championship trophies, pictures of all these great players as you are walking down the hall. And for a twenty-one-year-old kid who would have played for a hamburger and a shake, it's pretty impressive. So we sit down in his office … across from Lombardi. I'm looking across at a legend. My attorney is trying to keep me calm. Remember. Twenty-four hours. And Arthur starts saying, 'Mr. Lombardi, we told you we wouldn't go back and forth, but you must know that the Miami Dolphins offer is considerably more than yours.' Lombardi, without hesitation, looked me right in the eye and said, 'Here's what we'll offer you. We'll give you a three-year contract. The amount is four hundred thousand. You can split it however you want. The only thing is your salary can't be higher than forty thousand because that's the highest salary on the team right now.' He looked me right in the eye and said, 'What do you think, son?' And I, without thinking, shook my head yes and said, 'Sure.' My attorney is hitting me under the table to remind me of the twenty-four hours. But I couldn't help but say yes. The instructions to me went right out the window. It was the way Lombardi looked at me and said, 'What do you think, son?' The look, the trophies, the pictures of the team, the legend, how can you not be influenced by this? I should have known then this was the first sign of the great psychologist he was."[1]

Neither Grabowski nor Lombardi was willing to publicly state just how much the rookie was going to be paid for his services, but it soon leaked out that Grabowski had signed a three-year contract on December 18 worth somewhere between $300,000 and $400,000. It was said to be the first rookie contract the Packers ever agreed to that extended beyond two years.[2]

Grabowski's contract, however, turned out to be chump change after the Packers signed Texas Tech halfback Donny Anderson on December 31 to a three-year deal worth $600,000. Green Bay's top choice in 1965, Anderson had been red-shirted for a year in college but was now ready to go pro. The combined one-million-dollar contracts earned the pair their regrettable nickname of "Gold Dust Twins."

Grabowski was aware that there were at least a couple of major obstacles to overcome. First and foremost was the fact that the Packers already had one of the greatest fullbacks of all time in Jim Taylor. Would Grabowski be able to unseat a future Hall of Famer on a team whose coach normally viewed rookies as practice fodder for his grizzled veterans? Lombardi played it cagey, not wanting to suggest that Taylor's days were numbered, while also not wanting to dampen Grabowski's confidence before he'd even met his new teammates. "He's a real fine rushing back," Lombardi told the press. "A good rushing back definitely can become a starter as a rookie in the National Football League. We're real happy to have him."[3]

Lombardi, however, knew that Grabowski was a work in progress. Taylor may have been nearing the end of a legendary career, but the coach sensed he still had enough left in the tank to allow Grabowski time to develop while watching Taylor and the Packers' other star backfield man, Paul Hornung, from the sidelines. "I think I'll learn a lot from them," said Grabowski, adding, "I'll do my best to break into the starting lineup."[4]

But one player who was not about to impart any nuggets of wisdom on the rookie was rugged, cantankerous Jim Taylor. Lombardi knew the contracts Grabowski and Anderson signed were going to cause sore feelings, and according to Lombardi biographer David Maraniss, none were sorer than Taylor's. "One Packer was furious and determined to get his due: Jim Taylor looked at the salaries Anderson and Grabowski were getting and decided that he would play in Green Bay one last year, finishing his contract, then get some big money of his own."[5]

Both Grabowski and Anderson played in their first pro football game *against* the Packers as members of the 1966 College All-Star team. With Coach Lombardi still smarting from Green Bay losing to the All-Stars in 1963, he drove his defending champions to a 38–0 rout of the Stars in 1966. Grabowski gained 11 yards rushing, while Anderson managed a mere four.

Grabowski didn't help his case with the rest of the veterans after finally reporting to training camp at St. Norbert College in August. He experienced some confusion in trying to keep all of the new faces straight. "I was introduced to Jerry Kramer and I called him Ron. Then I met Zeke Bratkowski and addressed him as Max. I thought he was Max McGee, just as I mistook Jerry for Ron Kramer. That must have made a good impression on them. A great way to start, wasn't it?"[6]

Most, however, such as All-Pro defensive tackle Henry Jordan, were gracious. "Kid," Jordan told Grabowski, "I don't care what you make just so long as you help me win. If you help us win, you'll fit in fine."[7] At the end of the preseason, Colts scout Dick Bielski averred, "Grabowski has really impressed me. He's going to be a great one. I think he can help the team right now. Anderson is going to be a superstar someday, but I don't think he can help the club the first year as much as Grabowski can."[8]

But Grabowski was of little help that first season as he lugged the leather only three times in the first six games for a grand total of ten yards. He didn't see his first substantial playing time until Week 7 against Atlanta, gaining 52 yards on seven carries in mop-up

Jim Grabowski.

duty as the Packers destroyed the expansion Falcons, 56–3. He wouldn't see a significant snap count again for another month, but made the most of his opportunity when the Packers visited the Vikings on November 27. Grabowski picked up 61 yards on seven carries (an 8.7 yard average) and scored his first NFL touchdown on a 36-yard run to daylight in the Pack's 28–16 victory. Unfortunately, Grabowski was entrusted with the pigskin only ten more times over the remaining three regular-season games.

The Packers faced the Dallas Cowboys in the Cotton Bowl at Dallas in that season's NFL Title Game. Though he had no carries, Grabowski contributed in a big way by returning a fumble 18 yards for a score in the opening frame to give the Packers a 14–0 lead. That touchdown was vital as the Packers escaped Dallas with only a seven-point victory (34–27) and thereby earned the right to represent the National Football League in the first world championship game against the top AFL team.

Lombardi's boys faced the Kansas City Chiefs in the first AFL-NFL World Championship Game (the game not yet officially called "Super Bowl") on January 15, 1967, at Memorial Coliseum in Los Angeles. The Packers crushed the Chiefs, 35–10. Grabowski had just two carries for two yards.

Taylor, true to his word, played out his option in 1966 and became a free agent. After the New Orleans Saints—a new franchise starting play in 1967—tapped Paul Hornung in the expansion draft, they lured Taylor with the opportunity to return to his native state of Louisiana and continue his partnership with the Golden Boy. Still seething over the contracts awarded to the Gold Dust Twins a year earlier, Taylor didn't hesitate. "I was still very angry with Lombardi regarding the money that Grabowski and Anderson had signed for," Taylor recalled. "On July 6, after nine years with the Packers, I signed with the Saints, and the Packers received a first-round draft choice."[9]

Grabowski and Anderson were now expected to become the Packers' next great backfield tandem. Anderson, though was still a backup as the 1967 season began. Grabowski was starting but got off to a slow start. Jim finally lived up to his rookie-season hype against the New York Giants in Week 6, when he rushed for 123 yards on 21 carries. He also scored two touchdowns, one on the ground and another on a 38-yard pass from Bart Starr. A thrilled Lombardi paid his new starting fullback the ultimate compliment: "He looked like Jimmy Taylor, didn't he? He really did."[10]

The accolades were short-lived, though; a knee injury suffered against Baltimore two weeks later would keep Grabowski hobbled for the rest of the season while bringing fame to backup fullbacks Ben Wilson and Chuck Mercein. Anderson would get his chance as well because starting halfback Elijah Pitts also was lost in the Colts game. The knee injury would, in fact, cause Jim to miss out on two of the most historic games in team history: the Ice Bowl and Super Bowl II.

Despite having missed five regular-season games and playing sparingly in several others, Grabowski was Green Bay's leading ground-gainer in 1967, picking up 466 yards on 120 carries.

Coach Lombardi stepped away from the sidelines at the end of the 1967 season, and tapped defensive coordinator Phil Bengtson as his successor. The Packers were, despite the youthful presence of backs Anderson and Grabowski, an aging team whose best years were now in the past. Under the comparatively low-key Bengtson, the Packers suffered their first losing season since 1958 and were destined to miss out on the playoffs for his entire three-year run. During that time, Grabowski, nagged by injuries, failed to record another 100-yard game.

Grabowski's time as a Green Bay Packer came to an unceremonious end during training camp of 1971 when new coach Dan Devine placed him on waivers. Grabo had never fully recovered from the devastating knee injury he had suffered in 1967, and was also hobbled by a pulled hamstring suffered during camp. In addition, the Packers had drafted fullback John Brockington of Ohio State with their top draft pick in 1971. They were building toward the future, and Grabowski was not part of the plan.

"If this is the end of my football career," said the 26-year-old Grabowski, "I'll have no regrets. I've had five enjoyable years with the Packers. When a coach has to make a decision like this, I can appreciate the problems he faces."[11]

But it wasn't the end. Grabowski was signed by his hometown Chicago Bears and played one season for the Packers' most detested rival, getting to play a season with his former Illini teammate Dick Butkus. He came back for one more go-round in 1972, but it was clear by then that there was nothing left in the tank. He announced his retirement on September 1, 1972.

In six NFL seasons, Grabowski gained 1,731 yards on 475 carries and scored eight touchdowns. He caught 82 passes for 675 yards and three more scores. He also earned two world championship rings. In retirement, he accumulated several additional honors. Grabowski was inducted into the College Football Hall of Fame in 1995, and is also enshrined in the Rose Bowl Hall of Fame as well as the GTE Academic All-America Hall of Fame. He is also a member of the University of Illinois All–Century Team and the National Polish-American Sports Hall of Fame (class of 1993).

Grabowski found his way into the broadcast booth in 1981, when he was hired by his alma mater to provide color commentary for Illini football games. He enjoyed a 26-year run before retiring in 2007. He now makes his home in Inverness, a northwest suburb of Chicago.

NOTES

1. David Maraniss, *When Pride Still Mattered: A Life of Vince Lombardi* (New York: Simon & Schuster), 383–384.
2. *Pittsburgh Press*, December 19, 1965.
3. *Lawrence (KS) Daily Journal-World*, December 21, 1965.
4. *Ibid.*
5. Maraniss, 384.
6. *Pittsburgh Press*, October 23, 1967.
7. Maraniss, 384.
8. *Milwaukee Journal*, August 30, 1966.
9. Jim Taylor with Kristine Setting Clark, *The Fire Within* (Chicago: Triumph Books, 2010).
10. *Pittsburgh Press*, October 23, 1967.
11. *Milwaukee Journal*, August 19, 1971.

Forrest Gregg

JOHN GRASSO

Among the distinctions in Forrest Gregg's 26-year professional football career (15 as a player, 11 as a head coach) was participation in two of the coldest games in National Football League history, the Ice Bowl and the Freezer Bowl.[1]

Alvis Forrest Gregg was born on October 18, 1933. He was given the name Alvis after his maternal grandfather and Forrest after his paternal grandfather. He was born and raised along with four brothers and six sisters on a farm in Birthright, Texas, a small unincorporated community of about 100 people in Hopkins County in the northeast corner of the state.[2]

After spending his freshman year at Miller Grove High School, Gregg left home to attend Sulphur Springs High School in Sulphur Springs, Texas. One reason for transferring was that unlike Miller Grove, Sulphur Springs High School had a football team and Gregg felt it might give him the opportunity to attend college. As was common with many athletes in that era, Gregg played baseball, football, basketball and competed in track and field while in high school.[3]

Gregg was originally not offered a full scholarship by Southern Methodist and was planning on attending Texas A&M. However, chief recruiter Herman "Sleepy" Morgan eventually convinced SMU to offer Gregg a full scholarship and Gregg went to the Dallas school. From 1952 to 1955 Gregg played for the Mustangs. As a lineman (both offensive and defensive tackle) he was a team co-captain in his senior year of 1955 and was named to the All-Southwest Conference team in 1954 and 1955. During that era SMU had mediocre teams, but despite their record, SMU still had five players selected in the 1956 NFL draft with Gregg being chosen by the Packers in the second round as the 20th overall selection.[4]

The Packers of the 1950s did not have winning records. Gregg suffered through losing seasons in both 1956 and 1958. During the 1956 season, the six-feet-four, 249-pound Gregg was a backup but played in 11 of the team's 12 games before being drafted into the U.S. Army. He served in the military until the start of the 1958 football season and was discharged three months early in order to resume his NFL career.[5]

When Gregg returned to the Packers in 1958, he was still a backup as the starting offensive tackles were Norm Masters and Ollie Spencer. The team featured several players who would become stars over the next few years—quarterback Bart Starr, halfback Paul Hornung, receiver Max McGee and middle linebacker Ray Nitschke. One element that was missing was an effective head coach. One of the few highlights of Gregg's season was a fumble recovery—the first of eight in his NFL career.[6]

In 1959 Vince Lombardi was hired as coach and immediately turned the team around.[7] Gregg became the starting offensive right tackle in 1959 alongside guard Jerry Kramer. Gregg was selected to play in the Pro Bowl, for the first of nine times in his career. He was also named to The Sporting News All-NFL First Team and the Associated Press and United Press International All-NFL Second Teams.[8]

In 1960 the Packers improved to 8–4 and finished in first place in the West with Starr as the primary quarterback. This began a span of eight seasons in which Green Bay reached the NFL championship game six times and won five of them. The 1960 team, however, was defeated by the Philadelphia Eagles, 17–13 in the NFL championship game. Gregg was again named to the Pro Bowl and was named to the NFL First Team All-Pro team by the AP and Second Team on three other media All-Pro teams.[9]

In 1961 the NFL changed from a 12-game to a 14-game schedule. The Packers finished with a record of 11–3, their most victories in a season since 1931. This time they won the NFL championship game with a one-sided 37–0 victory over the New York Giants—their first NFL title since 1944 and seventh in the team's history. Gregg again made the Pro Bowl and UPI All-NFL First Team.[10]

The 1962 Packers team had the best record in Green Bay history to that point as they won 13 of 14 games. This regular season record would not be bettered until 2011 when the Packers finished at 15–1 but were then upset by the Giants in their first postseason game. The 1962 team again defeated the Giants in the NFL championship game, 16–7, and were league champions for the second straight year. Gregg was selected for the Pro Bowl and was named to the All-NFL First Team by the three major newspaper wire services (AP, UPI, and Newspaper Enterprise Associates [NEA]).[11]

In 1963 the Packers were looking to become the first NFL team to win three consecutive championships since the Packers of 1929, 1930 and 1931. Despite an excellent record of 11–2–1, they were edged out by the Chicago Bears who finished at 11–1–2. The Packers' only two losses that season were to the Bears, who rightly deserved to win the Western Conference championship. In the NFL championship game the Bears defeated the New York Giants, 14–10. Gregg repeated as a Pro Bowl choice with multiple All-NFL First team selections.[12]

Forrest Gregg.

The 1964 Packers slipped to 8–5–1 and finished tied for second place in the NFL West. The Cleveland Browns defeated the Baltimore Colts for the NFL title, 27–0. Gregg again made the Pro Bowl and was selected for multiple All-NFL teams.[13]

In 1965 Green Bay regained the top position in the NFL West, finishing with a record of 10–3–1 and edging the Baltimore Colts in a divisional playoff game, 13–10. In the NFL title game Green Bay defeated the Cleveland Browns 23–12. Gregg was moved to left guard from his usual right tackle spot and consequently was not selected for the Pro Bowl—the first time since 1958 that he was not selected. He did, however, make the AP and UPI All-NFL First Teams.[14]

On June 8, 1966, the rival American Football League (AFL) agreed to merge with the NFL for the 1970 season. As part of the agreement an AFL-NFL world championship game would be played following the two leagues' seasons beginning with the 1966 season. Green Bay finished 1966 with a record of 12–2 and then defeated the Dallas Cowboys, 34–27 in the NFL championship game, and the Kansas City Chiefs, AFL champions, 35–10 in the first AFL-NFL World Championship Game on January 15, 1967. Gregg returned to his customary right tackle position in 1966 and was again named to the Pro Bowl and several All-NFL First teams.[15]

With the addition of the New Orleans Saints the NFL became a 16-team league in 1967. Rather than the two-division setup that had been the rule since 1933, the league switched to four divisions of four teams each with the alliterative names of Capitol, Century, Central and Coastal. The 1967 Packers again had an excellent team and led the Central Division with a record of 9–4–1. They defeated the Los Angeles Rams 28–7 in the playoffs and on December 31, 1967, defeated the Dallas Cowboys in the Ice Bowl. The

subsequent AFL-NFL World Championship Game (still not yet known as the Super Bowl) was easily won by Green Bay over the Oakland Raiders, 33–14, as the Packers won their third consecutive title. Gregg had another outstanding year with both Pro Bowl and All-NFL First team honors.[16]

The 1968 season began a decline in Green Bay Packers fortunes. Head coach Vince Lombardi resigned following the 1967 season and was replaced by his long-time assistant, Phil Bengtson. Lombardi did retain his general manager position though. Many of the Packers' stars of the previous nine years were now in their 30s, including Gregg at age 35, and not quite as capable as in previous years. Consequently the Packers had their worst season since 1958. Gregg was named to the Pro Bowl for the final time in his career but not to any All-NFL teams.[17]

In 1969 Lombardi left the Packers to become head coach/general manager of the Washington Redskins. Bengtson remained as the Packers coach. Although Green Bay improved to 8–6 they still finished in third place in their four-team division. The Packers again had a comparatively old team with many of their players from the previous year returning. For the first time in a decade Gregg did not receive any post-season plaudits.[18]

The NFL was shocked in 1970 when Vince Lombardi was diagnosed with cancer in July and died less than two months later. This would be Gregg's final year in Green Bay as the Packers again finished in third place in their four-team division with a record of 6–8. The season was noteworthy for Gregg as he recorded the only NFL offensive yardage of his career with two kickoff returns good for 21 yards with one of them for 16 yards.[19]

In 1971 Gregg was released by the Packers. Dallas coach Tom Landry convinced Gregg to play one more season. Gregg was used as a backup tackle and appeared in only six games, but he was able to go out on top as the Cowboys finished the regular season at 11–3 and went on to defeat the Miami Dolphins in the Super Bowl, 24–3.[20]

Gregg retired following the 1971 season after having set a record for consecutive games played with 188 from 1956 to 1971. The record has since been broken by many since the NFL has expanded its season to 16 games.[21]

Gregg did not remain out of football for long. After his retirement as a player he coached for a number of years, serving as an assistant with the Chargers and Browns, and as head coach with the Browns, Bengals, and Packers. Gregg also served as head coach of both the Toronto Argonauts and Shreveport Pirates of the Canadian Football League.[22]

The 1981 season was Gregg's finest as an NFL head coach. He took Cincinnati to the Super Bowl for the first time in franchise history. He became only the second former NFL player to reach the Super Bowl as both player and head coach. (Tom Flores in 1980 was the first; since then a number of former NFL players have also accomplished this.) In 1981 Gregg's Bengals had a regular season record of 12–4, the best season in their history to that point and one that has been matched only once since then. After defeating the Buffalo Bills in the division playoff round, they met the San Diego Chargers on January 10, 1982, in the AFC championship game at Riverfront Stadium in Cincinnati. With a game time temperature of -9 and average wind chills of -32 the game rivaled the Ice Bowl of 1967 as the coldest in NFL history. The Bengals won the Freezer Bowl 27–7 to reach the Super Bowl where they were defeated by the San Francisco 49ers, 26–21.[23]

In 1988 Gregg accepted one of the most difficult challenges of his career, returning to his alma mater, Southern Methodist University. On February 25, 1987, as a result of numerous violations of National Collegiate Athletic Association (NCAA) rules, SMU was forbidden to field a football team for the 1987 season. This so-called "death penalty" also banned home games in 1988. Gregg was hired to be the school's head coach for the abbreviated 1988 season. After seeing the undersized group of students (primarily freshmen) who went out for the 1988 team, the season was canceled. Back to the gridiron the next season, but clearly outclassed, Gregg's 1989 SMU team finished 2–9. Gregg was named athletic director in 1990, but after a 1–10 season relinquished his coaching duties. In 1994 he resigned as athletic director.[24]

In recent years, Gregg has begun to have symptoms of Parkinson's disease, probably the result of multiple concussions sustained during his years of football according to his neurologist, Dr. Rajeev Kumar. He has since worked with UCB, Inc., a pharmaceutical company, in promoting Parkinson's disease awareness. Although quite a few former NFL players have attempted to sue the league for their post-career physical problems, Gregg is not one of them. He has stated that he doesn't believe in holding others accountable for his well-being and that his NFL experience was good.[25] In retirement Gregg resides in Colorado.[26]

NOTES

1. www.profootballreference.com/G/GregFoOO.htm;en.wikipedia.org/wiki/1967_NFL_Championship_Game;en.wikipedia.org/wiki/Freezer_Bowl.

2. *en.Wikipedia.org/Wiki/Forrest_Gregg*;en.wikipedia.org/wiki/Sulphur_Springs,_Texas; en.wikipedia.org/wiki/Birthright,_Texas.

3. Forrest Gregg and Andrew O'Toole, *Winning in the Trenches: A Lifetime of Football* (Covington, KY: Clerisy Press, 2009).

4. en.Wikipedia.org/Wiki/SMU_Mustangs_Football; www.pro-football-reference.com/years/1956/draft.htm; www.pro-football-reference.com/schools/smu/.

5. www.pro-football-reference.com/teams/gnb/1956.htm.

6. www.profootballreference.com/players/G/GregFo00.htm; www.pro-football-reference.com/teams/gnb/1958.htm.

7. en wikipedia.org/wiki/Vince_Lombardi.

8. www.profootballreference.com/players/G/GregFo00.htm; www.pro-football-reference.com/teams/gnb/1959.htm.

9. www.profootballreference.com/players/G/GregFo00.htm; www.pro-football-reference.com/teams/gnb/1960.htm; www.pro-football-reference.com/teams/gnb/.

10. ww.pro-football-reference.com/teams/gnb/1961.htm.

11. www.profootballreference.com/players/G/GregFo00.htm; www.pro-football-reference.com/teams/gnb/;www.pro-football-reference.com/teams/gnb/1962.htm.

12. www.profootballreference.com/players/G/GregFo00.htm; www.pro-football-reference.com/teams/gnb/1962.htm;www.pro-football-reference.com/teams/gnb/1963.htm.

13. www.profootballreference.com/players/G/GregFo00.htm; www.pro-football-reference.com/teams/gnb/1964.htm.

14. www.profootballreference.com/players/G/GregFo00.htm; www.pro-football-reference.com/teams/gnb/1965.htm.

15. www.profootballreference.com/players/G/GregFo00.htm; en.wikipedia.org/wiki/AFL-NFL_merger;www.profootballreference.com/teams/gnb/1966.htm;en.wikipedia.org/wiki/Super_Bowl_I.

16. www.profootballreference.com/G/GregFoOO.htm;en.wikipedia.org/wiki/1967_NFL_Championship_Game;www.pro-football-reference.com/teams/gnb/1967.htm.

17. www.profootballreference.com/G/GregFoOO.htm; www.pro-football-reference.com/teams/gnb/1968.htm.

18. www.profootballreference.com/G/GregFoOO.htm; www.pro-football-reference.com/teams/gnb/1969.htm.

19. www.profootballreference.com/G/GregFoOO.htm; en wikipedia.org/wiki/Vince_Lombardi; www.pro-football-reference.com/teams/gnb/1970.htm.

20. www.profootballreference.com/G/GregFoOO.htm; www.pro-football-reference.com/teams/dal/1971.htm.

21. www.profootballreference.com/G/GregFoOO.htm; *en.wikipedia.org/Wiki/Forrest_Gregg.*

22. www.profootballreference.com/coaches/GregFo0.htm;en.wikipedia.org/wiki/List_of_Toronto_Argonauts_head_coaches;en.wikipedia.org/wiki/1979_CFL_season.

23. en.wikipedia.org/wiki/Freezer_Bowl; www.profootballreference.com/coaches/GregFo0.htm; www.pro-football-reference.com/teams/cin/.

24. en.wikipedia.org/Wiki/Forrest_Gregg; en.wikipedia.org/wiki/Southern_Methodist_University; en.wikipedia.org/wiki/Southern_Methodist_University_football_scandal; www.sports-reference.com/cfb/schools/southern-methodist/.

25. espn.go.com/NFL/Story/_/Id/9183208/Forrest-Gregg-Fighting-Parkinsons-Not-NFL.

26. Gregg and O'Toole, *Winning in the Trenches.*

Doug Hart

Joe Zagorski

Doug Hart would go through his pro football career making the most of his abilities. He would also in turn make the most of his opportunities. He played in the NFL for eight seasons, all with the Packers, and never missed a game. He was a member of three NFL championship teams and played in two Super Bowls. There is little chance, however, that even Hart himself would have predicted that he would attain such success after being left undrafted from Arlington State College (now the University of Texas at Arlington) in 1963.

Douglas Wayne Hart was born on June 3, 1939, in Fort Worth, Texas, the son of a plumber. After graduating from Handley High School, he spent two years laying carpet and going to night school before joining the Arlington State team as a walk-on in 1959. Doug quickly earned a scholarship and a starring role in the team's backfield.

Offered tryouts by the St. Louis Cardinals, the Pittsburgh Steelers and the Dallas Texans, "I picked the Cardinals because they had a pension," Hart described. "I went there and all of their defensive backs had returned, and I got cut."[1] Although he did not make the Cards, he did draw attention from Packers head coach Vince Lombardi. Packers personnel director Pat Peppler joined Lombardi and Hart in the team's hotel just prior to a preseason game at Dallas. The three men discussed the possibilities of Hart playing defensive back for the Packers.

"Lombardi went kind of quiet," Hart remembered, "and he was running his hand through his hair. I found out afterward that's what he did when he was trying to make a decision. They asked me to practice for two days in Dallas. I was thinking that I didn't want to miss this chance."[2]

Lombardi offered Hart a position on the team's taxi squad. Hart would be paid $500 a week for his rookie services. "That was more money than I'd ever seen in my life," Hart proclaimed.[3]

After a year on the Green Bay taxi squad, Hart was promoted to the 40-man roster in 1964. He became a starter at right cornerback in 1965 when Jesse Whittenton retired. Although Bob Jeter had won the position in the preseason, he got hurt, and Hart replaced him. Hart made the most of it, intercepting four passes in 1965, and even returning a fumble 20 yards for a touchdown against Minnesota in the tenth game of the year.

The Packers beat the Baltimore Colts in the Western Conference playoff game, and then defeated the Cleveland Browns by a score of 23–12 for the NFL championship. In the second quarter of that game, Hart was injured and replaced by Jeter, who played so well against Paul Warfield that he won the starting job back for 1966. Hart had gone from being cut by a mediocre team (St. Louis) to the taxi squad of a great team, to a full roster member of a world championship team in a few short years.

In 1966, Doug's lack of playing time resulted in his recording only one interception, versus Atlanta, but he made it count. Hart stepped in front of a fourth quarter Dennis Claridge pass and sprinted 40 yards to paydirt in a 56–3 rout of the Falcons. But as any true professional team player would affirm, it's the team success that matters. And this team—the 1966 Green Bay Packers—was one of the best of all time. The Packers would appear in the first AFL-NFL World Championship Game, a 35–10 victory in Los Angeles over the American Football League's Kansas City Chiefs. It was Hart's most memorable game.

"I think that might be the most revered win by everyone on those teams," Hart said. "We were representing the NFL, playing a new league that had been bad-mouthing us and we thumped them. Lombardi said to the press that the Chiefs weren't as good as they thought they were."[4]

Hart was part of a team effort in the game. His teammates in the defensive secondary shut down the Kansas City passing attack in the second half, thereby providing the Packer offense with more opportunities to score. Shutting down an opposing offense's passing game was par for the course for the 1966 Packer defense.

Green Bay's strategy on defense was simple, yet successful. "It was a disciplined, very controlled system and we knew how to win," Hart noted. "The way we played was very intellectual and we were always thinking on our feet out on the field. We believed in the system because of the success we had."[5]

From 1965 to 1967, the Packers defense limited their opponents to an average of only 14.2 points per game. Fellow defensive back Herb Adderley once commented that Packer defenders "could make adjustments on the field without going to Bengtson or Lombardi. If you see something, make the adjustment. Bengtson was okay with that."[6] Of course, that only works if the players make the correct adjustments. The Packers system on defense was to react to what the opposing offense was doing, then hustle to make the play. Very few defensive secondaries in NFL history were as sound as the Packer defensive secondary of the 1960s.

In 1967, Hart was comfortable with his role of substituting for starting cornerback Bob Jeter on occasion. He was also comfortable in winning championships. The Lombardi Packers won their final world championship by defeating the Oak-

Doug Hart.

land Raiders in Super Bowl II by a score of 33–14. Like most of his teammates, it was Hart's last pro football championship.

The 1968 season brought an abundance of changes for Hart and the Packers as Bengtson replaced Lombardi as head coach. Hart played both safety and cornerback positions in 1968. By 1969, several veterans from the championship years had retired or moved on to other teams. Hart became a starter at the strong safety position that season. The Packers had a different identity from the head coach down. "Bengtson was a brilliant technician," Hart recalled. "He could design defenses and he was a teacher, but Lombardi had a charisma that as a player you were taken in by. Phil didn't have that ability. Vince was very deliberate in telling us what we had to do to win, and I think we could have won one more championship had he remained head coach. It changed the team's character without him."[7]

One thing that did not change after Lombardi left was Hart's desire to play the game. Number 43 was given more opportunities to play, both as a starter and as a reserve. In 1968, Hart intercepted one pass versus Chicago in the final game of the season, a 28–27 victory over the Bears. In 1969, Hart intercepted three passes worth a career-high 156 yards in runbacks including an 85-yard return for a touchdown in a 9–7 loss to the Vikings. The following year, he intercepted another three passes, and ran those back a total of 114 yards. He returned one of those throws 76 yards for a touchdown against the Philadelphia Eagles. In 1971, Hart picked off the final two passes of his career. He almost scored on one of them against Denver, running for 69 yards before being tripped up. Hart also returned a blocked field goal attempt 57 yards for a score in a 28–21 loss at Atlanta. Altogether, the opportunistic Hart intercepted 15 passes in his career and scored five defensive touchdowns, fourth in team history.

Dan Devine became the new Packers head coach in 1971, and his plan was to bring in his own draftees and trade away players from the Lombardi era. Hart was one of the casualties, as 1971 was his final pro season. After retirement, Doug ran several successful businesses, including a snowmobile distributorship, a portable toilet manufacturer and a textile mill, as well as serving as a fly fishing guide. After retiring from business, Hart moved to Minnesota to be closer to his three children and today he keeps busy with golf and fishing.

A reliable role player like Hart was important in making the Packers a champion. Every team needs quality depth in order to stay competitive, and Hart was one player who provided that strong depth for the Packers defensive lineup for a number of years. A number of world championship years.

NOTES

1. Ricky Zeller, "Where Are They Now? Hart Made His Mark in Packer Secondary," Packers.com, June 29, 2011, www.packers.com.

2. *Ibid.*

3. *Ibid.*

4. *Ibid.*

5. *Ibid.*

6. Cliff Christl, "Herb Adderley Sounds Off on Lombardi-Era Packers," Packers.com, May 15, 2014. www.packers.com.

7. Zeller.

REFERENCES

Christl, Cliff. "Herb Adderley Sounds Off on Lombardi-Era Packers." Packers.com, May 15, 2014. www.packers.com.

www.pro-football-reference.com, 1964–1971 Green Bay Packers.

Wiebusch, John, editor-in-chief. *The Super Bowl Celebrating a Quarter-Century of America's Greatest Game.* National Football League Properties. New York: Simon & Schuster, 1990.

Zeller, Ricky. "Where Are They Now? Hart Made His Mark in Packer Secondary." Packers.com. June 29, 2011. www.packers.com.

Dave Hathcock

John Maxymuk

Dave Hathcock may well be the unlikeliest member of the 1966 Green Bay Packers. One would not expect someone who never played on a winning team in high school or college, only played college football in his senior year, switched from offense to defense midway through that year, and was drafted in the 17th round of the NFL draft to make the cut of the defending world champions, but Hathcock did. And he earned a Super Bowl ring in doing so.

David Gary Hathcock was born on July 20, 1943, in Memphis, Tennessee. Dave's father, James, was a trained welder who taught vocational school and his mother, Jeannie, was an artist. He also had two younger brothers. After playing eighth grade football for a demanding and inspirational coach who foreshadowed Hathcock's experiences with Vince Lombardi, he attended Kingsbury High School. In high school, Hathcock was primarily a track star who won state championships in the high hurdles and the decathlon. As for football, Dave did not play much till his junior year due to injuries, but then he played middle linebacker and fullback.

Hathcock's track exploits won him a full scholarship to his hometown Memphis State University in 1961, and he starred at track there for four years, while thinking about training to try out for the 1968 Olympics in the decathlon. Still needing one class to graduate and having used up his track eligibility in 1965, Dave convinced Coach Billy Murphy to give him a one-year football scholarship. Starting out as a receiver, Hathcock drew the attention of the defensive coaches in the second game of the year when he drilled the opposing defensive back to prevent an interception of an underthrown pass. By game four, Dave was the team's starting "Monster Man" (a hybrid safety/linebacker) at six feet, 195 pounds, and Memphis went on a five-game winning streak. Still, in November when he got a telegram from the Packers saying they had drafted him in the 17th round, "I thought it was a joke being played on me."[1]

Hathcock knew nothing about the Packers, but when they won the NFL title in December, he understood "I was going to be playing with the championship team. I had not realized they were that good until that moment."[2] Green Bay signed him to a $12,000 contract with a $6,000 signing bonus.

Hathcock finished his degree in Physical Education with a minor in Architectural Drawing and reported to training camp in July 1966. He had never played with black teammates before, but quickly realized, "The mindset of the Packers was there is no race; there's just an individual human being."[3] Dave primarily was a safety and backed up All-Pro Willie Wood. Wood told him, "I'm going to teach you everything I know. Too bad you'll never get a chance to use it. Dave, you're bigger than I am. You weigh more than

I do. You hit as hard or harder than I do. If I ever give you the opportunity, I'll never get my job back."[4] It was the way of the Packers. "[Wood] was willing to teach me every day. That was Willie Wood, and that was the whole defense that I was involved with. That was the way they all treated me."[5]

The main reason for the open attitude of the players was their coach, Vince Lombardi. Hathcock maintains, "Everything you've heard about him is true. He was a master of psychology. He was a very caring person. He wanted the very best out of you. He demanded the very best out of you. Not everybody is willing to go to such work to make people work hard."[6] Despite Lombardi's strong bark, Dave was comfortable with him. "I never feared him. I felt like he was a just man. He was honest and when you associate with people like that, you don't have a fear."[7]

With veteran defensive back Hank Gremminger having been traded in late June, Hathcock took advantage of the open slot and made the team. His primary duty was on kick coverage and return teams. The only game in which Dave got to play much on defense was week seven against the expansion Falcons. Green Bay beat Atlanta 56–3 that day, and Hathcock played about half the game at safety. That week, the *Milwaukee Journal* noted, "Hathcock has impressed the coaches with his quickness and hitting power."[8]

As part of the 1966 Packers, Hathcock earned an additional $15,000 by being on the winning team in Super Bowl I against the Kansas City Chiefs. Dave made a couple of tackles on returns in that game, but it also signaled the end of his time in Green Bay. Covering a punt in the closing minutes of the game, he was hit in the knee and suffered cartilage damage, although he was not aware of it at the time. Dave survived the expansion draft for the fledgling New Orleans Saints franchise in February, married his girlfriend Cheryl, and reported to training camp in 1967. Still not fully recovered, he was beaten out for the sixth defensive back slot by third round draft pick John Rowser. On September 11, 1967, a week before the start of the season, Hathcock was traded to the Giants for a tenth round draft pick.

During the 1,100-mile drive to New York, a disappointed Hathcock decided to view this as an opportunity to play more. When he arrived, Coach Allie Sherman told Dave he would be returning kickoffs for the Giants. Hathcock remembers being taken aback in New York. "It was a shock to my system because of the organization and the team—the way they treated each other. They were more for self than they were for team."[9] That stood as a strong contrast to Green Bay. "What made Lombardi great was he was able to get like-minded people together in a unit, as a workable unit. When you're able to do that, that's a sign of a great leader."[10]

Hathcock led the Giants in kickoff returns in 1967, but played less than half the season. In Week 6, ironically against

Dave Hathcock.

the Packers, Dave aggravated his bad knee on the opening kickoff and never played in the NFL again. He had knee surgery and spent the ensuing season on the Giants' injured reserve list, while finishing his master's degree in education from Memphis State and beginning his teaching career. New York cut Hathcock for good the following training camp on July 28, 1969. During the brief players' strike in July 1970, Hathcock tried out for the Saints, but his knee problem flared up, and he retired from the game for good.

After spending a couple of years working in the customer service industry, Dave returned to teaching. He spent 36 years teaching drafting and woodworking in a number of primarily black Tennessee high schools, while also coaching several state track champions and serving as an assistant football coach. To supplement his teacher's salary, he ran his own landscaping business on the side for 24 years before eventually turning it over to one of his sons. He and Cheryl, married for nearly half a century, have two sons and a daughter as well as eight grandchildren.

Since retiring in 2008, Hathcock has had some health problems—knee and hip replacements and six bypass surgeries—and had to be resuscitated from one heart attack. Dave read the Bible straight through, and now plays golf and works on his memoirs. As a man of faith, he looks at Lombardi in a unique way: "The law of love is giving. Lombardi gave to each of us, and we returned that love to him in giving our talents and commitment to him. That makes a great team."[11]

Despite playing just two years in the NFL, Hathcock has very special memories. "I was part of that organization, part of that group of teammates that were very special, that wanted to strive for a purpose in life. That purpose was to do their very best."[12]

NOTES

    1. Dave Hathcock interview with George Bozeka, September 19, 2014.
    2. *Ibid.*
    3. *Ibid.*
    4. *Ibid.*
    5. *Ibid.*
    6. *Ibid.*
    7. *Ibid.*
    8. Chuck Johnson, "Packer Rookies, All 8, More Experienced Now," *Milwaukee Journal*, October 27, 1966.
    9. Dave Hathcock interview with George Bozeka, September 19, 2014.
    10. *Ibid.*
    11. *Ibid.*
    12. *Ibid.*

Paul Hornung

GEORGE BOZEKA

Vince Lombardi once said of Paul Hornung, "He may not be the greatest football player in the world, but Paul has the ability to rise to the occasion and to be the greatest when the game is on the line." One of the finest and most versatile clutch performers in the history of the National Football League, the Golden Boy was in many ways the face of the Packer Dynasty under Lombardi.[1]

Paul Vernon Hornung was born in Louisville, Kentucky, on December 23, 1935. His parents Loretta and Paul Sr., an insurance executive, divorced when Paul was a toddler as a result of his father's drinking problem. Paul grew up in a tough Irish working class neighborhood in western Louisville. His mother was a hard working woman who took care of all of his needs. He never knew his father growing up.[2]

Hornung was an outstanding athlete at Bishop Flaget High School lettering in football, basketball, and baseball, and earning all-state honors in football and basketball. As a 6'2", 200-pound split T quarterback who could run, throw, and kick he led Flaget to a 9–1–1 record and Kentucky state championship during his senior season of 1952.[3]

Hornung was heavily recruited by a number of collegiate football powerhouses. He narrowed his choices down to two schools, Kentucky and Notre Dame. Hornung was very impressed by Kentucky's young coach Paul "Bear" Bryant, and his mother, a devout Catholic, favored Notre Dame. He finally decided on Notre Dame, joining his best friend and high school teammate Sherrill Sipes at South Bend. Hornung recalled, "It was hard to say no to Bryant…. In the final analysis, I did it for mom. She sacrificed so much for me that I felt I owed her at least this much. She was the kind of Catholic mom who could imagine no bigger honor than having a son who graduated from Notre Dame. To her, a football scholarship to South Bend was a blessing, almost a gift from God. If I hadn't picked Notre Dame, I think it would have broken her heart."[4]

Legendary Fighting Irish coach Frank Leahy also had a role in Hornung's decision. During a visit to the South Bend campus, Leahy told Hornung and Sipes, "Lads, Our Lady needs you here. Lads like you belong in a Catholic college. You belong to Notre Dame. You should matriculate at the finest university in the world. If you're going to play professional football there's a back door and there's a front door. This is the front door." He then told Hornung directly, "Not only will you get a good college education here. But I can make you the greatest football player in the country."[5]

Paul had a difficult first year at Notre Dame. Freshmen weren't allowed to play on the varsity, and Hornung and Sipes were homesick. They even considered transferring to the University of Miami, Florida. Football practice saved Paul. Leahy would allow Hornung to practice with the varsity, and this enabled Paul to discover that he could play at that level. The crowning achievement of Hornung's first year at Notre Dame was his performance during spring practice in the 1954 Old-Timers Game pitting the freshmen against the graduating seniors and players from the past. Hornung threw three touchdown passes in one quarter and Tommy Fitzgerald of the *Louisville Courier-General* christened Paul "The Golden Boy."[6]

Hornung was looking forward to his sophomore season with Coach Leahy when the Notre Dame administration dropped a bombshell. Coach Leahy was forced to resign for "health reasons." Leahy had experienced health issues during the 1953 season, but Hornung stated "that he was run off because [Notre Dame president Father Thomas] Hesburgh and [his vice president Father Edmund P.] Joyce felt he had gotten bigger than the university."[7]

Terry Brennan, Paul's freshman coach, became Notre Dame's new head coach. The 1954 Irish finished 9–1 as Brennan groomed Hornung to succeed All-American Ralph Guglielmi as the Notre Dame signal caller. Paul had always worn number 20 through high school, but at Notre Dame quarterbacks had to wear single digit numbers so Paul switched to number five in honor of his idol, Joe DiMaggio.[8]

Hornung had an outstanding 1955 season with Notre Dame. The Irish finished the

season with an 8–2 record as Paul, now the
starter at quarterback, ranked fourth nationally in total offense with 1215 yards, and was
named a consensus All-American.

During his time at Notre Dame, Hornung
was also making a name for himself off the field,
appearing in gossip columns as he enjoyed the
night life in Chicago and New York, frequent-
ing famous nightclubs and restaurants of the
day such as Chez Paree and Toots Shor's and
meeting celebrities Tony Bennett, Dean Martin, Sammy Davis, Jr., and Kim Novak. When
a date with Novak to the Stork Club in New
York fell through Paul instead went to the Stork
Club with one of his Notre Dame teammates
Don Schaeffer. Paul told Schaeffer, "Damn, I
could have been here with Kim Novak, instead
of an ugly son of a bitch like you."[9]

This set the stage for a memorable senior
season for Paul at Notre Dame. In 1956, the
Irish finished a woeful 2–8, their first losing

Paul Hornung.

season since 1933, but Hornung became the first player from a losing team to win the
Heisman Trophy. Despite dislocating both of his thumbs during the season, he had an
outstanding year, leading the Irish in almost every major offensive statistic and finishing
second in tackles. Hornung was second in the nation with 1337 total yards and named
to several All-American teams. Paul played in the East-West Shrine All-Star game and
the Hula Bowl, earning MVP honors in Hawaii.[10]

On November 27, 1956, the Packers had selected Hornung with the Bonus Pick as
the number one player in the NFL draft. Hornung had hoped to play pro football in
Chicago for either the Bears or Cardinals, but after weighing a $25,000 a year movie
offer from Twentieth Century–Fox and a Canadian Football League offer from the BC
Lions, he decided that the NFL was his choice. Again his mother's wishes were a key to
his decision. Hornung recalled, "My Mom weighed in on the subject, as she did with
most of the key decisions in my life. She wanted me to play in the NFL. So there really
was no decision to make."[11] Hornung signed a three year deal, for $15,000 in the first year,
$17,500 in the second year, and $19,500 in the third year plus a $2,500 signing bonus.[12]

Hornung's first season in Green Bay proved to be very frustrating for the Golden
Boy. Mired in a decade long run of mediocrity, the atmosphere in Green Bay was dis-
heartening. Head Coach Lisle Blackbourn did not like Paul and Paul did not like him.
Blackbourn sarcastically called him "Golden Dome."[13] Uncertain about how to best utilize
Hornung, Blackbourn shifted him back and forth between three positions—quarterback,
halfback and fullback. Hornung never knew where he was going to play. The Packers finished the season with a 3–9 record and Hornung gained 319 yards on 60 carries with
three touchdowns. The only bright spot of the 1957 season was his roommate assignment.
Upon his discharge from the Air Force prior to the last exhibition game, three year
veteran Max McGee became Hornung's roommate. Max and Paul would become lifelong
friends and cronies.[14,15]

After the 1957 season, Hornung was sent to Fort Knox to fulfill his military obligation with six months of army basic training. As a result, he arrived at 1958 training camp in the best shape of his life for new Packer head coach Ray "Scooter" McLean. Blackbourn had been fired in the off season after refusing a Packer board of directors offer to resign. Hornung soon discovered that McLean was in over his head as the Packers suffered through another miserable season. Hornung carried the ball 69 times for a team high 310 yards and two touchdowns, caught 15 passes for 137 yards and scored a team high 67 points as he became the team's full-time place kicker.[16]

During the off season, a discouraged Hornung seriously considered retiring and going into acting or the real estate business. Then a series of events occurred that would forever change Hornung's pro football fortunes.[17] McLean resigned as the Packers head coach. The Packers executive committee made key administrative reforms to the organization, and after an exhaustive search the Packers board of directors approved the hiring of then Giants offensive assistant Vince Lombardi as head coach and general manager.[18]

Lombardi knew that Hornung was a key player who had been misused and underutilized, but could make the team go. After watching films, he told his staff that Hornung's versatile ability to run, pass, and catch reminded him of Frank Gifford. Lombardi communicated with Hornung in the off season and told him he was going to be his halfback.[19,20]

As soon as training camp began, Hornung knew that things would be very different for the Packers and that he would finally be utilized in the correct fashion. In 1959, Paul blossomed under Lombardi. The Packers experienced their first winning season since 1947 as Hornung doubled his average annual rushing output from his first two seasons gaining a team high 681 yards on 152 carries with seven touchdowns. He also caught 15 passes for 113 yards, completed five of eight passes for 95 yards and two touchdowns, and led the Packers and NFL in scoring with 94 points. After the season Hornung stated, "I felt like a new player. He [Lombardi] had me concentrating on my position so heavily I forgot everything else…. There's only one thing I want to be. I want to be the best player in this league."[21] Hornung was rewarded for his turnaround with his first Pro Bowl selection.

In 1960, Paul and the Packers continued their success under Lombardi. Green Bay won the Western Conference title but lost to the Eagles in the championship game 17–13. Hornung had an amazing season leading the NFL in scoring with a then league record 176 points. Paul gained 671 yards on 160 carries for a league high 13 rushing touchdowns, and caught 28 passes for 257 yards and two more touchdowns, also giving him a league best 15 total touchdowns. He also completed six of 16 passes for 118 yards and two touchdowns. Hornung was honored with a second Pro Bowl selection and named first team All-Pro for the first time in his career.

Hornung and the Packers reached the promised land in 1961. The Packers again finished atop the Western Conference, and went on to defeat the Giants 37–0 in the NFL championship game, for their first championship of the Lombardi era. Paul had another outstanding season, leading the league in scoring for the third consecutive year with 146 points. He rushed for 597 yards on 127 carries with eight touchdowns, caught 15 passes for 145 yards and two more touchdowns, and passed for one touchdown. In an early season game against the Colts Hornung scored 33 points as he led the Pack to a 45–7 victory. Hornung was named the league's Most Valuable Player, the winner of the Bert Bell Award as the NFL Player of the Year, and first team All-Pro. Hornung was also named the Most

Valuable Player in the championship game, scoring a then record tying 19 points against the Giants as he rushed for 89 yards and a touchdown and caught three passes for an additional 47 yards. Hornung recalled that it could have been worse. "Hell, I wanted to match the 73–0 whipping the Bears had put on the Redskins in the 1940 title game. But Lombardi didn't want to completely humiliate his former team which really pissed me off. "After the game Lombardi told his squad that they were "the greatest team in the history of the National Football League."[22]

Making Hornung's 1961 campaign even more impressive was the fact that he was juggling football and military obligations during the season. With the Cold War raging, Paul was called up to the Army reserves in October with several of his Packer teammates. Hornung reported to Fort Riley on November 14, and despite getting weekend passes to play for the Packers, he missed two late season games against the Rams, and would have missed the championship game but for Lombardi's intercession.[23]

Throughout his career Hornung was known for his playboy lifestyle. During the 1961 season sportswriter Dick Schaap was in Green Bay to follow the Packers and Hornung for an article for *Sport Magazine*. Schaap later explained the Hornung experience. "Each morning Paul would get up around quarter to nine and be on the field by nine o'clock. They would practice until twelve and there would be meetings to three. At three he'd come home, mix a pitcher of martinis and drink martinis until six o'clock with Kramer [teammate Ron] and the others. Then they'd go to dinner, a group of players. Scotch before dinner. Wine with dinner. Brandy after dinner. Then back on scotch. Every day. I lost count by the time it had reached sixty just how many drinks he had in that week leading to the Browns game. Also, he went to bed before four in the morning, he never went to bed alone, and he never repeated himself…. It was part of his image that he was supposed to get laid every night. And therefore to live up to his image he would get laid every night."[24]

In 1962, Hornung was deactivated from the Army reserves just prior to training camp. Hornung got off to a solid start, but a knee injury in a 48–21 Week 5 victory over Minnesota caused him to miss a number of games and he was not the same player for the rest of the season. Jerry Kramer took over place kicking duties, and Hornung's three year reign as NFL scoring leader ended as he finished the season with 74 points. Hornung gained only 219 rushing yards on 57 carries with five touchdowns as Jim Taylor picked up the slack at running back leading the league in both rushing and scoring. Paul added two receiving touchdowns as he caught nine balls for 168 yards. Despite Hornung's slide, the Packers repeated as NFL champs.

On January 8, 1963, Hornung was summoned to New York by Commissioner Pete Rozelle. Rozelle and Hornung met on January 10 at the Plaza Hotel. Rozelle confronted Hornung with gambling allegations. Growing up in Louisville, home of Churchill Downs and the Kentucky Derby, Hornung had gambled for years, but never against the Packers. Further, after Rozelle had warned all NFL players about gambling during the 1962 exhibition season, Hornung had refrained from placing bets. Hornung admitted to his past indiscretions, and Rozelle told him to keep the meeting confidential, and that he would get back to him. Hornung could have implicated other players but he refused to do so. On April 17, the ax fell. Rozelle suspended Hornung and Lions defensive tackle Alex Karras indefinitely for gambling. Lombardi was devastated and disappointed, wishing that Hornung, his prodigal son, had confided in him. Lombardi angrily told Hornung, "I don't want to see you go to the racetrack. I don't want to hear about you going to the

Derby. I don't want to hear about you doing anything. Keep your nose clean and I'll do my best to get you back. But, mister, stay at the foot of the cross."[25]

Without Hornung, the 1963 Packers finished behind the Bears in the Western Conference, and had to watch from the sidelines as Chicago defeated the Giants for the NFL championship. Asked how much the Packers missed Hornung, Lombardi stated, "Obviously a lot. His blocking, his leadership, his 'devil may care' attitude, his field goal kicking, his intelligence on the field."[26]

On March 16, 1964, Rozelle reinstated Hornung and Karras. Lombardi told Hornung to arrive six weeks before camp so the coach could get him back into shape. Hornung and the Packers struggled through the 1964 season. Injuries and the year off took their toll on Hornung, particularly in the kicking game. Hornung only converted 12 of 38 field goal attempts. His kicking woes cost the Packers three key games as they finished second in the Western Conference to the 12–2 Colts. After the suspension, Hornung would continue to be a solid player for the Packers, with flashes of brilliance, but never the player he was from 1959 to 1961. He finished the 1964 season with 107 points, 415 rushing yards on 103 carries with five touchdowns, and nine receptions for 98 yards.

Following the 1964 season, rumors spread that Lombardi was unhappy with Hornung, and that Hornung would be traded. Lombardi vehemently denied the rumors stating, "I have no plans to trade Hornung … period."[27]

Newly acquired kicker Don Chandler would take over kicking responsibilities for the Pack for the 1965 season, allowing Hornung to concentrate on his running back duties. Hornung, again fought a variety of nagging injuries, finishing the season with 89 carries for 299 yards and five touchdowns and 19 receptions for 336 yards and three touchdowns. Lombardi even benched the struggling Hornung for a Week 12 game against the Vikings. Hornung responded to the benching and turned back the clock late in the season. Entangled in a close race with the Colts for first place in the West, the Packers defeated the Colts 42–27 in Week 13 to take a half game lead in the conference. Hornung gained 176 total yards and scored five touchdowns, three on the ground and two in the air to pace the Packers. In the Western Conference playoff game with the Colts, Hornung scored Green Bay's only touchdown in a 13–10 overtime victory. Hornung then outplayed the best running back in football, Jim Brown, to lead the Packers to a 23–12 championship game victory over the Browns. In cold, muddy conditions at Lambeau Field Hornung gained 105 yards on 18 carries and scored a key third quarter touchdown. Hornung recalled, "This kind of game, you just throw caution to the wind. Got to go in a game like this with little hurts and forget about them because you'll have a chance to rest anyway. The season's over. In the championship game, you play more recklessly…. For a washed-up old man I gave 'em a helluva game to remember for awhile, didn't I."[28] Despite the heroics, Hornung knew that time was running out on his career.[29]

Again slowed by injuries, Hornung's star faded in 1966. He played fairly regularly through the first half of the season, and hardly at all in the second half of the season, as the Packers won the first AFL-NFL world championship game. Hornung recalled the first Super Bowl. "Late in the game, Lombardi came up to me on the sideline and asked if I wanted to go in for a few plays. He wanted me to be able to say I had played in the first Super Bowl, but I said no. I was afraid I'd get clotheslined, and never play again."[30]

After the 1966 season, it was rumored that Hornung would sign a contract with Sonny Werblin's New York Jets, joining Joe Namath in an all hedonistic backfield.[31] The rumors were denied, and Lombardi placed Hornung on the list for the New Orleans expansion draft. The Saints surprised Lombardi and drafted Hornung. The loss of Hornung hurt Lombardi deeply. Lombardi figured that the Saints would not take the injured Hornung in the waning moments of his career. Jim Taylor followed, playing out his option and signing with the Saints. It appeared that Hornung and Taylor would be reunited in the Saints backfield. Hornung, however, never played a game for the Saints, retiring after doctors told him he would be risking permanent injury if he played.[32,33] Hornung stayed with the Saints for the 1967 season and helped coach the backs, but did not return for the 1968 season.[34]

For his career, Hornung rushed for 3711 yards on 893 carries and 50 touchdowns and caught 130 passes for 1480 yards and 12 touchdowns. He also threw five touchdown passes and scored 760 points. Paul was inducted into the College Football Hall of Fame in 1985, the Green Bay Packers Hall of Fame in 1975, and the Pro Football Hall of Fame in 1986. He also was named to the NFL 1960s All-Decade Team. Of his Hall of Fame induction in 1986, Hornung stated, "God did that feel good. I know it meant a lot to my mom too, who always backed me in everything I'd done. Without her, I'm not sure I would have accomplished anything. That was really the last thing in football that mattered to me. I did everything I wanted to do and I couldn't have asked for more."[35]

In retirement, Hornung went into various business ventures and broadcasting, working for CBS and doing color commentary for Notre Dame with Lindsey Nelson. After a failed first marriage, Hornung also remarried. Hornung and his wife, the former Angela Cervilli, have been happily married for many years.

As it was for many of the former Lombardi Packers, his coach's death in 1970 was a difficult time for Hornung. "I really never said good-bye to the coach. I couldn't. The last time I saw him, maybe a month before his death, he was optimistic and looking forward to the season and talking about what a helluva passer Jurgensen was. How could I not play along? How could I tell him that I knew we would not see each other again in this life…. All of us who were touched by Lombardi were defined by him. He taught us how to win, and winning gave us an identity that each of us carried through life."[36]

Hornung summed up his own legacy: "I was very fortunate. I don't look back and say I was a special type player. I think I did okay. I don't have many regrets, but I think you get to the point after we quit that, after a while, you're done being a celebrity. You don't want it anymore. Sometimes you wish you weren't Paul Hornung. Still, it's been pretty nice being Paul Hornung."[37]

NOTES

1. Don Smith, "Paul Hornung, 1986 Enshrinee," Pro Football Hall of Fame Press Release, April 1, 1986.

2. Paul Hornung and Chuck Carlson, *The Paul Hornung Scrapbook* (Chicago: Triumph Books, 2014), 21.

3. Tim Layden, "Golden Forever," *Sports Illustrated*, July 15, 2002.

4. Paul Hornung as told to William F. Reed, *Golden Boy* (New York: Simon & Schuster, 2004), 35.

5. Hornung and Carlson, *The Paul Hornung Scrapbook*, 28.

6. *Ibid.*, 35–37.

7. Hornung, *Golden Boy*, 41–42.

8. Hornung and Carolson, *The Paul Hornung Scrapbook*, 38–40.

9. Hornung, *Golden Boy*, 49.

10. *Ibid.*, 57.

11. Hornung and Carlson, *The Paul Hornung Scrapbook*, 58.

12. Hornung, *Golden Boy*, 61.

13. David Maraniss, *When Pride Still Mattered* (New York: Simon & Schuster, 1999), 282.

14. Hornung, *Golden Boy*, 63–65.

15. Hornung and Carlson, *The Paul Hornung Scrapbook*, 62.

16. Hornung, *Golden Boy*, 68–70.

17. Hornung and Carlson, *The Paul Hornung Scrapbook*, 67–70.

18. Michael O'Brien, *Vince: A Personal Biography of Vince Lombardi* (New York: HarperCollins, 1989), 135–138.

19. *Ibid.*, 142.

20. Hornung and Carlson, *The Paul Hornung Scrapbook*, 73.

21. Hornung, *Golden Boy*, 98.

22. *Ibid.*, 125.

23. Maraniss, 289–290.

24. *Ibid.*, 278.

25. *Ibid.*, 342.

26. Hornung, *Golden Boy*, 160.

27. Bud Lea, "Why Vince Won't Trade Hornung," *Milwaukee Sentinel*, January 7, 1965.

28. Bill Libby, "The Full Story of Paul Hornung's Comeback," *Sport Magazine*, April, 1966, 79.

29. Hornung, *Golden Boy*, 175.

30. *Ibid.*, 180.

31. Art Daley, "Hornung Denies Jet Bid to Meet with Vince," *Green Bay Press-Gazette*, June 8, 1966.

32. Maraniss, 408.

33. Hornung, *Golden Boy*, 184.

34. Bud Lea, "Won't Return to Saints: Hornung," *Milwaukee Sentinel*, April 23, 1968.

35. Hornung and Carlson, *The Paul Hornung Scrapbook*, 164.

36. Paul Hornung with Billy Reed, *Lombardi and Me* (Chicago: Triumph Books, 2006), xxiii.

37. Hornung and Carlson, *The Paul Hornung Scrapbook*, 167.

Bob Jeter

Michael D. Benter

"As a young boy and up to this day, I still tell people, my cousin Bob Jeter
is the best Packer in Football. Coming from Weirton, West Virginia, we
had someone we knew, and could really bragg [sic] about…. I still do!!"
—anonymous obituary condolence, *Milwaukee Journal Sentinel*[1]

Robert DeLafayette Jeter was born in Union, South Carolina, on May 9, 1937, but was raised in Weirton, West Virginia, a small, steel-manufacturing city situated in the northern panhandle of the state, sandwiched between Ohio and Pennsylvania. It was a hardworking and safe town, although with segregated schools.[2] His father was a steel-worker. There were six children in the house, and Bob was the oldest.

Jeter attended Weirton's Dunbar High, the area school for blacks, from 1952 to 1954, then the integrated Weir High as a senior in 1955. Jeter excelled in football at both schools. He was named to all-state teams following his junior and senior seasons and selected as a high school All-American during his senior year. He was also a member of his high school's basketball teams.[3]

Upon graduation from high school, Bob became an Iowa Hawkeye in 1956 under celebrated coach Forest Evashevski. Others from Weirton had played at Iowa, so it was a school local athletes gave serious consideration.[4] Jeter showed enough during the spring practices between his freshman and sophomore years to get the attention of a *Daily Iowan* sportswriter who wrote that fall, "up-coming Bob Jeter, taking a crack at left halfback on the second team, began showing the spark and flash that had him pegged as a stand-out at spring grid practices." Jeter ended up playing sparingly during his sophomore season, but when he did; his average-yards-per-carry numbers suggested he'd be given future work. In 1957, he carried a mere seven times, but gained 51 yards.[5]

Those numbers didn't increase markedly in 1958, a season that culminated with a Rose Bowl appearance for Iowa, as Jeter played in the shadow of another halfback, Willie Fleming, a player good enough to be All-Big 10 that year, and another back named Ray Jauch. Coach Evashevski ran a winged-T offense, behind Big Ten MVP Quarterback Randy Duncan, that required good running backs and lots of them. Even in his senior season, 1959, Jeter shared the left halfback job with John Brown.[6]

It was in the 1959 Rose Bowl against the University of California that Jeter truly shone. That New Year's Day, he gained 194 yards on nine carries. One carry resulted in an 81-yard touchdown jaunt, and Jeter was named "Outstanding Player of the Game" by the national writers attending the game.[7]

The following spring, he won the team's "Spring Football Award." Coach Evashevski said of Jeter at the time, "Bob won the award because of his fine attitude, his attendance and hard work. He worked just as long and hard as if he did not have a position clinched."[8]

That hard work paid off as Jeter's play his final two seasons was enough to garner him All-American honorable mention accolades. His speed, football acumen, and the fact that he could play both in the offensive backfield and at left halfback on defense made him attractive to the pros. He was drafted as a first selection in the 1960 AFL draft by the Los Angeles Chargers and in the second round of that year's NFL draft by the Packers.

In fitting bits of irony, Evashevski was one of the people weighed by the Packers in 1959 as a replacement for coach Scooter McLean, a job that eventually was filled by Vince Lombardi. And Jeter's teammate, quarterback Randy Duncan, was Green Bay's first round pick in 1959, the first overall in the draft. However, Duncan signed instead with the Canadian Football League's BC Lions, returning to the U.S. in 1961 to play one year with the Dallas Texans of the American Football League.[9]

Like Duncan, Jeter signed with the CFL's team in Vancouver, British Columbia, where he stayed for two seasons. According to Jerry Kramer in *Distant Replay*, Jeter injured his ankle during his senior season and thought his draft chances were diminished, so he signed a three-year contract with the Canadian team. In a *Milwaukee Journal* article a couple of decades earlier, Jeter said his reason for going to Canada was because he thought he was physically "too small" to play in the NFL.[10]

The British Columbia Lions were a terrible team during Jeter's two year stay there. Bob gained 377 yards rushing and 470 yards receiv-

Bob Jeter.

ing in his time in BC. The Lions traded him to the Hamilton Tiger-Cats after the 1961 season. Jeter became involved in a contract dispute with his new club and wouldn't report for the third year of his CFL contract. The Tiger-Cats apparently withdrew from negotiations before the season started.[11]

Understandably disappointed and a little shocked, he went to Pittsburgh, where he was making his off-season home, and worked out informally with the Steelers that summer. Perhaps concerned about tampering with a contracted player from another team, Pittsburgh coach Buddy Parker told Jeter to call Lombardi to see if he might try out there, since the Packers held his NFL rights.[12]

Lombardi was willing to take Jeter on. He'd have to spend the 1962 season on the team's taxi squad, however. The NFL and CFL wanted to protect the integrity of their respective contracts and since Jeter was technically still on his three-year CFL deal, he'd have to sit out with Green Bay or report to Canada under terms agreeable to the Tiger-Cats.[13]

When Jeter finally was able to compete for a spot on Green Bay's active roster, the team was loaded at halfback with Paul Hornung, Tom Moore and Elijah Pitts in the stable. While he did show some defensive ability, the Packer coaching staff decided to try him at wide receiver but he did not display the catching skills necessary to compete with starters Boyd Dowler and Max McGee and eventually evolve into a starting wide receiver. He only caught two passes for 25 yards during the 1963 and 1964 regular seasons.[14]

When cornerback Jesse Whittenton retired before the 1965 season, Jeter and Doug Hart competed for Whittenton's starting spot in the defensive backfield, with Jeter winning the job and Hart set as a very able reserve. A pleased Jeter told a *Milwaukee Sentinel* reporter that it had been "a disappointment not being able to play here. I had been a regular in college and in Canada."[15]

Unfortunately, Jeter would have to wait a while longer because he suffered an injury in the exhibition season, and Hart played in the corner sport opposite Herb Adderley for all of the 1965 season until the championship game at Cleveland. There, Jeter replaced an injured Hart and ended up keeping the job for the next five seasons.[16]

If the previous six seasons of Jeter's pro career were somewhat rocky and mundane, the 1966 season was magical. In the 1966 season opener against the Baltimore Colts, Jeter picked off a Johnny Unitas pass and raced 46 yards for a score in a game in which the Packers trounced their number one competitor, 24–3.

What he didn't mention that day to the Milwaukee reporters was that Coach Lombardi had spoken to a very nervous Bob Jeter, a man making his first regular-season start against one of the finest quarterbacks to ever play the game. He talked about it almost two decades later, the night he was inducted into the Packers Hall of Fame, "Before the game Coach Lombardi saw me with my head down in the locker room. Knowing that I had to face the great Johnny Unitas and Raymond Berry. He said, 'Jeter, when you go out there today I want those 50,000 people in the stands and millions watching the game on television to leave saying they saw the best defensive back in the NFL today.' That really pumped me up."[17]

He intercepted a pass against the expansion-club Falcons, thrown by former Packers reserve quarterback Dennis Claridge, in a game on October 23, a blowout won by Green Bay, 56–3.

In early December, he intercepted a John Brodie pass and blocked a 37-yard field goal attempt by Tommy Davis when the Packers clinched the Western Conference by defeating the San Francisco 49ers, 20–7.[18]

Against the Rams, on December 18, in the season finale, Jeter, fittingly, picked off another pass and returned it for a touchdown. His 75-yard return of a Roman Gabriel pass was "Green Bay's sixth touchdown interception of the season, tying a team record set by Cleveland in 1960."

Jeter explained his 75-yarder, "They had completed a few in front of me ... then we had the blitz on ... so I could play it a little tighter. Otherwise I would have had to lay back, but I cut in front because of the pressure, and there was the ball."[19]

Jeter was still a stalwart defender after the 1966 season, garnering consensus All-Pro honors in 1967. He and Adderley were starting corners in the Pro Bowl after the 1967 season.[20] Jeter also made the Pro Bowl in 1969.

Willie Wood, the Packers' superlative safety, noted that Jeter, 30 years old at the time of his first all-pro award, had made a gradual and not always seamless transition from offense to defense, all things considered. "He was a late bloomer. We had a hell of a time to get him to think defensively."[21]

Things changed in 1971. Jeter and new Packers coach Dan Devine didn't see eye-to-eye about his conditioning, so Devine worked out a deal with Chicago. Jeter had worked in the Chicago parks system during the off-season since 1965; before that, Bob and his family lived in Pittsburgh. He was traded to the Bears that July along with a draft choice for Chicago running back Ross Montgomery. Montgomery balked at going to Green Bay and the Packers received an undisclosed draft choice instead.[22]

Jeter played his final three seasons with Chicago and retired after the 1973 season. He played long and well enough to intercept 26 passes, including three with Chicago, during his 11-year NFL career. He had played with two of pro football's most storied franchises. And most dear to him, were the years he spent with one of pro football's most successful and united teams. "Those were the best years of my life. This was a team. We were like brothers—all of us, black and white. We were that close."[23]

Jeter stayed in Chicago after retiring from the game. He worked for a distributor of beauty products. He also worked as a "warehouse planner" for Unilever Best Foods.[24] At one time, he tried his hand at small business. He ran a small store and gas station operation in Chicago. He gave it up after he was robbed a few times, the last thief "stuck a gun in his stomach," ordered him to the back of the place and cleaned the till of its contents.[25]

Jeter was inducted into the West Virginia Sports Hall of Fame in 1980 and the Green Bay Packers Hall of Fame in 1985. He died of a heart attack on November 20, 2008, and was survived by his wife and two sons, Rob and Carlton. The Jeters also raised several foster children. As of 2015, Rob is the head basketball coach at the University of Wisconsin–Milwaukee.

Rob Jeter joked that his father operated on "Lombardi time" during his lifetime, being 15 minutes or so ahead of time for any and all appointments, gatherings or whatnot. He noted that his father was proud of his days with the Packers and that he wore his Super Bowl I and Super Bowl II rings all the time. "He'd switch off. He'd wear one one day, then the other the next. My father learned from Lombardi to give your best and he passed that on to me. It was all about competing. It really irritated him if you didn't go hard, compete, and accept the challenge. If you were nonchalant or didn't go at it hard enough it really bothered him. He told me that when he first came to the Packers, he was a wide receiver. And my father was fast. So in practice one day Bart Starr throws a pass that my father thought he could catch up to but didn't—didn't go all out—and Lombardi came running down the field and got in his face. He told him you won't last in Green Bay if you don't play to the best of your ability."[26]

A late-bloomer on the defensive side of the line of scrimmage, Bob Jeter did indeed give his demanding coach the best of his ability from that point forward, none more so than in 1966 and 1967, and he had the rings to prove it.

NOTES

1. "Robert Jeter," *Milwaukee Journal Sentinel*, Jsonline.com, December 4, 2009, accessed July 31, 2014, www.jsonline.com.

2. "Northern Panhandle," The West Virginia Encyclopedia, Wvencyclopedia.com, accessed October 20, 2014, www.wvencyclopedia.org/articles/1700.

3. Ralph Cox, "Jeter, a Great Person, Athlete," Heraldstaronline.com, December 4, 2008, accessed October 20, 2014,www.heraldstaronline.com/page/content.detail/id/512689.html?nav=5013#sthash.waEumBGP.

4. *Ibid.*

5. *Daily Iowan*, September 27, 1958.

6. *Ibid.*; *Daily Iowan*, September 4, 1959.

7. *Daily Iowan*, May 23, 1959.

8. *Ibid.*

9. "1959nflplayerdraft," Databasefootball.com, accessed 10/20/2014, www.databasefootball.com/draft/draftyear.htm?yr=1959&lg=NFL; Bud Lea, "Packer Insider How Does 'Evashevski Trophy' Sound?" *Milwaukee Journal Sentinel*, Jsonline.com, March 18, 2009, accessed November 3, 2014, www.jsonline.com/packerinsider/41390857.html.

10. Jerry Kramer and Dick Schaap, *Distant Replay* (New York: G.P. Putnam's Sons, 1985), 166–167; *Milwaukee Journal*, October 11, 1967.

11. Jerry Kramer and Dick Schaap, *Distant Replay* (New York: G.P. Putnam's Sons, 1985), 166–167; *Milwaukee Journal*, October 11, 1967.

12. *Ibid.*, 167.

13. *Milwaukee Journal*, October 11, 1967.

14. "Bob Jeter, 71: Football Star for Iowa Hawkeyes, Green Bay Packers," *Los Angeles Times*, www.latimes.com, accessed July 31, 2014,www.latimes.com/local/obituaries/la-me-jeter-obit23–2008nov23-story.html.

15. Bud Lea, "Jeter Scoots on Defense," *Milwaukee Sentinel*, August 10, 1965.

16. *Milwaukee Journal*, October 11, 1967.

17. Bud Lea, "Jeter Warmed by Return to Packer Spotlight," *Milwaukee Sentinel*, February 4, 1985.

18. *Milwaukee Journal*, October 24, 1966, December 5, 1966.

19. *Milwaukee Journal*, December 19, 1966.

20. Cliff Christl, "Packers Flashback: What Happened to Bob Jeter?" *Milwaukee Journal Sentinel*, November 13, 2002.

21. Kramer, 167.

22. *Milwaukee Sentinel*, July 26, 1971, May 24, 1983.

23. Lea, "Jeter Warmed by Return to Packer Spotlight."

24. Cox, "Jeter"; Kramer, 168; Christl, "Packer: What Happened to Bob Jeter?"

25. *Milwaukee Sentinel*, February 4, 1985.

26. Rob Jeter phone interview with author, November 21, 2014.

Henry Jordan

JOHN MAXYMUK

Remembering Hall of Famer Henry Jordan, teammate Dave Robinson joked, "He always said he wanted to room with [Bart] Starr because when the Packers hit town they'd call Starr's room, Henry would answer and get his name in the paper."[1] Indeed, Jordan was popular with the media because he was one of the leading quipsters on the team. Many of his lines are still familiar today. "[Lombardi] treats us all the same. Like dogs." Or "I play for the love of the game, the love of the money and the fear of Lombardi." Or "When [Lombardi] says, 'Sit down,' I don't look for a chair." Beyond the funny lines, though, was an intelligent man and one of the finest defensive tackles of his time, an essential player on the champion Packer teams of the 1960s.

Henry Wendell Jordan was born on January 26, 1935, at Emporia, Virginia. He was the son of a railroad car inspector and one of six children, four boys and two girls. His family moved to Newport News when Henry was six. When Henry matriculated at Warwick High School, he was 6'2", 230 pounds—just 10–15 pounds below his future NFL playing weight. However, his father was reluctant to let Jordan play football because he had "baby bones." Eventually, though, Henry lettered in three sports: football, track and wrestling. In football, he was a two-way tackle who was named All-State as a senior. In track, he put the shot and held the school record for the high hurdles. Wrestling was probably his best sport, though, and he was state champion in his junior year.

Jordan also excelled in academics as well as being class president for his freshman, sophomore and junior years. He graduated high school in 1953 and won an athletic scholarship to the University of Virginia. At UVA, he continued in the same three sports while earning a degree in commerce, making the dean's list and serving as vice president of his graduating class. As a senior, he was team captain of the football team and was named All-Atlantic Coast Conference. His wrestling prowess outshone his football exploits, however. In 1957, Henry went to the NCAA finals in the heavyweight division where he lost to Bob Norman of Illinois. He was named the University of Virginia Athlete of the Year in 1956–57.

Henry was drafted by the Cleveland Browns in the fifth round of the 1957 NFL draft, ironically with a pick Cleveland had obtained from the Packers for journeymen Don King and Gene Donaldson. Jordan was good enough to make the team, but could not fit into Paul Brown's scheme. Brown tried him at offensive tackle and guard as well as defensive tackle and end over the next two seasons, but Henry could not find a niche. Chuck Noll later told Murray Olderman for *The Defenders*, "In the old days a tackle would parallel and read. Henry Jordan couldn't make the Cleveland Browns when he started as a pro because he didn't have the ability to stay put and parallel and read like Bob Gain or Don Colo. But when he was traded and turned loose in the Green Bay Packers defense, he became an All-Pro tackle."[2] Jordan told Chuck Johnson for *The Greatest Packers of Them All* of a time when he slipped past Giants All-Pro tackle Rosey Brown to sack quarterback Charlie Conerly and was immediately benched by Brown because he had ignored his outside responsibility on the play.[3]

Henry Jordan.

When Vince Lombardi arrived in Green Bay in 1959, it was clear the defensive line was a real weak point on the team. So Lombardi shored it up with a pair of savvy deals with Cleveland. First, he snagged defensive end Bill Quinlan and versatile halfback Lew Carpenter for star receiver Billy Howton. Brown also offered Vince his choice of Jordan or defensive tackle Floyd Peters for a fifth round draft pick. Lombardi chose Henry and would never regret his choice. Len Wagner's *Launching the Glory Years: The 1959 Packers—What They Didn't Tell Us* quotes extensively from the player assessments each assistant coach handed in to Lombardi after 1959. All four assistants praised Jordan, with one summing up, "Likes to play the game and does a good job on the rush and very well on pursuit."[4] Pursuit was a particular point of emphasis of Lombardi.

Jordan was essentially set free in Green Bay. He told the *Milwaukee Journal*, "Coach Phil [Bengtson] told me, 'If you have any hunches, play them.' The coaches would give us the overall picture of the defense, then it was up to us to use our own techniques." Bengtson said of Jordan, "He's quick and strong. Henry isn't very big, but with a man like that, as has always been the case, he makes up for it in some other way."[5] Henry added to Chuck Johnson, "Coach Phil has told us that he expects us to get blocked on every play, but he doesn't expect us to stay blocked. Defensive tackle is no longer a position for just a big, strong football player. It has developed into a game of playing keys."[6]

Jordan began to draw national recognition in 1960 when he was a consensus All-Pro, being named to the first team of the AP, UPI and the *New York Daily News* (NYDN), with a second team notice from the Newspaper Enterprises Association (NEA). He would follow that up with three more years as a consensus All-Pro: in 1961 with first team notice with AP, UPI, NYDN, NEA and *The Sporting News*; in 1962 with first team notice from AP and SN and second team from NEA and UPI; and 1963 with first team notice from all five organizations. Beginning in 1964, Bob Lilly and Merlin Olsen began to dominate the All-Pro ratings for defensive tackle, but Henry still managed first team notices from AP, UPI and NYDN that year despite missing two games with injuries. He also drew second team notices in 1966 from AP, UPI and NYDN and in 1967 from NYDN.

During training camp in 1963, Lombardi experimented with moving Henry from right defensive tackle to right defensive end to replace the traded Bill Quinlan. With the development of rookie end Lionel Aldridge, that change was rendered unnecessary. Jordan was pleased. He once remarked to the *Milwaukee Journal*, "Coach Lombardi does very little substituting. He believes you should have pride in your position. I'm the right defensive tackle. I'm not supposed to get tired. I've played left tackle and I always feel as if I'm in left field. Everything is different there—the view, the angles."[7]

Lombardi assessed Henry in *Run to Daylight*. "He has a tendency to be satisfied, though, which is why I don't flatter him much and why often, when we're reviewing the pictures, I make him a target. Sometimes you will make a man a target to impress somebody else who can't accept public criticism, but I will call Hank because we both know his ability and know that I'm on him to bring it out and because he performs best when he's just a little upset."[8] For his part, Jordan told Jerry Kramer for *Lombardi*, "I guess it helped the team, but it didn't help me much. His yelling didn't motivate me. It just made me mad."[9]

Because Jordan was dwarfed by many of the larger star defensive tackles of his time, he used his speed, quickness and agility to knife past offensive linemen. His wrestling background made him an expert at finding and using leverage to get past bigger men. He would shoot any gap he could find.

On the eve of the 1965 championship game, Browns Coach Blanton Collier noted,

"Fellows like Henry Jordan and Willie Davis use that quickness and mobility to get the job done."[10] Linemate Willie Davis concurred in Vern Biever's *The Glory of Titletown*, "Jordan had the good quickness as an inside rusher, but he very seldom overpowered someone. He would just kind of slither through a crack or, almost off a movement of quickness, he was able to penetrate. He was very slender, and he could take a seam and split two offensive linemen.... He had very big and strong legs, and I think once he was able to split two guys, he was able to really power his way between them."[11]

In the biggest games, Henry made some of his best plays. In the 1961 championship game, he tipped a pass into the arms of Ray Nitschke whose interception led to the Packers' second touchdown that day. In the 1965 NFL title game, he blocked a field goal attempt by Lou Groza in the third quarter. He had a sack of Don Meredith in the 1966 NFL championship, and in Super Bowl I he had 1.5 sacks of Len Dawson and tipped a Dawson pass that Willie Wood intercepted in the third quarter, leading to the touchdown that put the game out of reach.

While Jordan had three tackles, including one for a loss, and two assists in the Ice Bowl, his most memorable game came the week before in the 1967 divisional playoff against the Rams. Henry was in the Los Angeles backfield all day, shooting past All-Pro guard Tom Mack for 3.5 sacks of massive Ram quarterback Roman Gabriel. Jordan once joked about the Rams, "They're a good team and their quarterback is bigger than I am."[12] On this day, he joked that he had extra motivation, "This was a money game, I'm broke, and I have an expensive wife."[13]

By 1966, Lombardi began substituting young linemen Bob Brown and Jim Weatherwax in more frequently with Henry and Willie Davis in their 30s. Jordan battled back problems for years and began to seriously decline in 1968. The following season, he only played in five games before hurting his hip and being dropped from the active roster. Both he and Davis retired at the end of the year. Henry lamented, "If I could, I would play another five years, but this year the pain was more acute than ever."[14]

In retirement, Jordan was named executive director of Summerfest, an annual Milwaukee festival that was hemorrhaging money and was deep in debt. Over the next few years, he remade Summerfest into a popular and financially-successful institution. The one blip under his leadership was the arrest of comedian George Carlin at the 1972 Summerfest for disorderly conduct due to Carlin performing his blue Seven Words You Can't Say on Television routine; six months later, all charges against Carlin were dismissed.

On February 21, 1977, the 42-year-old Jordan was working out at the Milwaukee Athletic Club when he collapsed from a heart attack. All efforts to revive him were unsuccessful. Just as Henry's teammates had begun to be elected to the Hall of Fame, he was the first of Lombardi's stars to die. He had been elected to the Virginia Hall of Fame in 1974 and the Packer Hall of Fame in 1975, but his posthumous selection for the Pro Football Hall of Fame had to wait another 18 years till 1995. At his induction his remarried widow, Olive, recalled her husband, "He would have loved this. He loved an audience. He was a people person. It didn't make any difference where you were in the social register; he enjoyed everybody. He would sit and have coffee with the women who cooked for him at the training camp at St. Norbert's or he would be equally happy talking to President Nixon."[15]

Henry Jordan lives on in many ways. First, of course are his three children and several grandchildren. In addition, the Henry Jordan Memorial Scholarship was established in 1985 to honor a high achieving Warwick High School senior. In 1995, Warwick High retired his number 49 and four years later named its new athletic field Henry W. Jordan

Field. Packer fans remember a good man, smart and witty, who was the best defensive tackle of the first half of the 1960s.

NOTES

1. Bud Lea, "Fun Loving Jordan Deserved Hall Niche," *Milwaukee Sentinel*, January 30, 1995.
2. Murray Olderman, *The Defenders* (Englewood Cliffs, NJ: Prentice-Hall, 1973), 298.
3. Chuck Johnson, *The Greatest Packers of Them All* (New York: G. P. Putnam's Sons, 1968), 133–41.
4. Len Wagner, *Launching the Glory Years: The 1959 Packers—What They Didn't Tell Us* (Green Bay: Coach's Books, 2001), 49.
5. Chuck Johnson, "Jordan Is Not a Big Tackle, but Quick," *Milwaukee Journal*, January 7, 1962.
6. Chuck Johnson, "Tackle Can't Stay Blocked," *Milwaukee Journal*, October 2, 1966.
7. Chuck Johnson, "Packers Jordan Tells of Struggle to Reknit a Team," *Milwaukee Journal*, April 2, 1966.
8. Vince Lombardi with W.C. Heinz, *Run to Daylight* (Englewood Cliffs, NJ: Prentice-Hall, 1963), 43.
9. Jerry Kramer, *Lombardi: Winning Is the Only Thing* (New York: World Publishing, 1970), 119–120.
10. "Browns Respect Packers," *Nashua Telegraph*, December 28, 1965.
11. Vernon J. Biever, *The Glory of Titletown,* ed. Peter Strupp (Dallas: Taylor Trade, 1997), 95.
12. Terry Bledsoe, "Couldn't Run, So Rams Never Could Control Ball," *Milwaukee Journal*, September 26, 1966.
13. "Packers Improving with Age—Lombardi," *Daytona Beach Morning Journal*, December 25, 1967.
14. Terry Bledsoe, "Jordan's Career Might End Sunday, Too," *Milwaukee Journal*, December 18, 1969.
15. "It's a Shame He Missed the Party," *Spokesman-Review*, July 29, 1995.

REFERENCES

Anderson, Dave. "A Packer in Pursuit of Football Fish." *Sport*, December 1964.
Biever, Vern, with Peter Strupp. *The Glory of Titletown*. Dallas: Taylor Trade, 1997.
Bledsoe, Terry. "Couldn't Run, So Rams Never Could Control Ball." *Milwaukee Journal*, September 26, 1966.
_____. "Jordan's Career Might End Sunday, Too." *Milwaukee Journal*, December 18, 1969.
"Browns Respect Packers." *Nashua Telegraph*, December 28, 1965.
"It's a Shame He Missed the Party." *Spokesman-Review*, July 29, 1995.
Johnson, Chuck. "Jordan Is Not a Big Tackle, But Quick." *Milwaukee Journal*, January 7, 1962.
_____. "Packers Jordan Tells of Struggle to Reknit a Team." *Milwaukee Journal*, April 2, 1966.
_____. "Tackle Can't Stay Blocked." *Milwaukee Journal*, October 2, 1966.
_____. *The Greatest Packers of Them All*. New York: Putnam, 1968.
Kramer, Jerry. *Lombardi: Winning Is the Only Thing*. New York: World Publishing, 1970.
Lea, Bud. "Fun Loving Jordan Deserved Hall Niche." *Milwaukee Sentinel*, January 30, 1995.
Lombardi, Vince, with W.C. Heinz. *Run to Daylight*. Englewood Cliffs, NJ: Prentice-Hall, 1963.
Olderman, Murray. *The Defenders*. Englewood Cliffs, NJ: Prentice-Hall, 1973.
"Packers Improving with Age—Lombardi." *Daytona Beach Morning Journal*, December 25, 1967.
Wagner, Len. *Launching the Glory Years: The 1959 Packers—What They Didn't Tell Us*. Green Bay: Coach's Books, 2001.

Ron Kostelnik

JAY ZAHN

Was Ron Kostelnik the least known of the 22 Packers who started the first Super Bowl? Teammate Jerry Kramer thought so.[1] Running back Elijah Pitts was a starter for fewer seasons, but had a colorful name and played a more glamorous position. Safety Tom Brown played major league baseball and made the big interception to nail down the 1966 NFL championship. Even fellow Polish-American Bob Skoronski was a team captain and played in a Pro Bowl.

Along with Lionel Aldridge, Dave Robinson, Lee Roy Caffey, Bob Jeter, and Tom Brown, Kostelnik was part of a second wave of Packer defenders that reinvigorated the defense after the championships of 1961 and 1962. That defense would be needed as the vaunted ground game of Taylor and Hornung began to lose steam due to age and injury.

Ronald Michael Kostelnik was born January 14, 1940, in Colver, Pennsylvania, a small town about 75 miles east of Pittsburgh. His parents were Mickey and Julie Kostelnik; Mickey was a coal miner. Ron didn't play organized athletics until high school, and didn't do that until Central Cambria head football coach Jim Cook spotted Ron in a physical education class. Coach Cook had to drive out to Colver from Ebensburg, where Central Cambria High School is located, to convince Ron's parents to let him give high school football a try.

Ron's career might have ended in high school but for a twist of fate. Ron got only two scholarship offers, a half scholarship from Shippensburg State Teachers, and a full one from the University of Cincinnati when UC staff spotted him in game film they were reviewing of an offensive lineman from neighboring Greater Johnson High School.

For a third time, Ron's football career almost came to a halt at Cincinnati when he tore his ACL and MCL his sophomore year. He successfully rehabilitated his injury by running the stadium steps and local country roads. Ron also worked on his academic performance by attending summer school to retain his scholarship; this paid an extra dividend when he met his future wife Peggy Fey in a music appreciation class.

His knee healed and by 1960 Ron made second team All-Missouri Valley Conference at tackle and honorable mention All-American. He capped off his college career by appearing in the North-South Shrine game in Miami and was named the game's outstanding lineman.

Due to his injury, Ron played only 20 varsity games at Cincinnati, but that didn't deter the Packers from drafting him in the second round of the 1961 draft. Ron was only 20 years old at the time, and thus his contract needed to be co-signed by his mother Julie. Ron signed for an $8,750 salary and $750 bonus; the bonus was used to buy an engagement ring for his fiancée Peggy.

Upon drafting Kostelnik, his new coach Vince Lombardi hyped up his draftee. "He's a mad Russian [sic], you've got to spoon-feed him with a steam shovel," Lombardi said at the time. "A big man who has excellent pursuit and is a good pass rusher, and he's still growing."[2]

Not all of Ron's teammates were sure he would even make the team. "I was absolutely convinced he wasn't going to make the cut," said Jerry Kramer. "Thought he had no shot. He was a little cherubic and didn't have a great deal of speed. But I couldn't measure his heart."[3]

Ron's first training camp with the Packers would give him first-hand experience with Lombardi's hard driving style, including his punishing grass drill. Later in his life, Ron reflected on his training. "You wanted to lay there and smell the grass for a minute or two, catch your breath and rest. But you had to jump back up and keep going and the only thing making you get back up again was that guy next to you, your teammate, was jumping up and doing another one too."[4]

Kostelnik injured his knee the second day of training camp in 1961, but the injury only kept him out a week. He had competition from 1960 backup John Miller and fellow rookie Jim Brewington. But Kostelnik took instruction on his "moves" from established starters Henry Jordan and Dave Hanner, and both Miller and Brewington were cut by the end of August.

As a Lombardi rookie, Kostelnik didn't figure to see much playing time behind Hanner and Jordan. But when Hanner underwent an appendectomy on September 19, Kostelnik got the first start of his career against the 49ers September 24. Kostelnik and the Packers' defense performed well against the 49ers and Head Coach Red Hickey's Shotgun offense, holding the 49ers to 233 yards and ten points in a 30–10 Packers victory. Kostelnik stayed in the lineup for the Packers' next game as well, a 24–0 shutout of the Bears.

Kostelnik continued to back up the Packers' defensive tackles and ends in 1962, despite being slowed by a dislocated shoulder suffered in a preseason game against the Bears. The shoulder was corrected with offseason surgery, though Kostelnik wore a shoulder harness in 1963. In 1963, he was also hampered by a broken wrist suffered early in training camp.

By 1964, Kostelnik was in his fourth season, and still waiting to break into the lineup. Moreover, giant 1964 first round draft pick Lloyd Voss loomed behind him. Ironically, it took an injury to Henry Jordan, not the older Hanner, to give Kostelnik his gateway to the starting lineup.

Jordan went out of the Packers' opening game against the Bears with a leg injury, and Kostelnik replaced him. Jordan later sat out with leg and groin injuries against the Lions and 49ers, both Packer victories. With Lombardi praising Kostelnik's work against the 49ers in particular, it was Hanner and not Kostelnik who was sent to the bench when Jordan recovered.

Kostelnik didn't waste any time becoming a productive part of the Packers' defense. That defense became much more active in the second half of the 1964 season, coming up with almost twice as many turnovers as the first half of the season (27 to 14). Those turnovers helped the 1964 Packers to a 5–1–1 second half after a 3–4 start.

Dave Hanner retired in 1965, leaving Kostelnik as a firmly entrenched starter. Early in the season, Kostelnik reflected on what had led to his breakthrough as a starter. "Experience is the answer—I played a lot last year and didn't get hurt. Playing between two all-pros [Davis and Jordan] and having another behind me in Nitschke, how can I go wrong? If I make a mistake, they cover for me. Dave's [Hanner] my roommate, you know. He can analyze a player a lot better than I can. That's where he helps me—he teaches me what to look for and that sort of thing."[5]

The Packers' offense was in a state of transition in 1965, with replacements and shuffled personnel at several positions due to injuries

Ron Kostelnik.

and age. After a 5–0 start, the offense endured a severe slump, averaging only 132 yards gained over the next four contests. To remain in the championship chase, the Packers' defense would have to carry more than its share of the load. Ron Kostelnik and the defense responded.

On October 24, the Packers beat the Cowboys in a classic defensive struggle that saw both teams wind up with negative passing yardage, due to 14 sacks (9 by the Packers.) Despite being outgained 191–63 in yards, the Packers won 13–3 due to five turnovers created by the defense. Kostelnik came up with his own when he pounced on a Craig Morton fumble at the Green Bay 19 in the fourth quarter. "I think our defense played a helluva game," Kostelnik said. "Each one of us took a turn at making the big play."[6]

On November 14, a big play by Kostelnik helped the Packers beat the Rams 6–3 and end a two-game losing streak. Kostelnik hit Bill Munson and forced a fumble, recovered by Lionel Aldridge, that led to the winning Don Chandler field goal. "I don't think he ever saw me coming," Kostelnik said at the time. "I circled around the center, and I came in at Munson at such a steep angle that he couldn't see me. I didn't grab his arm or anything. I just grabbed him—but after I saw the ball pop loose I sort of threw him away from it. I was trying to crawl toward it myself, but Aldridge got there first."[7]

After narrowly winning the Western Conference with an overtime playoff victory over the Baltimore Colts, the Packers won the 1965 NFL championship with a convincing 23–12 win over the defending champion Cleveland Browns. The defense more than held its own in the game, coming up with several key stops and holding Jim Brown to 50 yards rushing in his final game. Kostelnik did his part, stopping Brown for a one-yard loss on a key third-and-two play at the Browns' 47 in the second quarter.

One highlight for Kostelnik and the rest of the Packers' defensive line in 1966 was when they sacked Roman Gabriel eight times for 57 yards in a 24–13 Packer victory over the Rams on September 25. Vince Lombardi came out with special praise for Kostelnik and teammate Henry Jordan after the game. "The two [of them] were all over the place and it wasn't unusual to see Kostelnik making tackles near the sidelines," Lombardi said.[8]

A week later Kostelnik recovered a fumble by Amos Marsh of the Lions. "It was a draw play and I could see Marsh going to the outside. I got my arms around him but he slipped out. I got up again and Henry Jordan came up and really cleaned out his clock. I could see the ball—it was laying there in the open, behind Davis who didn't see it, and I went for it. It got me out of a hole, after missing the tackle. I lose a couple of points when I miss a tackle, but I get 'em back when I recover a fumble."[9] The fumble recovery set up a Don Chandler field goal in a 23–14 Packer victory.

An unusual sight later in the season saw Kostelnik dropping into pass coverage and knocking away a pass intended for Minnesota's Phil King. "That's part of our defense and we often have the ends [sic] go down with the receiver," said Vince Lombardi about the play.[10]

Despite these highlights, Kostelnik wasn't satisfied with his level of play. "I definitely haven't been having a good year—not nearly as good a year as I had last year. I've had a few problems. Up to this point, I'm not as satisfied as I was last year. I had a bad start this season. It's nothing specific, but I just haven't been playing as well as I felt I could be."[11]

Kostelnik went on to discuss his tactics as a defensive lineman. "I rely more on strength, I'm not quick enough to be as evasive as Henry [Jordan] can be. I have to play exactly the way my keys tell me. Henry's so quick he can afford to gamble a little more. We both follow the defensive pattern, but we often work out things together. On certain plays, for example, I'll hang back for a draw or a screen, and let Henry be the primary rusher."[12]

After the Packers won the West again in 1966, Kostelnik was a big part of their 34–27 victory over the Dallas Cowboys in the NFL championship game, being in on 14 tackles. In the first Super Bowl, he had three tackles in the second half, and collaborated on a sack of Len Dawson with Henry Jordan as the Packers pulled away to a 35–10 victory.

By 1967 Kostelnik was becoming a seasoned veteran, entering his fourth season as a starter. That experience would pay off when the Packers made their playoff run towards their third straight championship. Before the famous Ice Bowl game against Dallas, Kostelnik had some advice for Jerry Kramer. "With this cold it's gonna hamper us on defense. We won't be able to grab, to use our hands too well. You won't have to be afraid of popping people, Jerry. They won't be able to throw you with their hands," he said.[13]

Beyond advice, Kostelnik made his own on-field contributions. He combined with Henry Jordan for a sack in the Western Conference championship game against the Rams. In the Ice Bowl, he was in on tackles of Cowboys runners for no gain or a loss on four separate occasions. In Super Bowl II, he made a key block of Oakland's Gene Upshaw on Herb Adderley's interception return for a touchdown that capped off Vince Lombardi's final win as Packer coach.

In 1968, injuries caught up to Ron Kostelnik. Knee and ankle injuries took a toll on his performance. As he had at Cincinnati, Kostelnik worked hard to recover from his injuries in the offseason. But he faced a new challenge as the Packers drafted Villanova's Rich Moore, a defensive tackle, in the first round of the 1969 draft. After sitting out a preseason game against the Bears, Kostelnik was traded to the Baltimore Colts for what would be a fourth round draft choice in the 1970 NFL draft.

Kostelnik spent the 1969 season backing up Fred Miller and Billy Ray Smith in Baltimore, and got into only ten games, primarily on goal line stands. On August 4, 1970, Ron Kostelnik retired from the Colts and professional football.

Ron did well for himself in life after football. While he was still active, he completed his master's degree in education at Cincinnati. Ron and his family (he and Peggy eventually had a son and three daughters) settled in Wisconsin year round during his career.

During the football off-seasons, Ron began working at Mainline Industrial Distributors in Appleton, Wisconsin, doing public relations and sales. After his football career ended, he purchased Mainline. The company prospered under his leadership, growing from less than a million dollars of gross revenue to nine branches and over $18 million 14 years later.

Ron Kostelnik was never named All-Pro or selected for a Pro Bowl, but he was honored for his football playing after his career. He was selected to the Cambria County Sports Hall of Fame, the University of Cincinnati Hall of Fame, and in 1989 the Green Bay Packer Hall of Fame. With his daughter Laura, Ron prepared a speech for the latter honor and reflected back on football. "What do I miss about the game of football? My shoulders ache for the feeling of that last thrust as I go for the quarterback sack. I also miss the chess game. To me, the chess game is the mental contest that is played in the split second when the ball is snapped and that offensive man is coming towards you. You move towards him, and he looks at you and whole battles are fought in those few seconds…. I also miss the singleness of purpose that we develop as members of the Packers. The only thing we lived for was to play for the Green Bay Packers and to win football games. How simple that life seems to me now. Each week we practiced for a football game and our goal was to win. By Sunday night we knew whether we had achieved our goal or not, and we moved on. Unfortunately, life after football involves goals that are more complex and accomplishments not as immediate."[14]

Like many players, Ron struggled with his weight after his playing career, often topping 300 pounds. On January 30, 1993, while driving home from a Florida vacation with his wife Peggy, Ron suffered a heart attack while on I-75 and lost control of his car. The car overturned several times and Ron was pronounced dead at the scene. He was 53 years old. His wife Peggy suffered only minor injuries in the accident.

Ron Kostelnik did not receive individual honors during his career and was not a flashy player. But the defenses he was a part of were outstanding. In each of his five seasons as a starter (1964 through 1968), the Packers led the NFL in fewest passing yards allowed, a critical advantage for a team that was often protecting leads. Since coaches Lombardi and Bengtson did not like to blitz often, it was crucial that the defensive linemen pressured the quarterback sufficiently to allow the linebackers to concentrate on pass coverage. Each of the linemen had their own responsibilities in the defensive line, and his teammates recognized Ron's abilities.

Jerry Kramer, Ron's daily opponent in practice, put it best: "It wasn't glamorous work. There aren't statistics for steady dependable guys who plug up the middle and allow other guys to excel. But that's what Ron did. Henry and Willie and Lionel were able to rush the passer and freelance because Ron was in the middle doing the dirty work."[15]

NOTES

1. Jerry Kramer and Dick Schaap, *Distant Replay* (New York: G. P. Putman's Sons, 1985), 78.

2. Art Daley, "Packers Snare 'Big Three' in NFL Draft, Adderley, Kostelnik Nugent Give Needed Speed, Defensive Aid," *Green Bay Press-Gazette*, December 28, 1960.

3. Martin Hendricks, "Packer Plus: Kostelnik Got the Job Done Without a Fuss," Jsonline.com, November 20, 2012, www.jsonline.com.

4. Laura Biskupic, "Walk 100 Yards in These NFL Cleats," Mollybandme.com, January 29, 2014, www.mollybandme.com.

5. Lee Remmel, "Personality Parade," *Green Bay Press-Gazette*, September 15, 1965.

6. Mike Christopulos, "Vince Says: 'Defense Was Tremendous,'" *Milwaukee Sentinel*, October 25, 1965.

7. Terry Bledsoe, "Kostelnik Took Munson by Surprise," *Milwaukee Journal*, November 15, 1965.

8. Art Daley, "Packer Defense 'Almost Flawless,' Lombardi," *Green Bay Press-Gazette*, September 27, 1966.

9. Lee Remmel, "Defense Sparks Packers Past Detroit, 23 to 14—Wind Was Baffling, Chandler," *Green Bay Press-Gazette*, October 3, 1966.

10. Art Daley, "Vince Breaks Rule: 'Davis Played Outstanding Game,'" *Green Bay Press-Gazette*, November 29, 1966.

11. Lee Remmel, "Personality Parade," *Green Bay Press-Gazette*, November 23, 1966.

12. *Ibid.*

13. Lee Remmel, "Personality Parade, Kos Finally Feels Better," *Green Bay Press-Gazette*, November 20, 1968.

14. Laura Biskupic, "Hall of Fame Induction Speech Take Two," Mollybandme.com, February 27, 2012, www.mollybandme.com.

15. Martin Hendricks, "Packer Plus: Kostelnik Got the Job Done Without a Fuss," jsonline.com, November 20, 2012,www.jsonline.com.

Jerry Kramer

Kenneth R. Crippen

Jerry Kramer is arguably one of the best offensive guards in NFL history. The three-time Pro Bowler was named to the NFL's All-Decade team of the 1960s, the Green Bay Packer Hall of Fame and the NFL's 50th Anniversary Team. In his 11-year career with the Packers, the team won five NFL championships.

Born Gerald Louis "Jerry" Kramer on January 23, 1936, in Jordan, Montana, Kramer was the fourth of six children. While growing up, Kramer's family moved several times. At the age of six, they moved from Jordan to Salt Lake City. Six months later, they moved to Layton, Utah. In 1945, they moved to Sandpoint, Idaho, where he stayed until he left for college.[1]

According to Kramer in his book Jerry Kramer's *Farewell to Football*, he recalled, "The more I look back, the more it strikes me I had an almost perfect childhood, a good blend of fun and strictness and learning and hard work, not a thing that would ever hurt me."[2]

Kramer started playing football in the seventh grade. In high school, he went out for the freshman team. He recalled, "I played end on the freshman team, and I caught a grand total of one pass all year, a pass that somebody else deflected. The ball wobbled in the air and I caught it for a one-yard gain."[3]

The following year, Kramer made the varsity squad and played tackle.[4]

During his senior year in high school, several colleges were interested in him. His decision came down to Idaho, Washington, and Washington State. He chose Idaho to play for Coach Skip Staley. His sophomore season, he made the varsity squad. In his senior year, Kramer made second-team All-Pacific Coast Conference at guard.[5]

Kramer was taken 39th overall in the 1958 NFL draft by the Green Bay Packers. Kramer remembered an encounter with a former Packer lineman. "My line coach at the College All-Star game was John Sandusky, who had played in Green Bay [in 1956]. He took me aside in Chicago and said, 'Jerry, you probably won't make that Green Bay team. They have five returning guards. They had a couple injured last year and they picked up a couple of extra guys. Don't get discouraged. I think that you can play. You will probably play somewhere, but I don't expect it to be Green Bay. I think that you will get traded.' So, I went to Green Bay with that attitude and I accepted that."[6]

Kramer continued, "Scooter McLean was their coach, and Scooter called me in one day. I had been there about ten days. He said, 'What the hell is wrong with you?' I said, 'What are you talking about, coach?' He said, 'One day you look great. You run well. You move well. The next day you are looking over to the bench like you are checking the girls out and not paying attention.' I said, 'I was waiting to be traded.' He said, 'You're what?' I said, 'Well, John Sandusky said that I was going to be traded when we were at the College All-Star game. So, I was just kinda waiting for the trade.' He said, 'Well, I didn't draft you to trade you. You are starting Friday night.' This was like Wednesday, or something like that. I had a pretty good game."[7]

The 1958 season was a year before coach Vince Lombardi arrived. According to Kramer, "It was a hell of a lot more fun, initially. There were very few conditioning exercises. There were very few curfews. We had a very good time and enjoyed being a professional football player."[8]

However, the fun did not last. According to Kramer, "Toward the middle of the season, it became a little uncomfortable around town. We got beat by Baltimore 56–0 [November 2]. In Baltimore. Rainy day. It started early in the morning and lasted throughout the game. In the fourth quarter, we get across midfield on a scramble by our quarterback named Joe Francis. We moved down across the 35 [yard line]. All of a sudden, this roar erupts throughout the stadium. A roar of 'Hold 'em…. Hold 'em.' They really held us at that point. They scored on us again. It started to get so uncomfortable around town that we started to have our parties after the game in the locker room. Being 1–10–1 didn't leave much of a taste in your mouth."[9]

Kramer continued, "Winning was something I had experienced occasionally in college. I think my best year was a .500 season. That was the best year the university had in 29 years. [Paul] Hornung came from a 3–7 [sic] Notre Dame team. Bart came off an Alabama team that hadn't won a game his senior year and he was third string on that team. By and large, we didn't have guys that experienced and expected to win."[10]

After going 1–10–1 in the 1958 season, Coach McLean was gone and Lombardi was in. According to Kramer, he did not know much about Lombardi before he arrived. "I had heard that the only head coaching job that he had was high school. He had been an assistant with the Giants. But, I did not hear much more than that. I thought that the Packer board [of directors] had just made the biggest blunder ever by not bringing Curley [Lambeau] back."[11]

Kramer learned quickly about Lombardi's coaching style and temperament. "I remember meeting him for the first time. Joe Francis and I drove back from Wisconsin together. He was a west coast guy. Rookies reported three days early to training camp. Joe and I thought we would get some golf in and have a good time. We are standing in the Packer offices and we are arguing with Jack Vainisi about the dormitory. 'Jack, you need to open the dorm. We need a place to stay.' He replied, 'They do not open up until tomorrow.' Then, this short, full-head of hair guy walks by and said, 'What the hell is going on?' Jack said, 'They need a place to stay…' Lombardi interrupted, 'Rawwawwwrr,' and he turns and walks away. He doesn't say 'Hello' or 'Kiss my ass.' He just gave Jack a command and goes on about his business. So, Joe and I go golfing. Get back to the dorm and drink some beer and have some fun. The next morning, I am walking down the stairs with my golf clubs and Lombardi says, 'Where the hell do you think you are going?' I said, 'Well, I was going to play some golf.' Lombardi replied, 'Like hell you are. If you are in the dorms, you will make all meals, all meetings and all practices. Just like everyone else. Now, go get dressed!' He gave us two extra two-a-days. He was just killing us. So, that was my introduction."[12]

The 1966 season was much like the other championship seasons. However, one difference

Jerry Kramer.

was that for the first time, the NFL would face the rival American Football League in a championship game. According to Kramer, "We were aware of the AFL and a lot of us communicated with AFL folks about the possibility of playing or not playing. So, there was curiosity about them. We were aware that this was the first AFL-NFL championship. But, that is tomorrow. That is not now. We have Baltimore and Cleveland and other things to worry about now. You have a sense of excellence about you. And then, it almost became a journeyman quality that you expected and your team expected and the other guys expected to win, and it just became a way that you went about doing things."[13]

The Packers only lost two games in the 1966 season. Kramer recalled, "I don't even remember them. Even in '62, there was never a feeling of undefeated. We never talked about losing a game. We talked that sometimes the other team had more points than we did when the clock ran out. But, we had never lost a game. We had that philosophy. That is the way we felt. We just ran out of time. You just tried to learn what happened, then analyze it and put it away and don't let it happen again."[14]

Kramer continued, "We were thinking more about the NFL championship than we were the Super Bowl, or AFL-NFL championship."[15]

After beating the Cowboys in the NFL championship game, the Packers faced the Kansas City Chiefs in the AFL-NFL World Championship Game (later referred to as Super Bowl I). According to Kramer, "There were moments where we didn't respect them [the Kansas City Chiefs] like we should have. We actually made fun of them. There was a situation in the film room. The offensive group was together. Two of their defensive backs collided and knocked each other down. Max McGee said, 'Look at this. What is this?' Then he started to hum the Looney Tunes theme. We looked at things like that. We really did not have the understanding of how good a football team they were. Once you got a hold of Buck Buchannan, Bobby Bell, Johnny Robinson and all of those guys, they have a hell of a football team."[16]

Kramer recalled, "Years later, Lenny Dawson and I were having a beer together somewhere, and I said, 'You know, Lenny. There is something that I always wondered about. It seemed to me that when we came out in the second half, we had an interception by Willie Wood and brought it down to about the five-yard line and then scored. I just got the feeling that you guys played a good first half, then said, 'Well, we didn't embarrass ourselves. We stood up to the Packers and we did a good job.' He said, 'Jerry, I am not sure you are not right. Hell, we watched you guys from the time we were in high school. You were heroes of ours. We all wanted to be like you. So, just to play in a big game was a huge thrill for us.'"[17]

Kramer is known for "The Block" in the Ice Bowl, the 1967 NFL championship game against the Dallas Cowboys. With 16 seconds left, Bart Starr sneaked the ball through a hole created by Kramer and fellow lineman Ken Bowman to win the game and take the Packers to Super Bowl II against the Oakland Raiders. Kramer recalled, "That play started on Thursday in short-yardage films. The film guy separated all of the short-yardage plays from the rest of the plays. We studied our goal-line plays. We were looking at Dallas' last three weeks. I noticed that Jethro Pugh's first move was up. I watched that for several plays and it is consistently up. I said, 'Coach, we can wedge Pugh if we want to.' In his usual style, coach barked, 'What? We can wedge Pugh if we had to? Run it back.' We ran the film back about three times on this particular play. He said, 'That's right. Put in a wedge on Pugh.' You never expect it to be on the one-yard line. You expect it to be in the second quarter in the middle of the field. Jethro is actually a pretty good football player. He had a better game than I remember."[18]

However, Kramer felt that it was the entire series that should be remembered, and not just the block. "It is more about the drive than the block. The memory started in the huddle at the 35-yard line with four-and-a-half minutes to go. [Ray] Nitschke came by the huddle, 'Come on guys. Don't let me down,' as he went off the field. I asked Bart [Starr] years later, 'What possessed you to think that you could take that team 65 yards, when in the previous 31 plays, ten possessions, we gained minus nine yards?' He said, 'Jerry. I don't remember that. I don't believe that is true.' I looked it up. It was true. He said, 'I don't remember that.' I said to Fuzzy, 'Fuzzy. You remember that last drive?' He said, 'Yeah, Jerry.' I asked, 'Do you remember the 31 plays before that where we gained a minus nine yards?' He said, 'Oh. I don't think that is right.' I asked Bart again, 'What makes you think that you could drive us down 65 yards?' He said, 'The look in your eyes. The look in Forrest's eyes. The look in Bow's [Ken Bowman] eyes. I looked in that huddle and I knew that I didn't need to say anything. All I said was ok. Let's go.'"[19]

Kramer discussed 'The Block.' "It came down to the final play and it was my turn to contribute. I come off the ball and got into Jethro and the block is over. All of that bullshit about Kenny [Bowman] and I is not even in the conversation. Jethro is high. I am low. He is moving. It is over. Case closed."[20]

Kramer summed it up, "It is a series of plays in the drive that I remember the best. And I remember the most about my teammates and about the Green Bay Packers, I remember 'The Drive.' The character and the quality. The things that coach Lombardi stood for. The commitment. The discipline. The preparation. The consistency. The sacrifice. That is what we were all about. It is not 'The Play.' It was 'The Drive.'"[21]

During the 1967 season, Kramer was asked by sportswriter Dick Schaap to collaborate on a book. *Instant Replay* was published and became a best-seller. Kramer also wrote *Farewell to Football* in 1969 and *Distant Replay* in 1985.

In 1968, Kramer knew that it was time to retire from football. "We played the [Chicago] Bears. Odd man line. We had a split backfield. Fullback behind tackle. Halfback behind the other tackle. Spread formation, strong right. The tight end is right. On an odd man line, [Dick] Butkus was over me. A 245-pound defensive tackle named Dick Evey was over the center. Ray Wietecha, our line coach, drew a play up where I block down on Dick Evey with Bowman. We double-teamed the 245-pound defensive tackle. Jimmy Grabowski, the fullback, was 225 pounds with a bad leg. He took Butkus one-on-one. Butkus was 245 or 250 pounds. I said, 'Ray, let me have Butkus. Bow can stand up Evey, Grabo can hit him from the side and we will whack his ass out. I can handle Butkus. It is a much stronger play.' Ray said, 'I'm the coach and we are going to do it my way.' I said, 'Well, it's goddamn stupid!' He said, 'I'm the coach. We are going to do it my way.' It is only one play, but one play can make a difference. It seems like we were doing something stupid. We had a couple of other incidents like that during the season. It was defeating. It was demoralizing. Coach [Lombardi] was gone. My guys were gone. I thought it was time for me to do something else."[22]

After he retired from football, Kramer was involved with a myriad of activities, including as a color commentator for NFL games.

Currently, Kramer is keeping himself busy. "I fish a little bit. I golf a little bit. I am talking to a guy about hosting a casino at Packer home games. I am doing a lot of autograph sessions. I do speaking engagements."[23]

NOTES

1. Jerry Kramer, *Jerry Kramer's Farewell to Football* (New York: Bantam, 1969).
2. *Ibid.*
3. *Ibid.*
4. *Ibid.*
5. *Ibid.*
6. Jerry Kramer telephone interview with Ken Crippen, June 29, 2014.
7. *Ibid.*
8. *Ibid.*
9. *Ibid.*
10. *Ibid.*
11. *Ibid.*
12. *Ibid.*
13. *Ibid.*
14. *Ibid.*
15. *Ibid.*
16. *Ibid.*
17. *Ibid.*
18. *Ibid.*
19. *Ibid.*
20. *Ibid.*
21. *Ibid.*
22. *Ibid.*
23. *Ibid.*

Bob Long

RICK SCHABOWSKI

Bob Long's seven-year NFL career was highlighted by playing on two Packers Super Bowl championship teams and also being the only person to play a full season for Vince Lombardi in both Green Bay and Washington.

Robert Andrew Long was born on June 16, 1942, in McKeesport, Pennsylvania, and attended suburban Pittsburgh's Washington Township High School. In his senior football season, Long dislocated his elbow during the team's first game. To stay on the team, he volunteered to hold for extra points with his good arm. The coach didn't allow that, so while the football team was practicing, Long stayed in the gym practicing his jump shot with his good arm. The practice paid off. Long broke the school's scoring record and was offered a basketball scholarship to Wichita State. Long felt, "I wanted to get away from the steel mills in Pittsburgh. My dad was a steel mill worker, my grandfather was a coal miner and I didn't want to do that. I said I've got to get to college somehow, and that's how I got there."[1]

It is not common for a scholarship basketball player to get involved with football, but Long did: "The football team was in spring practice, spring of 1963. Our basketball team had an intramural football team. Dave Stallworth was our quarterback and I was a receiver, and it was fun! No one hit you, it was flag football, we had basketball hands, I could catch almost anything, great hands, and in one game I caught seven touchdown passes. The football coaches were supposed to be watching their team, playing the spring football game, but they turned around and watched our game. They needed a wide receiver, a split end at Wichita."[2]

The football staff offered Long a deal. "They didn't want me to get hurt learning and they said, 'Long, we don't want you to block.' At Wichita, I never blocked. They said, 'We don't want you to get hurt. Run an experimental pattern where you don't hit anybody and nobody can hit you, and you won't get hurt. Run a pattern straight downfield between the strong safety and the cornerback, they will stay with you because they respect your speed. You're taking two defensive players with you, that's better than a block.' Yeah, I like this deal. This is almost like flag football."[3]

Bob had 43 receptions and nine touchdowns in his only year of football at Wichita. He was drafted by the AFL's San Diego Chargers in the tenth round and by the Packers in the fourth. Packers personnel director Pat Peppler liked Long's talents. "He was a basketball player with limited football experience, but we took a chance on him. Vince [Lombardi] liked the bigger receivers with big hands."[4]

Long visited a Chargers workout. "I flew out there for a visit. I'm watching practice one day from the bleachers. There was a guy sitting beside me and I said, 'Who's that number 19? He looks pretty good.' He said, 'That's our new, young receiver. His name is Lance Alworth.' I said, 'Really.' So when I got back to Wichita, where I went to college, I called up Pat Peppler of the Packers and I said, 'Send me a program.' Pat said, 'We've never been asked for a program before. Why are you asking me?' I said, 'I'll tell you later.' So he sent me a program, and I said, 'I want to look at the ages of the Packer receivers.' I look at this program: Max McGee, 30; Boyd Dowler, 29. If I'm not going to make it—and no one thought I'd make it—if I'm not going to make it, what I want to do, I want to tell my grandkids someday, you were cut by the great Vince Lombardi."[5]

Long was elated with signing a contract with the Packers, saying, "This is one of the happiest moments in my life. This is the sort of thing one reads about in the land of make-believe. I never had any idea last fall that by Christmas I would be a member of such an established organization as the Green Bay Packers. I'm going to give the Packers the very best that is in me. That is all I can honestly do, and I hope that my very best will help in a small way to further the success of the Green Bay Packers on the football field."[6]

A week before going to the Packers training camp, Long met with his college coach and asked, "'Coach, I have an interesting question—am I going to have to block in Green Bay?' I didn't know how to block. I didn't block at Wichita. He looked up at me and said, 'Ray Nitschke is waiting for you!' I said, Uh-oh, I'm in deep trouble."[7]

Having played only one season of college ball, training camp was a learning process for Long, but Bob was truly impressed with his coach: "Lombardi was a great coach, and the greatest motivator of all time in my opinion, but he had the ability to take a player and say, 'Herb Adderley, you're not playing offense for me, you're playing cornerback.' Lombardi had the ability to put players in their right positions. They weren't all defensive players. A lot of them were offensive players in college. I think that's one of the real abilities that people miss when all these books are written and they talk about him."[8]

Long earned a roster spot on the 1964 team, but got very little playing time, catching just one pass for 19 yards.

In 1965, Long had a great season, getting some opportunities to start because of injuries to Boyd Dowler and Carroll Dale. Long made the most of the opportunity with 13 receptions for 304 yards with a team-high 23.4 yards per catch average. His four touchdown receptions tied for the team lead with Boyd Dowler.

Before the 1966 season, Long reflected about his 1965 performance, "Last year really helped me. Your rookie year you don't play much. The second year, you get a chance to show the coach what you can do, or you sort of drift out of the picture."[9] He was also excited about the upcoming season. "I came in a little heavier this year—I came in at 203. I only played those seven games of college football because I had come to Wichita as a basketball player, so I feel my body is still adjusting and I'm just picking up a little weight."[10]

However, injuries limited Long's playing time in 1966 as he finished the season with only three receptions for 68 yards. Although he didn't catch a pass in the first AFL-NFL World Championship Game, Long was still involved in the game's first touchdown. Boyd Dowler was injured on the Packers' first series, requiring Max McGee to enter the game. McGee, who didn't expect to play, had left his helmet in the locker room, so Bob let McGee use his helmet. McGee caught a 37-yard pass from Bart Starr for the first score of the game wearing Long's headgear: "So I think I had a little part of that first touchdown too. I tell my kids that I was part of Super Bowl history—that's my helmet Max was wearing!"[11]

Lack of playing time continued to be an issue for Long in 1967. "I had trouble getting playing time because Lombardi loved his veterans and we had a lot of veterans."[12] Long played in ten games with eight receptions for 96 yards.

On September 2, 1968, Long was traded to the Atlanta Falcons for defensive end Leo Carroll, Bucky Pope, and a draft choice. Long was leading the Falcons in receiving through the first nine games. Unfortunately he got in an automobile accident on Interstate Highway 75 in Georgia that left him with a broken back, a broken foot, and a mangled elbow. The head-on collision resulted in the death of the driver of the car that hit Long's vehicle. There was considerable doubt if Long would ever be able to run again. Long decided to move on. "I was mentally and physically depressed. I decided to quit football. A year later, Coach Lombardi, who had moved to Washington, called me. He asked me to what degree I had recovered. I told him about 80 percent. Lombardi said, 'That's good enough for me,' and I reported to the Redskins in 1969."[13]

Lombardi had changed Bob's mind. "He said that even though I'd been hurt, I'd still be able to help him, and he said he'd help me, mentally and physically. I told him I'd spent four years sitting on the bench for him, and he said he wasn't asking me to come back to sit on the bench. He said I'd be a starter."[14] This time around, being a veteran was helpful for Long. "He said, 'Bobby Mitchell is retiring and I need a veteran.' You don't turn down Vince Lombardi, so I went to Washington. Being a veteran paid off for me with Coach Lombardi in Washington, and Sonny Jurgensen was the quarterback, so I had a great experience there."[15]

Long was a major contributor to the Red-

Bob Long.

skins' resurgence to a 7–5–2 record, their first winning season since 1955. He caught 48 passes, more than he had caught in his five previous seasons combined, ranked 14th among NFL receivers, and also caught more than any Packers end that year.

Long did note some differences in Lombardi's coaching style in Washington. "Minor things, very minor things. He allowed the Redskins to wear long hair, and he didn't yell as much with the Redskins as I remember him yelling at Green Bay, the reason being he didn't even come close to the talent he had at Green Bay. The Redskins had a few great players, Jurgensen, Charley Taylor and Jerry Smith."[16]

When Lombardi was in the hospital, fighting his battle against cancer, Long remembered visiting him. "I was on National Guard duty and got a long lunch hour to go to the hospital. I tried to thank him for all he'd done. He just reached out and squeezed my hand."[17] The death of Lombardi left many people devastated. Long was among many commenting, "Mentally, his death almost destroyed me. He had brought me back when I was at the height of my career, and now he was dead."[18] The Redskins had an exhibition game with the Dolphins on Saturday, September 5, 1970. Long said the game would go on. "We'll play this game Saturday because that's the way Coach Lombardi would have wanted it. You had to have known him to realize why we must play."[19]

Thinking back, Long says, "I kind of lost my spirit to play and was thinking about retiring right after that happened. I kind of pushed the Redskins to release me in 1970. I wanted to go back to selling pizzas, start making some money, have fun, and not getting hurt. Then Boyd Dowler, who was the end coach for the L.A. Rams, called me. George Allen was the coach. Boyd Dowler was my hero, great receiver, and a great guy. So I went out and played for the Rams for four or five weeks."[20] Long played for the Rams in 1970, making three receptions for 35 yards, and was happy to play under Dowler. "Boyd Dowler was my hero. He was 6–5 with long arms and legs, kind of a Randy Moss of his era. I'd watch him in practice and games."[21]

Long caught his last NFL touchdown, a 15-yard pass from Roman Gabriel, on November 1, 1970, at Tulane Stadium in New Orleans. Long recalled, "At Tulane Stadium, at the end of one of the end zones, they had a bunch of shrubs, high shrubs. So I went up in the end zone, I jumped, caught the pass, landed in the shrubs and kind of disappeared."[22]

A broken back, many injuries, and three knee operations took their toll on Long, so, after failing his physical examination with the Los Angeles Rams on July 14, 1971, he retired from the NFL. His career in business, though, was already launched. At Wichita State, Long had majored in business administration and earned some extra cash by making pizzas at a pizzeria near campus. The store's name was Pizza Hut, and it was the first one in the U.S. When Long's boss wanted to expand the franchise around the country, he offered Long the exclusive rights to franchises in northern Wisconsin for $20,000. Teammates who invested with Bob did well. Fuzzy Thurston and Max McGee each put up $2,000, and in 1975, when Pepsi took over Pizza Hut, they both cashed in for almost $250,000.

Many of Vince Lombardi's players became successful in their post-football endeavors. Long gives Lombardi credit for "a lot of it, a whole bunch of it. I definitely think having played for Coach Vince Lombardi he taught me how to act, how to be a good citizen, and how to interact. After you deal with Lombardi, you're not really scared of anybody! You could go on and deal with a tough attorney, a tough banker, it doesn't really bother you that much. I've been to the mountaintop, so everything after him isn't really too much.

He taught us discipline, and he taught us mental toughness, which is a big one. My employees, I would laugh sometimes, they would come up to me when I owned the Pizza Hut franchises, after a meeting, or telling what to do and what not to do, and one of the employees came up to me and said, 'You're just like Vince Lombardi—in pizza!' I said, 'Well, that isn't all bad. I bet we'll win.' I've learned the guidelines to win. Loyalty, mental toughness, teamwork, everybody helping each other, and no egos."[23]

In 1976, Long married Joan, whose first husband had been killed in an accident, and adopted her son, Christian. The Longs had two additional children, Bree and Andrew.

On the morning of January 15, 1991, Long began his most important battle. Long suffered a stroke. He couldn't open his eyes or speak. He spent two months in Elmbrook Hospital, but after a lot of hard work, learned to eat, walk and talk all over again. He says, "I consider myself lucky. I can walk. I can see. I can get around. The only thing wrong with me is that I can't talk real well, and my balance is real bad. I'm trying to get better."[24]

Long was inducted into the State of Kansas Hall of Fame in 1965, the Wichita State Hall of Fame in 1972, and the Western Chapter of the Pennsylvania Sports Hall of Fame in 2008. Bob is also proud of his involvement with a number of charities, including the Ray Nitschke Foundation, the Special Olympics, the Task Force Against Family Violence, and the Alzheimer's Foundation. He also has served as the president of the NFLPA Retirees for Wisconsin.

Hall of Fame teammate Willie Davis summed up Long as "a speedster who instantly dedicated himself to the Packers' cause. Bob never became a superstar for any of the teams he played for, but he was always regarded as a decent receiver, a reliable option who took some of the pressure off the top guys. He'd also go down as one of the luckiest of Green Bay Packers, staying with the team for three championships before moving on."[25]

NOTES

1. Bob Long interview with author, October 22, 2014.
2. *Ibid.*
3. Dave Robinson and Royce Boyles, *The Lombardi Legacy: Thirty People Who Were Touched by Greatness* (Louisville, KY: Goose Creek Publishers, 2009), 317.
4. Martin Hendricks, "Ex-Basketball Player Bob Long Caught on as a Receiver for Vince Lombardi," *Packer Plus*, July 30, 2013.
5. Bob Long interview with author, October 22, 2014.
6. Bob Overnaker, "Wu End Long Signs Packers Pact," *Wichita Beacon*.
7. *Ibid.*
8. Bob Long interview with author, October 22, 2014.
9. Lee Remmel, "Long Will Be Best End in League, Says Herb," *Green Bay Press Gazette*, July 15, 1966.
10. *Ibid.*
11. Hendricks.
12. Bob Long interview with author, October 22, 2014.
13. Bud Lea, "From Flake to Tycoon," *Milwaukee Sentinel*, February 24, 1975.
14. Jerry Kramer, *Lombardi: Winning Is the Only Thing* (New York: World Publishing, 1970),159.
15. Hendricks.
16. Bob Long interview with author, October 22, 2014.
17. "The World Mourns Death of Lombardi," *Spartanburg Herald,* September 3, 1970.
18. Lea, "From Flake to Tycoon."
19. "Lombardi Knew How to Be a Champ," *St. Petersburg Times*, September 4, 1970.
20. Bob Long interview with author, October 22, 2014.
21. Hendricks.
22. Bob Long interview with author, October 22, 2014.

    23. *Ibid.*
    24. Bud Lea, "Ex-Packer Bob Long Won't Quit," *Milwaukee Sentinel,* November 26, 1991.
    25. Willie Davis with Jim Martyka and Andrea Erickson Davis, *Closing the Gap: Lombardi, the Packers Dynasty, and the Pursuit of Excellence* (Chicago: Triumph Books, 2012) 188.

Red Mack

Gary Sarnoff

Red Mack proved that it is not what life does to you; it's what you do with life. Things never came easy for the redhead from Pennsylvania, but he always found a way to beat the odds: through hard work, perseverance, and the support of others. He also received a few breaks along the way—the biggest of his six-year NFL career coming in 1966, when he was claimed off waivers by the Super Bowl-bound Green Bay Packers.

William "Red" Mack was born on June 19, 1937, in Oconto, Wisconsin, a town located 35 miles north of Green Bay. "My parents moved [the family] to the Pittsburgh area in 1943," according to Mack, but that would not be the last time his family would relocate.[1] The Macks were forced to move every month since the parents were unable to pay the rent and eventually divorced. The authorities stepped in and considered sending the Mack boys to Boys Town in Nebraska and placing the girls with a foster family. However, the final decision was to send the children to the St. Paul's Orphanage in Crafton, Pennsylvania. During his two-year stay at St. Paul's, Mack was noted for his red-hot temper. "Have faith, son," the nuns would tell him whenever he was overcome by anger. "Have faith and things will get better."[2] Two years later, Mack went to Indianapolis to live with an uncle, before all of the Mack children were finally reunited in Pennsylvania to live with their grandparents in Allison Park. That proved to be a good break as Mack's grandparents stressed discipline and kept a close eye on him.

Mack entered Hampton High School, a small school of 350 kids. "There were just fifty-seven in my class."[3] He starred in football, basketball, and track, and was named to the All-Western Pennsylvania gridiron team three years in a row. "I was also the state's hurdles champion." To top it off, Mack was tabbed as a "model student and leader" by Hampton High line coach Ed Fay, who insisted that "Red could do just about anything."[4]

Following three outstanding athletic school years at Hampton, Mack had reason to be excited about his senior year. His final high school year would offer a chance for him to be named to the All-Western Pennsylvania team for a fourth consecutive season. In addition, there were several college scouts who were interested in watching Mack during his senior season. However, Mack had a big problem. "I was ineligible my senior year because I turned nineteen three months too soon."[5]

Due to his absenteeism caused by his family's constant migration during his grammar school days, he was placed two years below his actual grade.

He may have been unable to play at Hampton High School, but Mack found a way to compete in athletics during his senior year, thanks to the Naval Academy. With interest in having Mack play college football in Annapolis, Navy paid Mack's way to Bullis Prep, a boarding school located in Silver Spring, Maryland, that scheduled their seasons against major college freshman football teams. In addition to playing football, the college prep school served another important purpose: helping Mack boost his grades. "I learned a lot of good study habits and discipline at Bullis Prep," said Mack.[6] Although he did not have the solid academic educational background the other students had at Bullis, Mack managed to keep up by working harder and keeping late hours to study. On the football field Mack scored 12 touchdowns in six games and was named the prep player of the year by the Washington Touchdown Club.

The success of Mack's high school football career attracted the interest of several college scouts. Navy was also in pursuit until Mack declared that the military college life would not suit him. He visited several universities, Michigan, West Virginia, Pitt, Michigan State, but decided those schools were big, "like cities," and did not appeal to him.[7] Coach Fay, a Notre Dame alumnus, told Mack that there was a spot for him in South Bend. "I was a teammate of [Terry] Brennan, the Notre Dame coach at the time, and he was interested in Red," said Fay.[8] Mack paid a visit to South Bend, fell in love with the campus since it was "small and compact," and was impressed with Terry Brennan.[9] But the most influential coach for Mack at Notre Dame was Fighting Irish backfield coach Hank Stram. Before meeting Stram, he was forewarned by Len Dawson who had played for him at Purdue. "Dawson lived in Allison Park, and we would work out together. I would run pass patterns and he would throw passes. He told me that I could expect to work my butt off for Stram."[10]

And Dawson was right. Mack worked hard, much to Stram's appreciation. "He was like a dad to me," Mack said about his collegiate coach. Stram liked the fact that Mack made the best of his size. He weighed just 165 when he entered college. He was knocked around a lot, but always stood up for himself. "If they knocked me down, I'd get right back up and somehow get back at them."[11]

In 1957, Mack's first year on the South Bend campus, college freshmen were prohibited from playing on the varsity, however, Mack practiced everyday with the Notre Dame varsity. "Red could have been in the Notre Dame starting backfield [as a freshman]," according to Coach Fay. "That's what Brennan told me."[12]

The Fighting Irish posted just one winning season during Mack's three varsity seasons. "My sophomore year was my best," said Mack. Notre Dame posted a 6–4 record, and Mack rushed for 429 yards on 71 carries for an average of six yards per carry. He also scored four rushing touchdowns and caught one touchdown pass.

Before Mack's junior season, Joe Kuharich was hired as the new head coach at Notre Dame. The new head coach inherited Red as his top-rated returning running back, but Mack twisted his knee two weeks prior to the season's first game. After missing the first two games, Mack returned, but saw limited action. It was then reported that when stepping off the team's bus following Notre Dame's 20–19 upset win at

Red Mack.

Iowa, Mack's knee locked. Surgery was immediately recommended and performed, ending his junior season. Mack returned for his senior season, but his season and career at Notre Dame ended with another knee injury just two games into the season.

Following the 1960 season, Mack was surprised when the Pittsburgh Steelers drafted him in the tenth round. "Art Rooney [Steelers owner] made one personal draft pick each season, and I guess I was his pick in 1960." Why did Rooney choose a player who saw limited action during his last two college seasons? Mack believes that Rooney remembered him from years before, when the Steelers' owner took Mack and his grammar school football teammates to the Elk Club for dinner and purchased new football shirts and pants for every player.[13]

His chances of making the Steelers appeared to be slim, and Mack knew it. "Why do they want me?" Mack asked, and probably for good reason. He was undersized, injury-prone, had a limited college career, and had slowed down since the days he could run the 100-yard dash in 9.8 seconds during his sophomore season. "Don't tell yourself you are not good enough," someone suggested. "Let them tell you."[14]

Dave Brady later wrote in the *Washington Post*, "Red Mack came to the pros thankful for small blessings even though he didn't have a leg to stand on."[15] Would Mack make it? One day during preseason practice in his rookie season, he went up against a rookie defensive back from Northwestern University named Fred Williamson. "Williamson was signed as a free-agent wide-receiver but they moved him to defensive back, which did not make him happy," said Mack.[16] One day on the practice field, Williamson sent Mack to the ground with a blindside hit, and Mack responded. "I got up and cold-cocked him," said Mack. Pittsburgh veteran quarterback Bobby Layne, who saw the play and what had followed, told Steelers head coach Buddy Parker, "We have to keep that crazy S.O.B." Parker must have agreed, because Mack made the team as a reserve wide receiver.[17]

In his rookie season, Mack had eight receptions, two of which resulted in touchdowns. He also benefited from the tutoring of Bob Schnelker, a veteran wide receiver the Steelers picked up in mid-season. "He coached me for two and a half months before he got cut," said Mack.[18] During their short time as teammates, Mack made an impression on Schnelker that would pay off later in his career.

In 1962, Mack worked hard to become a starter in the Steelers three-wide-receiver offense. In Week 3 of the 1962 season, Buddy Dial went out with an injury and Mack took his place in the starting lineup. Taking advantage of his opportunity, Mack scored a touchdown. "Coach [Buddy Parker] told me I made a nice catch," Mack said after the game. "He's not an outspoken guy. If he wants to tell you something, he usually tells you through his assistants."[19] When Dial returned to health, Mack went back to the bench until one month later when Harlon Hill was released, and Mack went back into the starting lineup.

A starter in the Steelers offensive attack in 1963, Mack made 25 catches for 618 yards, an average of 24.7 yards per reception. But after the season, an incident in a basketball game put Mack in hot water with the Pittsburgh management. "Lou Michaels [six-feet-two, 235-pound defensive end and place kicker for the Steelers, and the Colts later in his career] hit me with a sucker punch and I beat the heck out of him." The altercation may have been the reason why Mack was included in the Steelers and Eagles four-player deal that sent him to Philadelphia where he was reunited with his college coach Joe Kuharich. Mack rode the bench with the Eagles during a season in which he sustained an injury and was limited to one touchdown catch. The following season he was cut by the Eagles but was asked by head coach Kuharich to serve on the team's taxi squad. Mack declined, much to Kuharich's dismay, and was claimed off waivers by the Steelers.

The 1965 Pittsburgh Steelers went 2–12 while Mack warmed the bench due to a shoulder separation. He was then left unprotected after the season and was claimed in the 1966 expansion draft by the Atlanta Falcons. Mack reported to the NFL's newest franchise at Black Mountain, North Carolina. "It was the hardest camp I had ever been in," he said. "There was just one dirt road into what had been a YMCA camp. We slept in a hot, tin-roofed Quonset hut. Boy, did we work."

Mack made the team, played in the season opener, then was told to see the coach and bring his playbook. "Well, after the Atlanta Falcons cut me, I was out in the cold with a one-game paycheck, wondering what I was going to do next."[20]

Mack headed back to his home in South Bend, believing that his NFL career was over. He arrived home on Tuesday, and then destiny came calling the next day in the person of Vince Lombardi. Green Bay needed another wide receiver, and Packers assistant coach Bob Schnelker, the same person who had taken Mack under his wing in Pittsburgh, had put in a good word for him. Lombardi told Red they had a spot for him on the Packers roster and asked when he could be in Green Bay. "When is practice?" Mack asked. Lombardi told him during the afternoon of the following day. Mack assured Lombardi that he would be there.

"Lombardi told me that I probably would not see much action at wide receiver," said Mack. The plan was to play Mack on special teams and serve as an emergency wide receiver. "Lombardi convinced me that I was just as important to the team as Bart Starr," said Mack. "He told me that one good play on special teams could make the difference in the outcome of a game," and Mack and the Green Bay special teams did not permit a single kickoff or punt return for the touchdown during the entire season.[21] The Packers also took care of Mack by giving him an overdue pay raise increasing his yearly salary from $12,000 to $15,000.[22]

In Super Bowl I Mack did his part by snuffing two Kansas City kickoff returns by making the tackles. After the game, in an emotional Green Bay locker room, Red recalled, "Fuzzy Thurston, who was crying, came over and gave me a kiss."[23]

"This is the greatest moment in my life," Mack said in the victorious locker room. "Thank you for letting me be a part of this," he told Lombardi. "Red, if you didn't belong here, you wouldn't be here," answered the legendary head coach.

"I'm so happy," Mack said on the plane ride back to Green Bay, "I've never been a part of anything like this."[24]

For winning the Super Bowl, Mack and his teammates received $15,000, which doubled his 1966 salary. He also received a ring that he will never part with. "A guy offered me a Porsche for it once," Mack said at the twentieth Super Bowl I reunion in 1986, "and I wouldn't trade it. I wouldn't give it up for all the money in the world."[25]

In the summer of 1967, Mack was back in Green Bay and worked hard at the summer training camp with a determination to make the team and be a part of the Packers' quest for a third consecutive NFL championship and a second Super Bowl win. When the first cuts of the Packers' 1967 training camp came prior to the start of the exhibition season in late July, Pat Peppler, the Packers' player personnel director, told Mack that he was going to drive him to the Oneida Country Club. When they arrived, they sat down at a table with Vince Lombardi. During lunch, Lombardi explained the situation. The Packers had a few talented rookie wide receivers, and they wanted to go with more youth at that position. Lombardi told Mack that the Lions were willing to claim him. There was also a player-coach position with a team in the Atlantic Football League (minor leagues). Mack appreciated the fact that there were other options, and thanked Lombardi for finding other jobs in football, but said he was going to pack it in. He said he was going to retire from professional football. Lombardi assured him that he could use him as a job reference. "I was really fortunate that I got a chance to play for him," Mack said of Lombardi. "He was a coach, a teacher, and like a father to me."[26]

Was there something that Mack learned from Vince Lombardi that he applied to his life after football? "Yes," replied Mack. "If you can't give one-hundred percent everyday, find a different job."[27]

Mack worked for the Bendix Corporation in South Bend for nearly 36 years. Today, he still lives in South Bend with his wife Jean and is enjoying his life in retirement.

NOTES

1. *Pittsburgh Post-Gazette,* September 17, 1987.
2. *Washington Post*, January 11, 1967.
3. Red Mack interview with author, October 24, 2014.
4. *Pittsburgh Post-Gazette*, September 17, 1987.
5. *Washington Post*, November 22, 1962.
6. *Ibid.*
7. Red Mack interview with author, October 24, 2014.
8. *Pittsburgh Post-Gazette*, September 17, 1987.
9. Red Mack interview with author, October 24, 2014.
10. *Ibid.*
11. *Ibid.*
12. *Pittsburgh Post-Gazette*, September 17, 1987.
13. Red Mack interview with author, October 24, 2014.
14. *Ibid.*
15. *Washington Post,* November 22, 1962.
16. Red Mack interview with author, October 24, 2014.
17. *Ibid.*
18. *Ibid.*
19. *Washington Post,* November 22, 1962.
20. *Washington Post,* January 11, 1967.
21. Red Mack interview with author, October 24, 2014.
22. *Ibid.*
23. *Ibid.*
24. Jerry Kramer and Dick Schaap, *Distant Replay* (New York: G. P. Putnam's Sons, 1985), 176.
25. *Ibid.*
26. *Pittsburgh Post-Gazette*, September 17, 1987.
27. Red Mack interview with author, October 24, 2014.

Max McGee

JOHN MAXYMUK

Max McGee is a legend among Packers fans on a number of counts. As a raconteur, he was the charismatic wingman to Golden Boy Paul Hornung on their well-publicized night life explorations of the big cities of America. As a teammate, he was hot-headed coach Vince Lombardi's dry-witted foil who was often able to defuse tense situations with a sly retort that even Lombardi seemed to appreciate. On the field, Max was a clutch receiver especially noted for his ability to make big plays in the clutch. All of these elements combined in his fabled performance in Super Bowl I when McGee came off the bench to catch seven passes for two touchdowns despite having spent the entire night before out on the town in Los Angeles. That performance with its roguish backstory quickly became part of the enduring lore of the NFL.

William Max McGee was born on July 16, 1932, in Sexton City, Texas, as the youngest of six brothers, all of whom played football at some level. The most accomplished aside from Max was Coy, a 5'9", 160-pound scatback who spent one year at the University of Tulsa before transferring to Notre Dame in 1945. Max's brother was drafted in the 25th round of the 1948 draft by Detroit, but stayed at Notre Dame that year. In 1949, he signed with the Chicago Hornets of the All-America Football Conference, but did not make the team.

That same 1949 season, Max was a senior at White Oak High School and became the first Texas schoolboy athlete to rush for over 3,000 yards in a single season with a total of 3,048 yards and also intercepted 17 passes on defense. Assistant coach Cotton Miles recalled decades later to the *Longview News-Journal* that Max "played fullback in '48 in our short punt formation, and then moved to tailback. He played linebacker all the time, and he was our punter and kickoff man."[1]

Although Notre Dame Coach Frank Leahy leaned heavily on brother Coy to recruit Max for the Fighting Irish, Max instead elected to attend Tulane University in New Orleans where his high school freshman coach Winlon Knowles was an assistant. At Tulane, the 6'3", 200-pound halfback led the Green Wave in rushing in 1951, 1952 and 1953, but the team never achieved a winning record during Max's time there. Being in New Orleans had other benefits, though, for someone with a taste for revelry, and McGee was said to take full advantage of that. One story holds that Packer personnel man Jack Vainisi was scouting in the area and went to the Tulane dormitory where Max lived late one night and yelled up, "I'm looking for Max McGee." A young man called back, "What?" Vainisi screamed, "Max McGee." The student responded wearily, "Just leave him there. We'll come down and haul him up."[2]

Max also was married for the first time while an underclassman. The ill-fated marriage would not last long, but would produce two daughters, Mona and Maria.

McGee played in the 1954 Senior Bowl where he hooked up with future Packer teammate Zeke Bratkowski for a 60-yard touchdown reception to give the South a 14–13 third quarter lead in a game eventually won by the North squad. Three weeks later, Jack Vainisi drafted Max for Green Bay in the fifth round of the NFL draft. Coming off a 2–9–1 season, the 1954 Packers were led by new coach Lisle Blackbourn, a longtime Wisconsin high school coach whose coaching record at Marquette University for the four previous seasons was a mere one game over .500.

Blackbourn converted Max to end, and McGee later told newspaper writer and Packer historian Cliff Christl, "I kind of liked his passing attack."[3] As a rookie in 1954, Max learned from veteran receivers Billy Howton, an All-Pro, and Bob Mann. When Mann got hurt in Week 2, McGee took over at left end. Max caught his first NFL touchdown the next week against San Francisco, and Mann never got his job back. McGee caught three touchdowns against the Eagles in Week 6 and two more against the Bears in Week 7, ending up with nine touchdown receptions for his rookie year while averaging 17 yards on his 36 catches for the season. He also held down the Green Bay punting job and finished fifth in the league with a 41.7 yard average.

After such a promising rookie season, Max was called for active duty by the Air Force and spent 1955 and 1956 as a pilot, while also playing service ball with Zeke Bratkowski and Jim Dooley of the Chicago Bears. In his autobiography, *Starr: My Life in Football*, Bart Starr repeated another popular story about McGee's Air Force experience. It seems that on his first solo flight from Laredo, Texas, Max was blown off course by high winds and landed in Mexico where he obtained some fuel and a highway map and resourcefully made his way back to base where he found himself in deep trouble, but somehow managed to talk himself out of it.[4]

Two years later, he was discharged and returned to Green Bay, but struggled in his second season as a pro in 1957, catching just 17 passes for only 273 yards and one touchdown. In 1958, McGee told Bud Lea of the *Milwaukee Sentinel*, "When I got back to Green Bay one week before the opener last season I felt as though I was playing about one-half of my normal potential. My legs were not in shape."[5] The one positive from 1957 was meeting rookie Paul Hornung, a kindred soul. The two began a lifelong friendship, although that did not necessarily look like a positive for the team at the time as the duo seemed to make bigger headlines with their after-hours activities than their on-the-field efforts. Max would later crack, "Anyone who has roomed with Paul Hornung for ten years and can still play football has to be a superman."[6]

That 1958 season was the worst in team history, but it was a return to playing form for McGee. "Maxie the Taxi" averaged 17.7 yards on his 37 catches and scored seven touchdowns, while finishing fourth in punting with a 42.3 average. All would change for the team the next season, and Max was one of the first veteran Packers to see how different things were going to be under new Coach Vince Lombardi in 1959. McGee and fiery teammate Howie Ferguson got to Green Bay a couple days before the opening of training camp that summer and stopped in to eat at the training table. They went out on the town that night and returned to the cafeteria the next day where Lombardi lit into them, telling them once they ate a meal under his roof, they were subject to training camp rules. Ferguson got into a heated argument with the coach and was soon gone, but Max decided discretion was the better part of valor and kept quiet. When the veterans did report, Lombardi addressed them for the first time and then called McGee aside privately to ask how he came across to the team, suggesting the coach held a certain amount of respect for the high spirited end.

McGee thrived with the revitalized Packers in 1959. Although his catches dropped to 30 in the run-oriented offense, he led the league with a 23.2 yards per catch average

Max McGee. Photograph by Laughead Photographers.

and snagged five touchdowns. Still, he was considered suspect by all four assistant coaches. Len Wagner's *Launching the Glory Years: The 1959 Packers—What They Didn't Tell Us* quotes extensively from the player assessments each coach handed in to Lombardi in the offseason. All four said essentially the same about Max. To quote one, "Max could be a great end. Excellent runner after he receives the pass. Good Speed. Poor attitude and a bad actor off the field. Would trade him if we could get a good pro football player. Very unpredictable on what to expect from him."[7]

However, Lombardi saw it differently. A couple years later, Vince wrote in *Run to Daylight*, "If Max were a perfectionist there is no telling how great a receiver he might be, but then, pressing all the time as perfectionists must, he would probably lose one of his greatest assets, the ability to relax. He can relax before, during and after a game, and it makes him a great clutch player, although it also contributes to his tendency to be a little careless."[8] Furthermore, McGee employed his relaxed nature to help the team better function under the demands of perfectionist Lombardi. One of the most often told stories about Max is the time that Lombardi grew so angry with the team's performance that he told them they were going to start all over from the beginning. Vince snapped, "Gentlemen, this is a football." To which McGee called out, "Slow down, Coach, you're going too fast." Lombardi was sharp enough to realize that characters like McGee and Hornung could help the team stay loose as long as they bought into Lombardi's leadership, and they did that.

Looking back years later in 1977, McGee told the *Chicago Tribune*, "I would just pay the fine and a couple days later Lombardi would punch me playfully in the ribs. I figured one thing early. He wanted to win. If you made a big play for him, you could go a long way."[9]

The Lombardi promise began to come to fruition in 1960 as the team went to the NFL championship game that year. McGee upped his catches to 38 while still averaging over 20 yards per catch in Green Bay's power running attack. The coach favored big receivers for his offense to help in the blocking scheme. While Max was not known as a great blocker, he could at least cause enough of an obstruction to be serviceable. In that title game against the Eagles, McGee showed not only his coolness in the clutch, but also his fearlessness. Late in the third quarter with Green Bay trailing 10–6 and facing a fourth-and-ten from the Packer 11, Max dropped into punt formation. He took the snap, looked up and saw no Eagles rushing and bolted up the sideline for 35 yards to the Green Bay 46. The decision was entirely his and a surprise to Lombardi who praised McGee's intelligence after the game. Eight plays later, he caught a seven-yard bullet from Starr for the only Packer touchdown of the game that they ultimately lost.

The 1961 Packers won it all and McGee went to the Pro Bowl for the only time based on a career high 51 receptions and seven touchdowns. That year, he joked to the *Milwaukee Sentinel*, "I'm still learning. I'm learning to catch the easy ones."[10] He was tougher than some gave him credit for. Despite cracking his ribs in the season finale, he played in the title game against New York. The 1962 team even repeated as league champions with Max catching 49 passes and three touchdowns.

In 1963, his catches dipped to 39, but his average per reception rose back to 19.2 and he caught six touchdowns as the Packers came up a bit short in their quest for a third straight championship in the season that Paul Hornung was suspended for gambling on football. Not surprisingly, Hornung's roommate was known to lay a few bets as well. In 2008, it came out that Max's gambling had been investigated by the FBI in the early 1970s, but the matter was dropped. The 1964 season would be McGee's last as a starter. Despite his catches dropping further to 31, he again averaged more than 19 yards per reception and snagged six touchdowns and was named to the *Sporting News* All-Pro team, the only All-Pro notice of his career. The 1964 Packers had slipped to an 8–5–1 record, and Lombardi retooled several positions for 1965's championship run, including wide receiver where newly-acquired Carroll Dale took over for McGee. Max caught just ten passes on the year, but his only touchdown proved to be a game-winner. In the September 26th victory over the rival Colts in Milwaukee, McGee's 37-yard reception from Zeke Bratkowski with 2:48 to play gave Green Bay a 20–17 lead that would prove to be the final score. Bratkowski said after the game, "I asked Max what would go? What do you have? Will a zig-out go? He said, 'Yes' and I called it."[11]

Indeed, McGee was often noted for his intelligence. In Vern Biever's photography book, *The Glory of Titletown*, Boyd Dowler asserted, "You know Max is always being characterized as a free spirit and all that kind of stuff, but Max was very disciplined about what he was doing, very disciplined about his football. He wasn't loose about it at all. He was also very, very smart."[12] Regarding McGee's game shrewdness, Gary Knafelc added that when Bart Starr would ask Max what was open. "He'd say, 'It's second-and-nine and we're on the near hashmark, so I could run a turn-in at twelve and a half.'"[13]

In 1966, the eleventh NFL campaign for the 34-year-old McGee, his catches dropped to four for the season, one in each of four different games. His 50th and final regular season touchdown catch came on a 24-yard pass from Bratkowski against Atlanta on October 23; it would not be his final touchdown, however. The Packers faced the Cowboys in Dallas for the NFL championship on January 1, 1967. Despite breaking out to a big lead, Green Bay had to fight off the inspired Cowboys right to the end. The Packers' winning touchdown came on a fourth quarter 28-yard out pattern from Starr to McGee on a third-and-19 to up the lead to 34–20 in the eventual 34–27 victory. In a bit of foreshadowing, McGee entered that game to replace an injured Boyd Dowler.

Two weeks later, the NFL champion Packers faced the AFL champion Kansas City Chiefs in the first Super Bowl game. McGee did not figure on playing, so he skipped out after bed check the night before the game and wasn't seen again until breakfast when Bart Starr greeted Max coming in from his night out. As the game began, McGee sat on the bench next to his pal Hornung, who would be the only player to not appear in this historic game. During the first series of downs, though, Dowler hurt his shoulder, and McGee was sent in wearing a teammate's helmet since Max couldn't find his own on short notice. After an exchange of punts, Green Bay took over at its own 20 and drove 80 yards in six plays with the touchdown coming on a third-and-three pass to McGee from the Kansas City 37. Starr's pass was behind Max, so he had to reach back and snag it one-handed at the 19 before racing in for the first score in Super Bowl history.

After the Chiefs tied the score at seven, the Packers started another drive from their 27 with 10:40 to play in the first half. During the 13-play 73-yard drive, Max caught a ten-yard pass to convert a third-and-five, and Green Bay took a 14–7 lead on a Jim Taylor touchdown run. In the third quarter, the Packers scored quickly after a turnover to take a 21–10 lead. Max caught a 14-yard pass the next time Green Bay had the ball. After another exchange of punts, the Packers drove 56 yards in ten plays, highlighted by McGee's catches of 11 yards, 16 yards (on third down) and the 13-yard scoring reception that Max juggled before securing despite it being accurately delivered. McGee's seventh and final catch on the day went for 37 yards and led to the final score of the day by Elijah Pitts in the fourth quarter.

Although Starr was named MVP of the game, McGee was featured on the cover of

Sports Illustrated the next week. When asked about how he managed to catch the off-course pass easily while juggling the easy one, McGee smiled puckishly toward Starr and said, "I don't get to practice the easy ones."[14] Max also said after the game, "I can't think of a better way to go out. I caught more passes than I caught all year. So I think it's about time to quit."[15]

It was a short-lived retirement, though. McGee returned for his twelfth season in 1967 as the aging Packers made their final push toward a three-peat championship run. His only three receptions for the season came in Week 14 against the lowly Steelers. He made no receptions in the playoffs against the Rams or the Cowboys, but got one last catch in Super Bowl II against the Raiders. In the third quarter with Green Bay up 16–7, Dowler was shaken up and Max came in for a third-and-one play from the Packer 40. Starr read the tight defense and went with a play-action deep pass to McGee for a 35-yard gain to the Oakland 25. Seven plays later, Donny Anderson scored, and the game was essentially over.

At this point, Max made good use of his Tulane business degree. A few years before, he and teammate Fuzzy Thurston had partnered for a Wisconsin restaurant franchise called The Left Guard. McGee moved from that experience to co-found the Chi Chi's restaurant chain that made him a multimillionaire when he eventually sold his stock well before that chain went under. Inducted into the Packer Hall of Fame in 1975, he returned to the Packers as the color man on the team's radio broadcasts in 1979, teaming with play-by-play man Jim Irwin for the next 20 years. McGee's amiable and sardonic delivery made him even more beloved by Packers fans, as his presence made a number of sad football seasons bearable before the Pack returned to prominence in the 1990s.

Along the way, McGee married for a second time in 1981 at age 49, and he and his wife Denise had two sons, Maxwell and Dallas. In the wake of Green Bay's two Super Bowl trips in the late 1990s, Irwin and McGee retired from broadcasting together following the 1998 season. Nine years later, the 75-year-old McGee died after falling from his roof, which he was clearing of leaves. At his funeral, Denise revealed that Max had been dealing with the ravages of Alzheimer's Disease.

Fifty years after his late career heroics in Super Bowl I, Max McGee remains in the team's all-time top ten in receiving yards. His career stat line reads 345 catches for 6,346 yards, an average of 18.4 yards per catch for 50 touchdowns. Moreover, he remains an integral part of Packers history and lore, for his contributions on the field, in the broadcast booth and in the hearts of Green Bay fans. He personified grace under pressure and exuded affable humor and joyful life.

Notes

1. Bob Ward, "Ex-White Oak Coach Credits Mcgee's Competitive Desire for Success," *Longview News Journal*, June 19, 2003.

2. Mike Miller, "Jack Vainisi: The Drafting Genius Behind the Packers Dynasty," *Capital Times*, April 23, 2009.

3. Cliff Christl, "An Oral History: Max Mcgee." Packers.com, accessed August 14, 2014, www.packers.com.

4. Bart Starr with Murray Olderman, *Starr: My Life in Football* (New York: William Morrow, 1987), 82.

5. Bud Lea, "Mcgee Bay Key?" *Milwaukee Journal*, September 25, 1958.

6. William N. Wallace, "The Golden Boy Frets," *New York Times*, July 20, 1967.

7. Len Wagner, *Launching the Glory Years: The 1959 Packers—What They Didn't Tell Us* (Green Bay: Coach's Books, 2001), 31.

8. Vince Lombardi with W.C. Heinz, *Run to Daylight* (Englewood Cliffs, NJ: Prentice-Hall, 1963), 60.

9. Cooper Rollow, "The Packers Had Superswingers, Too," *Chicago Tribune*, February 22, 1977.

10. Bud Lea, "Taxi Double Clutch Man," *Milwaukee Journal*, November 22, 1961.

11. Terry Bledsoe, "Bratkowski-Mcgee Pass Gives Packers 20–17 Victory Over Colts," *Milwaukee Journal*, September 27, 1965.

12. Vernon J. Biever, *The Glory of Titletown*, ed. Peter Strupp (Dallas: Taylor Trade, 1997), 11.

13. *Ibid.*

14. Allie Shah, "Goodbye to Max," *Minneapolis Star-Tribune*, October 29, 2007.

15. Murray Olderman, "Packers: Look of Superb Champs," *Times News*, January 20, 1967.

References

Biever, Vernon J. *The Glory of Titletown*. Edited by Peter Strupp. Dallas: Taylor Trade, 1997.

Bledsoe, Terry. "Bratkowski-Mcgee Pass Gives Packers 20–17 Victory Over Colts." *Milwaukee Journal*, September 27, 1965.

Christl, Cliff. "An Oral History: Max Mcgee." Packers.com. Accessed August 14, 2014. www.packers.com.

Lea, Bud. "Mcgee Bay Key?" *Milwaukee Journal*, September 25, 1958.

_____. "Taxi Double Clutch Man." *Milwaukee Journal*, November 22, 1961.

Lombardi, Vince, with W.C. Heinz. *Run to Daylight*. Englewood Cliffs, NJ: Prentice-Hall, 1963.

Miller, Mike. "Jack Vainisi: The Drafting Genius Behind the Packers Dynasty." *Capital Times*, April 23, 2009.

Olderman, Murray. "Packers: Look of Superb Champs." *Times News*, January 20, 1967.

Rollow, Cooper. "The Packers Had Superswingers, Too." *Chicago Tribune*, February 22, 1977.

Shah, Allie. "Goodbye to Max." *Minneapolis Star-Tribune*, October 29, 2007.

Starr, Bart, with Murray Olderman. *Starr: My Life in Football*. New York: William Morrow, 1987.

Wagner, Len. *Launching the Glory Years: The 1959 Packers—What They Didn't Tell Us*. Green Bay: Coach's Books, 2001.

Wallace, William N. "The Golden Boy Frets." *New York Times*, July 20, 1967.

Ward, Bob. "Ex-White Oak Coach Credits Mcgee's Competitive Desire for Success." *Longview News Journal*, June 19, 2003.

Ray Nitschke

Rich Shmelter

On July 29, 1978, five proud men who made up the Professional Football Hall of Fame's 16th induction class were on the verge of immortality after a stellar body of work left on the football field and in the history books. Like all other Hall of Fame members, past, present, and future, the class of 1978 possessed a life's journey filled with influential sagas of inspiration, perseverance, and talent. Ray Nitschke was one of the five awaiting enshrinement that July day in 1978.

Raymond Ernest Nitschke was born on December 29, 1936, in Elmwood Park, Illinois, a working class suburb of Chicago. Ray was the youngest of three sons born to his German father Robert and Danish mother Anna.[1]

The turbulent days of the Depression affected the Nitschkes. Despite their financial woes, Robert and Anna always made sure the boys were fed and had clean clothes. Ray's father worked for the Chicago Surface Lines, which was the street railway system in Chicago from 1913 to 1947 and the predecessor of the Chicago Transit Authority.[2]

Unfortunately, in addition to financial struggles, the Nitschkes' problems increased due to personal tragedy. In 1940, an automobile accident killed Robert Nitschke. This left Anna alone to raise three children while working two jobs. To help ease some of the burden, Ray's 14-year-old brother Robert found employment as a laborer. When Ray got a few years older, he worked any odd job he could find.[3]

Ray attended Proviso High School in Maywood, Illinois. Nitschke's name would rise to prominence in Proviso's history, but during his early time at the school, his life was once again torn apart. This time it was when his mother died at age 41 after developing a blood clot. The loss left 13-year-old Ray and his brothers orphaned. Relatives looked to help the boys by taking them into their families, but the three Nitschke boys would have had to be split up. Ray's 21-year-old brother Robert refused to allow the separation to occur. He took it upon himself to raise Ray along with help from his 17-year-old brother Richard.[4]

Anna's death left Ray confused and angry. He became a loner, mad at the world and everyone in it. His interest in sports was beginning to grow, but even then, he practiced alone.[5]

Proviso's motto "Peace, pride, and power" truly reflected what Ray Nitschke's life would eventually represent. Power helped earn him recognition as a great football player.[6] Pride was reflected in his work under the legendary coach Vince Lombardi, and peace came in family as the years went along. However, long before all this occurred, Nitschke was an undersized 100-pound 13-year-old. Despite his small stature, he displayed a fearless attitude that allowed him to battle his way through older and heavier opponents as a fullback on offense. On defense, he inflicted pain on opposing offenses from his linebacker position. Football was a way to release the fury stemming from his mother's death, and gave him the chance to show his worth.

Ray had no problems athletically. Unfortunately, he lacked enthusiasm in the classroom. It became a chore for him to attend school, and this negative approach saw his grades slide downward. After falling below a C average, Ray was declared ineligible for sports during his sophomore year. He then began to focus on his studies, and got his grades up so that he could compete in sports.[7]

Not only did the year away from sports improve his grades, but also helped his physical stature. A growth spurt took Ray from 5'9" to 6'0" with large hands that made it very easy for him to get a sturdy grasp on any type of ball. This allowed him to eventually showcase his prowess as a strong-armed quarterback, a basketball center, and pitcher for the baseball team.[8]

Proviso's football coach Andy Puplis, a former All-American quarterback at Notre Dame, served as a father figure and role model to Ray when it seemed that he was on the verge of destruction.

Another surge in his physical size took

Ray Nitschke.

Ray to a 6'1", 200-pounder with extraordinary arm strength. As a hard-throwing quarterback, he led the Pirates to a league championship his senior season while earning honorable mention on the 1953 High School All-America Team. In basketball, he set a school single-game scoring record with 36 points that lasted 20 years. He also helped Proviso win the 1953 state baseball championship, and earned second team All-State honors.[9]

Ray's athletic talents were too good to ignore, but he did not look to college as an option, at first. He did not take the proper courses needed in high school to prepare for college, and did not enjoy schoolwork. His only goal was to finish high school and not focus too far ahead. As the years went on, Ray's lackadaisical approach to schoolwork was something he regretted.[10]

Despite his previous thoughts of not going to college, his mind began to change after numerous offers started to present themselves. He also received an offer to play professional baseball for the St. Louis Browns for what was then an impressive sum of $3,000. He even thought about getting a blue-collar job or joining the military.[11]

Puplis convinced Nitschke not to take the offer from the St. Louis Browns, but go to college for an education. The idea of giving up the $3,000 offer was tough, but Ray knew that Puplis was right. It was then that he decided to stay close to his roots by committing to the University of Illinois.[12]

In the fall of 1954, Nitschke travelled to Champaign, Illinois, to begin the next phase of his life. College life at the University of Illinois did not settle well with Ray, as he was intimidated by the faster pace of his classes, and the hands-on approach by teachers was not there as in high school. After being a well-known star athlete at Proviso, he was now just another college freshman. These circumstances once again made Ray a loner just looking to make sense of his new environment.[13]

Nitschke chose physical education as his major. However, other courses were required, and he struggled until getting a grip on the academic side of college. On the athletic side, Ray's freshman year went well. He was named the freshman team's quarterback, and earned a reputation as a tough player to bring down while carrying the football.[14]

Before the 1955 season Illinois head coach Ray Eliot felt that Nitschke would better help the team as a hard-charging fullback. The news was not well received by Nitschke, whose eyes welled up with tears upon hearing the coach's decision, but the move proved to be the best one of his football career.[15]

Eliot recognized Nitschke's toughness as a fullback, and how brutal he was on defense. During this time in college football, players performed on both sides of the ball. It was common for anyone playing fullback on offense to move over to linebacker when the team switched to defense. Even though he was still an offensive-minded player at heart, Nitschke enjoyed blasting unfortunate opponents. Over 200 pounds by his sophomore season, Nitschke readied himself for punishing runs on offense, and punishing runners on defense.[16]

During Nitschke's three seasons on the varsity the Fighting Illini posted a mediocre 11–13–3 record.[17] In 1957, Ray was selected Second Team All-Big-Ten, and picked to play in the College All-Star Game and Senior Bowl. In addition, Nitschke received a sterling compliment from legendary coach Paul Brown who praised Nitschke for being the top college linebacker in the country.[18]

It seemed apparent that Ray would find his way onto a professional roster. Of the 12 teams that comprised the NFL in 1958, only one was the focal point of Nitschke's desires—his hometown Chicago Bears. On December 2, 1957, the Bears, who were already solid at linebacker, did not draft him. With their third round selection, obtained in a trade with the New York Giants, the Green Bay Packers selected the 6'3", 235-pound line-backer, making him the 36th overall player picked in the 1958 NFL draft. This draft went down in Green Bay history as possibly the greatest ever. Along with Nitschke, the Packers got fullback Jim Taylor, guard Jerry Kramer, and center/linebacker Dan Currie.[19]

Over the course of the next 15 seasons, Nitschke's number 66 was the cornerstone of the Packers defense. However, his reign of terror from the middle linebacker position almost never materialized. Ray attempted to play in the Canadian Football League for the Toronto Argonauts following a contract dispute with Green Bay's head coach Lisle Blackbourn. Blackbourn presented a contract offer of $7,000, which Nitschke found out was quite a bit lower than other college players were getting. Feeling that the offer was a slam on his abilities, he refused to sign.[20]

Just as he was about to go to Canada, Nitschke received a phone call from Jack Vain-isi, an administrative assistant and scout for the Packers. Vainisi sold the idea of playing in Green Bay to Nitschke, and he came away signing for slightly more than Blackbourn had offered, plus a $500 signing bonus.[21]

The Packers at this time were in shambles. The once proud franchise, winners of six NFL championships up to that time, had fallen on hard times. Before the start of the 1958 training camp, Blackbourn was fired and replaced with Ray "Scooter" McLean.

Prior to getting fired, Blackbourn told reporters that he wanted to try Nitschke out at either defensive end or linebacker. Ray also felt that he could have been a fullback. He might not have had the skills at running the ball like others, but he was good at catching passes and blocking. He quickly realized that his skills were better suited at linebacker due to his size, aggressiveness, and ability to track where the ball was going. When McLean took over as coach, he placed Nitschke at outside linebacker, but it was in the middle that the rookie, dubbed a "mean cuss" by Blackbourn, looked to wind up.[22] The 4–3 defense was quickly becoming prevalent in the NFL by 1958, and the middle line-backer was the leader of the defensive unit. The position carried a huge amount of respon-sibility, and the hard-nosed rookie was more than ready to take on that task.

Tom Bettis stood in Ray's way at landing the starting job at middle linebacker. Ray came into his first training camp with a nasty attitude. He remained a loner, and his type of seek-and-destroy nature turned most of the veteran players off, but the coaching staff loved it.[23]

At first, he was assigned to the special teams unit, but Bettis went down with an injury in the team's first pre-season game, forcing the Packers to start the rookie. The Packers finished Nitschke's rookie season with the worst record in team history, and McLean was fired.

Despite all the negativity surrounding the team, the Packers had a solid core of young players. They just needed someone to pull everything together. That someone was Vince Lombardi, the Packers' new head coach in 1959.

Over the course of the first few years under Lombardi, everything was not congenial for Nitschke and the coach. Lombardi saw Nitschke as a problem to coach. He was still an overly aggressive individual who caused problems in bars and eateries around Green Bay. Lombardi saw the actions as immature and stupid, and constantly reprimanded Nitschke. Under Lombardi, Nitschke was reduced to second-string linebacker. This did not sit too well with Nitschke, and he was highly vocal about his dislike of the situation. The outbursts got Lombardi mad, but he saw that Nitschke had the makings of a solid football player.[24]

In time, even though Lombardi remained tough on Nitschke, the pair put together a legendary union that made the Packers one of the greatest dynasties in all of American sports history. Winning helps cure many problems on a team, and under Lombardi, the Packers and Nitschke saw the benefits of the coach's harsh teachings. The Packers reached the NFL championship game in 1960, their first in 16 years, but lost to the Philadelphia Eagles. The following year, the Packers won the championship in convincing fashion over the New York Giants.

Ray's life made a complete turnaround. Not only was he on the cusp of becoming a full-time starter with a championship-caliber team, but also he found the love of a good woman who tamed his wild side. Nitschke got married to Jackie Forchette in 1961, and she helped him become a gentle giant off the field. Jackie got him to quit drinking alcohol, which mellowed him out. In time, the turnaround allowed Nitschke to become an intelligent, caring individual, and one of Green Bay's most beloved citizens who always lent a helping hand for local charities. In time, the couple adopted three children, which also allowed Nitschke to express more love.[25]

Despite the change in Nitschke's personal life, he was still one of the most volatile performers on the field. He became the starting middle linebacker in 1962, and helped the Packers repeat as champions. In the NFL championship game against the New York Giants, Nitschke recovered two fumbles and deflected a pass that was intercepted. His stellar play earned him the game's MVP award, and his legacy as one of the greatest was well on its way to maturation.

Nitschke was a strong, fast, vicious tackler that gave 100 percent on every play. During Lombardi's tenure from 1959 through the 1967 season, he anchored a defense that allowed slightly over 262 yards and 15 points per game, en route to five NFL championships and two Super Bowl titles. He not only intimidated physically, but also served as a psychological weapon, constantly weighing on the minds of opponents as to where he was on the field.

By the 1966 season, Nitschke was at the pinnacle of his successful career. With the front four doing such a great job keeping blockers away from him, Nitschke was able to roam from sideline to sideline looking for ballcarriers. Nitschke's efforts allowed him to be selected First Team All-Pro for the third straight year. He also received Second Team All-Pro honors four times (1962, 1963, 1967, 1969).

To commemorate the NFL's 50th season in 1969 the league released the top players at each position, and Nitschke was named all-time top linebacker. He was the only linebacker to be honored on both the NFL's 50th and 75th Anniversary Teams.

Following the 1972 season, at age 36, Nitschke retired after 190 games. He became a successful businessman, worked in commercials, and had a memorable role in the film *The Longest Yard* in 1974.

On July 29, 1978, along with Lance Alworth, Weeb Ewbank, Larry Wilson, and Tuffy Leemans, Ray Nitschke was enshrined into the Professional Football Hall of Fame in his first year of eligibility. He was the first Green Bay defender from the Lombardi era to be so honored. In 1983, he had his famed number 66 retired by the Packers.

On March 8, 1998, while returning to his winter home in Naples, Florida, Nitschke suffered a fatal heart attack at age 61. The day prior to each induction ceremony, the Hall of Fame holds a luncheon with many Hall of Famers present. Nitschke was a constant presence at the affair, and spoke to each new induction class about the honor that came with one's acceptance into the sport's hallowed shrine. Following his death, the Hall of Fame honored his memory by naming the annual luncheon after him.[26]

Nitschke rose up to become one of the greatest at his position. If there is a football league beyond this world, it would be a good bet that Ray Nitschke is lined up at middle linebacker. And if this is true, the next sound of thunder heard from the heavens might not be an act of inclement weather, but the result of a brutal Nitschke tackle.

NOTES

1. Edward Gruver, *Nitschke* (Lanham, MD: Taylor Trade, 2002), 3.
2. *Ibid.*, 2.
3. *Ibid.*, 3.
4. *Ibid.*, 4.
5. *Ibid.*, 5.
6. *Ibid.*, 7.
7. *Ibid.*
8. *Ibid.*
9. Ray Nitschke as told to Robert W. Wells, *Mean on Sunday: The Autobiography of Ray Nitschke* (Boulder: Big Earth, 1998) 18.
10. *Ibid.*, 21.
11. *Ibid.*
12. Gruver, 14.
13. *Ibid.*, 15.
14. *Ibid.*, 17.
15. *Ibid.*
16. *Ibid.*, 19.
17. University of Illinois Football, en.wikipedia.org.
18. Gruver, 31.
19. *Ibid.*, 32–33.
20. *Ibid.*, 33.
21. *Ibid.*, 34.
22. *Ibid.*
23. *Ibid.*, 36.
24. *Ibid.*, 46.
25. *Ibid.*, 63.
26. Ray Nitschke, en.wikipedia.org.

Elijah Pitts

MICHAEL D. BENTER

"If you don't go to Green Bay and try it, you're not half the man I think you are."
—Ruth Bellinger, 1961[1]

Shortly after the 1961 draft, Jerry Kramer wondered if his team had drafted Elijah Pitts from Philander Smith or vice versa. And there was the time Rams coach George Allen mistakenly referred to Pitts as actress ZaSu Pitts after Elijah helped defeat Allen's Rams with an 80-yard pass reception for a touchdown. Some teammates, according to Kramer, called him "Olive, Gravel, and every kind of pit" as well.[2]

His fellow Packers and fans knew him quite well, though, as a very reliable and steady backup halfback (6'1", 204 pounds) who could fill the shoes of, say, a Paul Hornung so adequately that the Green Bay offense often didn't miss a beat.

Elijah Eugene Pitts was born in Palarm, Arkansas, a small community along the Arkansas River near Mayflower and 17 miles north of Little Rock, on February 3, 1938. He was the son of sharecroppers, Samuel and Gertha Pitts. He had a brother Samuel and a sister Tressie. Their father died while Elijah was in his early teens.[3]

Pitts attended Pine Street High School in Conway, Arkansas, ten miles up the "old, old highway," Sturgis Road. He was remembered as a good student who ran track and "played a little basketball." When the Pine Street Polar Bears played their home games at Hendrix College's Young Memorial Stadium, Elijah Pitts lined up at halfback. A feat in itself because "he had never seen a football until he attended Pine Street." The segregated school had so few students that when the band played at halftime, Pitts played in it, too, on either the trombone or tuba.[4]

After high school, Elijah played college football from 1958 to 1960 at Philander Smith, a tiny, black, Methodist college with an enrollment of 600 students in Little Rock. Pitts had offers to play from larger schools, but chose to stay close to home; he had an aversion to large cities. It also helped that his older brother Sam had attended Philander Smith and his high school football coach, Mike Summerville, had become head coach at the school in 1956.[5]

Philander Smith wasn't exactly a football landmark like some other black colleges at the time, such as Jackson State, Southern and Grambling. The Panthers hadn't won a football game in the ten years before Pitts got there. In fact, three years after he left the school, its football program was discontinued in 1964.[6]

Pitts was a two-sport athlete at Philander Smith. As a track athlete, he ran the 100-yard dash in 9.6 seconds and the 440 in 47.1 seconds. On the gridiron, he set a Gulf Coast scoring record.[7] It was while Elijah was participating in a track meet at Grambling that he was recommended either by Summerville or track coach A.H. Morrow (there are differing versions) to an AFL scout from the Boston Patriots. The Patriots offered Pitts more money than the Packers, who selected him in round 13 of the 1961 draft. The Packers had spotted Pitts on game film they obtained from Arkansas A&M&N, a previous opponent of Philander Smith. Elijah's future wife Ruth Bellinger convinced him to spurn the better financial offer from the Patriots and report to Green Bay instead.[8]

Ruth was the daughter of a minister from Pontiac, Michigan. They married in 1962 after Pitts received his degree in education. The couple eventually raised a daughter and two sons.[9]

Pitts made the 1961 Packers but not without some trepidation. "I felt like a little fish in a big pond. The Packers ... were pretty well set at every position. I had the most trouble following the guards. I must have looked awful," Pitts confessed to a *Milwaukee Sentinel* reporter in 1965.[10]

For the first five seasons at Green Bay, Pitts played primarily behind Paul Hornung, though, he did find his way to the field to demonstrate a variety of talents. He was as good a blocker and

Elijah Pitts.

receiver and occasional option-passer as he was a special teams standout. Elijah was such a devastating tackler on special teams that Lombardi made him special teams captain.[11]

The 1966 season was a special year for Pitts. He was the recipient of a short Starr pass that turned into an 80-yard touchdown, the clinching score in a 24–13 victory over the Los Angeles Rams on September 25. A few weeks later, subbing for an injured Hornung who was out with a pinched nerve in his neck suffered against Chicago in the sixth game of the season, Pitts gained 188 rushing yards in games eight and nine vs. Detroit and Minnesota, respectively, assuaging the concerns the team and fans had about Hornung's absence. It was Pitts' two rushing touchdowns against Baltimore on December 10, 1966, that won that game for the Packers, thereby eliminating the Colts from the Western Conference title race. He also caught a 17-yard throw from Bart Starr for a touchdown and was the leading rusher (12–66) in the NFL title game against Dallas on January 1, 1967, a 34–27 Green Bay victory.[12]

He rushed and caught passes for 853 total yards in 1966, scoring ten touchdowns. He capped off the season by rushing for two second-half touchdowns vs. the Kansas City Chiefs in the inaugural Super Bowl, as the Packers won convincingly, 35–10. After the game a jubilant Pitts told the press, "The biggest thrill is winning the game for the NFL."[13]

During the off-season, Pitts worked in public relations for Milwaukee's Pabst Brewery. He and his wife also ran a personnel agency and a temporary help firm in the city, as the couple then lived in Brown Deer, a Milwaukee suburb. During the season, he roomed with other African American players in Green Bay in an apartment behind "an exterminating business that was owned by the family of former Packer and eventual Hall of Famer Tony Canadeo. Before 1967, Pitts and his family had lived in Chicago."[14]

His stellar play on a national stage at the Super Bowl was the impetus behind an Elijah Pitts Day in Little Rock. Held on January 21, 1967, the celebration was attended by the mayors of both Little Rock and North Little Rock, numerous fraternal organizations from Philander Smith, and civic groups from the local community. There was a parade with marching bands and drill teams and a luncheon at the Holiday Inn in his honor. Quite a feat for an African American in a city that was still reeling from school integration demonstrations.[15]

Racial matters were of paramount concern in Milwaukee by 1967, too. Milwaukee's race riots in the summer of 1967 had tensions high on the city's black north side. A few white south siders, some of them Polish, expressed their concern over the north side demonstrations—some marred by looting and vandalism—with less than civil behavior and words.

The *Milwaukee Journal*'s editorial staff on September 14, 1967, tried to quell things by noting the racial mix of the Green Bay Packers as it related to a report about Green Bay's offensive backfield for the season opener: "The starting runners for the Green Bay Packers when they open their National Football league season against the Detroit Lions in Green Bay are expected to be fullback Jim Grabowski and Elijah Pitts…. Without saying so … Coach Lombardi obviously picked the two men because he thought they would make the best combination…. They were picked strictly on their merits." The story did not mention that Pitts was black, or Grabowski of Polish extraction, because that was beside the point.

Incongruously not mentioned in the editorial was the fact that Jim Grabowski was a member of the Wisconsin National Guard and had done guard duty on a Milwaukee street corner that summer.[16]

Pitts' play and durability, not his race, though, were what mattered most in Green Bay, and to the Packers' fans in Milwaukee. As evidence to his worth to the team, a picture of Pitts running with the ball behind guard Fuzzy Thurston adorned the cover of the 1967 Packers press guide. Another highlight of Elijah's career came on opening day 1967 against the Lions when his 84-yard reception on a third-and-19 from the Green Bay three in the closing minutes of the fourth quarter led to the Packers eking out a tie with a Don Chandler field goal.

Unfortunately for Pitts, his career zenith was the 1966 season. Though he played three more seasons with the team, including the first couple of years that Phil Bengtson served as head coach, his playing time and overall value to the team eroded due to age, injury, and young, high-priced backs Donny Anderson and Jim Grabowski.

Pitts suffered an Achilles tendon injury in the eighth game of the 1967 season that shelved him for the rest of the year. The Packers had thoughts of passing him through 30-day injured waivers and then adding him to the active roster if he'd regain his health, but Otto Graham of the Redskins put in a claim for him to derail Green Bay's plan. Graham was seething from the Packers' recent signing of Chuck Mercein from their taxi squad (as Pitts' replacement, no less) and undoubtedly got some measure of revenge in doing so. Graham's maneuver forced the Packers to have Pitts miss the rest of the year rather than keep an injured player who might not return at all on their roster.[17]

In 1968, after suffering knee and thigh injuries in preseason games against the College All-Stars and Dallas, Pitts fell out of the mix at halfback. As a result, he was shifted to fullback, where he played behind Jim Grabowski. Grabowski was injured at times during the season so Pitts managed to accrue 72 carries, 17 pass receptions, and two rushing touchdowns.[18]

After a lackluster 1969 season in which he carried the football only 35 times, he was traded along with reserve center Bob Hyland and starting linebacker LeRoy Caffey for the Bears' first pick (second overall) in the 1970 draft. The Bears had tied the Steelers for the worst record in the league in 1969 and lost a coin flip for the first selection.[19]

Pitts never appeared in a game with the Bears; he was cut by Chicago as the team trimmed its roster to the then 40-man limit. He did play some in 1970, though. He appeared in two games with the Los Angeles Rams before he was traded to the Saints, for whom he appeared in six games before being waived in early December.

In 1971 Pitts returned to Green Bay where he was used solely as a return man in the punting and kicking game. Realizing his time as an active player was up when he didn't carry the ball a single time from the line of scrimmage that season, he retired. A veteran of 11 NFL seasons, Pitts left the game having amassed 1,788 yards rushing while scoring 28 touchdowns. He scored an additional six touchdowns as a receiver, having caught a total of 104 passes.[20]

Shortly after the 1971 season ended, he was named a Packers scout by head coach Dan Devine. He scouted for a couple of seasons before turning to coaching, something he then said he "always wanted to do." He definitely had experienced a change of mind, because years later he told Jerry Kramer that during the last few years of his playing career he thought coaching was "the last thing I would do."[21]

Pitts served as an assistant coach with the Rams, Oilers, Hamilton Tiger-Cats, and Buffalo Bills.[22] He was a member of Marv Levy's Buffalo Bills coaching staff while the

Bills made four Super Bowl appearances during the 1990s and was promoted to assistant head coach in 1992. In 1995, when Levy was ill with cancer, Pitts assumed the head coach's job for three games on an acting basis. Just three years later, Elijah died of stomach cancer at the age of 60 on July 10, 1998, at Mercy General Hospital in Buffalo.

Said Wade Phillips, who succeeded Levy in 1997 and had retained Pitts on his staff: "The passing of Elijah Pitts is a great loss not only for the Buffalo Bills but the entire National Football League.... The number of players and coaches that he has touched throughout the league are too many to name. His legacy will certainly carry on through them."[23]

Bart Starr, his erstwhile teammate said of Pitts, "[he was] one of the greatest gentlemen I have ever known."[24] Elijah was inducted into the Green Bay Packers Hall of Fame in 1979 and the Arkansas Hall of Fame in 1980. Fittingly, Pitts' younger son, Ronnie, a defensive back, played for the Bills from 1986 to 1987 and with the Packers from 1988 to 1990, the two teams with whom Pitts spent most of his 36 years in the NFL.

Notes

1. *Arkansas Gazette*, January 22, 1967, clipping provided by Philander Smith College library archives.

2. Jerry Kramer and Dick Schaap, *Instant Replay: The Green Bay Diary of Jerry Kramer* (New York: New American Library, 1968), 29.

3. "Elijah Eugene Pitts (1938–1998)," Encyclopedia of Arkansas History & Culture, Eycyclopediaofarkansas.net, accessed October 21, 2014, www.encyclopediaofarkansas.net/encyclopedia/entry-detail.aspx?entryID=5943; *Arkansas Gazette*, January 22, 1967; "Philander Smith College and Elijah Pitts," *The Panthernaut*, February 1966, clipping provided by Philander Smith College library archives.

4. "Elijah Pitts: A Polar Bear, a Panther and Now a Packer," *The Panthernaut*, February 1966, article courtesy Philander Smith College library archives; Joe Mosby, "Elijah Pitts: The Answer to Super Bowl Trivia," Thecabinetstories.com, accessed October 2, 2014, www.Thecabinet/Stories/052 099/Gre_0520990010.Html.

5. *Ibid.*; Jerry Kramer and Dick Schaap, *Distant Replay* (New York: G.P. Putnam's Sons, 1985), 124.

6. "Elijah Eugene Pitts (1938–1998)," Encyclopedia of Arkansas History & Culture; "Philander Smith College," *The Panthernaut*.

7. Green Bay Packers Press Guide, 1966, 25.

8. "Elijah Pitts: A Polar Bear," *The Panthernaut*; Encyclopedia of Arkansas; "Elijah Pitts," *The Panthernaut*; "Philander Smith College and Elijah Pitts," *The Panthernaut*.

9. *Ibid.*

10. *Milwaukee Sentinel*, September 9, 1965.

11. Kramer, *Distant Replay*, 124.

12. *Milwaukee Journal*, September 26, 1966; November 15, 1966. Pitts was pictured rushing for one of his two touchdowns against Baltimore on the front page of the *Milwaukee Journal* on December 11, 1966.

13. *Milwaukee Sentinel*, January 16, 1967.

14. *Milwaukee Sentinel*, July 16, 1969, September 9, 1965; Kramer, *Distant Replay*, 124; *The Panthernaut*.

15. *Southern Mediator Journal*, January 20, 1967, clipping courtesy Philander Smith College library archives.

16. *Milwaukee Journal*, August 1, 1967; Kramer, *Instant Replay*, 53.

17. *Milwaukee Sentinel*, November 16, 1967; *Milwaukee Journal*, July 17, 1968.

18. "Elijah Pitts," Databasefootball.com, accessed November 24, 2014, www.databasefootball.com/players/playerpage.htm?ilkid=PITTSELI01.

19. *Ibid.*

20. *Milwaukee Sentinel*, October 12, 1970; *Milwaukee Journal*, December 5, 1970; databasefootball.com.

21. *Milwaukee Journal*, February 14, 1974; Kramer, *Distant Replay*, 125.

22. "CBS Sportsline: Elijah Pitts Dead at 60," Cbsnews.com, July 10, 1998, accessed October 2, 2014, www.cbsnews.com/news/former-packer-pitts-dead-at-60/.

23. *Ibid.*

24. Encyclopedia of Arkansas, "Elijah Pitts."

Dave Robinson

John Maxymuk

Longtime Packer player and assistant coach Dave Hanner told local reporter Cliff Christl in 2004, "I know people think I'm crazy, but if you had to pick between Nitschke and Dave Robinson, I'd take Dave Robinson."[1] While that may be surprising to some, Packer fans have long been well aware of what a great linebacker Robinson was and were delighted in 2013 when Dave finally was elected to the Pro Football Hall of Fame. It was well deserved and long overdue.

Richard David Robinson was born May 3, 1941, in Mount Holly, New Jersey, and grew up in nearby Mount Laurel. Dave was the youngest of nine children, six boys and three girls, born to laborer Leslie Robinson and his wife Mary. Before Leslie died at 52 from a heart ailment when Dave was a freshman in high school, he encouraged Dave to play all sports because they would help sharpen his talents on the football field: "He said that basketball would help me develop my linebacker skills, that a baseball leaving the bat would be like a ball leaving the quarterback's arm. And he was right."[2]

At Moorestown High School, Dave earned 12 letters and played on three undefeated teams: a state champion football team in 1957 and state champion basketball teams in 1958 and 1959. Upon graduation in 1959, he was offered athletic scholarships to 46 universities, including Penn and Columbia, and chose Penn State. For the Nittany Lions, Robinson was something of a trailblazer. In 1961, he was the first African American to play in the Gator Bowl, where he made the defensive play of the game with a timely quarterback sack. A year later, he became the first black player from Penn State to be named All-America as an end in his senior year. An intelligent man and a serious student, Dave would earn a B.S. in Civil Engineering with a minor in Economics at Penn State. He also married his high school sweetheart, Elaine.

Robinson was drafted 14th overall by the Packers in 1963 and also 17th overall in the AFL draft by the Chargers. Green Bay outbid San Diego to sign Dave and it was money well spent, although Dave wondered how welcome he was when he first reported to training camp in August. Robinson played in the 1963 College All-Star game a couple days before in a game the Packers lost 20–17. Robinson had played well in the game and looked forward to getting praised for his play as the team viewed the game films. When Coach Vince Lombardi stopped the projector after a play in which Robinson beat tight end Ron Kramer to throw Tom Moore for a loss, Dave was all ears. However, an infuriated Lombardi screamed, "KRAMER! Look at that rookie get rid of you! That kid probably won't even make the team that drafted him!"[3] Veteran safety Willie Wood leaned forward and chuckled to Dave, "I wouldn't buy a house if I were you."[4]

Robinson was shifted from defensive end to linebacker as a rookie and was taken under wing by 12-year veteran right linebacker Bill Forester, playing in his final year. Dave later told Ken Hartnett, "Everything else was a refinement of what he taught me."[5] Dave was ready to start in 1964, the year he and Elaine had twin sons Richard and David. Robby was inserted as the left, or strong side, linebacker, with incumbent left linebacker Dan Currie replacing the retired Forester on the weak side. Thus, the Packers' celebrated defensive Left Side of the 1960s was formed; it featured Hall of Famers at defensive end (Willie Davis) linebacker (Robby) and cornerback (Herb Adderley) and would prove nearly impregnable for the remainder of the decade, particularly in pass defense.

But first the players had to learn to work together. Robinson told reporter Chuck Johnson, "When I came here Willie and Dapper [Dan Currie] had been playing together, and they both liked to free-lance a lot. I'm not that kind of player, and when I took Dapper's place, we had some adjustments to make. Now Willie plays it more by the book than he used to. I've got to know where my help is coming from on every play and in every defense."[6]

Robinson had some knee problems that year, missed three games and underwent surgery in the offseason. He came back at full strength in 1965 and began to demonstrate his special talent for pass defense and his propensity for making big plays. At 6'3", 245 pounds, Dave was, in the words of Sports Illustrated's Paul Zimmerman, "one of the first of the truly great size and speed outside linebackers in history."[7] He was agile, rangy and had a great wingspan. Ever the engineer, Robby used his analytical mind during film study to precisely determine the depth of his drops so that he was nigh impossible to throw over. He told Murray Olderman, "To clear me, a pass has to be at least ten feet high and short enough so the corner behind me can't get it."[8] San Francisco 49ers coach Jack Christiansen famously quipped, "With his arms and reactions, it's like trying to pass over the Empire State Building. If it were a banana tree going past him, he'd strip it clean with the first grab."[9]

Robinson demonstrated that extraordinary pass defense facility in the Week 13 showdown in Baltimore against the rival Colts in 1965. The Packers were leading 14–13 late in the first half, when backup quarterback Gary Cuozzo tried a swing pass from the Green Bay two-yard line. Robinson leaped, tipped the ball to himself and returned it 87 yards to the Colt ten. The Packers scored a quick touchdown to close out the half up 21–13, rather than down 20–14. That crucial 14-point swing enabled them to go on to win easily 42–27 on the path to the 1965 NFL championship.

In 1966, Robinson tied with Bob Jeter for the team lead in interceptions with five and was selected for the Pro Bowl. Defensive coach Phil Bengtson said of him, "Robbie handles tight ends as well as anybody in the business. He has the strength and quickness that are the keys to holding those guys at the line to delay their patterns. And Dave doesn't often get cut down when the other team blocks down on the linebacker on off-tackle slants."[10]

In the NFL championship game against Dallas, Dave made the most famous and important play of his career. In the final minutes of a back-and-forth contest that Green Bay led 34–27, the Cowboys mounted a last drive that took them to a first down on the Packer two-yard line. Three downs later, it was fourth-and-goal from the two, with the game hanging in the balance of one play. Quarterback Don Meredith rolled out as Robinson blew past Bob Hayes and smothered Meredith who lobbed a pop-fly into the end zone where Packer safety Tom Brown made the game-clinching interception. Robinson likes to tell the story that he was graded poorly on the play by Lombardi because "I should have gotten in front of the [pulling] guard and shut off the run before I thought of anything else."[11] Dave added to Chuck Johnson, "I tried to pin both [Meredith's] arms, but all I could get was his left. As I grabbed him, I thought that I hadn't done what I was supposed to do. Under Coach Lombardi, you always try for perfection, and if I had played this perfectly, I would have had both his arms."[12]

Cowboys assistant Ermal Allen saw it differently, though: "We had never run the play out of a Brown left [formation]. So Robinson didn't have any films or coaching tips to go by. He just made the play by himself, on instinct and good football sense. That's why we think he's the best outside linebacker around."[13]

Vince had the final word in the posthumous volumes *Vince Lombardi on Football* published a few years later. "The man who had to make the play for us was the linebacker. He did. Dave Robinson, as he was taught to do, analyzed before reacting and, reading rollout, fought through the blocker protecting Meredith and then chased Meredith with his hands up high, screening him off from his receivers, and when Dave got to him he tried to pin both arms and forced Meredith to throw the ball up for grabs. We intercepted and that was that."[14]

Green Bay went on to win the first Super Bowl two weeks later, and then topped that in 1967 by winning their third consecutive world championship in Super Bowl II, Lombardi's last game as Packers coach. Robinson had another excellent year in 1967, intercepting four passes, being selected to a second Pro Bowl and earning All-Pro honors for the first time. He also came up with another big play in the first round of the playoffs when he blocked a field goal against the Rams that kept the game in hand during the first half before the Packer offense got going.

Under new coach Phil Bengtson, Robinson continued his excellent play, earning All-Pro honors in both 1968 and 1969 and going to the 1969 Pro Bowl. Perceptive defensive tackle Henry Jordan once described Robby's football skills: "He has exceptionally good hands, good speed and he's a good tackler. What makes a linebacker successful is being able to analyze real quickly and, if it's a run, to fill his hole and, if it's a pass, to go deep. Dave can do all this."[15] Cleveland Brown receiver Gary Collins put it more piquantly: "I played against Dave Robinson in college, too. He was an end at Penn State. He knocked the shit out of me when we played the Packers. He got you. He was very underrated."[16]

In 1970, Bengtson's final dispiriting year as head coach, though, Dave tore his Achilles tendon in Week 4 and missed the rest of the season. When he returned, fully rehabbed, in 1971, Dan Devine was the new coach. Robinson, like most Packers from that time, did not respect Devine and thought he was a poor coach. By this point, Dave was a team leader and was instrumental in developing young linebackers Fred Carr and Jim Carter as well as new left

Dave Robinson.

defensive end Clarence Williams into a divisional championship unit in 1972. At that point, Robinson retired. He told the *Milwaukee Sentinel* in 1988, "I played here for ten years, then Dan Devine ran me out of town."[17]

One thing that Devine did that irked Robinson was removing Dave when the team shifted into nickel defense, since pass defense was always a strength and source of pride for Robinson. Although Robby had announced his retirement in the offseason, Devine traded his rights to Washington, and George Allen persuaded Dave to play again in 1973. In Washington, Robinson started for two years, was a part of two more playoff teams and then retired for good in 1975. His 27 interceptions, 21 with Green Bay, still ranks in the all-time leaders among linebackers. He was selected to the NFL's All-Decade team for the 1960s and was inducted into the Packer Hall of Fame in 1982.

Post-football, Dave started his own beverage distributorship in Akron, Ohio, and became a very successful businessman, like so many of his former Packer teammates. His marriage to Elaine lasted 44 years until her death in 2007. He himself survived colon cancer in 2011. Sadly, though, two of their three sons have also passed away, Richard (one of the twins) and the youngest, Robert. Son Dave, Jr., however, was able to present his father for induction to the Hall of Fame in August 2013, and Dave Sr. gave a moving and humorous acceptance speech.

Looking back, defensive coach Phil Bengtson ranked Dave Robinson second only to Ray Nitschke of the great players he coached. Bengtson aptly stated, "No one I've ever met within pro football has within him a higher degree of intelligence plus a higher degree of aggressiveness than Dave Robinson."[18] Robinson was a brainy, analytical hitter, stout at the point of attack, with the athletic litheness to range deep down the field in pass defense. He is at home in Canton.

Notes

1. Mike Vandermause, "Green Bay Packers Legend Dave Robinson Reflects on Life, Career," *Green Bay Press Gazette*, July 19, 2011, www.archive.packernews.com.

2. Walt Burrows, "Moorestown's Robinson Starred with the Packers," *Courier-Post* (Camden, NJ), December 17, 2002.

3. David Maraniss, *When Pride Still Mattered* (New York: Simon & Schuster, 1999), 347.

4. Rob Reischel, "Standing Out in a Crowd," *Milwaukee Journal Sentinel*, March 13, 2002, www.jsonline.com.

5. Ken Hartnett, "Doubting Dave," *Packers Yearbook*, 1967, 35.

6. Chuck Johnson, *Greatest Packers of Them All* (New York: G. P. Putnam's Sons, 1968), 159.

7. Paul Zimmerman, "Inside Football—Hall of a Task," *Sports Illustrated*, SI.com, August 1, 2003.

8. Murray Olderman, *The Defenders* (Englewood Cliffs, NJ: Prentice-Hall, 1973), 88.

9. *Ibid.*, 257.

10. *Ibid.*

11. Paul Zimmerman, *The Linebackers: The Tough Ones of Pro Football* (New York: Scholastic, 1973), 80.

12. Johnson, 162.

13. *Ibid.*, 163.

14. George Flynn, ed., *Vince Lombardi on Football: Volume II* (New York: New York Graphic Society, 1973), 71–72.

15. Hartnett, 35.

16. Alan Natali, *Browns Town: 20 Famous Browns Talk Amongst Themselves* (Wilmington, OH: Orange Frazer Press, 2001), 525.

17. Bud Lea, "Former Packer Robinson's Return a Letdown," *Milwaukee Sentinel*, September 15, 1988.

18. Zimmerman, *The Linebackers*, 84.

REFERENCES

Burrows, Walt. "Moorestown's Robinson Starred with the Packers." *Courier-Post* (Camden, NJ), December 17, 2002.

Flynn, George, ed. *Vince Lombardi on Football: Volume II*. New York: New York Graphic Society, 1973.

Hartnett, Ken. "Doubting Dave." *Packers Yearbook*, 1967.

Johnson, Chuck. *Greatest Packers of Them All*. New York: Putnam, 1968.

Lea, Bud. "Former Packer Robinson's Return a Letdown." *Milwaukee Sentinel*, September 15, 1988.

Maraniss, David. *When Pride Still Mattered*. New York: Simon & Schuster, 1999.

Natali, Alan. *Browns Town: 20 Famous Browns Talk Amongst Themselves*. Wilmington, OH: Orange Frazer Press, 2001.

Olderman, Murray. *The Defenders*. Englewood Cliffs, NJ: Prentice-Hall, 1973.

Reischel, Rob. "Standing Out in a Crowd." *Milwaukee Journal Sentinel*, March 13, 2002. www.jsonline.com.

Vandermause, Mike. "Green Bay Packers Legend Dave Robinson Reflects on Life, Career." *Green Bay Press Gazette*, July 19, 2011. www.archive.packernews.com.

Zimmerman, Paul. "Inside Football—Hall of a Task," *Sports Illustrated*, SI.com, August 1, 2003.

Zimmerman, Paul. *The Linebackers: The Tough Ones of Pro Football*. New York: Scholastic, 1973.

Bob Skoronski

RICK SCHABOWSKI

Bob Skoronski had an 11-year career in the NFL, all with the Green Bay Packers, and was an important part of five NFL championships over a seven-year span, which included victories in the first two Super Bowls.

Robert Francis Skoronski (originally Skowronski) was born in Ansonia, Connecticut, on March 5, 1934, to Francis and Sophie Skoronski. Both of his parents worked at a B.F. Goodrich rubber mill near New Haven, Connecticut. Reflecting on his childhood, Skoronski says, "My grandparents came over on a boat [from Poland]. The values I grew up with were that you worked like hell to get ahead. My folks didn't have a lot, so the only way I was going to college was on a football scholarship."[1]

When Bob's family relocated from Ansonia to nearby Derby, Skoronski attended Fairfield Prep, a Catholic high school. After attaining All-State honors in football, Skoronski was courted by several colleges, but he planned to attend Admiral Billard Academy in New London, Connecticut, before attending Holy Cross. Skoronski notes, "I didn't have the academic qualifications to go to Holy Cross after graduating from Fairfield Prep, but I got financial assistance from Holy Cross to go to Billard Academy. My intention was to go to Holy Cross the next year."[2]

Skoronski's coach at Billard, Sal Amanti, recalled the first time he met Bob. "He was 17 years old, stood 6–4, and weighed 240 without an ounce of fat. The first thing he ever said to me was that he was going to be a professional football player."[3]

During Billard's 2–2 season in 1951, they played Aquinas Institute, and even though they lost, 33–12, Skoronski's play so impressed Aquinas' coach, Mickey Connelly, that when Connelly was offered an assistant coach's position at Indiana University, he recruited Bob for Indiana. Skoronski's older brother Frank was tired of his job working at a mill and wanted to go to college, too. Frank was an athlete, although not as good as his younger brother, but Bob informed the colleges pursuing him that he'd like to go to a school that would also take his brother. Indiana was the only school that offered the brothers the package they wanted. There, Bob majored in business marketing, while his brother worked his way through school after giving up football.

Skoronski started as an offensive lineman for Indiana in his sophomore season, and during his senior season, in which he recovered eight fumbles, he was the team's captain and Most Valuable Player. He also was a two-time selection to the All-Big Ten team at tackle. While attending Indiana he met Ruth Ann Asher from Wayne, New Jersey. The two married in 1956.

It seemed like a career in the NFL loomed in Skoronski's future. The first three rounds of the NFL draft took place in Philadelphia on November 30, 1955, with Forrest Gregg from SMU being selected by the Packers in the second round. Skoronski had to wait until the draft resumed in Los Angeles on January 17, 1956, to be selected by Green Bay in the fifth round. Although Skoronski was offered a contract for more money to play in Canada, he signed with Green Bay for $7,500 with a $500 bonus.

Skoronski was not happy going to Green Bay. He recalls, "One of the things I didn't want to do was go to Green Bay. When I got drafted by Green Bay, I didn't even know where it was. I'd never been north of Chicago in my life. When I flew up to Green Bay, we landed in this field and there wasn't even a building there. I thought, why did we stop here? Someone must have to go to the bathroom. But someone said, 'Here we are.' That was it. The first meal was hot dogs. I hadn't eaten hot dogs in years. At Indiana we had steaks."[4] John Sandusky was traded from Cleveland to Green Bay during the training camp and Skoronski greeted him with "John, welcome to the end of the earth."[5]

The adjustment to Green Bay was so difficult that on the night of Sunday, August 12, 1956, Skoronski, along with Packers top draft pick halfback Jack Losch from the University of Miami, left the club's Stevens Point training camp and headed home. After a 36-hour manhunt, the team found them in their homes back east and persuaded the rookies to rejoin the club.

Along with Gregg, Skoronski started on the offensive line for head coach Lisle Blackbourn's 1956 Packers team that tied for last place with the Rams in the Western Conference. Blackbourn was pleased with Skoronski, touting him as "a fast, quick big man with lots of ability."[6]

Despite the good rookie season, the pro game gave Skoronski new challenges. "The main difference is the way the defenders in the pros use their hands. In college, you get hit by a shoulder or they try to overpower you. But up here everybody's so strong, so they have to use their hands They try to grab you and twist you and throw you and get you off-balance. You don't have the same thing in college at all—lots less passing, and then a lot of roll-outs when you do throw."[7]

Over the next two seasons, Skoronski fulfilled

Bob Skoronski.

his military commitment, serving 23 months in the United States Air Force. He still managed to get some football playing in, for the Bolling Air Force Base squad in 1957–58, and was named to the All-Military Service All-Star team. He was given an early release for seasonal occupation.

Bob returned to Green Bay in May 1959 and met his new coach, Vincent T. Lombardi. Skoronski noticed a big change on the playing field from his rookie year of 1956. "It wasn't a democracy. It was his way and he knew what he wanted. He had an enormous knowledge of the game and what the opposition was trying to do. My rookie year, some of the guys traveled to away games in T-shirts. With Vince, the start of his discipline thing was that every player traveled in a jacket and tie. And that tie doesn't come off until you were up in your hotel room."[8]

The coaching change and the maturing of the team resulted in the Packers winning the Western Conference in 1960, earning the right to play the Eagles for the NFL title. When Lombardi found out that Skoronski's in-laws lived in nearby New Jersey, he extended an invitation to Skoronski to bring his wife and three sons along for the flight out east. "Vince carried one of my boys off the plane, and that picture ran in several newspapers. Still got the photo somewhere in my house."[9]

The Packers lost to the Eagles, but they would not fail in 1961. Skoronski recalled the 1961 championship game victory over the Giants. "It was a special game. Usually players don't realize what is happening to them when they are playing in a big game like that. They are sort of in a daze. We realized everything. We knew it did no good to go that far and lose. We had been so infused with Lombardi's philosophy. We were loose and focused at the same time. It was a bit frightening."[10]

In the early years, Skoronski didn't always start but shared the left tackle position with Norm Masters. He also filled in when Masters moved to right tackle to replace Forrest Gregg. Skoronski saw extensive action in 1961 when Masters replaced Jerry Kramer who was sidelined with an ankle injury. In addition, Skoronski occasionally played center.

However after Jim Ringo's trade to the Philadelphia Eagles on May 5, 1964, Skoronski was shifted to center. Lombardi praised Skoronski, noting, "We know he can play it regularly. He'll add a great deal of size to our line."[11] Skoronski weighed 250 pounds, 20 more than his predecessor. The Packers' confidence in Skoronski playing center was because of a trial run they conducted. Skoronski recalled, "They called me down and asked me to snap the ball. I did it maybe eight or ten times and they said, 'Okay, we've seen enough.' Well then the next thing I know they trade Ringo and I'm the starting center. I had no idea what they had been up to."[12]

After the retirement of Norm Masters in July 1965, Skoronski returned to his left tackle position full time, with Ken Bowman taking the starter's job at center. Before the season, Skoronski was named the Packers' offensive captain by Lombardi. The Packers returned to the NFL title game meeting the defending champion Cleveland Browns at Lambeau Field on January 2, 1966.

The Browns hung close to the Packers, down just 13–12 at halftime until the game's decisive touchdown was scored in the third quarter. The Packers were on the Browns' 13-yard line when Bart Starr handed off to Hornung. He followed perfect blocks by both Jerry Kramer and Skoronski and ran through the muddy field and across the goal line, giving the Packers a 20–12 lead. They went on to win, 23–12, returning the NFL title to Green Bay after a two-year absence.

They repeated as champs in 1966, defeating the Cowboys, 34–27, in a 1967 New Year's Day game at the Cotton Bowl. That day the Packers changed how they normally ran out of their formations. On the game's first play from scrimmage, Elijah Pitts gained 32 yards to the Dallas 44-yard line. Skoronski gives credit to Coach Lombardi. "Actually, it was an old play, but the blocking was different. Vince was very good at watching film and designing a game plan. He had a good eye for that. He really could find things. It was completely backwards to what the Cowboys must have expected. They had no idea what we were doing to them. Vince was excited all week that it was going to work, and it did. No one ever noticed the flex defense like he did. That was his baby."[13]

Their victory over Dallas gave the Packers the right to represent the NFL in the first world championship game, AFL vs. NFL (no Super Bowl title or Roman numerals yet). Their opponent was the American Football League's Kansas City Chiefs. The Packers were under a lot of pressure carrying the NFL's reputation into this game, and Lombardi drove them hard. Skoronski says about Lombardi, "He was miserable that week. He liked to have killed us. I personally thought he was going to leave the game on the practice field, the only time I ever thought that."[14] In the second half, the Packers broke open a close 14–10 halftime advantage, defeating the Chiefs, 35–10.

The next year, Green Bay returned to the playoffs, again tangling with Dallas in the 1967 NFL championship game. Skoronski has fond recollections of that day's Ice Bowl. The Packers got the ball with 4:54 remaining in the fourth quarter. Skoronski recalls, "When it [the final drive] began, when we were 67 yards away or whatever it was, we were gathered together on the sidelines and someone said, 'Well, we got it.' That's all anyone said. We didn't do a lot of shooting off at the mouth."[15]

The final drive required all the effort these experienced veterans had left in them, in sub-zero conditions. Skoronski recalls the game-winning quarterback sneak by Bart Starr. "On the last touchdown, I just tried to keep my guy in his position so he couldn't get across the inside to stop whoever had the ball. I didn't know Bart was going to keep the ball. He decided that because of the slippery handling, it was best not to take a chance on a handoff. I didn't see Bart go over the goal line. We were not the kind of team who was looking at where the ball was going. Everybody was trying to do their block to the best of their ability."[16] Skoronski also notes it was the most focused he had ever seen the offense on any drive in all his time with the Packers.

The victory against Dallas earned the Packers a berth in Super Bowl II versus the Oakland Raiders. Skoronski noticed a change in Lombardi's behavior before the game. He even allowed the players' wives to accompany the team, breaking a long-standing rule. "I'm not saying he didn't have the urgency to win, that was obvious, but he was more melancholy about it. He'd dwell on some things more than he would have before. He was so business-like, so professional most of the time, and now—I don't want to say he was a more loving guy—but he was a little more gentle."[17]

Before the game, Skoronski, the offensive captain, spoke to his teammates, noting that if they lost, everything they had worked so hard for the entire season would be gone. "I don't have any damn intention of losing this ballgame, and I don't think anybody else here does."[18] The entire team agreed with Skoronski, posting a 33–14 victory for the Packers' second Super Bowl victory and their third consecutive pro football championship.

In the locker room after the victory, Skoronski noticed a different type of reaction from Lombardi. "Normally, he would have been very, very excited about winning and saying, 'We'll do it again, boys.' There was no talk like that. He was very reserved."[19]

Indeed, on Thursday, February 1, 1968, Lombardi would relinquish the head coaching job to Phil Bengtson, retaining the job of general manager.

Skoronski's last game at Lambeau Field as a player, on December 7, 1968, against the Baltimore Colts, was an emotional one. Before the game, because of his role as offensive captain, Skoronski spoke first. "We've dedicated games to the fans and to the coaches and to individual players, but let's play this game for the guys who've made this team what it's been. A lot of us are playing our last game at Lambeau Field."[20]

On June 10, 1969, Skoronski formally announced his retirement, saying it was best for his family, the Packers, and his business interests.[21]

Retirement from the field did not end Skoronski's tight connection with his teammates. In his book, *Closing the Gap,* Willie Davis wrote, "Bob was a very caring individual and still is, even today. As the Packers hold team functions for their former players over the years, if by some chance I miss one, I'll still get a call from Bob making sure I'm okay. He's a dear friend who cared for each and every one of his teammates, showing an unmatched loyalty."[22] Davis also praised the job Skoronski did as the offensive captain. "He was also someone who believed in boosting morale. He was always quick to congratulate teammates on a good play, offer encouragement, and even bring in some gifts.... Bob gave it his all in every game, leaving nothing on the field. He looked at his role as a team leader to make sure that other players were doing the same thing. He was a player we could rally around."[23]

After retiring, Skoronski was involved with a number of successful business ventures. The work ethic and commitment to excellence Lombardi had instilled paid off. Skoronski is proud to say, "No one could have worked harder than I did, but it was a labor of love. I can't think of a day I didn't look forward to going to work. I didn't think I could find anything nearly so exciting after football, but it was the thrill of victory all over again. To me, the greatest thrill was seeing people who worked for me start a family, buy a home, and begin raising and educating their kids."[24]

In 1976, Skoronski was inducted in the Packers Hall of Fame, and in 2000 he was inducted to the Polish-American Hall of Fame. Reflecting on his NFL career, Skoronski is thankful. "I was very lucky to be where I was and a member of those teams in Green Bay. I played with a great group of teammates for a great coach. There was a helluva lot of love there, and that's what made it special. It wasn't all about the money you took home. I'll treasure the experience for the rest of my life."[25] He is also proud. "Did we always run to the right side? The captaincy of the Packers wasn't an elected position. Why did Lombardi select me? I've evaluated myself alongside the guys who were the greatest of all time, and I can sleep, I can sleep."[26]

NOTES

1. Martin Hendricks, "Skoronski Recalls Early Efforts to Represent Players," jsonline.com, *Packer Insider,* March 23, 2011. www.jsonline.com/packerinsider/118437609.html.

2. Roger Montgomery, "Bob Skoronski May Begin New Career," *The Day,* February 3, 1975.

3. *Ibid.*

4. Chip Malafronte, "Derby's Bob Skoronski Made Packers Hall of Fame, But Bart Starr Thinks He Belongs in Canton," *New Haven Register,* October 17, 2012.

5. David Maraniss, *When Pride Still Mattered* (New York: Simon & Schuster, 1999), 192.

6. Chuck Johnson, "Blackbourn Rates His Packers as 'Better" Tempers Enthusiasm with a Look at West," *Milwaukee Journal,* September 18, 1956.

7. Chuck Johnson, *Greatest Packers of Them All* (New York: G. P. Putnam's Sons, 1968), 122.

8. Hendricks.

9. *Ibid.*

10. Maraniss, 292.

11. "Lombardi Says Green Bay Might Not Be Through Yet," *Sarasota Herald-Tribune*, May 7, 1964.

12. Leroy Butler and Rob Reischel, *Packers Pride* (Chicago: Triumph Books, 2013), 136.

13. Bud Lea, *Magnificent Seven: The Championship Games That Built the Lombardi Dynasty* (Chicago: Triumph Books, 2002), 95.

14. Maraniss, 392.

15. *Ibid.,* 143.

16. Michael, 84.

17. Lea, 168.

18. Edward Gruver, *Nitschke* (Dallas: Taylor Trade, 2004), 185.

19. Lea, 181.

20. Jerry Kramer, "Packers Couldn't Even Win One for Themselves Sunday," *Sarasota Journal,* December 10, 1968.

21. Bud Lea, "Retirements Force Pack to Revamp Line," *Milwaukee Sentinel,* June 11, 1969.

22. Willie Davis with Jim Martyka and Andrea Erickson Davis, *Closing the Gap* (Chicago: Triumph Books, 2012), 77–78.

23. *Ibid.,* 78.

24. Kramer, *Distant Replay,* 133.

25. Hendricks.

26. Kramer, *Distant Replay*, 132.

Bart Starr

John Vorperian

The five-time NFL Title game and Super Bowl I and II champion quarterback played with the Green Bay Packers from 1956 to 1971. Selected four times to the Pro Bowl, named to the NFL's 1960s All-Decade Team, Starr led the league in completion percentage in 1962, 1966, 1968, and 1969. He was the NFL's MVP in 1966. With a 9–1 playoff record, Starr's 104.80 playoff passer rating has kept him listed as the top quarterback in NFL playoff history for decades. The two-time Super Bowl MVP went on to coach Green Bay from 1975 to 1983. Starr was inducted into the Pro Football Hall of Fame in 1977.

Bryan Bartlett Starr was born on January 9, 1934, in Montgomery, Alabama, to Benjamin Bryan Starr and Lulu Inez Starr (nee Tucker). His parents, married October 1932, rarely referred to him by his first name but rather by his middle name given to him in honor of the doctor, Haywood Bartlett, who delivered the child. In 1936, the couple had a second son whom they named Hilton. Ben worked as a blacksmith and served in the Army National Guard. Lulu was a homemaker. Ben pursued his military career in the Army Air Corp.

The family moved from Montgomery to Columbia, Tennessee, and back. Prior to World War II, Ben was assigned to Fort Blanding near Gainesville, Florida, and then to Fort Ord in California. In each move the family came along as well. Bart later said of those frequent moves, "I will always be grateful for the things I learned from having to adapt to different circumstances and environments."[1] In 1942, Ben was shipped off to combat. During those war years, Bart and Hilton became an inseparable pair. Lulu, a loving mother but firm disciplinarian, taught the boys to appreciate the importance of responsibility and orderliness in conducting themselves with life's daily tasks. A devout

Methodist, Lulu ensured the Brothers Starr attended church. More than an attendee, Bart at an early age was a true believer in the faith.

At war's end, the family reunited and returned to Montgomery. Master Sergeant Benjamin Starr continued service in the newly created U.S. Air Force. He and Lulu purchased a house for $3,500 in a middle-class neighborhood.

Both boys loved sports. It was common for them to play sandlot baseball and tackle football with other youngsters. They also played on youth teams sponsored by the local Veterans of Foreign Wars chapter. Bart, a fan of Yankee outfielder Joe DiMaggio, followed the Yankee Clipper's exploits by reading newspaper articles and listening to radio broadcasts. He even got to see DiMaggio play during a visit with his aunt in Detroit.

As for football, University of Alabama halfback Harry Gilmer was Bart's favorite player. Gilmer was known for his spectacular ability to leap into the air and pass the ball way down field. Having seen Gilmer during one of Alabama's annual games at Montgomery's Cramton Bowl, Bart would continually practice the jump pass. He later reflected, "I was fascinated by Harry Gilmer and wanted to learn to throw the ball just like him."[2]

Hilton, nicknamed "Bubba," was Ben's favorite athlete. Fiery and uninhibited, Bubba reflected many of his father's personality traits. In his autobiography, Bart wrote, "He would knock your block off with a tackle. I had to learn that. Hilton just did that naturally.... Bubba was aggressive, with a mean streak. I was an introvert."[3] Ben lavished praise upon Bubba's sports exploits but often chided Bart's athletic endeavors. Bart recalled Ben stating, "If you had your brother's guts and your talent, you'd be all right."[4] Ben allowed for no disagreement whatsoever to his views. Ben's criticisms led to Bart containing his emotions. Despite the constant reproaches Bart later said, "My father was my first football coach."[5] Ben's treatment prepared Bart for a football coach he would meet later on in his life.

During the summer of 1947, tragedy struck. While barefooted and playing outdoors, Hilton stepped on a dog bone, infection set in and he died of tetanus. Grief, guilt, and loneliness consumed the Starr family. Lulu wallowed in remorse. She had balked at bringing Bubba in for a relatively new medical procedure—a tetanus shot. Bart was racked with tremendous guilt for his past resentment of Ben's attention upon his little brother. Ben became bitter, despondent, and even more distant from Bart both emotionally and physically. A week after the horrific incident, Ben departed for a tour of duty in Japan.

Upon his return, Ben obtained a second job with Montgomery's South Atlantic League baseball club as a ticket taker. He even got Bart a ball boy job with the team. Ben helped Bart's development and enrich-

Bart Starr.

ment, yet the negative judgments and criticisms were ever present. Bubba's specter hovered over Bart. Ben's verbal assessments would include how Bubba would have accomplished in better fashion whatever Bart had just done. Faced with this adversity Bart relied on his faith which led him to move forward and honor Bubba's memory. Starr said, "Many times I've thought of him in a tough game and set myself, dedicated myself to do … some task for Hilton, even today."[6]

In 1949, Bart attended Sidney Lanier High School, an all-white school in Montgomery. The football coach was Bill Moseley, a disciple of then Kentucky coach Paul "Bear" Bryant. The Poets ran the T-formation. Bart quarterbacked but was relegated to the junior varsity.

Disappointed, Starr almost quit the team, but over time Moseley noticed the small, polite youngster was a good listener, alert and determined. Moseley remarked, "He absorbed coaching so well, we could put in a new wrinkle or new play and I knew when he got home, he would be out in the yard [working on it]. He had the desire to do the job right."[7]

In 1950, Bart was promoted to varsity back-up quarterback. Lanier was 2–0 going into the season's third game against Tuscaloosa, a powerful team with a 17-game win streak. Over 12,000 fans at Montgomery's Cramton Bowl saw quarterback starter Don Shannon gang-tackled and suffer a broken leg. To that point in the year Starr had taken three or four game snaps. Moseley sent the 150-pound 16-year-old into the scoreless game. Once in the huddle, teammates were shocked how the unassuming Starr immediately asserted himself and took charge. Starr directed two touchdown drives and led the Poets to a stunning 13–0 upset. Lanier teammate Nick Germanos commented, "One guy goes down and another guy gets his chance. You could tell Bart had been preparing for that opportunity for a long time."[8] Lanier finished the season undefeated with Bart at quarterback.

During the Summer of 1951, Bart was personally tutored by Kentucky quarterback Vito "Babe" Parilli. Moseley was a former Kentucky assistant coach and his brother was Parilli's center. He contacted Bear Bryant to secure the private training sessions in Lexington. Moseley said, "It was a selfish move on my part, because I wanted Bart to be the best quarterback for us."[9] Parilli, only a few years older than Starr, was impressed by Bart's respectful behavior and tremendous desire to learn the position. The All-American felt Starr's detailed approach in mastering the instruction placed him above most interscholastic athletes. In turn, Starr simply idolized Parilli.

In 1951, Lanier missed a consecutive undefeated season with a 9–1 record. Due to his consistent and brilliant play, Starr was named All-State and All-American. With the exception of Tennessee he was recruited by every Southeastern Conference school. His first choice was Kentucky. Coach Bryant wanted him, and Parilli was part of the Wildcats' wooing efforts. But the senior was impacted by a social consideration.

Bart had found love. He was attracted to classmate Cherry Louise Morton. They dated and went steady. However, when Cherry told him she would be attending Auburn, Starr rethought going to Kentucky. Instead he accepted a Crimson Tide football scholarship offer.

Due to the Korean War, freshmen were deemed eligible for varsity play for the 1952 college football season. Alabama was headed by Coach Harold "Red" Drew. In 1947, Drew took over from famed coach Frank Thomas and installed the Split T as the Crimson Tide's key offensive formation.

Bad news for the 170-pound 18-year-old as that particular offense placed a higher emphasis on a quarterback's running ability than passing skill. Yet, Bart persevered and by 1953 he was Alabama's primary quarterback and punter, and a starter on defense. Sports writers were comparing Starr's passing acumen to Harry Gilmer. Starr's 870 yards fell short of Gilmer's 1945 mark by just 80 yards and Starr missed one game due to an injury.

Alabama nabbed the Southeastern Conference championship and a New Year's Day date with Rice in the Cotton Bowl Classic. The Owls stopped the Crimson Tide 28–6 behind running back Dickie Moegle's three touchdowns,

Entering his junior year, Bart enrolled in the Air Force ROTC program. Starr planned to make the military his career, but he was concerned about his relationship with Cherry. Cherry had left Auburn and returned to her parents' Jackson, Missouri, home. On May 8, 1954, Bart and Cherry eloped. They were married in Columbus, Missouri. This was during an era when coaches took a dim view of married athletes and were known to revoke scholarships from such players. Bart and Cherry tried to keep their union a secret. They returned to their respective households but by July the marriage became known. Bart wrote a letter to Cherry and had unwittingly addressed it to "Mrs. Bart Starr." The couple found a $15 a month apartment in Tuscaloosa. Cherry got a clerical job. And Bart ceased to be Alabama's starting quarterback.

Prior to the 1954 season, Bart's back was severely injured during a hazing incident. At the time, Bart claimed that punting practice caused the injury. Doctors determined he had a lower back sprain. Playing football only exasperated the condition and further increased the pain. Starr forced himself to continue and endured the agony. The pain got to the point where he could barely raise his arms. Traction was the only solution. His 1954 season became truncated. Bart threw a mere 41 passes for 24 completions as Alabama finished 4–5–2.

Starr's misfortune continued in 1955. Coach Drew resigned and was replaced by Jennings Bryan "Ears" Whitworth. Starr found himself on the bench as Alabama ended the 1955 season without a single win.

Starr's NFL hopes could have ended then, but Alabama basketball coach John Dee willingly got involved. Starr had often talked with Dee about his pro football dream. Dee came to admire Starr's quiet dignity and tremendous self-control during the 1955 season. Dee knew Jack Vainisi, Green Bay's player personnel director. Dee informed Vainisi that Bart was a fine NFL prospect. In preparation for the NFL draft, Vainisi had Bart try out for Packer assistant coach Lou Rymkus.[10] Dee never wavered in his support for Bart because he had observed the young man had character and intellect.

Starr was selected by Green Bay in the 17th round of the 1956 NFL draft (200th overall). Nine quarterbacks were chosen before him. Green Bay dispatched assistant coach Ray "Scooter" McLean to Tuscaloosa. There he offered Starr a $6,500 contract. The Hamilton Tiger-Cats of the Canadian Football League offered Bart nearly $7,500 to come north and play for them. Starr asked McLean for $7,500. McLean got approval from Green Bay to change the offer. Starr signed with the NFL club. He was given $1,000 upon signing, but later learned it was an advance against the sum of $6,500.

In May 1956, Bart graduated and received an Air Force ROTC commission with the rank of lieutenant. In June 1956 Starr went to Green Bay for rookie practice. The clubhouse was 33 lockers in an area barely the size of Ben Starr's garage. The training room was a tub with a rusted pipe. Players waiting to be taped had to line-up outside the room. Starr said, "Nonetheless, the inconveniences failed to diminish my exhilaration over the opportunity to play in the National Football League."[11] After the four day experience, he was at the pre-season camp in Stevens Point, Wisconsin.

Starr's initial jersey number was 42. In all previous drafts, no quarterback chosen so low ever made the team. Expectations were that Bart would not break the trend. Starr was competing with three other quarterbacks for the lone reserve position, two rookies and second year man Paul Held.

The Packers' starting quarterback was Tobin Rote. A second round 1950 draft pick from Rice University and cousin to New York Giant Kyle Rote, Rote took a liking to Starr. During an era when veterans rarely spoke to rookies, Rote advised Bart on how to improve his passing ability. Starr adhered to the vet's sage counsel. Bart repeatedly practiced strengthening his arm and making his fly ball passes into speedy line drives. He intently studied game film of opponents and would continue to do so throughout his career.

In the first preseason game against the Philadelphia Eagles at Milwaukee's Marquette Stadium, Head Coach Lisle Blackbourn used both Starr and Paul Held after starter Rote suffered an elbow injury. In a 27–6 victory, Starr completed three of four passes for 31 yards and led two touchdown drives. In exhibitions and scrimmages the coaching staff noticed Starr's confidence, steady demeanor and how his teammates positively reacted to the rookie. On the final cut day Green Bay released Held and issued a number 15 jersey to Starr. The 1956 Packers finished with a 4–8 record. The second-stringer completed 24 of 44 passes for 325 yards, two touchdowns and three interceptions.

On January 3, 1957, Lieutenant Starr was called to active duty and assigned to Eglin Air Force Base near Valparaiso, Florida. After a physical, it was determined he had a back problem. A second exam by an orthopedic doctor resulted in a postponement as to his fitness to serve. The commanding general refused to sign a medical waiver for Starr. Six weeks later, he was discharged.

Before training camp opened in July of 1957 Green Bay dealt Tobin Rote to the Detroit Lions. Afterwards, the Packers traded for Starr's quarterback tutor Babe Parilli. Through the season Starr and Parilli split the quarterback duties.

On September 29, 1957, Green Bay's new City Stadium was officially opened, as the Packers beat the defending Western Conference champion Bears 21–17. A week later Cherry gave birth to the couple's first child, Bryan Bartlett Starr, Jr. The Packers went 3–9. Bart closed out 1957 completing 117 of 215 passes for 1,489 yards, eight touchdowns and ten interceptions.

In January of 1958, Blackbourn resigned. Green Bay promoted Scooter McLean to the head coaching position. McLean as an assistant coach was a poker playing buddy with many Packer veterans. In his new job he continued in that fashion. Viewed as a nice guy, McLean could not discipline or control his charges.

It was a disillusioning season for Bart. Quarterbacking was a three way musical chair arrangement with Starr, Parilli, and rookie Joe Francis, a fifth round Green Bay draft pick from Oregon State. Bart recalled, "If you made an error you went out and if the other guy made an error you went back in. Not only does it test your resolve, it tests your reasoning…. It was a tough terrible year."[12]

The 24-year-old pondered his future. Lisle Blackbourn, now Marquette University head coach, contacted Starr. Blackbourn informed Bart that he would go no further than just an NFL back-up, but Blackbourn felt Starr had the ability to teach and invited Bart to be his quarterback coach. Starr rejected the offer. It was a wise decision, because in 1960, the school, without warning, terminated football. More importantly, Bart would soon meet the coach who would turn his professional playing career around and make the Green Bay Packers into a dynasty.

On February 4, 1959, Vince Lombardi became the Packers Head Coach. Lombardi's life view encompassed the tenets of duty, obedience, and responsibility. Whereas McLean's game plan was full of complex schemes and verbose codes, Lombardi issued a playbook half the size and in a simplified format. In one of his first team meetings Lombardi told his players, "Gentlemen we are going to chase perfection knowing full well that we won't catch it, because nobody is perfect but we're going to relentlessly chase it, because in the process, we will catch excellence."[13]

During a break in that meeting, Bart phoned Cherry to elatedly state, "Honey, we're going to begin to win."[14]

Lombardi's initial assessment of Starr matched Blackbourn's thinking. Not sold on Starr, he named former Chicago Cardinal quarterback Lamar McHan as his starter. Francis and Starr were reserves. Mid-season McHan went out with injuries. In game seven Lombardi inserted Starr as his starter. The Pack lost 28–17 to the Bears, but the next week Lombardi stayed with Starr, who completed 14 of 40 passes for 242 yards but showed tremendous tenacity in a 28–24 loss to the reigning NFL champion Colts. Starr remained as the starter and Green Bay won their last four games to finish with a 7–5 record. After the season, Lombardi said on Frank Gifford's radio show, "In Bart Starr we're going to have one of the great quarterbacks in football."[15]

Entering the 1966 season, Starr had fulfilled Lombardi's prophecy. Over the previous six seasons Bart developed into one of greatest field generals in the NFL as he led the Packers to four Western Conference titles and three championship game victories. In 1960, 1961, and 1962 Starr was named to the Pro Bowl. In his personal life, Bart and Cherry had welcomed a second son, Bret Michael, in 1964.

In 1966 Starr had perhaps his finest season. He led the NFL in passing, completing 156 of 251 passes for a 62.2 percent completion rate and 2257 yards, which translated to 9.0 yards per attempt. He had 14 touchdowns with only three interceptions. His passer rating was a career best 105.0. Starr was named the NFL's Most Valuable Player. Green Bay captured the Western Conference for a fifth time during Starr's career.

On January 1, 1967, in the NFL championship game at the Cotton Bowl against the Dallas Cowboys, Starr had one of the greatest games of his career. He completed 19 of 28 passes for 304 yards, with four touchdowns passes to four different receivers: Elijah Pitts, Carroll Dale, Boyd Dowler, and Max McGee. Two weeks later in the First AFL-NFL World Championship Game against the Kansas City Chiefs Starr connected with Max McGee early in the first quarter for a touchdown and found McGee again in the third quarter as the Packers dominated the Chiefs for a 35–10 victory. In this initial Super Bowl, Starr was named MVP.

In 1967, the conferences were split into divisions. The Packers were placed in the Western Conference's Central Division. They finished atop the Central and met the Coastal Division leading Los Angeles Rams in the conference playoffs on December 23. That day at Milwaukee's County Stadium, Starr was 17 of 23 passes for 222 yards, one touchdown and one interception as Green Bay corralled the Rams 28–7.

On December 31, the NFL championship game known as the Ice Bowl was a rematch with the Cowboys. Starr had attended an early church service with his father, and later said, "It was so cold that neither of us talked about it. Nobody wanted to bring it up."[16] The Packers held an early 14–0 lead as Starr connected with two touchdown passes to

Boyd Dowler. But as the weather further deteriorated the Pack fumbled twice (once by Starr as he was sacked by Cowboy Willie Townes) and both fumbles resulted in Dallas scores. In the fourth quarter with 4:54 left the Packers trailed 17–14. The Pack had one last chance to pull off a third consecutive NFL title, and Starr engineered a miraculous scoring drive. With 16 seconds left Starr called Green Bay's final time out and went to the sideline and told Lombardi, "The backs are slipping and sliding. But I'm upright. I can shuffle my feet … and sneak the ball in."[17] Lombardi emphatically replied, "Then run it! And let's get the hell out of here!"[18] Lombardi's playbook did not have a quarterback sneak play. At the huddle Starr opted to keep the plan to himself and called for a Brown right, 31 wedge play which meant a handoff to Mercein. Upon the snap Starr lunged behind the wedge of center Ken Bowman and guard Jerry Kramer into the end-zone for the winning touchdown.

The 33-year-old veteran was 14 of 24, for 191 yards and two touchdowns for the day. Most football analysts would have expected the Packers to try a pass as an incompletion would have stopped the clock and the Packers could try again or go for a game-tying field goal. In later years, Ken Bowman said, "That's one of the reasons it was such a smart call by Bart because a quarterback sneak was the last thing the Cowboys expected. Bart made a lot of brilliant calls in his time, and that was one of the smartest."[19]

In Super Bowl II at Miami's Orange Bowl, Green Bay handily defeated the Oakland Raiders 33–14. Starr was 13 of 24 for 202 yards and one touchdown. He was named Super Bowl MVP for a second consecutive year.

Starr finished the 1967 season completing 115 of 210 passes for 1823 yards, nine touchdowns and 17 interceptions.

On July 21, 1972, Starr retired but remained with Green Bay as quarterback coach. For his career he threw 3149 passes with 1808 completions for 24,718 yards, 152 touchdowns, and 138 interceptions. In 1973 he became a sports analyst for the CBS network. That same year the Packers retired his number 15.

On December 24, 1974, Starr accepted a three year deal as Green Bay's head coach and general manager. The Alabama Sports Hall of Fame inducted him in 1976. A year later Starr was elected to the Pro Football Hall of Fame.

As for his pro coaching experience, the Packer quarterback who directed the team over his playing career to a 94–57–6 record could not do the same from the sidelines. Starr as head coach of the Packers from 1975 to 1983 notched a 52–76–3 mark and in December 1983 Green Bay unceremoniously released him.

In 1984, after 31 years in Green Bay, Bart and Cherry moved to Phoenix, Arizona. He was not out of football for long. Thomas Stoen, chairman of the board of Pacific Energy and Mineral Ltd and a primary force for an NFL team in Phoenix, recruited Bart to become head coach, general manager and minority partner of the Arizona Firebirds. The proposed club sought NFL approval but was rebuffed once the St. Louis Cardinals were permitted to move to Arizona.

Bart has been involved in a number of business ventures, and numerous charitable and community organizations including the nonprofit Rawhide Boys Ranch for at risk youth.

In September 2014 Starr suffered an ischemic stroke followed by a hemorrhagic stroke and a mild heart attack. He overcame this health setback to attend a Thanksgiving game at Lambeau Field in 2015 honoring Brett Favre.

Jerry Kramer put Starr and his legacy in perspective. "As the years passed, as other careers faded, Bart became the personification of our team, the personification of Vince's coaching. We all tried to play up to one hundred percent of our ability, and none of us quite made it, but Bart came the closest. Without awesome physical equipment, he made himself the finest football player he could possibly be. That was all that Vince asked—that you use your God-given talent to the utmost."[20]

NOTES

1. Keith Dunnavant, *America's Quarterback* (New York: Thomas Dunne Books/St. Martin's Press, 2011), 9.
2. *Ibid.,* 12.
3. David Claerbaut, *Bart Starr* (Lanham, MD: Taylor Trade, 2004), 20.
4. Dick Schaap, *Quarterbacks Have All the Fun* (Chicago: Playboy Press, 1974), 85.
5. *Ibid.*, 19.
6. *Ibid.*, 22.
7. Dunnavant, 18.
8. *Ibid.*, 19.
9. *Ibid.*, 20.
10. Claerbaut, 47.
11. *Ibid.*, 53.
12. *Ibid.*, 71–72.
13. Dunnavant, 81.
14. *Ibid.*
15. Claerbaut, 99.
16. en.wikipedia.org/Wiki/1967_NFL_Championship_Game.
17. Dunnavant, 230.
18. *Ibid.*
19. *Ibid.*, 232.
20. Jerry Kramer, *Lombardi: Winning Is the Only Thing* (New York: Pocket Books, 1971), 91.

REFERENCES

Allen, George, with Be Olan. *Pro Football's 100 Greatest Players.* Indianapolis: Bobbs-Merrill, 1982.
Claerbaut, David. *Bart Starr.* Lanham, MD: Taylor Trade, 2004.
Dunnavant, Keith. *America's Quarterback.* New York: Thomas Dunne Books/St. Martin's Press, 2011.
Eisenberg, John. *That First Season.* New York: Houghton Mifflin Harcourt, 2009.
Epstein, Eddie. *Dominance.* Washington, D.C.: Brassey's, 2002.
Goska, Eric. "Wilson Tops Rodgers, Starr as Best Postseason Passer." *Press-Gazette Media*, January 16, 2015.
Herskowitz, Mickey. *The Quarterbacks.* New York: William Morrow, 1990.
Hyland, Bob. Interview with author, April 16, 2015.
Korth, Todd. *Greatest Moments in Green Bay Packers History.* Lenexa, KS: Addax Publishing Group, 1998.
Kramer, Jerry. *Lombardi: Winning Is the Only Thing.* New York: Pocket Books, 1971.
Maraniss, David. *When Pride Still Mattered.* New York: Simon & Schuster, 1999.
Michael, Jackson. *The Game Before the Money.* Lincoln: University of Nebraska Press, 2014.
Polvetich, William. *Green Bay Packers.* Madison: Wisconsin Historical Society Press, 2012.
Schaap, Dick. *Quarterbacks Have All the Fun.* Chicago: Playboy Press, 1974.
Starr, Bart, with Mark Cox. *Quarterbacking.* Englewood Cliffs, NJ: Prentice-Hall, 1967.
Wise, Bill, comp. *1964 Official Pro Football Almanac.* Greenwich, CT: Gold Medal Books Fawcett, 1964.
www.encyclopedia.com/doc/1G2–3407900531.htm/.
www.encyclopediaofalabama.org.
www.jsonline.com/sports/packers/bart-starrs-legacy-will-last-forever-b99107830z1–225665201.html.
www.packernews.com.
www.profootballhof.com/hof/member.
www.sports.jrankr.org/Starr-Bart-Determination-Pays-Off.

Jim Taylor

Neal Golden

Fullback James Charles "Jim" Taylor enjoyed a ten-year NFL career during which he amassed what was, at the time of his retirement after the 1967 season, the second most rushing yards in NFL history. Taylor made the Pro Bowl five times and was voted a member of the NFL 1960s All-Decade Team. In 1976 he became the first of the "Lombardi Packers" to be inducted into the Pro Football Hall of Fame.

Born on September 20, 1935, in Louisiana's capital city (and site of LSU itself, Louisiana State University), Jimmy starred in two sports for Baton Rouge High—basketball, his favorite sport,[1] for four years, and football for his final two years. During his senior year, he received more college scholarship offers in basketball than football.[2] A 5'11" guard, Taylor made All-State in his senior year for the Bulldogs and helped the team achieve a 25–3 record and the Class 2A state basketball championship. He also played in a national all-star game in Murray, Kentucky.

One reason for Taylor's love of basketball came after his father died, when Jim was only ten. He could shoot baskets in solitude, to cope with the loss. Jim credits basketball for improving his agility, his quickness and his pass catching ability.[3]

Jimmy was also a pioneer in using weight training to improve as an athlete, becoming one of the first students to train at Alvin Roy's Health and Strength Studio in Baton Rouge. One reason he had received little attention in football was that he weighed less than most players until his senior season. Thanks to Roy's weightlifting program, though, "I developed to 205. I got a little more muscular, and I didn't get hurt. I could take the licks and run like a 220 or 230 pounder. And hit people. Drop that shoulder and not let one tackler take me down."[4]

Taylor decided to accept LSU's offer of a football scholarship so that he could stay close to his widowed mother. After his father died, he had sold peanuts and soft drinks at Tiger Stadium to help support his family, and now he was going to play football there; but his career as a Tiger nearly ran off the tracks before it got started. After playing on the freshman team, he had to transfer to Hinds Junior College in Mississippi in order to raise his grade average. Jim returned to LSU after playing one year at Hinds, and started on the varsity team. In that era of limited substitution, Taylor played middle linebacker as well as running back, and served as the defensive captain who called the signals. He had amassed 1,314 yards in two seasons, and he scored more points than any LSU player since the great Steve Van Buren. In addition to his 20 touchdowns, he kicked the points after and the field goals as well. Jim made some All-America teams and was selected to play in the Blue-Gray Game in Montgomery, the Senior Bowl in Mobile, and the College All-Star Game in Chicago.

The Green Bay Packers made Taylor their second pick in the 1958 NFL draft and he was selected 15th overall. Jimmy admitted in his autobiography that "I didn't even know where Green Bay was, much less the fact they had a team!"[5] The Pack had not had a winning record since 1947. Since legendary coach Curly Lambeau had retired after the 1949 season, Green Bay had gone through four head coaches. Taylor had been drafted in December while Lisle Blackbourn (who had compiled a four-year record of 17–31) was still head coach, but by the time Taylor arrived in Wisconsin, he went to work for new coach Ray "Scooter" McLean, the replacement for Blackbourn.

Another draftee who played both fullback and linebacker in college, Illinois' Ray Nitschke, arrived in Green Bay with Taylor. However, the Packers had no interest in Nitschke as a fullback because they had their eye on Jimmy for that position. Taylor recalls now, with a laugh, "I was a ball carrier. I could catch the ball and make yardage. But Nitschke thought *he* was going to be a fullback or running back on the team, and they said, 'No, Ray, you're going to be our middle linebacker!' You know, he was 6'3" and weighed 220, and here I was, 205."[6] Taylor found McLean's training and practices "lackluster" and far less demanding than Coach Paul Dietzel had expected at LSU. As he recalled, "Instead of utilizing film reviews as a teaching tool, the coaching staff basically just ran the film. The film sessions were useless."[7] The result was predictable, and the 1–10–1 record was the worst in franchise history. As for the rushing champ of the SEC, he played mostly on special teams until late in the season. Jimmy finally got a chance to start in the second to last game, against the 49ers in San Francisco. He gained over 100 yards in the 48–21 defeat. In the finale against the Rams in the Los Angeles Coliseum, the Packers dropped their seventh game in a row 34–20, but Taylor ran for 106 yards on 22 carries. That gave him 247 yards for the season, almost all in the last two contests.

McLean resigned before the board of directors could fire him. Team administrator Jack Vainisi consulted NFL commissioner Bert Bell and Cleveland coach Paul Brown concerning a replacement. Both recommended the same man—Vince Lombardi, the Giants' offensive coach.

It wouldn't take long for Green Bay rooters and football fans everywhere to discover who Lombardi was—a winner. Taylor gained respect for Lombardi even before the season began, after the new head coach sent assistant Red Cochran to spend a month with him in Baton Rouge to teach him the Lombardi offense that had propelled the Giants to the championship game twice in the previous three years. When training camp began, Taylor learned the hard way that the coach meant what he said about enforcing rules. At 11 p.m. one night, he was sitting on the edge of his bed with his socks and shorts on when Lombardi entered the room. Since players were supposed to be *in* bed at that hour, the coach fined Jimmy $25. Taylor recalls, "I never made that mistake again!"[8]

To eliminate errors, Vince simplified the offense to ten runs and eight passes. His most famous play became known as the "Green Bay Sweep." The quarterback handed off to either halfback Paul Hornung or fullback Taylor, and whichever one didn't have the ball

Jim Taylor.

would lead the runner around end, behind guards Jerry Kramer and Fuzzy Thurston. As Taylor noted, "Like many of Lombardi's plays, the sweep relied on a minimum of deception but a maximum of effort."[9] It was the first play Lombardi installed, telling the offense, "Gentlemen, if we can make this play work, we can run the football."[10] He began and ended every practice with the power sweep until the players could run it in their sleep.

The new system paid dividends immediately. After gaining confidence by winning four of six exhibition games, the Packers began the regular season by upsetting the Bears, whose longtime coach, George Halas, was Lombardi's idol. Improved conditioning helped Green Bay score nine points in the fourth quarter to overcome a 6–0 deficit, and Taylor scored the winning touchdown. "Sloshing through the mud, I followed pulling guards Thurston and Kramer on a sweep left from five yards out to give us a 7–6 lead."[11] When the final gun sounded, the Packers jubilantly carried their coach off the field. Arriving at the locker room, Lombardi proclaimed, "We're on our way now!"

The momentum continued with upsets of the Lions and 49ers the next two weeks, but enthusiasm can take you only so far. The Rams came to Milwaukee and clobbered the Packers 45–6 in Week Four, the start of a five-game losing streak. With Bart Starr under center permanently in place of Lamar McHan, the Pack won their last four games to finish 7–5, Green Bay's first winning season in 12 years. When the team returned from the final game in San Francisco, 7,500 fans stood in freezing rain to greet the plane. Taylor missed three games because of injury but still compiled these statistics for the 1959 season: 452 yards on 120 attempts (3.8 average), nine receptions for 71 yards, and eight touchdowns (six running, two receiving).

When Lombardi's second training camp opened in 1960, Taylor recalls, "I saw more veterans arrive earlier than I could remember, and they were in better physical condition. They all knew what to expect and came prepared."[12] At age 25, Jim hoped to stay healthy and play in all 12 games of the regular season.

At a press conference during that year, Lombardi bestowed nicknames on his backfield duo. The crashing Taylor was "Thunder," and the speedy Paul Hornung was "Lightning." Said the coach, "Taylor and Hornung are about results, nothing more. Other backfields around the league may be bigger and faster, but none produce like Thunder and Lightning. Taylor loves contact so much that if no defensive back is in his way, he will go and find one. To watch Hornung running at midfield may be nothing special, but near the goal line he is the best."[13] Taylor ran for 1,101 yards that season and gained another 121 receiving to make the Pro Bowl for the first time.

The Packers won their last three games, all on the road, to capture the Western Conference. That put them into the 1960 championship game against the 10–2 Philadelphia, kings of the East. The Eagles won a hard-fought contest at Franklin Field 17–13. The game famously ended with linebacker Chuck Bednarik tackling Taylor in the open field on the Eagle ten, then holding him down while the last seconds ticked off. When the gun sounded, Chuck stood over Jimmy and said, "You can get up. This damn game is over!"[14] As Taylor and Hornung walked off the field, Bednarik embraced them and told them they would be back in the championship game the next year.

Taylor earned a place in NFL lore with not one but two memorable performances in championship games. The 1962 final against the Giants in Yankee Stadium was played in Arctic conditions—temperature dropping from 20 to 10 degrees with swirling winds of 20–30 mph. Taylor wasn't feeling good and had dropped 15 pounds the previous few weeks. He would learn a week later that he had been suffering from hepatitis. Nevertheless, Jim carried the ball 31 times for 85 yards and scored a touchdown in the 16–7 victory. Taylor repeatedly ran for first downs, something he describes more than a half century later as "moving the chains." Fans still remember his one-on-one collisions with Giants middle linebacker Sam Huff during the fray. Taylor recalls, "It was just mind over matter. We had conditioned ourselves for that, and Lombardi was such a tremendous leader and a motivator. He would get into the players' heads and really get them to get the job done."[15]

The championship of the 1965 season brought the Cleveland Browns and Jim Brown to Green Bay. That morning, three inches of snow fell on Lambeau Field before turning to rain and, as things got colder, sleet. With passing attacks dampened by the conditions, Taylor toted the leather 27 times on the slippery field for 96 yards and caught two passes for 20 more as the Packers prevailed 23–12. The Green and Gold defense held Brown to just 50 yards on 12 tries. Afterwards, Hornung, who gained 105 yards on 18 carries, told the press, "Taylor and I are just a couple of old-timers trying to hang on."[16] Jimmy was voted the Most Valuable Player for the game.

Taylor's production declined sharply after five straight 1,000-plus yard seasons from 1960 to 1964. His running style inflicted pain on defenders but also caused him wear and tear on his own body. Lombardi, knowing that Jimmy was fading, offered him only a one-year contract after the 1965 season. Seeing how much the Packers paid rookie running backs Jim Grabowski and Donny Anderson, Jimmy privately decided he would move on after the 1966 season. Midway through that campaign, the Associated Press picked up a story from a Milwaukee reporter, who quoted him as saying that he would play out his option and become a free agent at the end of the season. "We just haven't negotiated a contract [for 1967] to my satisfaction," Taylor said. Asked if the bonus paid to Grabowski influenced his demands, Taylor replied, "Sure it does. It has a bearing on both your pride and your performance as an individual." While denying he was trying to obtain a contract that matched Grabowski's, Taylor expressed skepticism that he would sign anything before the season ended.[17]

Despite what other commentators noted as an unjust difference between the pay for one of the NFL's top rushers, and the bonus for a 1966 rookie (an editorial writer noted that "one of the hardest working football players in the business is understandably miffed that his understudy came to the Packers on a bonus arrangement far in excess of what he is earning") Taylor showed class that would be almost unheard of 50 years later. After the Atlanta game that day, he praised Grabowski's play, and said he had no quarrel with the new kid's bonus.

Regardless of his future plans, the 31-year-old fullback contributed to the Packers' 1966 championship season. He led the team in rushing attempts (204) and yards on the ground (705, almost double Elijah Pitts' 393). In the thrilling NFL championship game at Dallas, Jim gained 37 yards on ten attempts and caught five passes for 23 more. Then, in the very first Super Bowl (and his very last game as a Packer), he carried 17 times for 56 yards and a touchdown.

As a free agent, Taylor signed a long term contract (20 years including the front office) with the expansion New Orleans Saints for their maiden voyage in 1967. Jim gave it one more go for the excited fans in his home state but threw in the towel after just one season, during which he toted the pigskin 130 times for 390 yards.

His career tally ended like this: 1941 attempts, 8597 yards, 4.4 yards per carry, 83 touchdowns, and 225 receptions for 1756 yards. When he retired, Jim ranked second in All-Time NFL rushing behind another Jim, Brown of Cleveland. It took nine years before O. J. Simpson overtook Taylor. (Joe "The Jet" Perry amassed more yards than Jimmy, but 1,345 came in the AAFC.)

After Taylor's playing days ended, the rest of his 20 year deal with owner John Mecom, Jr., bound him to various duties for the Saints, including color commentator on radio broadcasts, scouting college prospects, supervising and playing in golf tournaments, and speaking at civic clubs locally and around the country. "Whatever job the Saints asked me to do, I did … and that was for 19 years!"[18]

Taylor was elected to the Pro Football Hall of Fame in 1976 after being a finalist the previous three years. He was especially pleased that Vince Lombardi's widow, Marie, spoke on his behalf in Canton. Among the excerpts from her speech:

"Not everybody knows of those fine records that Jimmy made in Green Bay—those magnificent five years where he gained over 1,000 yards. I know he did because I saw him gain every single one of them. But I have to say, today is the day he will be most proud of because, you see, he is the first—the very first of the great Packer players of what is known as the Lombardi era to be inducted into the Hall of Fame…."

"I have a tape at home … and he [Vince] says this about Jimmy, and I quote: 'Jim Taylor isn't big for a fullback, but when you bump against him it's like bumping against an iron statue—in fact, he likes that feeling. The thing about Jimmy is that he really likes people. I don't know anyone on the squad that has a greater need or a greater capacity for friendship and understanding than Jim Taylor.'"[19]

Taylor spoke about Lombardi in his acceptance speech. "He gave me the admiration, dedication, discipline, and determination to become the kind of football player that he wanted. He not only developed me into a football player, but he developed me into a man."[20]

Jimmy Taylor lives in Baton Rouge where he still attends games in Tiger Stadium and is rehabbing from open heart surgery. In 2014, he summarized his NFL career with these words. "We had some great players, and I loved playing with them, and I tried to be the best player I could be. I was really focused on being productive. You know, I look back on my career and I feel very pleased with the complete finish, with me at the Packers, and then finishing up with the Saints."[21]

NOTES

1. Jim Taylor interview with author, August 2014.
2. *Ibid.*
3. *Ibid.*
4. *Ibid.*
5. Jim Taylor with Kristine Setting Clark, *The Fire Within* (Chicago: Triumph Books, 2010), 4.
6. Jim Taylor interview with author, August 2014.
7. Taylor, 21.
8. *Ibid.*, 32.
9. *Ibid.*, 35.
10. *Ibid.*, 37.
11. *Ibid.*, 39.
12. *Ibid.*, 42.
13. *Ibid.*, 48.
14. www.phillybirdstalk.com/2015/03/eagles-great-chuck-bednarik-passes-away.html.
15. Jim Taylor interview with author, August 2014.
16. Taylor, 114; other sources (for example, Keith Dunnavant, *America's Quarterback: Bart Starr*

and the Rise of the National Football League, New York: Thomas Dunne Books/St. Martin's Press, 2011, 164) attribute the quotation to Taylor, not Hornung.

17. Ken Hartnett, "Jim Playing Out Option," *Milwaukee Sentinel*, October 24, 1966.

18. Taylor, 153.

19. *Ibid.*, 161.

20. *Ibid.*, 162.

21. Jim Taylor interview with author, August 2014.

Fuzzy Thurston

Rick Schabowski

Frederick Charles Thurston had a distinguished career in the National Football League, which included being on six championship teams and playing a vital role as the left guard on the renowned Green Bay Packers teams of the 1960s.

Thurston was born at Luther Hospital in Altoona, Wisconsin, a small town near Eau Claire, on December 29, 1933. His father, Charles, worked at Eau Claire Sand and Gravel, and his mother, Marie, was a homemaker. He was the youngest of eight children, the only one born in a hospital, and was probably the biggest, ten pounds and 22 inches. One of his sisters, Dorothy, nicknamed him "Fuzzy" because when he was a baby he had dark, curly locks. When Fuzzy was four, his father died from a heart attack. Thurston recalled, "I had a loving mother and great brothers and sisters. From my perspective at an early age, I had everything I needed in life. Looking back, I realize that I really didn't have much."[1]

He attended Altoona High School and was the family's only child to graduate. Thurston explained, "they quit school and went to work because our mother needed their help and because they wanted to give me a chance to earn a high school diploma, go to college, and have a better life. They loved me, and I loved them. They sacrificed a lot for me. The fact that they didn't graduate from high school didn't embarrass me. It motivated me. I didn't want to let them down."[2]

Thurston played basketball four years at Altoona and earned a basketball scholarship to Valparaiso University in Indiana. At Valparaiso, Thurston's Physical Education professor, Walt Reiner, told Fuzzy that he was very impressed with Thurston's play on the basketball court and that he thought he'd be an excellent football player because of his strength and agility. Thurston took Reiner's offer and participated in spring football practice during his sophomore year.

Head Coach Emery Bauer used Thurston at defensive end during the spring drills, but moved him to the offensive line when the 1954 regular season began. During both the 1954 and 1955 seasons, Thurston was named to the All-America team and to the Indiana Collegiate Conference all-conference team. He was also named Most Valuable Conference Lineman in 1955. Pro scouts took notice of his abilities, and he was chosen in the fifth round of the 1956 draft by the Philadelphia Eagles. "They tried me at tackle, and I thought I was going to make the team," Thurston said. "Hughie Devore was the coach. Then a week before the season started, Frank Wydo came back from retirement, and I got my army draft notice. The Eagles let me go, and two weeks later I was in the army."[3]

During the summer of 1956, before going to the Eagles camp, Thurston met Susan Eggleston on a beach where Thurston was working out. They started dating and communicated by mail while he was at the Eagles camp and on the army base. On October 3, 1956, they were married at the First Lutheran Church in Eau Claire.

While serving in the U.S. Army, Thurston spoke with Wayne Robinson, a teammate when Thurston was with the Eagles who was now coaching with the Winnipeg Blue Bombers, and Robinson invited Thurston to try out when he was discharged. Also in Thurston's army unit was Harlon Hill of the Chicago Bears. Hill told George Halas about Thurston, and the Bears signed him in July 1958 but cut him September 1, because they had a surplus of guards. The Eagles reclaimed him.

Thurston recalled, "The day before the season opened, the Eagles cut me again. I headed for Winnipeg. The Colts tried to get in touch with me, but I was already on my way to Canada. The Colts finally got the license number of my car and tried to have me intercepted at the border, but I got to Winnipeg and spent the night in the hotel. The Colts reached me there by phone the next morning. I went to Robinson and talked it over. He said he thought I ought to join the Colts because he was sure I was good enough to play in the NFL."[4]

Thurston made the Colts roster at guard, backing up Art Spinney and Alex Sandusky. He started the last two games of the regular season, when Sandusky was out due to injury. The Colts won the NFL championship that season, defeating the New York Giants in an exciting "sudden death" overtime thriller. However, in July 1959, Thurston drove all the way to Baltimore, only to find out that he had been traded to Green Bay.

At first, Thurston was very upset, especially with Colts coach Weeb Ewbank. "I didn't understand why he couldn't have told me this before I got in the car and drove eighteen hours. I was pissed off."[5] During the long ride back home his emotions settled down. "I was going home. I was a Wisconsin native, born and bred in Altoona, home of the Railroaders. I was going to be playing for the Green Bay Packers, the team I idolized and dreamed about growing up in that tiny town in northeast Wisconsin. All I ever wanted when I was a kid was maybe, just maybe a chance to watch a Packers game at City Stadium. How faraway it seemed. How wonderful it would be. I was going to be playing for the team I loved while I was growing up. I wasn't going to be a loser. I was coming home.

It was just a matter of rearranging my attitude and my expectations, and it was going to be all right. In fact, it was going to be fantastic."[6]

Thurston made the 1959 Packers and started as one of the guards, the other being Jerry Kramer. Vince Lombardi liked the deal for Thurston because he thought bringing in a player from a championship team would give the Packers a boost, and he was also a vocal, enthusiastic player who got the team psyched up and ready to play.

Lombardi was appreciative of Thurston. "You need an intelligent clown on a pro football club, and Fuzzy is that. He

Fuzzy Thurston.

has a talent for rhyming, and when he bellows out calypso accounts of his personal heroics, he doesn't need a mike."[7] Packer reporter Bud Lea recalled, "I remember attending evening meals with the Packers at St. Norbert College when Lombardi would get upset with the rookies who were supposed to sing. He would turn to Fuzzy, who took over and he'd sing, 'He's Got the Whole World in His Hands,' always referring to Coach Lombardi."[8]

Lombardi assessed Fuzzy in *Run to Daylight*. "He made it big with us. When we traded for him we'd seen just enough of him in the movies to know he could handle the pass block, but we didn't know if he had the speed to pull and we knew nothing of his personality. He's not quite as good as a pulling guard as Jerry Kramer, but he's a good short-trap blocker and he's got enough quickness, size, strength and determination so that, when he and Jerry come swinging around the corner together like a pair of matched Percherons, you can see that defensive man's eye-balls pop."[9]

On the Packers' legendary sweep, numbers 63 and 64 paved the way for the ground game. Kramer waited for the tight end to block the outside linebacker, then he took out whoever was in the running lane, with Thurston following Kramer, looking for anyone he could knock out of the way. Hornung followed Fuzzy so closely that, at times, he would have his hand on Thurston's hip.

Kramer had high esteem for his blocking partner. "Fuzzy was very smart, the guards are always pulling in Lombardi's offense. A lot of trapping, a lot of sweeps and a lot of pull plays. Fuzzy never pulled the wrong way. Not even once. And I never pulled the wrong way. The two of us together always knew what the hell we were doing. We did that as good as we possibly could. I had a faith and a trust that Fuzzy would do the right thing. He was very consistent. I don't remember a mistake Fuzzy ever made."[10]

Despite the loss of Jerry Kramer for the last half of the 1961 season due to two separated bones and stretched ligaments in his left ankle, the Packers won the Western Conference. Forrest Gregg took over Kramer's spot, and Norm Masters and Bob Skoronski, who'd been sharing the left tackle spot, now both started at the tackles. Green Bay became "Titletown" again after a 37–0 pasting of the New York Giants in a game played at City Stadium on December 31, 1961. Thurston was named to the AP First Team All-Pro in 1961, which led Thurston to comment, "I know now that the only way for me to be the best guard in this league is for me to break my buddy's leg."[11]

In 1962, the Packers suffered their only loss in a 26–14 Thanksgiving Day game against Detroit. It had been a difficult week for Thurston. He separated his shoulder against the Colts the Sunday before, and on Monday his mother passed away. The Lions, led by defensive linemen Roger Brown and Alex Karras, played ferocious defense. Thurston recalled that in the first half of the game he perfected a new play, the "lookout" block. The lookout block was when Thurston was beaten on the play, he would look over his shoulder and yell, "Look out, Bart!"[12]

The Packers repeated as world champions in 1962, and Thurston was named AP second team All-Pro for the 1962 season. The Packers fell short of the playoffs in 1963 and 1964, but in 1965 the Packers advanced to the NFL title game defeating the defending champion Cleveland Browns. Recalling that game against the Browns, Thurston said, "We thought we were the best club. I thought we were. But I wasn't sure. And to beat a good ball club like Cleveland, you've got to be sure. So Paul came back to the huddle and said, 'Hey, this is 1962 again.' And all at once you could feel everybody in the huddle come up. All at once we didn't just think we could win. We knew damn well we would win."[13]

Thurston injured his ankle late in the 1966 season, allowing rookie Gale Gillingham to get some playing time. Praising Gillingham, Thurston noted, "Maybe it's about time for me to hang it up. I'm glad there's a good one to take my place."[14]

Playing with a heavily wrapped ankle and a cortisone shot, Thurston started in the title game against Dallas. Coach Lombardi said, "I think I owe it to a veteran like Thurston to start him in the title game."[15] The Packers defeated the Cowboys 34–27, and one of the reasons was Thurston's play. Fuzzy was matched up for most of the afternoon against the Cowboys' Bob Lilly. Thurston had a great game, both pass blocking and run blocking. "I have great respect for Lilly's ability," said Thurston after the game, "but I wasn't about to concede anything."[16]

The victory over Dallas landed the Packers a spot in Super Bowl I against the AFL champion Kansas City Chiefs. Thurston was concerned with his matchup against the Chiefs' 6'7", 287-pound defensive tackle, Buck Buchanan. Thurston noted, "He's about the biggest I ever played against. His big trouble is going to be finding me when we line up against each other. Maybe he'll trip over me."[17]

Despite his concerns, Thurston was proud of his performance against Buchanan, as the Packers overcame tremendous pressure to defeat the Chiefs, 35–10.

Gale Gillingham replaced Thurston in the Packers' starting lineup in 1967, with Thurston going to play on the special teams. Thurston's career had gone full-circle. "I remember, as a rookie with the Colts, receiving compliments from some of the veterans because I played so hard on special teams and never complained. I also received letters of admiration from Packers fans when I played so hard on special teams and never complained at the end of my career."[18] Super Bowl II, a 33–14 victory over the Oakland Raiders, proved to be the final game in Thurston's career, and also the last game for Lombardi as the Packers' head coach. They were together from Lombardi's first game in 1959 until the end in 1968.

On July 4, 1968, Thurston followed teammate and business partner Max McGee in retirement, but retirement didn't go smoothly for Thurston. The restaurants he owned collapsed, and in the late 1970s he was forced to file for bankruptcy.

Thurston later resurrected the restaurant/bar business and gave credit to Lombardi. "I played for a guy [Lombardi] who never thought to fail was the end of the world, but he thought never to come back is the biggest sin in the world, and I want to make it back."[19] Indeed, Fuzzy's #63 Bar & Grill is still a thriving establishment in Green Bay.

After a long, courageous bout with not only cancer but also Alzheimer's disease, Fuzzy passed away on December 14, 2014, leaving behind his children, Mark, Griff and Tori, and his grandchildren, Olivia and Fred Thurston and Joey Kluck. His wife had passed away on October 23, 2012.

At the funeral, longtime teammate and friend Jerry Kramer summed up Thurston's spirit. "Well, I love Fuzzy, first of all, and I admire his attitude and spirit. He's always been to me like a five-year-old boy on Christmas morning, and he got a bucket of horseshit for Christmas and shouted, 'Yippee!' When everyone asked why he was so happy, he'd say, 'With all this horseshit, there's got to be a pony around here somewhere.' He will find the good and right in everything."[20]

Notes

1. Bill Wenzel, *What a Wonderful World: Fuzzy Thurston, a Story of Personal Triumph* (Example Product Manufacturer, 2006), 28.

  2. *Ibid.*, 33.

  3. Chuck Johnson, *Greatest Packers of Them All* (New York: G. P. Putnam's Sons, 1968), 117.

  4. *Ibid.*

  5. Wenzel, 58.

  6. *Ibid.*, 60–61.

  7. Bud Lea, "Thurston's Comeback Helped Packers Capture Crown," *Milwaukee Sentinel,* January 5, 1967.

  8. Author's correspondence with Bud Lea.

  9. Vince Lombardi with W. C. Heinz, *Run to Daylight* (Englewood Cliffs, NJ: Prentice-Hall, 1963), 56.

  10. Bob Fox, "Green Bay Packers: Remembering Fuzzy Thurston," *The Bleacher Report,* December 15, 2014.

  11. Chuck Johnson, "Kramer Boys Help Packers Cream Foes," *The Sporting News,* September 22, 1962.

  12. David Maraniss, *When Pride Still Mattered* (New York: Simon & Schuster, 1999), 319.

  13. Bud Lea, *Magnificent Seven: The Championship Games That Built the Lombardi Dynasty* (Chicago: Triumph Books, 2002), 76.

  14. Art Daley, "Limping Fuzzy Glad He Has Good Understudy," *Green Bay Press Gazette,* December 6, 1966.

  15. Bud Lea, "Thurston's Comeback Helped Packers Capture Crown," *Milwaukee Sentinel,* January 5, 1967.

  16. *Ibid.*

  17. Chuck Johnson, "Vintage 'Twins' Packer Roomies," *The Sporting News,* August 12, 1967.

  18. Wenzel, 90.

  19. Avrum D. Lank, "Fuzzy Thurston Guarding Against Bad Luck This Time," *Milwaukee Sentinel*, June 3, 1983.

  20. Wenzel, 103.

Phil Vandersea

Ed Bryant

Phil Vandersea was one of the younger 1966 Green Bay Packers, and hardly the most celebrated. Those Packers include several members of the Pro Football Hall of Fame. Even so, the story of the versatile rookie and how he seized his opportunity is a good one, and a good way to revisit a very different era, when there were still two distinct leagues playing on Sundays.

Philip John Vandersea was born in Whitinsville, Massachusetts, on February 25, 1943. Phil's father Sid was a machinist who worked his way up to foreman at a textile mill.[1] After graduating from Northbridge High School in 1961, Phil attended the University of Massachusetts and played fullback for the Minutemen. Versatility was his strong suit at UMass. When Vandersea was injured in 1963, and otherwise sidelined, he was still able to help UMass as a punter. After sitting out the 1964 season, Vandersea put in a full year in 1965 and was named to the All-Yankee Conference team. In his last year of college ball, Phil finished third on the team in points scored, trailing only Greg Landry and Milt Morin, who both went on to long NFL careers; Vandersea was also the third leading receiver, and the second leading rusher. While playing fullback with Landry, Vandersea had plenty of chances to show he was willing and able to block. At the time of the 1965 draft, Lombardi projected Vandersea as a back-up to Jim Taylor.

In November 1964, knowing that Vandersea would play one more year for the University of Massachusetts, Green Bay had taken Vandersea in the 16th round of the 1965 NFL draft with the 220th pick as a futures pick and the Denver Broncos had selected Phil during the 9th round of the 1965 AFL Redshirt draft.[2]

Vandersea chose Green Bay. The seeds of the decision were sown before Vandersea was born, when his college coach, Vic Fusia, who played for Manhattan College, got to know Vince Lombardi, from Fordham, one New York borough to the north. Fusia had good things to say to Vandersea about Lombardi, and Vandersea wanted to play for him, but in addition to signing a contract, he would still have to win a job.[3]

By the time the Packers opened training camp in 1966, though, a great deal had changed. In the 1966 NFL draft, the Packers drafted another celebrated college back, a fullback, Jim Grabowski, and outbid the expansion Miami Dolphins, who were awarded the first pick in the 1966 AFL draft and used it on Grabowski. The Packers gave one rookie, Donny Anderson, the richest contract in football history, and Grabowski commanded a hefty check as well.

In another time, Vandersea would have been slotted third at the start of camp behind Taylor and Grabowski and hoping for a chance to practice with Starr, Hornung and company, but the other players were not in camp to crowd him out. Grabowski was obligated, before reporting to his rookie season with his pro team, to perform in Chicago for the College All-Stars, at a time when the first professional game of the summer was the All-Stars against the defending NFL, champions, in 1966, the Packers.

Jim Taylor was offended by the money offered to Anderson and Grabowski; he thought he should be paid for proven performance. Taylor came to camp in time to play in the All-Star Game, but until Taylor arrived, the only fullbacks in Packers training camp were second year player Allen Jacobs and the rookie Phil Vandersea.

Phil Vandersea.

Given a chance to impress the coaches, Vandersea seized it. Jacobs had only carried the ball three times as a rookie, but he dressed for all 14 regular season games in 1965. Vandersea was held to two yards in two carries playing for the defending champion against the rich rookies in Chicago, but by then, he had been praised for his crisp execution in practice.

With Taylor and Grabowski now on hand, though, Vandersea and Jacobs were probably competing for one job, and that only if Green Bay kept three fullbacks.

Before the Packers' first pre-season game against an NFL team, the Chicago Bears, the coaches introduced Vandersea to the defense, with Vandersea studying to be a Packers linebacker. Some pre-season work on the defensive side of the ball improved his chances to make the team. Vandersea recalled the experience. "I was real nervous, but the veterans went out of their way to be nice. I'll never forget Hornung giving me advice at linebacker. He didn't have to do that. He was a superstar. There were egos on that team, but no individuals. Lombardi controlled egos."[4]

For 1966, the NFL allowed each team only a 40-player roster. As the cut to 40 neared, Wisconsin papers speculated and printed leaks from time to time. Vandersea was thought to be vulnerable to the numbers game, but at the last moment, the Giants traded for Allen Jacobs, and Phil Vandersea made the cut. When the roster was set, it was reported that Vandersea was "awarded" number 37, and in that jersey, he can be found in the first chapter of NFL Films' excellent *America's Game* series.[5]

Vandersea was available to play fullback and linebacker, but he made his mark on special teams. The unlikely "up" man enjoyed a month when the other team kept kicking off to him, and when the season was done, Phil Vandersea was the Packers' third leading kickoff returner. For 1966, his total kick return yardage trailed only two Packers, Hall of Famer Herb Adderley, and Anderson, the richest rookie ever!

In 1967, the Packers had to expose a certain number of players when the NFL sought to stock the brand-new New Orleans Saints, who selected Bill Curry, Paul Hornung and Phil Vandersea.

After a year with the Saints, Vandersea returned to Green Bay in 1968, and the Packers, now coached by Phil Bengtson, used him as a tight end.

He played a full season in 1969 at defensive end, and then was moved to defensive tackle in 1970, but he ended up on injured reserve after hurting his ankle. Fifteen pounds heavier than his rookie season, he was slotted to play offensive tackle and center in 1971. Vandersea quipped, "I kept eating my way closer to the ball."[6]

The Packers released Vandersea before the 1971 season and Phil moved to the Canadian Football League for one final season with the Montreal Alouettes.

After that? Let's let Jerry Kramer describe Vandersea's life after football: "after his playing days, Phil Vandersea put in time as a salesman, a high school science teacher, a college football coach, an assembly-line worker and, for the Massachusetts Department of Corrections, a counselor to adult felons."[7]

Vandersea is now retired from the Department of Corrections, and enjoying a life that takes him out on the golf course from time to time.

NOTES

1. Jerry Kramer and Dick Schaap, *Distant Replay* (New York: G.P. Putnam's Sons, 1985), 226.
2. *Complete Pro Football Draft Encyclopedia* (St. Louis: Sporting News Books, 2004).
3. Phil Vandersea interview with author, August, 2014.
4. Kramer, 226.
5. *America's Game, the Super Bowl Champions: 1966 Green Bay Packers*, NFL Films.
6. Kramer, 226.
7. *Ibid.*, 225.

Jim Weatherwax

MATT REASER

Defensive lineman Jim Weatherwax had a short but eventful NFL career with the Green Bay Packers from 1966 to 1969. Weatherwax was born January 9, 1943, in Porterville, California. He was a three sport athlete at Redlands (California) High School where he played football, basketball and competed in the high jump in track. After two years of junior high school football experience, Weatherwax struggled initially at the high school level. "When I was a sophomore, I played on what they called the B Exponents, a special classification for boys too small or younger. It was designed to give small seniors and younger boys, like sophomores, a chance," Weatherwax said. "When I was a sophomore, I was only 5'8" and weighed 151 pounds. And when I was a junior, I was 6'4" and 170. I didn't play varsity football until I was a senior, when I was 6'5" and 215. I didn't stop growing until I was 21." He added, "I was a little uncoordinated as a junior and the first part of my senior year, but it worked out all right."[1]

He was also not a varsity basketball player until his senior year—when he became the starting center for the RHS Terriers. During his senior season he played for legendary basketball coach Jerry Tarkanian who coached at Redlands High School for two years.

Weatherwax also had a great football coach: Frank Serrao. "I wasn't a starter at Redlands High until my senior year. It was Frank Serrao who guided me along. I had a great time my senior year," he said, adding, "Coach Serrao led us into the CIF [California Interscholastic Federation] playoffs."[2]

During his senior season the Terriers had a 9–2 overall record and were undefeated in the Citrus Belt League. They were the 1959 CBL champions and made it all the way to the semifinals of the CIF playoffs. Weatherwax started at both offensive and defensive tackle, and was selected as the first-team tackle on the All-CBL team. He also won Redlands' Most Improved Player Award. For his athletic contributions, Jim Weatherwax was one of the first inductees into the Redlands High School Athletic Hall of Fame.[3]

After high school, Weatherwax enrolled at nearby San Bernardino Valley College because, he said, "I was only 17 years old and didn't want to be too far from home."[4] He played for Coach Buck Weaver and was the second youngest player on the team as a freshman. His young age did not hurt him, at least on the football field. "Not football wise, but study wise," said Weatherwax. "When I was a freshman I came to college to play football and goof around. I found out you have to study, too."[5] His first season with SBVC was cut short when he injured his knee late in the season.

During the 1961 football season Weatherwax scored his first ever touchdown, against Mt. San Antonio College. The ball was at the six-yard line and the quarterback rolled out and fumbled. He explained what happened: "I was just starting to throw a block, when I saw [the quarterback] out of the corner of my eye. The ball just squirted loose and I fell on it. I thought I was on about the ten-yard line. When I saw the referee's hands go up, I was surprised to death." After that game Coach Buck Weaver made Weatherwax a co-captain and said of him, "Wax has great potential, and he's just now started to play up to it. It takes a big fellow longer. In the hot weather he was carrying around 240 pounds, and he had been tiring. Now that it's cooler he should be able to play more defense." Weaver added, "Wax is one of our youngest players, just 18 as a sophomore. He may have been our best lineman last year, but he was hurt twice and missed a lot of recognition."[6] In a late October game he re-injured his knee, it forced him to have a knee operation the next day and he was out for the season.

In 1962 he went to play football at West Texas State College, but he was plagued by his knee injury. So he returned to San Bernardino Valley College to play basketball. He played one season for the Indians under head basketball coach Ray Blake.

Jim Weatherwax is part of the San Bernardino Valley College Athletic Hall of Fame;

he spent two seasons on the football field and one season on the basketball court for SBVC.[7]

After a year out of football in 1963, he played his junior and senior seasons for California State College at Los Angeles. Weatherwax was coached by Homer Beatty and he was a key player for the Diablo championship football teams of 1964 and 1965. In 1964 Cal State L.A. went undefeated with a 9–0 record (5–0 in conference) and they were selected as the small college national champions in the United Press International poll.

In 1965, Cal State L.A. repeated as California Collegiate Athletic Association champions and accepted an invitation to the Camellia Bowl, where they defeated the University of California, Santa Barbara, 18–10. Weatherwax said about the game: "We played the Camellia Bowl with only 26 players. As a matter of fact, there were only three games I didn't play 60 minutes."[8] The Diablos finished the season with a 9–1 overall record and again were an undefeated 5–0 in conference play. During the season Jim earned the Golden Helmet Award for his performance against Fresno State in a game where he had ten tackles. After the season he was selected as first-team All-CCAA, was named to the UPI Little All-Coast second-team as an offensive lineman and he was Associated Press Little All-America honorable mention. He was also named his team's Most Valuable Lineman. Jim Weatherwax was inducted into the Cal State L.A. Athletics Hall of Fame in 1990.[9]

Before his senior season in college, Weatherwax was selected as a futures pick by the Green Bay Packers in the 11th round of the 1965 National Football League draft. He was also selected by the San Diego Chargers in the 5th round of the 1965 American Football League redshirt draft—a separate draft from the regular AFL draft. After his senior season, in December of 1965 he chose to sign with the Packers. Weatherwax was scouted and signed by Packers assistant Tom Fears. He explained his decision to sign with Green Bay: "I was also drafted by San Diego, but I signed with the Packers to be with the best. It was a chance in a lifetime."[10]

Weatherwax got the attention of the local sportswriters after he reported to Packers camp in 1966. He was dubbed "Jumbo Jim" by one Green Bay sportswriter, but linebacker Tommy Joe Crutcher liked to call him "Jungle Jim." His size was a common topic, as he was one of the largest linemen in the NFL.[11]

In an interview as a rookie, he noted the challenges he faced. "In college, I'd get by on brute strength. Here, everyone is big." He also said, "The biggest thing for a rookie defensive tackle to learn is reacting to movements of the offensive line. For instance, I've got to study how a guard sets up, his stance. These are my keys."[12] In another interview Weatherwax said, "Just a few years ago, I was working as a laborer and never expected to even play college football again. With the Packers I honestly didn't think I had much of a chance. They had nine defensive linemen and I thought I must have been number

Jim Weatherwax.

nine but I was determined to make a try of it and do my best. There were some pretty big names ahead of me and I knew I had my work cut out."[13] He made the team as a reserve defensive tackle and played special teams for the 1966 world champions.

In 1967, after Lionel Aldridge fractured his leg during the preseason and his replacement Bob Brown pulled his groin muscle, Weatherwax filled in at defensive end early in the season. He discussed it in an interview with the *Wisconsin State Journal* after the first two games of the season against the Lions and Bears. "It's different than playing tackle, but I like it out there. When you're in the middle of the line at tackle, you're watching three guys. At end, you're playing against the tackle on the weak side and against two guys, the end and tackle, on the tight side. When the opposing quarterback sees a new guy out there, they like to run over there and see what you can do. Caffey, Jordan and Nitschke also helped me a lot…. I like playing both spots, I don't mind moving around."[14]

Weatherwax won a second NFL championship with the Packers in 1967. He discussed playing in the famed Ice Bowl: "Dallas scored a touchdown right before halftime to pull within 14–10, and then tried an onside kick that I recovered about midfield. It was like an ice rink on the field that day. The field was soft before the game, but after the first quarter, your cleats wouldn't even go into the ground. The Super Bowl was the final goal, but beating Dallas both those years for the NFL championship meant as much if not more than winning the Super Bowl."[15]

After two consecutive world championship seasons, the next couple of years were tough for Weatherwax. In 1968 an injury in a game against the Bears in the preseason led to him having knee surgery and he sat out the entire season. He had a second knee operation in January 1969 and he had to start the 1969 season on the injured list. He made his season debut when he was reactivated a half-hour before the Falcons game and he spent the rest of the year as a part-time player. He was waived by the Packers in 1970 and was claimed by the St. Louis Cardinals on September 3. The Cardinals sent him back to Green Bay on September 4 after he failed his physical. He sat out the 1970 season and retired from professional football.

After his professional football career was over Jim and his wife Jo Ann owned a restaurant in El Toro, California. One day Ray Nitschke coincidentally came into the restaurant and noticed Jim was not wearing his Super Bowl rings. "He told me to put my championship ring on and never take it off again. I have done that," Weatherwax said.[16]

Weatherwax discussed Vince Lombardi in a 1997 interview with the *San Bernardino County Sun.* "I still think about him almost every day. He taught you football, but he also taught you how to live. He taught us that the three most important things in life are family, religion and career, and to do all of them the best that we could." An incident in 1967 he said epitomized Lombardi: "You never wanted to let him know you were hurt because you feared what might happen. We were in St. Louis for an experimental Monday Night Football game against the Cardinals. I had broken several ribs the week before in practice but I was afraid to tell Lombardi. Our defense was on the field for the first series of the game, and St. Louis ran 12 or 13 plays. I came off the field and could hardly breathe. Lombardi saw me and chewed me out. The next day, I was still in a lot of pain and tried to avoid him when I arrived at Lambeau Field for practice, Lombardi saw me and said, 'Weatherwax, I've reviewed the film, and I want you to know you're going to play next Sunday against Detroit.' He didn't believe in being hurt."[17]

A two-time Super Bowl champion, Jim Weatherwax shared his favorite Super Bowl memories in a 2011 interview with the *Milwaukee Journal Sentinel*: "In Super Bowl I, I played about half the third and all the fourth quarter backing up Henry Jordan and Ron Kostelnik. That was quite a thrill … then in [Super Bowl II], I played a little bit earlier in the game, but also got my snaps in the third and fourth quarter. That year, everybody heard the rumor this was going to be [Vince Lombardi's] last game. We had a cloud over us and there was a kind of a different feeling. When it was over, we had a good feeling because we were the world champions. But we also had a bad feeling because we were going to lose our coach, and he was the backbone of everything."[18]

Notes

1. Lee Remmel, "Weatherwax 6–7, Pack 'Answer' to Lundy, Andrie?" *Green Bay Press-Gazette*, July 21, 1966.
2. Harvey M. Kahn, "Ex-Redlands, Sbvc Football Player Jim Weatherwax Appeared in First Super Bowls," *IE Community News Group*, Iecnwww, January 29, 2015, www.iecn.com/ex-redlands-sbvc-football-player-jim-weatherwax-appeared-in-first-super-bowls.
3. Vanessa D. Overbeck, "Rhs Inducts Five into Hall of Fame," *Redlands Daily Facts*, Redlandsdailyfacts.com, May 31, 2008, www.redlandsdailyfacts.com/sports/20080601/rhs-inducts-five-into-hall-of-fame.
4. Bud Lea, "Jumbo Jim Beefs Up Packers," *Milwaukee Sentinel*, August 16, 1966.
5. Jim McKone, "Sbvc Giant Scores Td," *San Bernardino Daily Sun*, October 12, 1961.
6. *Ibid.*
7. Kahn.
8. Remmel.
9. California State University, Los Angeles Athletics, www.calstatelaathletics.com/hof.aspx?hof=56&path=&kiosk.
10. Lea.
11. Remmel.
12. Lea.
13. "Packer Rookies Surprised, Wary," *Wisconsin State Journal*, August 1, 1966.
14. "Weatherwax Likes New Spot," *Wisconsin State Journal*, September 28, 1967.
15. Danny Summers, "Hometown Hero with Lots of Heritage," *San Bernardino County Sun*, January 26, 1997.
16. Kahn.
17. Summers.
18. Rob Reischel, "Memory Lane with Former Packers," *Milwaukee Journal Sentinel*, jsonline.com, February 6, 2011, http://www.jsonline.com/sports/packers/115396629.html.

Willie Wood

Joe Zagorski

One of the key victories that made the Green Bay Packers the Team of the Decade in the 1960s was their win in the first Super Bowl, the very first showdown between the rival National and American Football Leagues. While Max McGee and Bart Starr received the most acclaim, safety Willie Wood made the most vital play. Early in the third quarter of Super Bowl I against the Kansas City Chiefs, a full-fledged Packer blitz by linebackers Lee Roy Caffey and Dave Robinson caused a wobbly pass by Chiefs quarterback Len Dawson. Willie Wood stepped in front of the intended receiver in the left flat, Kansas City tight end Fred Arbanas, easily intercepted the pass, and began a return that changed the course of the game. He ran straight for 23 yards before changing directions and running toward the middle of the field. Kansas City offensive tackle Dave Hill then got close enough to Wood to force him to veer to his right before being tackled at the Kansas City five-yard line by Chiefs halfback Mike Garrett, completing a 50-yard interception return. "I don't think I was gambling," said Wood when describing the play. "I was playing him [Arbanas] on his outside shoulder, so if he had caught the ball, he wouldn't have had a first down."[1] One play later, Green Bay running back Elijah Pitts ran off left tackle and into the end zone. The touchdown gave the Packers a 21–10 lead en route to a 35–10 triumph. Willie Wood had provided the turning point of the game that solidified the Green Bay dynasty.

It seemed as if William Vernell Wood was always making big plays for the Packers. In his 12 years with the team, Wood accumulated 48 interceptions, many of which turned games around or saved games for Green Bay. Wood played in six NFL championship games and the first two Super Bowls. During his career, he was named to eight Pro Bowl squads and was first team All-Pro five times. But the beginning of Wood's fantastic career had many more question marks than exclamation points.

He was born in Washington, D.C., on December 23, 1936, to John and Amanda Wood who both worked for the federal government. Willie spent a great deal of time at the local Boys Club and excelled in sports despite his slight 5'10" size. After high school, he spent one year at Coalinga Junior College in the San Joaquin Valley of California before transferring to USC in 1957. At USC, Wood became the first black quarterback in what was then called the Pacific Coast Conference. However, the NFL had no interest in black quarterbacks, or short ones for that matter, so Wood was ignored in the 1960 player draft. He had to resort to writing letters to various pro teams in order to obtain a tryout. He even enlisted the aid of former coaches and associates to write letters on his behalf. Only one pro coach, Vince Lombardi, decided to take a chance on Wood and give him a tryout. Lombardi offered Wood a free agent contract worth $6,500, then watched the native from Washington, D.C., excel beyond anyone's expectations. The Packers quickly saw that with Wood's speed and leaping ability (he could touch the crossbar of the goal posts with his elbow) he was capable of playing in their defensive backfield.

He was just below average in size for his time (5'10" and weighing in the 170s before bulking up to 190), but he made the most of his abilities. But like most longshot success stories in the NFL, Wood's beginning in the league had its share of questions.

"We had 24 defensive backs in camp that first year," Wood recalled. "We knew the Packers would only keep six."[2] The numbers were there for him to gauge his abilities. Wood would have to beat out 18 other men, each with dreams similar to Wood's. "There was a lot of anxiety, a lot of sleepless nights," said Wood. "I didn't know much about playing defense, but I do

Willie Wood.

know that my experience as a quarterback eventually helped me as a safety because I could understand what the quarterback was thinking."[3]

Wood survived training camp and made the 1960 Packers roster. Like most rookies, he would first have to prove himself on special teams. This he did with hard-nosed desire, and in the time span of only a couple of years, Wood became known as one of the league's hardest hitters. Lombardi considered him the team's surest tackler. He also exhibited another trademark of Packer players from the 1960s—the ability and willingness to play with pain. On one occasion, Wood played with both a collarbone injury and a shoulder injury. When asked by a teammate if he wanted to come out of the game, Wood fearlessly responded "No. I'm all right. I've got another shoulder."[4]

Taken under wing by roommate and future Hall of Famer Emlen Tunnell, Willie took Tunnell's starting slot in 1961. Wood intercepted five passes throughout the 1961 season and led the league in punt return average (16.1 yards).

The more Wood saw action, the better he became. He was used extensively by Lombardi throughout 1962, and even saw duty as a placekicker on kickoffs that season. Their defense gave up a miserly total of only 148 points that season, their best mark during the Lombardi years, and Willie Wood was a major reason why. Wood intercepted nine passes that year, the highest mark in the league. In the 1962 NFL championship game victory over the Giants, Wood made a key shoestring tackle of Johnny Counts on a New York kickoff return in the second quarter which saved a certain touchdown. Unfortunately, Willie also accidentally bumped an official while protesting an interference call and was ejected from the game in the third quarter. The temperature on that day reached 13 degrees above zero, but the hitting on both sides warmed things up. Packers reserve wide receiver Max McGee quipped that "this was the hardest hitting game I ever saw, and I watched most of it."[5]

The following two years were good years for Wood, but not so good for the team. Green Bay could not repeat their success from 1961 and 1962, finishing second both years, but Wood managed to intercept five passes in 1963 and three more in 1964. Wood also scored a touchdown in 1964 with a 42-yard interception return against the Los Angeles Rams in a 27–17 loss. The Green Bay defense was in flux with young players like Dave Robinson, Lee Roy Caffey and Ron Kostelnik taking on larger roles, but in 1965, the transition was complete. Green Bay recorded a 10–3–1 record in 1965 and defeated the Browns for the NFL championship. The Packers defense permitted only 224 points, the lowest mark in all of professional football. Wood picked off six passes during this comeback season for the Packers.

Wood earned four All-NFL honors during the years 1962–1965. He had come from practically nowhere to become known by his teammates and contemporaries as perhaps the best free safety in all of professional football. But he was not satisfied. He made the All-NFL team once again in 1966, despite intercepting only three passes. One of those interceptions went for a 20-yard touchdown against Chicago in a 17–0 victory. Wood also made a great play in the 1966 NFL championship game at Dallas, when he raced to deflect a pass intended for Dallas setback Dan Reeves on a circle route that, if it had been completed, would have resulted in a sure Cowboys touchdown. Add Wood's great play in Super Bowl I, and you have a most memorable year for a super player.

Willie Wood played five more seasons of pro football after Super Bowl I. He helped the Packers repeat as world champions with a resounding 33–14 victory over the AFL's Oakland Raiders in Super Bowl II. That game would mark the final postseason game for

Wood and for the great Packer dynasty of the 1960s. Wood's last four years in pro football would see him achieve more individual honors, but would be devoid of any more playoff appearances. A true professional always gives his best effort, however, even in the midst of losing seasons. Wood intercepted a pass in a Monday night game at San Diego in 1970 which helped the Packers pull out a 22–20 win over the Chargers. Wood intercepted seven passes in that season, the second-highest yearly total of his career. In 1971, Wood's final year in pro football, his diving stab of a Bobby Douglass pass helped preserve a 17–14 win over the hated Chicago Bears. It marked the final interception of Wood's stellar career.

During that career, Wood received many accolades and praises from his foes. Hall of Fame Baltimore wide receiver Raymond Berry once said that "Wood sets the style for the Packers type of defense. Willie gives them the ability to call one defense and get many interpretations of it. He smells a play and takes off, strictly on his own, to break up a play he should never have been near."[6] Even "Iron Mike" Ditka, the Hall of Fame tight end for the Chicago Bears, admitted that Wood hit him as hard as any of his much bigger opponents.[7]

Willie's coaches were equally willing to sing his praises. "Willie has good hands and great reactions," admitted Packers defensive backfield coach Norb Hecker. "He can play a man loose, which tempts the quarterback to throw the ball. But once the ball is in the air, Willie reacts quickly and he goes after the ball. And he will hit as hard as anyone on our team."[8] Lombardi, after watching Wood blossom into one of the game's best defenders over the 1960s, put it more succinctly. "He is the most natural defensive back we have," Lombardi said.[9]

Wood retired at 35 following the 1971 season, when he knew that his body could no longer perform at the level to which he was accustomed. In 1972, He joined Harland Svare's coaching staff in San Diego as the Chargers' secondary coach. After three years, Willie was hired as head coach of the Philadelphia Bell in the World Football League, making him the first black head coach of a major football league since the 1920s. The team was 4–7 when the league folded midseason. Wood then went into the construction business.

In 1979, he returned to football as a member of former teammate Forrest Gregg's staff for the Toronto Argonauts of the Canadian Football League. When Gregg backed out of his contract to take the head coach job for the Cincinnati Bengals a year later, Wood succeeded him, the first black coach in CFL history. Under Willie, Toronto finished 6–10 in 1980 and then lost the first ten games in 1981 before he was fired. He left football for good at that point and started an HVAC business in D.C. Wood's later years have been marked by bad health—knee replacements, diabetes, high blood pressure and dementia. In 1989, Wood was elected into the Pro Football Hall of Fame and in 2012, a D.C. street was renamed Willie Wood Way in his honor. One of his two sons, Willie Jr., carried on the family tradition by playing and coaching in the Arena Football League.

Notes

1. Lee Remmel, "Greatest Packer Games: No. 2," *Pro!* November 30, 1975, 56–59.
2. Don Smith, "Willie Wood," *The Coffin Corner*, Volume 11, No. 2, 1989.
3. *Ibid.*
4. *Ibid.*
5. Remmel, 42–45.
6. Smith.

7. *Ibid.*
8. *Ibid.*
9. *Ibid.*

REFERENCES

Remmel, Lee. "Greatest Packer Games: No. 7." *Pro!* September 21, 1975, 42–45.
_____. "Greatest Packer Games: No. 2." *Pro!* November 30, 1975, 56–59.
Smith, Don. "Willie Wood." *The Coffin Corner*, Volume 11, No. 2, 1989.
"Willie Wood." www.profootballhof.com.
"Willie Wood—Class of 1989." www.packers.com.

Steve Wright

GARY SARNOFF

An offensive lineman often is the least noticed player on the roster. Steve Wright was an exception to the rule, despite being a second string offensive tackle during five of his nine NFL seasons. Wright gained recognition for his wry sense of humor, as the model for the NFL's Gladiator Award trophy, as a member of the 1960s Packers dynasty and for being the target in Vince Lombardi's most publicized temper-tantrum. The University of Alabama alumnus had the privilege of playing on three NFL championship teams and two Super Bowl winners, and was able to extend his career for two additional seasons by playing in the short-lived World Football League. Looking back on his career, though, Wright finds it hard to believe that he played for seven different teams (make that eight, "if you consider the University of Alabama")[1] during his 11 seasons of professional football (nine in the NFL and two in the WFL). "When I watch it on television, I can't believe I even played the game. It's really hard to believe I did it for all those years."[2]

Steve Wright was born on July 17, 1942. His dad, an engineer, worked hard to provide his children an upper middle class environment. Wright played high school football at duPont Manual High School (in Louisville, Kentucky), where he earned All-State honors as a defensive tackle and received over 70 football scholarship offers. He visited the University of Georgia and the University of Tennessee, but was unimpressed. He also received a visit from Notre Dame assistant coach Don Doll.

"It's an all-male school?" Wright asked the Fighting Irish assistant coach.

"Yes," replied Doll.

"Well, what do you do for fun?" Wright asked.

Doll explained that the boys catch a bus for St. Mary's, a girls' college on the other side of the lake. Wright then asked if he could have a boat. Doll didn't find that to be funny. "You understand, we're interested in serious minded boys who want to play football," Doll clarified. "Boy, do you have the wrong guy,"[3] replied Wright.

Wright chose Alabama, mostly because three of his high school coaches, who had played for Bear Bryant at Kentucky, encouraged him to attend Alabama, but also he knew that everybody wants to be somebody, and at Alabama you are somebody. He liked the idea of being somebody, but he was most comfortable being his own person, something that would not sit well with the Tide coaching staff.

The coaching staff at Alabama was tough and expected a lot. When a player did not execute, a coach would grab that player by the facemask and give a blistering lecture. Wright, refusing that kind of treatment, would respond by grabbing the coach by the arm and pulling his hand away from his face mask.

During summer sessions prior to Wright's sophomore season something happened that would change the course of his life. During a three-on-one drill, Wright, a defensive lineman, and the one against the three, was to submarine off the line of scrimmage in order to stack up the offensive linemen. Wright properly executed the drill, but while on his hands and knees after piling up the three offensive linemen, an assistant coach walked up and said, "That's pretty good, Wright, except for one thing."

"Yeah, what's that?" asked Wright.

"You're not mean enough!" responded the assistant coach, along with a hard swing of forearm into Wright's facemask. The blow gave Wright a split lip and busted nose. The collegian was too stunned to react, but it was that incident that helped him decide that nobody was going to ever push him around, and that he would always be his own person.[4]

At Alabama, Wright did not start a single game, and saw little playing time. However, by the time he was a senior, he was attracting attention from professional teams, based on his size and the strong work ethic he displayed during team practices. Wright was unaware that he was being scouted by the pros, although one AFL team had sent him a questionnaire. He also heard from two semipro teams. Thinking that pro football was unlikely, he considered enlisting in the Marines in order to avoid the draft and being sent to the jungle in Vietnam.

In the early 1960s, the two leagues held their college player drafts before the season ended in order to try to beat the competition to the new talent. On December 3, 1963, Wright awoke to a radio report that he was drafted in the fifth round by the Packers; he had been drafted in the eighth round by the AFL Jets two days before. Wright responded by pressing the off button and going back to sleep.[5]

Would it be the Packers or Jets for Steve Wright? He was fortunate to have the option of choosing between Vince Lombardi's two-time NFL champs and the upstart AFL. While recovering from food poisoning in Mobile, Alabama, where the Crimson Tide prepared for the 1964 Sugar Bowl, Wright received a visit from George Sauer, Sr., a scout from the Jets (as well as a former college football coach and the father of future Jets receiver George Sauer). The meeting went well, and Wright was very impressed. However, he soured on the Jets when the team assigned a different scout to sign him, one who did not give Wright a good impression.[6]

Red Cochran, an assistant coach with the Packers, was also in town, and he wanted to meet with Wright, who was willing, but he had heard that Bear Bryant disapproved. "This is my business deal and it does not involve Bryant,"

Steve Wright.

Wright told an Alabama school official. He secretly met with Cochran in a hotel parking lot one night, and the two went back to the Green Bay assistant coach's room to chat. Wright, loving the idea of playing for Lombardi and the Packers, made a tentative deal to sign with Green Bay following the Sugar Bowl game for $12,000, plus a $9,000 signing bonus.

After the game, the Jets scout hounded him and kept asking if he had signed with Green Bay. Wright told him it was not that scout's business. He signed with Green Bay.[7]

Before reporting to the Packers for his rookie season in the summer of 1964, Wright spent time in his hometown of Louisville, where he worked out with a few established NFL players. "Don't mess with the veterans," they warned him. "They'll be trying to screw you because you will be trying to take away from them."[8]

Wright's first meeting with Lombardi was during training camp at St. Norbert College, where the legendary head coach greeted all the rookies outside of the dorm. "Boy, you're a big one,"[9] Lombardi said to Wright.

Wright was drafted as a defensive end, but learned that the position differed from how it was played at Alabama. In college, he played in a two-point stance, but in the pros the defensive end lined up in a three-point stance. His first day of practice was a tough one, and the next day he was switched to offensive tackle. The Packers, known to be like a family, were kind to the rookie. Fellow offensive linemen Forrest Gregg and Jerry Kramer worked with him. Gregg took him under his wing and tutored him by teaching the finer points of the tackle position and how to use quickness to win over the defensive player lined up against him.

Like the rest of the Packers, Wright benefited from playing for the league's greatest coach, being well prepared week after week and being in top physical shape. Wright, always willing to work hard, worked his tail off for Lombardi, and survived his grueling training schedule, especially the Packers well-known grass drills. In those torturous drills, usually conducted in the sweltering summer heat when the temperature was in the upper 90s, the players would run in place, drop to the ground on Lombardi's command, and then get back up on their feet. "Pick 'em up," Lombardi would holler. "Run! Run. Faster … you're not getting up fast enough … faster!"[10]

"He set his goals and worked toward them with more dedication than anyone I ever met," Wright said of Lombardi. "The way he went about it made a lot of people mad, but he did what he thought was right. He loved football, and he wanted to be the best. And his philosophy was to be the best you've got to give a whole lot."[11]

Although Wright's happy-go-lucky attitude would get under Lombardi's skin once in a while, the great Green Bay head coach held a place for him on his team. Lombardi believed that Wright was a good player and understood his style. Two or three times during a season, Lombardi would put his arm around Wright and tell him, "I know that everybody is a bit different. You're a good player."[12] However, there would be times when Wright would feel the wrath of Vince Lombardi. "I had a knack for making Vince mad," Wright would later admit, "and I mean pissed."[13]

Following his first season as a reserve and special teams player, Wright broke into the starting lineup in 1965, which seemed to baffle the sports world. "It makes one wonder—that second year man Steve Wright can be good enough to release [Forrest] Gregg of his old tackle post," wrote a *Baltimore Sun* sportswriter. "It makes one wonder that Gregg, the former all-pro offensive tackle, replaces Fuzzy Thurston, a former all-pro guard."[14]

Perhaps believing that his offense needed younger players and more speed after a second place finish in 1964, Lombardi opted for several changes. Max McGee, slowing up with age, was benched, Boyd Dowler was switched from flanker to split end, and Carroll Dale, obtained in a trade with the Rams, became the Packers' starting flanker. The revamped offense and Packers started fast by winning their first six games of the 1965 season. However, following a mid-season offensive slump Lombardi decided to make changes. Thurston was inserted back into the starting lineup at left guard, Gregg was moved back to right tackle, and Wright went to the bench. The Green Bay offense found its stride again, and the Packers went on to win the first of three successive championships.

As the Packers prepared for the 1966 season, Lombardi displayed his most famous temper tantrum on the Oneida Street practice field, located across the road from Lambeau Field. The story would become known publicly when it was sensationalized a year later by *Look Magazine*. "Suddenly, I was rushing one of my players and flailing away at him with my fists," Lombardi said. "I'm fifty-four years old now, and he's eight inches taller than I am and outweighs me by fifty pounds. If he had brought both hands down on me, he would have probably driven me into the ground, but he just stood there, warding off my blows because he understands me. Do I hate him, or even dislike him? No, not for a minute; I'm fond of him. He's one of the most likeable men on the squad. That's his problem. He has all the size and ability to be a great one, but he loves everybody. So what was I doing? I guess I was trying to get him to hate me enough to take it out on the opposition, because to play this game you must have that fire in you, and there is nothing that stokes that fire like hate."[15]

During that 1966 season, the Packers won their second consecutive NFL championship and earned the right to represent the established league in the first Super Bowl against the AFL champion Kansas City Chiefs. Wright remembers the tension of the week leading up to the game, and recalls that Lombardi was fully aware of it. The Green Bay Packers were representing not only the vaunted Packers dynasty, but the entire NFL as well. Everything that Lombardi and his team had established at Green Bay was riding on the outcome of the game. "I understand there are a lot of distractions," Lombardi said in a team meeting during the week of preparation for the game, "but the rules are going to be the same."[16]

The rules may have been the same, but the fines would be higher. "A fine for breaking the 11:00 curfew, during the week of the Super Bowl would cost a player an entire paycheck," said Wright. "Lombardi told us that if we were going to break curfew to come get him, because he wanted to see what was worth $15,000."[17]

The Packers won the Super Bowl, 35–10, and then faced a bigger challenge in 1967: to win a third consecutive NFL championship. The Green Bay team was a year older, the rest of the league would be gunning for them, and they would be minus Jim Taylor, who had played out his option and signed with the Saints. To make things even tougher, the Packers lost their starting backfield of Elijah Pitts and Jim Grabowski during the season.

With a patched up running attack, the Packers continued to win, though, and owned a 7–2–1 record when they traveled to Chicago to take on the Bears with a chance to clinch the Central Division with a win. With the score 14–10, in favor of Green Bay, Donny Anderson punted from deep in his own territory early in the second half. The wind caused the punt to twist in the air and made it difficult for Gale Sayers of the Bears to catch. Steve Wright came up with the subsequent fumble, and the Packers offense then drove for a decisive field goal in a 17–13 win.

The win clinched first place in the division and a spot in the playoffs for Green Bay, and the Packers went on to win their first playoff game over the Rams in Milwaukee. The Packers then met the Cowboys for the NFL championship in the frigid conditions of the game we now know as the Ice Bowl. During that game, Wright was sitting in a makeshift dugout with his teammates when one of the heaters malfunctioned. The heater let off steam or smoke, and the players quickly evacuated in case the dugout was on fire. Just then, Wright heard his name called. Bob Skoronski, the starting left offensive tackle, was injured on a play, and Wright needed to replace him. As a frantic search continued, Wright heard his name called again. Having to go into the game, he borrowed Lionel Aldridge's helmet, which was at least a size too big. At the line of scrimmage, as Wright lined up across of George Andrie, the towering defensive end of the Cowboys, the crown of the oversized helmet slid down Wright's forehead and covered his eyes. He managed to cut down Andrie on the play, and the play gained two yards, with Skoronski returning for the next play.

The Packers went on to beat the Cowboys, and then win the second Super Bowl. After the season, Wright, making just $2,500 more than his rookie season, asked Pat Peppler, the man who handled salaries for Green Bay, about a salary increase; however, Peppler balked at Wright's request of $18,000 per season. Hearing that, Wright told Green Bay line coach Ray Wietecha he wanted a trade. "Was it a mistake to ask to be traded? You bet it was, baby," Wright would later say. Other teams were far from the family that Lombardi had taught. "I never saw that anywhere but in Green Bay," Wright would later say. "Everywhere else, they were fractioned and cliquish."[18]

Traded to New York, Wright received $20,000 for the 1968 season from the Giants, a substantial raise of his $14,500 salary in Green Bay. In an unsurprising move, the Giants rewarded him with the starting right tackle job. The word around the league was Wright, although a back-up in Green Bay, was good enough to start for any other team in the NFL.

As expected, the Giants had a good offense that year, highlighted by the Fran Tarkenton to Homer Jones passing combination, and a strong offensive line, anchored by Pro Bowl center Greg Larson, guard Pete Case, and tackles Willie Young and Steve Wright. In Week 11, with New York's playoff hopes alive with a 7–3 record, the Giants ventured to Los Angeles to take on the Rams. Wright, going against Deacon Jones, sustained a groin injury on the game's third play. "They took me into the locker room and gave the groin a shot of Novocain," said Wright, "I then went back and finished the game."[19]

The Giants lost on a last second field goal. Wright played a solid game against Jones, but the injury ended his season. The Giants lost their last three games to finish with a 7–7 record.

Following the 1968 season, Wright was selected to model for "The Gladiator," the trophy for the NFL Man of the Year, an award given to the player considered the league's most "outstanding citizen athlete." Wright posed while dressed in his full uniform and wore a cape over that uniform. "The guys who won the award would turn in their graves if they knew it was me."[20]

In the summer of 1970, the Giants waived Wright, and the Washington Redskins, now coached by Vince Lombardi, claimed him.

Wright arrived in Washington, but Lombardi was not there. Instead, the all-time great coach was in the hospital, terminally ill with cancer. A few weeks later, Lombardi died at the age of 57.

The Redskins camp had the look of a Lombardi team when Wright arrived, but that faded as the season progressed. When players noticed that Lombardi was not there, discipline crumbled, and the Redskins limped through a 6–8 season. Wright played as a backup tackle, but moved into the starting lineup for the last two games of the season, both of those games resulting in wins by the Redskins. Before the last game of the 1970 season, the captains spoke at the team's pre-game meeting.

The Redskins traded Wright to the Chicago Bears prior to the start of the 1971 season. When told of the trade on the practice field, Wright replied, "I wish they hadn't waited until after wind sprints to tell me."[21] When asked what he would miss most about Washington, Wright quipped, "Central Liquors."[22]

In Chicago, Wright started at right tackle for the Bears, and in the opinion of one sportswriter, had his best pro season. "Wright played well, and he was a good team relaxer," said Bears head coach, Jim Dooley.[23]

Wright returned to the Bears in 1972, but was traded to St. Louis. He started for the Cardinals in 1972, and that would be his last season in the NFL. He returned to his home in Washington and bartended, "but that got depressing."[24] He also took the time to write his autobiography, *I'd Rather Be Wright*. Unsure what he wanted to do or where he wanted to live, he hit the road in his camper, settling in Montana where he tended bar. He then learned of the new World Football League and arranged to try out with the team in Anaheim, but opted to sign with the Chicago Fire instead.

Life started off well in Chicago and the new league, but with the economic recession and undercapitalized ownership, the league began to decline. The following year, the WFL attempted a comeback. Wright signed with the Chicago Winds. However, five games into the season, the Winds went under, and that concluded Steve Wright's professional football career.

After football, Wright relocated to Florida and sold veterinary pharmaceuticals. He got remarried and enjoyed life. "I'm living where I want to live and doing what I want to do," he said at the Packers' twentieth Super Bowl reunion. "I'm never going to be rich, but I am happy."[25]

As a salesman, Wright continued to live on Lombardi time by being at every appointment ahead of time. "If I have an appointment, I will be there fifteen minutes early."[26]

Steve Wright, now enjoying the life of retirement, lived his life his way without acquiescing to the demands of others. For better or for worse, Steve Wright was always his own person.

Notes

1. Steve Wright, *I'd Rather Be Wright: Memoirs of an Itinerant Tackle* (Upper Saddle River, NJ: Prentice Hall, 1974).
2. *Ibid.*
3. *Ibid.*
4. *Ibid.*
5. *Ibid.*
6. *Ibid.*
7. *Ibid.*
8. *Ibid.*
9. *Ibid.*
10. *Ibid.*
11. *Ibid.*
12. *Ibid.*
13. *Ibid.*

14. *Baltimore Sun*, September 25, 1965.
15. *Look Magazine,* September 5, 1967.
16. Steve Wright interview with Ken Crippen, 2014.
17. *Ibid.*
18. Wright.
19. Steve Wright interview with Ken Crippen, 2014.
20. Wright.
21. *Washington Post,* September 1, 1971.
22. *Ibid.*
23. Wright.
24. *Ibid.*
25. Jerry Kramer and Dick Schaap, *Distant Replay* (New York: G. P. Putnam's Sons, 1985).
26. *Ibid.*

Taxi Squad

John Maxymuk

From time to time on the Internet, one will come across a 1966 autographed football available for sale. A review of the list of players who signed the ball, though, reveals some unfamiliar names: Jeff White, Roy Schmidt, Sonny Redders, Larry Moore, Kent Nix … who are these guys? They aren't listed on the team roster for the season. Are they front office types? Wait a minute, Kent Nix sounds familiar. Didn't he play quarterback for the Steelers?

Yes, Nix did begin his playing career with Pittsburgh in 1967, but he spent 1966 on the taxi squad of the world champion Green Bay Packers along with the other four players listed above. Taxi squad players are ghosts in the team's official record book. They are nowhere to be found in the team's media guide, although practice squad players back to 1989 have their own listing, but those assigned to the practice squad when it was called the taxi squad are ignored and need to be culled from stray newspaper articles from the distant period.

The taxi squad originated with Cleveland Coach Paul Brown in 1946 when he had more good players than the All-America Football Conference's roster limit of 33. Wanting to retain these players, he had team owner Mickey McBride add them to the payroll of McBride's taxi cab company. Although not members of the Browns, they were paid by the team owner and practiced with the team. Used haphazardly throughout the league in the 1950s, the taxi squad began to be utilized more heavily in the 1960s. Then, there was no limit on the number of players stowed on the squad, but they did add to the team's payroll. As just noted, the Packers' media guide does not list taxi or practice squad players prior to 1989 when the league formalized a five-man development squad. The name was changed to Practice Squad in 1990 and the player limit was raised to eight in 2004.

The Packers had some taxi squadders in the 1950s, but Vince Lombardi had no members in his first season in Green Bay, although recently waived defensive back Bill Butler replaced halfback Tim Brown after the first week of the season, and former Giants guard Mike Falls was claimed during the season and went to training camp in 1960 with the Packers. Lombardi did assign two players to injured reserve in 1959: fifth round pick

Andy Cvercko, a guard, and Steve Meilinger, the starting slot back in 1958. In 1960, defensive tackle John Miller, whom the Pack signed after he was cut by the Redskins, was assigned to the taxi squad, while quarterback Joe Francis was assigned to injured reserve. Miller was activated in the week of November 14 for the last five games of the year, replacing defensive end Jim Temp who dislocated his shoulder.

Vince began to make more use of the taxi squad in 1961, carrying three men during his first championship season. Halfback Ed Sutton had played for the Redskins from 1957 to 1959 and the Giants in 1960; defensive back Don Ellersick had spent 1960 with the Rams; and quarterback Val Keckin was an 11th round pick of the Packers in 1961. Fifth round pick Jack Novak, a guard, spent the year on injured reserve. None of these men were ever activated by the team.

The repeat champions of 1962 carried two men on the taxi squad: undrafted free agent defensive back Howie Williams and Bob Jeter, a halfback/end who was drafted by Green Bay in the second round of the 1960 draft but opted to play in Canada for two years. When promising linebacker Nelson Toburen suffered a career-ending neck injury in his first-ever start on November 18 against the Colts, Lombardi tried to activate Jeter, but found that the CFL still owned his playing rights, so Williams was activated instead.

Both Jeter and Williams would make the team in 1963, a year that featured several inactive players on the roster. Halfback Paul Hornung, of course, was under league suspension. Second round draft pick Tom Brown, a back, decided to play major league baseball instead of reporting to Green Bay. Seventh round pick Gary Kroner, a kicker, was placed on the injured list first and then later on the taxi squad. Fourteenth round pick linebacker Ed Holler spent the first 12 games on the taxi squad before being activated to replace injured middle linebacker Ray Nitschke for the team's closing West Coast swing against the 49ers and Rams. The last two taxi squad men, fullback Frank Mestnik and defensive back Doug Hart, both were signed by Lombardi after having been cut by the Cardinals. Mestnik replaced tight end Jan Barrett on the active roster on October 4, but Hart spent the whole season as a cab man.

In 1964, the roster size was increased to 40 from 37, and Green Bay carried just one man on the taxi squad, linebacker Gene Breen, who was drafted as a future in the 15th round of the 1963 draft. Breen was activated at the beginning of November to take ailing Jerry Kramer's roster spot. Another future pick from 1963, third rounder Dennis Claridge, was on the 1964 active roster all year, but is not listed on any official league roster because he never appeared in a game. Claridge was the third quarterback, but would not appear in a game till 1965.

Lombardi restocked the taxi squad in 1965 as the team headed to its third championship. Fourth round pick Syracuse quarterback Wally Mahle, fresh from handing off to Floyd Little and Jim Nance, was converted to a defensive back. Sixth round pick halfback Bill Symons tore up his knee and spent the year on IR and the taxi squad, while third rounder Allen Brown was assigned to IR, too. Undrafted free agents Eli Strand, a guard, and Larry Moore, a kicker/defensive back, were solely cab men.

Strand was featured in an article in the 1966 *Packers Yearbook* in which he described the life of the anonymous men on the taxi squad, "My duties were simple. I went to practice every day. I ran other teams' plays, as well as going through the drills they had. On all games I travelled with the team. I stood [or jumped] on the sidelines during the games."[1] All five of the 1965 inactives returned to Green Bay for training camp in 1966, but only

Allen Brown made the team. Larry Moore became the first Lombardi Packer to serve a second season on the team's taxi squad and was joined by two undrafted free agents—quarterback Kent Nix and flanker Sonny Redders—as well as two future draft picks from 1965—13th rounder Roy Schmidt, a guard, and 18th round end Jeff White.

Nix (number 18) is the best remembered of the 1966 taxi squad; he had the best and longest NFL career of the group. Nix's father Emery was a passing tailback for the New York Giants during World War II. Kent had a big arm, but completed fewer than half of his passes for just ten touchdowns in his junior and senior seasons at Texas Christian. Former Packers assistant coach Bill Austin would give Lombardi a fifth round pick for Kent in 1967, and Nix became the Steelers' starting quarterback when Bill Nelsen got hurt that year. Kent spent three seasons in Pittsburgh, two in Chicago and one in Houston, mostly as a backup, and then hung on the taxi squads of Houston and New Orleans for a couple more years. He completed just 46 percent of his passes (a lower percentage than his father achieved 25 years earlier) for 23 touchdowns and 49 interceptions. His won-lost record as a starter was 4–14, but with some very bad teams. One win with Pittsburgh was over the Packers in 1967, though.

Roy Schmidt (number 65) was from Long Beach State and essentially took Eli Strand's place as the extra lineman on the taxi squad for 1966. In 1967, he was a late cut of the Packers, 10 days before the start of the season. He was signed by the Saints, coached by former Packers assistant Tom Fears, and spent two seasons in New Orleans, followed by one in Atlanta, one in Washington (coached by Bill Austin) and a final partial season in Minnesota. He played in 43 games over five NFL seasons and fought through some injury problems.

Jeff White (number 47) played with end Dave Parks and halfback Donny Anderson at Texas Tech and was a future pick in the 18th round of the 1965 draft, when Anderson was a future pick in the first round. White had been a junior college All-America at Glendale, California. At Tech, the thin speedster was a two-year letterman, but was never a starter and was never the team's leading receiver. He returned to training camp in 1967 and was noted in the *Sports Illustrated* football preview issue that year along with draftee Dave Dunaway as two youngsters who provided solid receiving depth for the defending champions.[2] Instead, Jeff was cut on September 6 along with Dunaway and Roy Schmidt. Atlanta claimed White, but then cut him a week later.

Sonny Redders (number 48) starred at Wisconsin Stevens Point as an all-conference running back. Redders hailed from Madison and played local semipro ball after college before winning a tryout with Green Bay in 1966. The Packers converted him to flanker and his biggest highlight was catching an option pass from Ron Rector for a touchdown in an intrasquad scrimmage in August. He was cut in late July 1967 and signed with the Vikings for a week before they cut him. The Falcons, coached by former Packers assistant Norb Hecker, signed him, but they cut Sonny as well. Redders returned to the semipro Central States Football League in 1967. He was elected to the Stevens Point Hall of Fame in 1985.

Larry Moore (number 42) was signed as a free agent halfback out of Central Michigan in 1965. He played some at defensive back in training camp, but as the lightest man in camp at 177 pounds, he was trying out primarily as a kicker. He stayed on the taxi squad in both 1965 and 1966 as insurance should anything happen to place kicker Don Chandler. An article in the *Milwaukee Sentinel* in October 1966 mentions him as part of a deer hunting party with Packers Jerry Kramer, Doug Hart, Steve Wright and Allen

Brown.[3] On August 16, Green Bay traded Moore to Atlanta, coached by former Packers assistant Norb Hecker, for a draft choice. Moore competed for the kicking spot with Bob Jencks for three weeks until being cut on September 6. Hecker had said that Moore was hitting them from 48 yards in practice, but ended up cutting both kickers and going with Lou Kirouac as the Falcons' first placekicker. Moore returned to Packers training camp in 1967 as a kicker, but was an early cut and never played in the NFL.

Lombardi's final team in 1967 made extensive use of the taxi squad, and not just his own, to replace injured players for the push to the fifth championship. Fullback Ben Wilson joined Green Bay from the Rams' taxi squad, while fullback Chuck Mercein was headed to the Redskins' cab team during the season when Vince intercepted him to replace an injured Elijah Pitts. Veteran defensive tackle Jim Colvin was claimed from the Cowboys and sat on the taxi squad for a few weeks in September while Lionel Aldridge's broken leg heeled. Colvin later ended up playing with the Giants that season.

Two players remained on the Packers' taxi squad all through 1967: second round pick, speedy receiver Dave Dunaway, and fifth round pick, center Jay Bachman. Dunaway would appear in just two games with the 1968 Packers before being cut during the season. He spent the rest of 1968 with Atlanta and then was the punter for the Giants in 1969 to conclude his disappointing career. Bachman played for Denver from 1968 to 1971 as a sometime starter. Fourteenth round draftee receiver Claudis James, a converted college quarterback, began the season on the roster, but when receiver Bob Long recovered from knee surgery James moved to the taxi squad on October 1. That same date, defensive end Lionel Aldridge returned to the active roster, and tight end/linebacker Dick Capp moved to the taxi squad as well. Capp had spent 1966 with the minor league Lowell Giants, which had a working agreement with the Packers. In fact, Green Bay sent two players to Lowell in 1967: defensive tackle Leon Crenshaw and running back Willy Ray Smith, Bubba's older brother.

On Friday, January 12th, just two days before Super Bowl II, Capp was reactivated by Green Bay to replace the injured tight end Allen Brown, and enthused, "Imagine me, a Boston Patriot cut, playing for the Packers in the Super Bowl."[4] Green Bay was his favorite team when growing up, and he played a key role in that game by recovering a muffed punt at the end of the first half that led to a Don Chandler field goal that put the Packers firmly in control of Vince Lombardi's swansong triumph in Miami.

NOTES

1. Lee Remmel, "Eli Strand and the Taxi Squad," *Green Bay Packers Yearbook*, 1966, 8–9.
2. Tex Maule, "Runaway in Central," *Sports Illustrated*, September 18, 1967.
3. Joe Pecor, "Pack Duels Deer to Scoreless Tie," *Milwaukee Sentinel*, October 6, 1966.
4. "Packers Fill Roster with Linebacker," *Milwaukee Journal*, January 12, 1968.

REFERENCES

Johnson, Chuck. "5 Get Second Chance with Packers." *Milwaukee Journal*, July 19, 1967.
_____. "Nix, Once Packer, Stars with Steelers." *Milwaukee Journal*, October 27, 1967.
Maule, Tex. "Runaway in Central." *Sports Illustrated*, September 18, 1967.
"Packers Fill Roster with Linebacker." *Milwaukee Journal*, January 12, 1968.
Pecor, Joe. "Pack Duels Deer to Scoreless Tie." *Milwaukee Sentinel*, October 6, 1966.
Remmel, Lee. "Eli Strand and the Taxi Squad." *Green Bay Packers Yearbook*, 1966, 8–9.

Race and the Packers

JOHN VORPERIAN

In 1959 the newly named Green Bay head coach and general manager Vince Lombardi challenged the Packer franchise with the goal of chasing perfection and brought with him a color-blind employment policy for all playing positions. Lombardi was highly intolerant towards losing and racism. He was no stranger to bigotry. As an Italian-American he encountered his fair share of direct prejudicial incidents.

Lombardi was a starting lineman at Fordham University. Yet despite being one of the famed "Seven Blocks of Granite" he was accorded no special favors. The cultural attitudes of anti-diversity were ever present on campus. Once on a date with his future wife Marie Planitz, he arrived at one of her sorority dances and was greeted by a group of men, one of whom piped up, "Who's the little wop?" Lombardi immediately punched the fellow in the mouth. Then there was a time after football practice when Lombardi was showering and another player loudly instructed another teammate of olive complexion to go stand by Lombardi. Using a racist epithet he wanted to see which one looked more like a Negro. Lombardi knocked out the loudmouth.

Aside from social settings, Lombardi had to contend with discrimination in business. After college Lombardi went into coaching and for many years was an assistant coach at various schools and colleges. He sought a head coaching position. While an assistant coach for West Point's Red Blaik, Lombardi interviewed for head coach at Wake Forest. Lombardi felt the interview went smoothly. However he later received a phone call from a North Carolinian. "Vince, I have to tell you, I don't want you to play out a charade. They had several number [*sic*] of people interview and you were one of them. But they are not going to give this job to anyone whose name ends in a vowel."[1]

Prior to 1959 of the 12 NFL franchises only three had employed an Italian-American as a head coach, Pittsburgh (Luby DiMeolo in 1934); the Cleveland Rams (Buff Donelli in 1944) and Green Bay (Gene Ronzani 1950–1953).

Upon his arrival in Green Bay Lombardi set forth to radically alter the team's culture of defeatism into a winner's attitude and to do so shaped the Packers by his key principles of discipline, hard work, and responsibility. A devout practicing traditional Roman Catholic, Lombardi put tolerance into the clubhouse and brought diversity onto the field. He was not a social worker but with football operations he wanted the best players regardless of race, color, creed or sexual orientation.

Although he had been the assistant coach in charge of the New York Giants offense, one of the first major player moves by Lombardi was to strengthen the Pack's porous secondary. He enticed All-Pro safety Emlen Tunnell to leave the Big Apple and come to Green Bay. Tunnell, a 34-year-old bachelor and African American, who had played in every Pro Bowl from 1951 to 1957, was highly reluctant to come to the NFL's northern outpost. No jazz clubs. No available black women. Tunnell was also aware of the housing problems Packer Nate Borden endured. Borden had lived in a shack outside of Green Bay which Tunnell later described as a place "you wouldn't keep your dog in."[2]

Lombardi convinced the first African American to play for the New York Giants in 1948 to come to the Pack with the promise he could find jazz and women in Chicago and he would stay at the Northland Hotel with the Packers taking care of the accommodation bill.

Four African American players were in 1959 training camp: Nate Borden, Em Tunnell, A.D. Williams, a receiver and 1956 Los Angeles Ram draft pick from the University of the Pacific, and rookie running back Tim Brown from Ball State. Brown struck up a friendship with a young white girl. In friendship the girl invited Brown over to her parents' house for dinner. Brown went and some Packers reported such news directly to Lombardi.

Some sport historians tag this story as the precursor to one of Lombardi's legendary addresses to his squad. At a team meeting Lombardi told his charges, "If I ever hear nigger or dago or kike or anything like that around here, regardless of who you are, you're through with me. You can't play for me if you have any kind of prejudice."[3]

By his second season, four years before enactment of the Civil Rights Act of 1964, St. Vince let it be known to Green Bay tavern and restaurant owners that establishments that barred service to his African American players would be declared off-limits to the entire team. Lombardi also sent word into the NFL grapevine that he would no longer split his team on road trips. Any hotel that would not house all Packers would get no Packers.

Green Bay's final 1960 pre-season game was in Winston-Salem against Washington. The all-white Washingtonians had no problems whatsoever with accommodations. However due to Jim Crow discrimination the Packers had to scramble to find suitable lodging for their four African American players. They were eventually housed in a dormitory at North Carolina A&T, a historically black college 35 miles away in Greensboro. Although there's no written verification, many Lombardi chroniclers cite that during the time period of this particular game Lombardi himself was denied service at a Winston-Salem area restaurant. Wait staff believed him to be black. Some contend Lombardi contacted Washington team owner George Preston Marshall to complain of these racist incidents. The next year with a game in Dixie at Columbus, Georgia, Lombardi made arrangements for the Packers to stay at Fort Benning, Georgia, an integrated army post.

The African American Packers did joke among themselves that over the course of summer training camp Lombardi was a secret brother. From time to time he did permit the players to go to Milwaukee or Chicago for what we now term "mental health days." Lombardi saw the bigger picture; life was God, family and the Green Bay Packers. Cohesion was paramount to a team's success. Division and bigotry had no place in the work place or in living.

In Green Bay Lombardi belonged to the Oneida Golf and Riding Club, a country club which used members of the Oneida Indian tribe as caddies except in the summer when the Native Americans would be released and local high school teenagers used for those jobs. The first time he was made aware of this hiring policy and practice. Lombardi publicly berated the club pro and insisted that the Native Americans be used year round. "If they're good enough for spring and fall, they're good enough for summer."[4] Needless to say, whenever he golfed at Oneida Lombardi always had a Native American caddy.

On December 27, 1960, Lombardi selected Herb Adderley of Michigan State as Green Bay's number one draft pick. Adderley became the first African American to be the Packers' top selection. In the 1963 draft, Lombardi again picked an African American as his number one draft pick: Dave Robinson from Penn State.

The executive board of the 45-member Green Bay board of directors called for a meeting with Lombardi. Their thrust and concern was he was wasting number one draft picks on black players. They argued black players could be selected in the third round. Lombardi met the board's racial resistance directly and forcefully. "I'm drafting football players. I'm not drafting white or black, I'm just drafting the best players out there. You guys run the business end of the thing, and I'll run the Green Bay Packer football operation."[5] There were no further meetings by the directors on the topic.

Defensive end Lionel Aldridge who joined Green Bay in 1963 came to Lombardi. The African American Packer had been dating a white Mormon woman named Vicki Wankier and they had decided to get married. In 1965 interracial marriage was a hot-button issue for the country and for the National Football League. Rumors did circulate that the NFL had barred such married players from competing in the circuit. Lombardi put it simply to Aldridge, "You know what, I don't care who you marry, as long as you keep the Green Bay Packer team clean, your nose clean, and play good football."[6]

NFL Commissioner Pete Rozelle personally met with Lombardi on the pending Aldridge marriage looking for the franchise to help find a way to stop it. The Commissioner was rebuffed by the Pope of Green Bay with "Absolutely not; this is my team. My team is who my team is and nobody can tell me what I can and cannot do."[7]

Lombardi's practical "football and only football" orientation which resulted in five NFL championships in seven years forced other teams to set aside arbitrary racial codes and practices. Hall of Famer Herb Adderley said, "Back in the day, there were quotas on how many black players were on an NFL roster, maybe six or seven total. Lombardi started playing six or seven just on defense. Other teams eventually started doing the same thing and because of that bold move, it opened the door for more black players to earn a spot on an NFL roster."[8]

The 1960s were a turbulent time with riots and unrest as America began to come to grips with the civil rights movement. Titletown in Green Bay, Wisconsin, already was running towards daylight in fostering racial equality and furthering human rights.

Notes

1. Ernie Palladino, *Lombardi and Landry* (New York: Skyhorse Publishing, 2010), xxviii.
2. John Eisenberg, *That First Season* (New York: Houghton Mifflin Harcourt, 2009), 82.
3. David Maraniss, *When Pride Still Mattered* (New York: Simon & Schuster, 1999), 241.
4. *Ibid.*, 242.
5. David Claerbaut, *Bart Starr* (Lanham, MD: Taylor Trade, 2004), 71–72.
6. Herb Adderley, David Robinson, and Royce Boyles, *Lombardi's Left Side* (Olathe, KS: Ascend Books, 2012), 3.
7. *Ibid.*, 14.
8. *Ibid.*

References

Adderley, Herb, David Robinson, and Royce Boyles. *Lombardi's Left Side.* Olathe, KS: Ascend Books, 2012.
Eisenberg, John. *That First Season.* New York: Houghton Mifflin Harcourt, 2009.
Maraniss, David. *When Pride Still Mattered.* New York: Simon & Schuster, 1999.
Palladino, Ernie. *Lombardi and Landry.* New York: Skyhorse, 2010.
Piascik, Andy. *Gridiron Gauntlet.* Lanham, MD: Taylor Trade, 2009.
Schaap, Dick. *Green Bay Replay.* New York: Avon Books, 1997.
www.en.wikipedia.org/wiki/Bob_Mann_(American_football).
www.en.wikipedia.org/wiki/Charlie_Brackins.
www.nflretirees.blogspot.com/2006/10/bob-mann-first-black-player.html.

www.packernews.com.
www.packers.com.
www.packershistory.net.
www.Packerville.Blogspot.Com/2007/09/Charlie-Choo-Choo-Brackins.Html.
www.profootballhof.com/history/story.
www.pro-football-reference.com.
waketheherd.wordpress.com/2012/11/27/black-white-and-red-all-over-detroits-history-of-racis.

PART 4

The Stadiums

Lambeau Field

Randy Snow

Lambeau Field. Chances are, you can't say the name without thinking of "The Frozen Tundra" and hearing the voice of John Facenda, or, perhaps, the voice of ESPN's Chris Berman, trying his best to imitate the voice of John Facenda while dropping the phrase "The Frozen Tundra." Since 1957, Lambeau Field has hosted pro football games for more than 58 years in a row, the longest continuous run of any stadium in the NFL.

By 1956, the teams of the National Football League were unhappy with visits to Green Bay's City Stadium. There were 24,500 wooden seats, and no more than 26,000 if people wanted to be part of a standing room only crowd. While that had been fine in prior decades, the rest of the NFL had moved ahead by the 1950s. All of the other Western Conference teams had room in their ballparks for between 50,000 and 80,000 fans, and Milwaukee County Stadium could accommodate 45,000 for Packers games. The visitors' share for a game at Green Bay averaged $161,000 in 1955, about $100,000 less than anywhere else in the conference. No longer was the talk about whether the Packers needed a nicer place to host. "We are deciding whether we want to keep the Packers in Green Bay," an official for the Packer Corporation said on January 29. The rest of the league had let him know that they would prefer playing their road games against the Milwaukee Packers.[1]

So it was that, on February 9, the Green Bay City Council scheduled a referendum on a bond issue in order to raise nearly one million dollars to finance a new stadium, the vote to take place on April 3.[2]

It was no exaggeration to say that the city's voters would decide the Packers' future. As the day got closer, there were suggestions that the Packers might leave Wisconsin altogether and move to Minneapolis—or Buffalo—or Miami.[3]

On March 31, the Saturday before the polls would open, the team staged a pep rally, and the crowd was addressed by five men who would be among the Pro Football Hall of Fame's charter class in 1963, and another who would be enshrined later. Founder Curly Lambeau was there, along with Packer greats John "Blood" McNally, Don Hutson and 1974 inductee Tony Canadeo. George Halas came up from Chicago to exhort the voters to build a place where more fans could boo him and the Bears. A telegram was read aloud to the crowd, letting the voters know that there was some truth to rumors that the town could easily lose its team, the word coming straight from NFL Commissioner Bert Bell. "It would be good business judgment to approve the referendum," the wire said. "We have firm offers for a franchise from many cities whose stadiums can accommodate large crowds. There is no doubt in my mind that the Green Bay Packers could sell their franchise, God forbid, for a maximum of $750,000." God forbid. Not many sermons could have scared a Packer fan more.[4]

The vote on the referendum had at one time been considered a toss-up, since opponents pointed out that money could also be spent on schools, hospitals and city services. Come Tuesday, April 4, though, the citizens approved borrowing for a new stadium by more than two to one,[5] not only "sight unseen," but "site unseen" as well, because the location had yet to be determined in a town whose East vs. West hostility was topped only by the one going on over in Berlin. Ultimately, the new stadium was placed southwest of the city, not as close to downtown Green Bay as it was to the town of Ashwaubenon.

Wisconsin's license plates proclaim its nickname as "America's Dairyland," so it's appropriate that the Packers play on what was once a dairy farm. Voters hadn't decided on where a stadium would be. They had simply approved a municipal bond issue to raise $960,000 and left it to a committee to decide how to spend the money wisely. The choices were narrowed down to expanding the existing City Stadium on the east side; building a stadium on the grounds of Perkins Park on the west side; or finding a new location in Brown County rather than in the city limits. The Osborn Engineering Company, based in Cleveland, Ohio, was hired to scout a location, and found it on a 56 acre dairy farm owned by Victor and Florence Vannieuwenhoven. The location—at Ridge Road and Highland Avenue (now called Lombardi Avenue)—was accessible from old U.S. Highway 41, the north-south route which ran from Milwaukee to Green Bay. The topography was ideal for stadium construction, because the sloping hillsides formed what geographers call a massive "natural bowl" that could support the stands. Best of all, the Vannieuwenhovens were the only persons with whom the Packers had to negotiate.[6] Victor and Florence were reasonable folks, and they sold their 56 acres for $73,305 in August, subject to the conditions that construction would not interfere with the harvest of that year's corn crop, nor with the harvest of the 1956 and 1957 alfalfa crops.[7]

The city and the team wanted a stadium whose capacity could easily be expanded as the years went by, and that was designed solely for professional football. Green Bay's Somerville architectural firm was hired to do the design, making for a stadium designed by Packers fans. John Somerville's team included Dick Gustafson, who was inspired by the gridiron at his alma mater, the University of Michigan. The Wolverines played at Michigan Stadium, which had been designed for the possibility of an expanded capacity (it was preparing to increase its seating to 100,001) and intended solely for football. What Gustafson added to the original vision was sightlines like the Wolverines fans enjoyed, where every seat could provide an unobstructed view of the entire field (including obstructions from the spectators in the next row down), and the action could be appreciated even from the highest rows.

The actual construction took only about nine months at a cost of $960,000 (a very reasonable $8.4 million in 2014 dollars), paid for by the selling of municipal bonds. The Packer Corporation shared costs with the city in paying the bondholders, providing $634,700 in interest and principal, and the original debt would be paid off in May 1978 (and was celebrated with a mortgage-burning ceremony).

The stadium was officially dedicated on September 29, 1957, when the Packers played their season opener at the site. Commissioner Bell was there, and he told the crowd of 32,132 (a record for Green Bay) that a decade earlier, a sportswriter had told him that Green Bay was too small to keep supporting an NFL team. Said Bell, "Here's a new stadium, built by a city of 60,000 while big cities of two or three million argue about it." Richard M. Nixon, vice president at the time, spoke as well, noting, "You folks did this yourselves," without asking any help from Washington, D.C. George Halas, who had urged

Green Bay voters to vote yes on the stadium, returned to town for the dedication, and this time he brought the Chicago Bears with him. Before the game, he told the audience, "You grew up with the National Football League. We of the Bears congratulate you."[8] To thank Halas, the Packers scored a come-from-behind touchdown in the fourth quarter to defeat the defending Western Conference champions, 21–17. "What a way to dedicate a new stadium!" the *Milwaukee Sentinel*'s Bud Lea wrote the next day.

For its first eight seasons, the facility was called the "new City Stadium" to distinguish it from City Stadium, where the Packers played from 1925 to 1956. When Packers founder Curly Lambeau died on June 1, 1965, the Green Bay City Council voted on August 5 of that year to rename the eight year old stadium in his honor, and the name became official on September 11. As for the old City Stadium, its name hasn't changed. Because the Packers have so many season ticket holders, their games have been sold out in advance every year since 1960. The *Milwaukee Journal-Sentinel* noted in 2011, that the waiting list of 86,000 and a turnover of only 90 season tickets per year mean that a newcomer to the list would have to wait "oh, about 955 years."[9] Shortly after that, the list had grown to more than 110,000. When the stadium expanded for the 2013 season, there were 5,000 people at the top of the list whose wait had ended. Most of the newcomers to the 105,000 in line will have to wait for more than a millennium.[10] Some people have been waiting for 30 years or more just to acquire their very own season tickets. There are people on the waiting list from all 50 states and even Canada. Few single game tickets are offered for sale, although the Packers point out that "from time to time, a visiting team returns tickets for a game at Lambeau Field. When such an occasion occurs, the tickets will be made available immediately on Ticketmaster.com."[11] That's not to say that the stands are always filled. On some particularly cold December days, fans have been known to stay home during the regular season, and two 1987 games with replacement players brought in less than 36,000. On the other hand, the 2007 NFC championship game at Lambeau saw 72,740 show up in subzero temperatures and frostbite inducing windchills.[12]

The 1956 plans for an easily expandable stadium proved to be farsighted, and have been taken advantage of again and again. Original seating capacity in 1957 was 32,150 and during that first season, the fans sat on temporary wooden bleachers, replaced the next season with permanent aluminum seats in the stands. This would be the first of many renovations, upgrades and expansions the stadium would experience. In fact, they are still continuing to this day.[13]

The stadium has hosted NFL championship games in three seasons (1961, 1966 and 1967) and NFC championships in two (1996 and 2007), all played in early winter. It was in preparation for that first title game that the Chamber of Commerce posted signs unofficially renaming the city "Titletown, U.S.A."[14] The name had been dreamed up by some local businessmen earlier in the month[15] and stuck. The weather has varied from "below freezing" to "below zero," and the wind chill factor has ranged from numbness to frostbite.

The stadium capacity as of 2015 is 81,435 seats, a little less than 20,000 short of the 100,001 seat Michigan Stadium that inspired Dick Gustafson nearly 60 years ago. This put the stadium in the top five among NFL stadiums along with the Dallas Cowboys' AT&T Stadium, MetLife Stadium, home of the New York Jets and New York Giants, FedEx Field, home of the Washington Redskins, and Memorial Coliseum, home of the L.A. Rams. Currently, these are the only five stadiums in the NFL that seat 80,000+ fans for games. No matter how big it becomes, Lambeau Field will always be the legacy of the people of Green Bay.

NOTES

1. "Packers Ask New Stadium at Green Bay," *Racine Journal-Times*, January 13, 1956.
2. "Green Bay Stadium Is Put Up to Voters," *Milwaukee Journal*, February 10, 1956.
3. "Approve Bonds or Lose Packers, Voters Told," *Janesville Daily Gazette*, March 29, 1956.
4. "Packers Stage Rally to Push Bond Vote 'Yes,'" *Racine Journal-Times*, April 1, 1956.
5. "Bay Votes a Big 'Yes' on Stadium," *Milwaukee Journal*, April 4, 1956.
6. "Propose New Packer Site," *Milwaukee Sentinel*, July 11, 1956.
7. Tony Walter, "Green Bay Packers Facilities Have Come a Long Way from a Farm Field," *Green Bay Press-Gazette*, August 1, 2010.
8. "Nixon Applauds 'Do It Yourself' Effort in Building Packer Stadium," *Sheboygan Press*, September 30, 1957.
9. Gary D'Amato, "Packers Season Tickets Worth the Wait—955 Years for Some on the List," *Milwaukee Journal-Sentinel*, January 29, 2011.
10. Tyler Dunne, "Lambeau Field Waiting List Shrinks," June 27, 2013.
11. "Single Game Tickets," www.packers.com.
12. PFRA Linescore Project, www.profootballresearchers.org.
13. "Packers Seek 5,000 Extra Seats," *Sheboygan Press*, March 26, 1960.
14. "'Titletown' Braces for Mass Influx," *Chicago Tribune*, December 31, 1961.
15. "Lew Cornelius' Scorebook," *Capital Times* (Madison WI), December 9, 1961.

Milwaukee County Stadium

Mark L. Ford

Located at 201 South 48th Street, Milwaukee County Stadium was the other home of the Green Bay Packers for 41 seasons from 1953 to 1994. During most of the 1950s, when the NFL was a 12-team league with a 12-game schedule, the Packers' six home games were split equally, three and three, between Milwaukee and Green Bay.[1] After 1961, when the NFL went to a 14-game season and each team got an additional home date, Lambeau got the benefit, and a four-three split that continued for the next 16 years, including the 1966 championship campaign. In 1978, the 16-game schedule was approved, and, for that year and the years 1980 and 1982, four of the eight home games were scheduled in Milwaukee. With those exceptions, Milwaukee's share of games remained at three until the relationship was terminated at the end of 1994.

With the exception of 1958 and 1960 (when only two Milwaukee games were set), the Packers scheduled at least three regular season games each year at County Stadium (as well as the annual Midwest Shriners Game in the preseason to benefit the Milwaukee Shrine Temple, and even a postseason matchup, the 1967 Western Conference title game).

There was actually one season (1982) where the Packers played *more* games at Milwaukee than at Green Bay, and that was when a strike canceled seven of each team's 16 scheduled games. Three of that year's four County Stadium dates (against the Rams, Vikings and Bills) were played as scheduled, while only one scheduled game at Lambeau (the December 12 date against the Lions) took place. Luckily, the opening round of the playoffs brought the Cardinals to Lambeau Field for a second game. The Packers' relationship with Wisconsin's largest city began as far back as 1922, when Milwaukee had its own NFL team, the Badgers (the University of Wisconsin hadn't yet trademarked that name, which was appropriate for any club in "The Badger State"). Green Bay and Milwaukee played home and away for five seasons, from 1922 to 1926, and when the Badgers hosted the Pack, it was at "Athletic Park," renamed in 1928 as "Borchert Field." From October 22, 1922, to November 7, 1926, the Packers never lost any of their games at Milwaukee (though the first one was a 0–0 tie), playing a couple of times before a sellout crowd of 6,500. On December 3, 1922, the Packers and Wisconsin's other NFL team, the Racine Legion, arranged a match at Athletic Park as a neutral site, with the Packers winning, 14–0. The Badgers folded, along with ten of the NFL's 22 teams, at the end of the 1926 season.

After that, the Packers came back for a couple of non-league exhibition games, beating the independent Milwaukee Eagles on October 30, 1927 (22–7 at Athletic Park), and the Ische Radio Stars on December 12, 1931 (44–0, the stadium having been renamed Borchert Field). In 1933, the Packers were invited to play in Milwaukee, and started with a 10–7 loss to the Giants on October 1, 1933, before 12,457 people at Borchert, the Packers' largest home crowd that year.[2] Given that type of welcome from the folks of Milwaukee, the Packers began playing some home games in the area, albeit not at Borchert. Instead, the team leased the larger capacity State Fair Park in West Allis, a suburb of Milwaukee, starting on September 30, 1934, with a 20–6 win over the Giants.

Because of the demand for tickets, and the larger capacity of State Fair Park, the Packers elected to move the 1939 NFL championship to West Allis and attracted their largest gate ever, with 32,279 watching them beat the Giants, 27–0. Earlier that year, Green Bay's 20,000 seat City Stadium had attracted its largest attendance ever that year, with standing spectators bringing the crowd to 22,558. For the next 18 seasons, until 1951, the Packers played two, and sometimes three games each year at State Fair Park. The exception was the war year of 1944, when no games were played there. On the other hand, the Packers shared the stadium in 1940 and 1941 with the Milwaukee Chiefs, one of the franchises of what historians refer to as "the third American Football League." The NFL team's final year at West Allis was 1951.

By then, each NFL team played a 12-game schedule, and the Packers agreed to play three games a year (half of their home schedule) at Milwaukee County Stadium. The first publicly-funded ballpark in the United States, Milwaukee County Stadium had been proposed decades earlier and wasn't ready in time for 1952 because of construction delays. Hence, the Packers played their three games that year at the stadium of Marquette University, which still had a football team in those days. County Stadium opened on April 6, 1953, in time for the new National League baseball season, when the newly-relocated Boston Braves made their debut as the Milwaukee Braves.

On September 27, 1953, the Green Bay Packers would play their home opener at the brand new facility. There were 22,604 fans in the 36,000 seat stadium when the team faced the Eastern Conference champion Cleveland Browns, and they lost, 27–0 (the Packers had played an exhibition game at the new stadium two weeks earlier, where 16,859 people watched them narrowly lose, 26–23, to the Steelers). Their worst home crowd of the year (16,378) came on November 22 at Milwaukee for a 37–7 loss to the 49ers, and the Packers went on to finish last in the conference, at 2–9–1. It would take until October 17, 1954, for the Packers' first win at County Stadium, a 35–17 victory over the visiting Rams. By then, new seats brought the capacity to 44,000 (compared to 22,500 at Lambeau in Green Bay), and in 1955, a Packers record home crowd of 40,199 turned out for a game against the Colts. After Vince Lombardi's turnaround took the Packers to the 1960 title game, County Stadium began having sellout crowds in 1961. With the events now "standing room only," the stadium began selling an additional 2,000 "standing room tickets."[3] For 1965, bleachers were added to provide 2,150 additional seats, so for 1966, County Stadium never had fewer than 47,000 customers, even for preseason contests.

The 1966 season is described in greater detail in Part 2 of this book, but all three of the Milwaukee games bear mentioning here. The Packers opened the 1966 campaign on September 10 against Baltimore, and the game was televised nationally.[4] It was the first major game in the stadium in nearly a year because the Braves had moved to Atlanta after the 1965 baseball season. CBS promoted the meeting as a rematch of the 1965 division tiebreaker that had been decided, 13–10, by a controversial Don Chandler field goal that went higher than the uprights, and which the Colts thought had gone wide. This time, there was no doubt about the winner, as the Packers beat the Colts, 24–3.

On October 23, the Packers hosted the NFL's newest team, the Atlanta Falcons, who were guided by former Lombardi assistant, Norb Hecker, and quarterbacked by former Packers' third-stringer Dennis Claridge. The defending champions pulled no punches for Hecker, Claridge, or the first-year Falcons, giving the new guys a 56–3 drubbing.[5]

Finally, there was the December 4 game against the 49ers. Milwaukee's 48,725 fans sat that afternoon through freezing rain and gusts of up to 25 miles an hour (for a 10° wind chill) and watched Green Bay win 20–7.[6] Now at 10–2–0 with two games left, the Packers were guaranteed a piece of the Western Division title a couple of weeks early. The second-place Colts could finish no better, and the Packers could finish no worse, than 10–4–0.

The 1967 playoff was the only postseason game ever played at County Stadium, against the Los Angeles Rams. That was the first year of a realignment of the NFL into four divisions. When it meant two playoff games instead of just the NFL championship game, the league decreed that for the first year, the Central Division winner's city would host the finalist of the Coastal Division for the Western Conference title game.

It being an odd-numbered year, the Western Conference winner was already scheduled to host the Eastern finalist for the NFL championship. Before the season began, the Packers announced that, if they made the playoffs, the semifinal game would be played at Milwaukee County Stadium, and the Milwaukee season ticket holders would get the first shot at tickets.[7,8] If they won the semifinal, then Lambeau Field would host the league championship. The Packers clinched the Central Division crown with 9–4–1 record, and were host to the 11–1–2 Rams, who had to play on the road despite having the best record in the NFL. Thus, for the first and only time, the thousands of Milwaukee season ticket holders got to see a playoff game without having to drive several hours to Green Bay. The 49,981 in attendance watched the Packers shut down an NFL team that had lost only one game, beating the Rams, 28–7.[9]

The Packers relationship with Milwaukee would go on for 26 more years, but their problems with Milwaukee's playing grounds were never resolved. County Stadium had been configured for baseball, and, as with many baseball parks, it didn't afford a very good view for football fans. Unlike other baseball venues, this one—with the left field and right field walls 315 feet from home plate—was barely large enough to accommodate a 120-yard by 53⅓ yard gridiron. The facility had been designed for baseball fans to watch more than 75 home games per season, while the Packers only came there three times a year. As one author described it, "there was little room beyond either end zone, and if a pass went long and a receiver didn't stop, he could end up in the front row with the fans and the popcorn"[10]; one could say it was an unintended variant of Green Bay's Lambeau Leap.

Rather than being separated by the width of the field, both teams had to share the same sideline. In games in August and September, the area between the hashmarks on the north half of the field was covered with the dirt of the baseball infield, which could turn into a slippery quagmire in the rain. The locker rooms were "too small for the 25 players on a baseball team, and positively agonizing for the 45 on a football team."[11] Worst of all for the fans were the sightlines. The majority of seats afforded a wonderful view of the diamond during baseball games. During a Packers game, these same seats looked down on the north end zone. Fifty-yard line seats were a long way from the gridiron, with a few hundred feet of grass separating the fans from the action, a safety feature for the protection of Braves and Brewers spectators, but an inconvenience at Packers home dates, not at all like the more cozy arrangement at Lambeau Field.

For the players, a trip to Milwaukee was little different from a game on the road, traveling by bus and staying in a hotel the day before. Still, team management (and Packers president Bob Harlan) put up with the inconveniences for years, until financial considerations led to a tough decision. Bud Selig, owner of the Brewers, commented "Bob Harlan has been incredibly loyal to Milwaukee…. The Packers are the only sports organization in the country, maybe the only one in the entire world, that would have stayed in Milwaukee this long, taking the hit that they were taking."[12]

As early as February of 1986, Harlan had talked to Selig about replacing County Stadium, as NFL teams began adding luxury boxes and expanding their capacity and revenue. Eight years later, Harlan would renew the Packers' lease for one more year, but commented, "We discussed our needs, and the thought was something might be done by 1991. Well, here we are in '94, and ground hasn't been broken. We don't want this situation to continue."[13]

By the early 1990s, the Packers and the visiting teams were losing potential money every time they played in Milwaukee instead of Green Bay, because of the difference in the revenue from County Stadium and Lambeau Field, and the grim figures were presented to the team's board of directors on the afternoon of October 12, 1994. That year, the lost revenue for the three games was estimated to be $1,600,000, or more than half a million dollars per game.[14] Worse, since Lambeau would have 90 additional private boxes for 1995, and County Stadium would still have none, the difference was forecast at more than $800,000 per game, or a total of $2,500,000 a year. At meeting's end, the board voted and Bob Harlan delivered the news that Milwaukee fans had hoped they wouldn't hear.[15] The Packers were ending their 62-year relationship with the city at the end of the season. Even Harlan reluctantly agreed to the unanimous, 45–0 vote.[16]

The end of the season in Milwaukee was on December 18, 1994, with a game against the Atlanta Falcons. A banner, made by a cynical fan, was hung behind the Packers' bench, with the parting shot "Goodbye Packers. And take the Brewers with you."[17] Before the two minute warning, the Falcons had taken a 17–14 lead, and the Packers were on the verge of their eighth loss, which would mean elimination from the playoff race against the many teams that could finish 9-7-0. As time was winding down, PA announcer Gary Knafelc chose a poor moment to tell the crowd, "The Packers extend a sincere thanks to our Milwaukee fans for their loyalty and support over the last 62 years."[18] Many of the 54,885 folks in the stands began booing, perhaps a bit cynical about the sincerity of the Packers' gratitude. The game wasn't over yet. The Packers were in their third year with both Coach Mike Holmgren and quarterback Brett Favre, and drove 58 yards, reaching the nine-yard line in the final minute. After calling the team's last time out at 0:21, Favre scrambled to find an open receiver while eluding a Falcon's blitz, then ran toward the end zone, diving in for the last touchdown ever scored at County Stadium. The Packers won, 21–14, and clinched a wild card berth the following week. Never again would the Packers play in Milwaukee, not even in the preseason.

Including the 1967 playoff game, the team had played 125 games at County Stadium, posting a 75–47–3 (.612) record.[19] Though the stadium had been built for baseball, it had served the Packers well. Capacity had increased from 28,000-plus to slightly over 53,000, and there had been the threat in the 1950s that the Packers might leave Green Bay and play all their games in Milwaukee, one of the incentives for Green Bay voters to approve what's now Lambeau Field. What had been "state of the art" in 1953 when County Stadium had opened, however, was out of step with the NFL of the 1990s. The loyalty of Milwaukee's Packers fans was unquestionable, and to that end, team president Bob Harlan didn't cut Milwaukee's Packer fan base out of the team's future. Season ticket holders in Milwaukee got the option of the "Gold Package" (Green Bay fans have the "Green Package"), the right to season tickets at Lambeau for one preseason and two regular games each year. Up through 1994, there weren't that many season tickets available for County Stadium because most of the lower level seats were offered on a per-game basis because there were few in the baseball park that were both close to the football sidelines and that offered an unobstructed view; as columnist Cliff Christl (now the official Packers historian) noted in 1999, "nobody wanted bad seats to watch a bad team in the 1970s, '80s and early '90s."[20] The number of County Stadium season ticket holders who were offered the Gold Package was less than 7,000—4,800 ticketholders and another 2,000 who had been on a waiting list—and people who had the second best seats (those in the bleachers) at County Stadium were now getting end zone seats at Lambeau, and the rest of the Gold Package season tickets were offered to people on the Lambeau Field waiting list, which was then a mere 19,000.[21] By 1998, however, the conventional wisdom was that most of the people at the Gold Package games were from the Milwaukee area, though others say that it isn't quite true.[22]

Whether they hail from Milwaukee or not, however, those that can buy the Gold Package are guaranteed the second and fifth home games every year, as well as the preseason Shrine game[23]; those with the more expensive Green Package get the other six regular season games and the preseason Bishop's Charities Game. Thus, because of the team's historical ties to Milwaukee, the Packers are the only team in the NFL that is community-owned and that has an almost completely different set of fans in the stands for some of their home games.

Notes

1. Data for the number of home games played at Milwaukee and Green Bay, as well as attendance information, was drawn from the website of Tod Maher and Maher Sports Media, Pro Football Archives, www.profootballarchives.com/index.html.

2. Information about sites other than County Stadium was drawn from the article "Other Homes of the Packers, 1919–94" on the official Green Bay Packers website, www.packers.com.

3. "Propose Added County Stadium Packer Seating," *Sheboygan Press*, May 22, 1964.

4. "Packer-Colt Showdown a Natural," *Milwaukee Sentinel*, September 10, 1966.

5. "Packers Cut Up Falcons, 56–3," *Milwaukee Sentinel*, October 24, 1966.

6. "Packers Win, 20–7; Ice Title Tie," *Milwaukee Sentinel*, December 5, 1966.

7. "Gb Cut to NFL Limit," *Daily Northwestern* (Oshkosh, WI), September 12, 1967.

8. "Packers' Playoff Tickets Plan Bared," *Capital Times* (Madison, WI), November 28, 1967.

9. "Packers 'Ran Off' with Title," *Milwaukee Sentinel*, December 25, 1967.

10. Chuck Carlson, *Tales from the Packers Sideline: A Collection of the Greatest Stories Ever Told* (Champaign, IL: Sports Publishing, 2013), 129–130.

11. *Ibid.*

12. "Packers Didn't Have Luxury of Staying," *Milwaukee Journal*, October 13, 1994.

13. "Stadium Concerns Packers," *Milwaukee Sentinel*, May 26, 1994.

14. "Packers Seem Set to Bolt Milwaukee," *Milwaukee Journal*, October 12, 1994.

15. "Pack Won't Be Back: Financial Reasons Cited for Pullout," *Milwaukee Sentinel*, October 13, 1994.

16. "Packers Pack Up, Go: Green Bay Leaves Milwaukee County Stadium," *Wisconsin State Journal* (Madison), October 13, 1994; "Harlan Finally Agrees Move Is Best for Team," *Milwaukee Journal*, October 13, 1994; "Packers to Desert Milwaukee; Tradition Since 1932 Will End When All Games Are at Lambeau in '95," Associated Press report in *Kansas City Star*, October 13, 1994.

17. "This One's for You, Favre Tells Fans in Milwaukee," *Milwaukee Sentinel*, December 19, 1994.

18. *Ibid.*

19. *Ibid.*

20. Cliff Christl, "Myths About Tickets Lead to Criticism of Packers," *Milwaukee Journal Sentinel*, November 17, 1999.

21. "Packers Ticket Recipe Sours Some Palates," *Milwaukee Journal Sentinel*, April 9, 1995.

22. Bob Wolfey, "Sportsday," *Milwaukee Journal Sentinel*, September 16, 1998.

23. Green Bay Packers website, www.packers.com/tickets/season-tickets.html.

PART 5

The Press

Bud Lea and Chuck Johnson
The Milwaukee Beats

RICK SCHABOWSKI

During the 1960s, Milwaukee, like most large U.S. cities at the time, was served by two major newspapers, the *Sentinel* in the morning and the *Journal* in the afternoon. Those two papers were blessed with two very different, but very skilled sportswriters who manned the Packers beat during the Lombardi era. The personable Bud Lea wrote for the *Sentinel* and the analytical Chuck Johnson for the *Journal*. The two competed with each other and also with Lee Remmel and Art Daley of the *Green Bay Press-Gazette* to provide excellent coverage of the team in its glory years. The two Milwaukee papers merged in 1995 to form the *Milwaukee Journal-Sentinel*.

Bud Lea spent 42 years as a sportswriter, editor and columnist for the *Milwaukee Sentinel*. He retired in 1995 but continued writing columns for *Packer Plus* for another 17 years.

Merlyn Lea was born in Green Bay on December 6, 1928. Nobody called him Merlyn as he began a writing career. Even his twin sister, Marilyn, called him Bud. He attended Green Bay West High School and began writing about sports for the school's newspaper, *The Purple Parrot*.

As a youngster growing up, Lea and his father, Dewey, attended Packers games at old City Stadium. "I'm so glad I got a chance to see Packer greats like Don Hutson in their heyday," Lea said, recalling those memories. "Hutson was my favorite player. My dad worked for the Railway Postal Service and we didn't have a lot of money, but he took me to City Stadium and we'd get in two for the price of one."[1]

Lea's interest in writing led him to the University of Wisconsin–Madison, where he majored in journalism. He wrote for the school newspaper, *The Daily Cardinal*, a paper that was published five times a week, and in his senior year, he was the paper's sports editor. While Lea was attending Wisconsin, the *Milwaukee Sentinel* asked him if he'd help cover Badgers football games. Lea enthusiastically took the job, and that would reap dividends later in his career.

After Lea graduated from Wisconsin, he was offered a position as sports editor of the *Rochester* (Minnesota) *Post-Bulletin*. Commenting on the assignment, Lea said, "Rochester was a unique experience. The whole city is geared to the Mayo Clinic. The paper had an agreement with the clinic that we would not call the Twin Cities' papers or wire services when we wrote about celebrities, but keep it right in Rochester. I remember doing features on Branch Rickey and Notre Dame Coach Frank Leahy, which were huge opportunities for a young writer."[2]

In 1953, the Boston Braves moved to Milwaukee, creating an opening for another reporter on the under-staffed sports department. *Sentinel* sports editor Lloyd Larson called Lea and offered him a job. "I accepted it at once," Lea said. "I knew it was a demotion in a sense, going from being a sports editor of a paper to being a cub reporter again, but I wanted to be in a big league city and with a big league paper. I was low man on the totem pole, I didn't have a beat of my own, but I was happy to have a job in a city that was jumping into the big leagues."

Lea worked from 4 p.m. to 1 a.m., editing copy and laying out the paper for changing editions.[3] He was given a beat in 1954, covering the Green Bay Packers. "The Packers were among the worst beats on the paper because the team was so lousy," Lea said. "Because I was born and raised in Green Bay, Larson assigned the Packers to me. Hell, nobody else wanted that beat because the paper didn't cover training camp, out of state preseason games and even some regular season games—pending on how the season was going."[4]

Lea elaborated further. "The Badgers, Marquette University, and even stock car racing got far more coverage than the Packers."[5] It might have seemed like a horrible assignment for most people, but Lea recalled, "At first I was overwhelmed. I bought a brand new Buick Special—my first car—$2,263, so I had wheels to get to Green Bay. But I was thrilled. I was the hometown kid writing about his favorite team for the largest morning paper in Wisconsin."[6]

There wasn't too much good news for Lea to write about the Packers in his first few seasons covering the team. Lisle Blackbourn's teams were 4–8, 6–6, 4–8 and 3–9 from 1954 through 1957. And 1958 was even worse under one-year coach Ray "Scooter" McLean. Lea recalled the horrible season, "1–10–1. The Packers had some talent, but under McLean, there was no discipline, no rules. Vince Lombardi changed that. He laid down the law."[7]

The Lombardi rules and discipline not only were for the team, but also the reporters covering the team. Commenting on the drastic change in policy, Lea said, "Well, before he got there, there were no rules. You did anything you wanted, talked to any players any time you wanted to—no rules at all. And this guy from New York comes in, and suddenly everything is changed. Now there are rules." Lombardi told Lea if he wanted to cover the Packers in training camp he had stay at the Packers' training site, St. Norbert College. "I asked Lombardi why I had to do that, and he said, 'Those are the rules.'"[8]

Lea followed Lombardi's edict, residing on the second floor of Sensenbrenner Hall with the rookies and sportswriters, dealing with one big bathroom at the end of the hall. The writer assigned to share the room with him kept him awake most of the night with his loud snoring. So Lea had had enough. "My parents lived in Green Bay," he said. "After two days, I just left. Lombardi was so wrapped up with his team, he didn't even notice I was absent."[9]

Lombardi also instituted a Five O'clock Club, which the media was invited to attend along with the coaching staff. Everything, he was warned, was off the record. Lea said, "It was almost like checking in. You had to go to that darn thing whether you wanted to or not. What power he had. The power was about as one-sided as anything I've seen in my reporting life."[10]

Lea recalled one memorable Five O'clock Club meeting in Lombardi's hotel suite on an out-of-town game. "We'd all have some drinks with the coach, and about five minutes to six, everyone cleared out—those are the rules. But I remember once, I think it was over in Cleveland, maybe I had a few scotches that night and I said, 'Ok, Coach, I'll put up with this under one condition.' He asked, "What's that?" I said, 'Don't lose.' he said, "Mister, I don't intend to." And he kept winning and winning and winning."[11]

The bus trip from the Hotel Manhattan to Yankee Stadium for the 1962 NFL championship game was one Lea would never forget. "Of all the things I've covered in sports, from Olympics to major league baseball, to the NBA, to college football to major golf tournaments, to auto racing, nobody can compare with him," Lea said. "I never saw a leader like that. I remember going out to Yankee Stadium for that 1962 championship game against the New York Giants. At that time, the writers could get on the Packer team buses. I remember sitting in the first bus, and there's Vince Lombardi and Marie Lombardi, and it was like going to war with the Fifth Armored Division, and there was General Patton in the first seat. They were that confident."[12] The Packers did indeed prevail winning their second consecutive NFL title over the Giants in a game played in windy, blustery conditions.

Bud Lea. Photograph by Jim Biever.

Something even more memorable happened during Lea's early years at the *Milwaukee Sentinel*; he met his wife, Filomena Volpintesta. Filomena graduated from Marquette University in 1951 with a Bachelor of Philosophy degree in Journalism, and joined the *Sentinel* in 1953. She was a feature writer, specializing in interior design. She worked days, and Bud worked nights.[13] They married in 1957 and were blessed with two sons, Dean, a jazz pianist, and Perry, an engineer/scientist for Hewlett-Packard in Boise, Idaho. After a courageous nine-month battle with brain cancer, Filomena passed away on July 25, 2014, at age 84.

Lea was privileged to have the opportunity to cover not only Packers games, but also many other sporting events. When asked about his favorite game, Lea answered, "The Ice Bowl, no question about it. Better than any of the 31 Super Bowls I've covered, better than any Packer game anywhere. The conditions, a wind chill factor of 46 below zero, the importance of the game, and then climaxed by Bart Starr's game winning plunge for a touchdown with only seconds left on the clock."[14] The weather was awful for the press corps. "We wrote from the press box, and our typewriters froze," Lea recalled. "Every time a guy opened the door it was like the Arctic Circle being blown in. It was incredible working conditions, and what a finish!"[15]

Lea covered the Packers through the 1972 season, when he was named sports editor of the *Sentinel*, replacing Lloyd Larson. Lea went on a project revitalizing the paper by hiring fresh aggressive sportswriters to compete with *The Milwaukee Journal*. In addition to being editor, Lea also became the paper's sports columnist, the two jobs resulting with often 14-hour workdays.

In 1987, Lea was named Wisconsin Sportswriter of the Year by the National Sportscasters and Sportswriters Association. He was elected to the Milwaukee Press Club Hall

of Fame in 2004 and has served on the selection committee for the Pro Football Hall of Fame and the Green Bay Packers Hall of Fame. In 2002, he wrote the book *Magnificent Seven: The Championship Games That Built the Lombardi Dynasty*. He also serves as vice president of the Milwaukee Braves Historical Association and writes for their publication, *The Tepee*.

Bud manages to get to Green Bay for an occasional game and takes a seat in the Lambeau Field press box. "I look around and nearly all the other writers are half my age or younger," he said. "I guess they look at me and wonder who's the old white haired geezer."[16]

The greatest tribute to a person's work is the respect that you receive from your peers. Cliff Christl, a former Packers beat writer for *The Milwaukee Journal* and *The Green Bay Press Gazette*, who now serves as the Packers historian, said of Lea. "I have a world of respect for Bud Lea. He set the standard for how to report on a football team, and I didn't work with Bud—we were with different papers. I read him as a kid, before I ever knew I was going to be a sportswriter and found him to be so informative, and I loved his personality. Bud has a cranky sportswriter side to him, which I love, but he's also one hell of a guy."[17]

Reflecting on his over half century of sports writing Lea said, "You know, it's been one heck of a ride. I was darn lucky to have been at the right place at the right time."[18] Packers fans were darn lucky to have had Bud Lea cover their team.

*   *   *

Chuck Johnson was a sports writer for *The Milwaukee Journal*, and covered the Green Bay Packers for 16 years among his assignments in 34 years at the paper.

Charles Raymond Johnson was born on September 16, 1925, in Williston, North Dakota, to Charles Andrew Johnson and Lena Johnson. He had an older sister, Eloise, who was born in 1917. After his high school graduation, Johnson served in the U.S. Navy from 1943 to 1946. He attended the University of North Dakota in Fargo, receiving a degree in journalism in 1948. Johnson then began working for *The Fargo Forum* and remained there until 1952, when he joined *The Milwaukee Journal*.

The *Journal* sports department was viewed as a "toy department," with very loose regulations and ethics until Johnson arrived. Mike Kupper, who worked for the *Journal* sports staff from 1959 to 1984, commented about working for Johnson: "When I was at a tender age and fairly new in the business, he explained some harsh realities to me. He was a grammarian, a stickler for detail and a very tough taskmaster, but he made everybody better. Sportswriters were a different breed back then. It was looser than other parts of the paper. He tried to get sportswriters to be better journalists, better newspapermen."[19]

Johnson was a perfectionist, rigid in his ways, and very demanding. These traits made it very difficult to work with him. Kupper, reflecting on his time working in the sports department, said about Johnson, "He had a short fuse and that's how you knew he was passionate. He couldn't stand slipshod work."[20] As a result of Johnson's striving for perfection, the employees who worked for him could take pride in their work.

While covering the Packers from 1953 to 1968 for the *Journal*, he also wrote two books about the team, *The Green Bay Packers: Pro Football's Power Team* in 1961, a history of the franchise to that point, and *The Greatest Packers of Them All*, published in 1968. Johnson wrote an article, "Anatomy of a Fumble," about the Packers victory over the Baltimore Colts, which was reprinted in a book, *Best Sports Stories 1967*.

When Johnson left the sports department in 1975, he wrote an article about the 10 biggest sporting events that he had the privilege to cover. Johnson listed as number one the 1972 Olympic Games held in Munich. Two Packers games made the list, the Ice Bowl at number four and Super Bowl I at number five. After Johnson left the sports department, he served as the *Journal*'s assistant news editor, news system editor, and Waukesha County editor, a job he held until his retirement in 1986.

Johnson's marriage to Lillian Hilmo lasted for 25 years, and he later married Corrine Johnson. Johnson had four children from his first marriage.

Johnson moved back to Grand Forks, North Dakota, and spent a lot of his time helping his alma mater. He also was involved with the University of North Dakota Alumni Association. Rob Bollinger, the university's director of athletic development and father of former University of Wisconsin quarterback Brooks Bollinger, said about Johnson, "He came back to serve as a volunteer, primarily as a writer of North Dakota athletics."[21]

Johnson's later years were complicated with health issues requiring stomach and heart surgeries. He passed away at the age of 79 in a Northwood, North Dakota, nursing home on January 13, 2005.

Chuck Johnson. Courtesy Bud Lea.

Notes

1. Martin Hendricks, special to *Packer Plus*, November 12, 2014.
2. Jack Pearson, "50 Plus," October 2004.
3. *Ibid.*
4. Drew Olson, "Milwaukee Talks: Veteran Sportswriter Bud Lea," Milwaukee.com, April 29, 2009.
5. Pearson.
6. Hendricks.
7. *Ibid.*
8. Dave Robinson and Royce Boyles, *The Lombardi Legacy: Thirty People Who Were Touched by Greatness* (Louisville, KY: Goose Creek Publishers, 2009).
9. *Ibid.*
10. David Maraniss, *When Pride Still Mattered* (New York: Simon & Schuster, 1999).
11. *Ibid.*
12. Robinson and Boyles.
13. Pearson.
14. *Ibid.*
15. Hendricks.
16. Pearson.
17. Hendricks.
18. Pearson.
19. Obituary, *Milwaukee Journal Sentinel,* January 14, 2005.
20. *Ibid.*
21. *Ibid.*

Art Daley and Lee Remmel
The Green Bay Beats

Joe Marren

On the field in 1966 the Green Bay Packers had two rookies in Donny Anderson and Jim Grabowski who would go on to be dubbed the Gold Dust Twins by the media. In the press box that same season the *Green Bay Press-Gazette* had its own "twins" covering the Packers with sports editor Art Daley and reporter/columnist Lee Remmel.

Although the championship season of 1966 was the rookie year for Anderson and Grabowski, Daley and Remmel had been around long enough to know defeat with prior Packers teams and strongly identified with the entire organization and its history. Daley even said he cried when the Packers lost a game, or several (well, more like many), prior to the Lombardi era: "I know that I got a reputation for crying in those bad years we had. I can laugh now, but I used to hear that the paperboys used to tell their customers on Monday, 'Here's Art Daley's tears.'"[1]

Both were also Packers fans before they started covering the team. Daley was born and christened Arthur J. Lunkenheimer in Minnesota, but his father died when he was two years old. His mother married John Daley and moved to Wisconsin and Art was using his stepfather's family name when he started working for the Fond du Lac *Commonwealth Reporter* at 19.

Daley was working at the *Press-Gazette* by the time he started covering the Packers in 1941 before going off to serve in World War II. Soon after being discharged he went back to the paper and was named sports editor, a job he held until 1968. He hired Remmel, a lifelong Packers fan, to be his assistant editor in October 1945.

Leland Remmel was born in 1924 in Shawano, Wisconsin, about 30 miles outside of Green Bay. He spent 62 years either covering the Packers, or working for the team.

Both Daley and Remmel had durability for a host of reasons. But the core of it is this: The duo knew their audience and covered the team like the professionals they were, but they were also fans and the readers appreciated that.

"Art has a folksy style that people enjoyed," Remmel reminisced in a *Milwaukee Journal-Sentinel* story shortly after Daley died in 2011.[2]

Remmel and Daley are both members of the Packers' Hall of Fame; the press box in the renovated Lambeau Field in 2003 was named for Remmel for many reasons, one of which was his encyclopedic knowledge of the team: "No one knows more about the Green Bay Packers than Lee Remmel," Daley once told a reporter. "He knows that franchise inside and out, warts and all…. Lee is the guru."[3]

Just as Daley was known for his down-home style of writing, Remmel was known as being more descriptive, or evocative, according to a 2014 article in the *Journal-Sentinel*: "Besides his remarkable memory, Remmel was a legendary wordsmith. He described the Packers-Bears rivalry as 'antediluvian' and a clash between 'venerable neighborhood enemies.' It was not unusual to see exotic words like primordial, invidious, and mellifluous in Remmel's news releases or Packers.com historical columns."[4]

And there were other trademarks, too, as former Packers quarterbacks coach (1992–95) and NFL network analyst Steve Mariucci mentioned in a 2012 *Journal-Sentinel* article: "Lee had that amazing memory and used those descriptive words, like Mike Holmgren was the 'monolithic Scandinavian,'" Mariucci said. "And he always used middle names, like Brett was Brett Lorenzo Favre."[5]

There isn't supposed to be any cheering in the press box because reporters are told to act dispassionately and record the game action. Such an antiseptic attitude may be fine for dentists, but it can be boring for football fans. Daley and Remmel were professionals, as judged by their subsequent accolades and their game stories, but they also knew how to write with vigor and to inject a little fun into their stories that reported not only the outcomes of game, but the context of it in the broader scope of a season.

But covering even the best teams isn't always fun because, frankly, sometimes they lose. And that's where the professionalism of Daley and Remmel came into focus. They had to contextualize a

Art Daley. Photograph by Jim Biever.

close loss for a fan base in the era before the NFL owned the airwaves and people paid closer attention to what was written in the papers.

Although one could say that Daley and Remmel took the journalism crowns during the Packer's 1966 championship season that season wasn't all either of them were known for. As has been noted, Remmel was associated with the Packers in one way or another from October 1945 to his retirement in December 2007. And Daley covered the Packers either for the *Press-Gazette* (he retired in 1979) or wrote about the team for *Packer Report* magazine almost right up until his death in 2011.

Daley and *Press-Gazette* promotions manager Jack Yuenger founded the Packers Yearbook in 1960 and got into trouble with Lombardi with a 1962 file picture of Curly Lambeau and Lombardi shaking hands on the cover of the 1965 edition after Lambeau's

death on June 1. Lombardi didn't like Lambeau and froze Daley out until October of the 1965 season after the publication came out in July, according to a February 11, 2011, story in the *Press-Gazette*: "Lombardi's disdain for Lambeau was legendary … and the coach wasn't happy to share the cover with him. Daley remembers the angry phone call when Lombardi saw the finished product: 'What do you mean putting me on the cover with him?' After he said, 'That was the worst yearbook you ever put out,' the phone clicked. Lombardi didn't speak to Daley for two weeks."[6]

But the more-or-less one-sided feud, such as it was, ended almost as abruptly as it began, wrote reporter Pete Jackel in the December 4, 2003, *Racine Journal Times*. Lombardi called Daley out to a team practice and shook his hand and apologized. But why the anger in the first place?

Lee Remmel. Photograph by Jim Biever.

It was all explained after the season: "'I ran into him out at the country club,' Daley said. 'We both belonged at the Oneida Golf and Riding Club. And he said, 'I've got to tell you. I do not like to share the spotlight. I did not like that with he and I on the cover.' 'See, that's the way he was.'"[7]

Lombardi's ire wasn't only directed at Daley. Remmel was also in the doghouse from time to time. For example, before a preseason game against the Cowboys at Dallas, Lombardi yelled at Remmel, who was writing down notes about something Lombardi didn't want publicized. "'Don't write that,' Lombardi bellowed. 'Be original!' After wondering whether Lombardi would even allow him on the plane to Dallas the following day.... Remmel was urged by Daley to go ahead as planned. 'We got to the Cotton Bowl for the game the next night and he allowed media in his locker room before the game...' Remmel said. 'I was walking around and he stopped me at one point and said, 'I'm sorry. I apologize for saying you're not original. I think you're as fine a writer as I've seen, ok?' And I said, 'Ok. What else are you going to say?'" Remmel considered that one of the most meaningful compliments he has ever received.[8]

Remmel died on April 16, 2015. He was 90. He was named Wisconsin's Sports Writer of the Year in 1967 and inducted into the Packers Hall of Fame in 1996. The Lee Remmel Sports Awards Banquet annually honors athletes from high school to the pros and has donated hundreds of thousands of dollars to Green Bay colleges and high schools.

Daley died February 19, 2011. He was 94. Daley was inducted into the Packers Hall of Fame in 1993 and was an original voter for the Pro Football Hall of Fame.

"This was really more than a job," Daley said in 1969 when he left the beat and the sports editor's job, according to the newspaper. "I took it ... maybe ... too much to heart. But in a town like this, I think you have to be that way."[9]

NOTES

1. Michael David Smith, "Art Daley, Packers Beat Reporter from Another Era, Dies at 94," Profootballtalk.nbcsports.com, February 21, 2011, accessed November 11, 2014, www.profootballtalk.nbcsports.com.

2. Amy Rabideau Silvers, "Covering the Packers Was Daley's Passion," *Milwaukee Journal Sentinel*, February 21, 2011.

3. Martin Hendricks, "Remmel a Packer for Life," *Milwaukee Journal-Sentinel*, January, 11, 2012.

4. Martin Hendricks, "Longtime Packers PR Director Lee Remmel Knew All the Greats," *Milwaukee Journal-Sentinel*, July 2, 2014.

5. Hendricks, "Remmel."

6. "For Art's Sake," *Green Bay Press-Gazette*, February 21, 2011.

7. Peter Jackel, "Old Friends: Veteran Writers Lee Remmel and Art Daley Have Enjoyed a Lifelong Love Affair with the Green Bay Packers," *Racine Journal Times*, December 4, 2003.

8. *Ibid.*

9. Brad Biggs, "National Football Post," February 21, 2011.

Ray Scott

JOE MARREN

There are some sports announcers who are known for a voice so deep and strong that one imagines it could easily be heard over cheering crowds without a microphone.

Others are known for speaking so much that they become as much of a story as the game they are announcing. Then there are the announcers who can use homey yarns or poetic imagery to describe a game and can make everything sound so quaint as the words come off the tongue and roll over the airwaves. And some sports announcers go on to become president of the United States.

Ray Scott, who called the Green Bay Packers games in 1966 for the CBS network, can't be as easily pigeonholed as any of them. Although he had a requisite deep voice, he was almost laconic by 21st century standards. He also had a keen sense of what to say and when, and he could come up with some pretty insightful comments when the occasion warranted. But he wasn't as flashy as contemporaries in his era of television sports broadcasters. What he was, however, was professional and precise in 12 seasons broadcasting the Packers. And, as he told interviewers, that's all he wanted to be when he called games for the 1966 team, one of the all-time great storybook teams in the National Football League and winner of the first Super Bowl at the end of that 1966 season. His was a big voice in a big season.

In a *Green Bay Press Gazette* story Bob Berghaus wrote that Scott's style when broadcasting games was to first set the formation, followed by a pause and a description of what was unfolding, maybe something brief like "Starr drops back to pass," followed by another pause and then the result "Starr, McGee, touchdown, Packers."[1]

What Scott never forgot was that people were watching as he was speaking and the style was explained in his *Washington Post* obituary in the March 23, 1998, edition. As Scott previously put it: "There was a highly respected high school coach there [in Johnstown, Pennsylvania] by the name of Pop Wenreich…. He said, 'Ray, don't insult my intelligence when you broadcast a game. Tell me something I can't see.' I've never forgotten that. My philosophy has always been let the action speak for itself. It doesn't need me getting in the way."[2]

That philosophy often clashed with others in his era. For example, Scott was not shy about criticizing ABC's Howard Cosell, as can be seen from a Joe Logan story in *Football Digest* from January 1982: "In my years in this business…. I don't know of any other broadcaster—with the endorsements of his employers, ABC Sports—who has deliberately set out to be obnoxious and succeeded so fantastically. I think he *tries* to be controversial so that people will talk about him. He *wants* to be the center of attention. Go some time to a city where there's a Monday Night Football game being broadcast that day. Go to the hotel where the broadcasters are staying. I will make any bet that sometime at the height of the traffic in that lobby, Howard Cosell will be somewhere so that people can stop him and gape at him and ask for his autograph. He *craves* attention [emphasis in original]."[3]

ABC fired back and an exchange from a radio show in Boston between Scott and Roone Arledge, then the sports boss at ABC, shows how tense things were, as reported by Jack Craig in the February 23, 1974, *Sporting News*: "Arledge: Well, I think that you're dull and inaccurate. You made more mistakes in the Super Bowl than Howard made all season … Scott: I'll tell you something. Monday Night Football in the past season has contained more mistakes of fact than a lot of high school broadcasts that I've heard. Arledge: Well, Ray, you're just jealous."[4]

Despite the debate about whether to talk too much or too little, Scott had the credentials to question the differences in style. His peers in the broadcasting booths twice voted him the National Sportscaster of the Year, in 1968 and 1971; he was inducted into the National Sportswriters and Sportscasters Hall of Fame in 1982; he was named Sportscaster of the Year not only in Wisconsin, but also in Minnesota, Florida, and Pennsylvania, winning the honor a total of 12 times; and in 1987 he won the Art Rooney Order of the Leather Helmet, the NFL Alumni's highest award.

The fascination with broadcasting began when Scott was 16 after graduating from high school in 1937 in Connellsville, Pennsylvania. "I was very much the frustrated high school athlete. I had all the desire and no ability. But I knew I had to work, and I'd won a couple of contests in extemporaneous speaking. So I went to a WPA [Works Progress Administration, a Depression-era government program] school for radio technique, and my teacher was a former Shakespearean actor.... I wrote letters to all the radio stations in the area looking for work. Finally, I decided to take the bull by the horns. I was going to crash radio in the big city, Pittsburgh."[5]

But the dream, well, didn't work out the way Scott hoped. A family friend got him back home and that's when fate intervened shortly afterward: "I soon got a letter from a station in Johnstown, Pennsylvania. There was a job for a summer replacement announcer and the pay was fifty-five dollars a month."[6] Scott started at WJAC four days after getting the letter in August 1937 and he stayed there until he left for the service in 1941.

After his discharge in November 1945, he went back to work for the station for another year and also did freelance work in Pittsburgh. In 1952 he did sports and commercials on a nightly news program for a DuMont station in Pittsburgh and also started doing radio play-by-play for the University of Pittsburgh football team. Scott began calling NFL games for the DuMont network in 1953.

Although the DuMont network faded into oblivion, Scott's career was just getting started on a regional, and then national stage with CBS. The network hired him in 1956 to do regional play-by-play of Packers games. "CBS offered me the assignment somewhat as an apology. They said if everything worked out with Green Bay, they would promote me to a larger region. Green Bay wasn't one of the prime NFL cities then. Of course, no one knew what would be happening there a few years later."[7]

Ray Scott. Courtesy Pavek Museum of Broadcasting.

He called the games until the end of the 1967 season when CBS stopped assigning announcers to specific teams. After that, Scott became the network's top announcer before he and CBS parted ways in 1974. "Parted ways" is a euphemism for something that Scott still felt uncomfortable talking about more than a decade later: "You could say that it was mutually agreed we would sever our relationship," he told an interviewer.[8]

But his broadcasting career wasn't over because he went on to do college and professional football and basketball, golf on radio and television, and baseball as the voice of the Minnesota Twins and other teams. Besides the Twins, he also at one time or another briefly did play-by-play for the Minnesota Vikings, Kansas City Chiefs and Tampa Bay Buccaneers. As late as 1994 Scott was a partner in a radio syndication service in Iowa that did pre- and post-game shows around Packers games.

So in more than 50 years of broadcasting experience, what is one of the best memories he had? The 1966 and 1967 NFL title games, he told writer Doug Kelly in a *Pro!* magazine article. "The way those two games ended, if you'd written a script for them beforehand, no one would have believed it. Those endings! In 1966, Dallas had the ball on the Packers' one-yard line and didn't score; then, a year later, the Packers had the ball on the Cowboys' one, no time outs left, and did score. I did both those games with Jack Buck. We each did a half. I had the second half of the game in Dallas, and he had the second half of the game in Green Bay."[9]

Green Bay's 1967 championship season was Lombardi's last as coach and Scott's last year calling play-by-play for the Packers. Lombardi, who wasn't always a fan of the beat writers assigned to the team, liked Scott and often invited him to his home for postgame parties.

Lombardi died in 1970. His legacy was five NFL titles and victories in the first two Super Bowls. Scott died March 23, 1998. He was 78. Although he was a man of few words while on the air, it was enough to get him elected to the Packers Hall of Fame and earn him accolades from his peers during the course of his lifetime.

Notes

1. Bob Berghaus, *Green Bay Press-Gazette.*
2. "Voice of Packers, Ray Scott, Dies," March 23, 1998.
3. Joe Logan, "Whatever Became of…," *Football Digest,* January 1982, 84.
4. Jack Craig, "Ego Evident in Sportscaster Debate," *The Sporting News,* February 23, 1974.
5. Doug Kelly, "Conversation with Ray Scott," *Pro!*
6. *Ibid.*
7. *Ibid.*
8. Logan, "Whatever."
9. Kelly.

Vernon Biever

Matt Foss

There's one man who didn't make a tackle, block an opponent, score a touchdown, or even call a play for the Green Bay Packers, but captured their legacy in a way nobody else could. In 1966, Vernon Biever was in his twentieth year as the official photographer of the Packers. As the year dawned, Biever's photos of the team's championship game victory over the Cleveland Browns on the muddy landscape of newly-renamed Lambeau Field became examples of some of his finest work. By the time the season was over, he captured the first Super Bowl champions, in the middle of three consecutive championships.

Vernon Joseph Biever was born on May 21, 1923, in Port Washington, Wisconsin, a small commercial fishing community on Lake Michigan.[1] As a teenager, his two major interests were photography and football. He took photos for the Port Washington High School Annual and the local newspaper *The Ozaukee Press,* and was an end for the Port Washington High School football team.[2] While his football career ended in high school, his career in photography was only beginning.

After graduating high school, Biever enrolled at St. Norbert College in De Pere, Wisconsin, a city just south of Green Bay and the future site of the Packers training camp. Before leaving for college, Vernon walked into the office of Stoney McGlynn—the sports editor of the *Milwaukee Sentinel*—and told him he could photograph the Packers for the newspaper. McGlynn, who saw Vernon's ambition and the opportunity to save money by using someone close to Green Bay, hired Vernon for the job.[3] This decision by McGlynn was surprising.

Not only did a major newspaper give a freelance job to an 18-year-old, but in 1941, photographers rarely covered sports, especially professional football, for newspapers and magazines. The main descriptions of sporting events were covered by writers, whose copy seemed to tell more of a story than a series of photos.[4] Biever took full advantage of the opportunity, photographing games at City Stadium, sending the film on a train to Milwaukee and then enjoying seeing the photos he took in the paper.

Unfortunately, his time working for the *Milwaukee Sentinel* was short lived. In 1942, as the United States was consumed in World War II, Vernon, like many young men at the time, decided to enlist. Leaving St. Norbert, Vern entered the army and became division photographer for the 100th Infantry Division. Soon his photos appeared in the division's weekly newspaper, *The Century Sentinel.*[5]

Besides being a combat division which liberated hundreds of towns and villages in Europe, the 100th Division was important in maintaining morale for soldiers and those at home. Although Vern encountered the sad results of war in Europe, he was proud of his work photographing entertainers like Jack Benny and Ingrid Bergman meeting the troops and also ceremonies where soldiers received medals for their actions in combat. Biever himself was awarded the Bronze Star for improving troop morale with his photography.[6]

After his service ended in 1946, Biever returned to college and continued his education and photography career. After earning a business degree, it was only natural for

Vernon J. Biever. Courtesy Vernon J. Biever Family.

Vern to return home and help his father Emil with the family Ben Franklin store in downtown Port Washington. While able to put his education to use, he wanted to continue photographing the Packers.

Unfortunately for Vern, the *Milwaukee Sentinel* joined forces with the Associated Press and United Press International and chartered planes to Green Bay to photograph games, eliminating the position Vern created for himself before the war.[7] Not deterred, Vern approached the Packers himself, offering photos of the team in exchange for a field pass. The price was right as the team agreed to the arrangement.[8]

With his Packer photography career renewed, Vern was able to focus on his personal life. In Port Washington, he met Frances Marsolek, a registered nurse at a local hospital. By October of 1948, Vern and "Frankie" were married, and soon had three children, Barbara, John, and Jim.[9] Over the years, the entire family would be involved in photographing the Packers in one way or another and contribute greatly to the success and popularity of Vern's photos.

One way family members contributed was by being

assistants on the sidelines. Assistants were necessary in the early years because Vern used a speed graphic camera to cover the action. The large camera used a plate with one negative on each side. So, to take 12 photos, you had to carry six plates, each the size of a small paperback.[10] Additionally, because Vern had to pre-focus the lens, he had to anticipate where the action in a football game was going to be. Biever said, "It taught you to be aware, you would follow the game very intensely."[11]

Assistants took notes on players in the photos and yards gained or lost during the play. His first assistant was his father Emil Biever.[12] Later, sons John and Jim became assistants, as well as co-photographers. Although photographing the team in the 1940s was not easy, the timing allowed him to capture some of the greatest players in Packers history during the Curly Lambeau era.

As good as Lambeau's teams were to photograph, the Gene Ronzani, Lisle Blackbourn, and "Scooter" McLean led teams of the 1950s were not. Although the team was not successful, Vern spent time developing a style which became his trademark. Some characteristics of his style included photographing fans watching from the stands, the players' and coaches' emotions and reactions on the sidelines, and action from an end zone perspective. Speaking about his style, Vernon said: "If you want to really chronicle a game, it requires shots other than just action. You've got to look for that sideline shot that tells the story. You have to look for action as well, you want to be there for the important touchdown, but I also like to watch the sidelines. You have to know your place, but in front of the bench you can do more observant work. The team allows me to do it, and I'm familiar to the players, so they are comfortable with my presence."[13]

Fans in stands. Vernon Biever was one of the first football photographers to turn his camera away from the field and onto the sidelines and into the stands. Here are loyal Packers fans enjoying the weather of an early season game. Photograph by Vernon J. Biever.

While other photographers simply captured the action, Vern turned his photos into artistic interpretations of all that was and is professional football. This was evident in the mood of many of Vernon's subjects throughout his career, but mostly during the Lombardi era. Although the roster retained several future Pro Football Hall of Famers and by 1966, had already won three world championships, many of Vern's most famous photos show Packer greats looking beat up, covered in mud, tired, and dejected. Vern was one of the first to accurately record the brutality of football and the toll that championship expectations took on players. Longtime Packers radio announcer Jim Irwin stated: "His strength is anticipation, but that's just knowledge of the game. It's the recognition of the human emotion of the event that comes through in Vernon's work."[14]

One of the reasons Vern was able to capture emotions, moods and feelings, and not just football action was because Vern had the routine of photographing the team down to a science. In the book *Young Sports Photographer with the Green Bay Packers* by son John Biever, John describes a typical Sunday in Green Bay with Vern. They would leave Port Washington at 9:00 a.m. after eating a hot breakfast.[15] Arriving in Green Bay around 10:30 a.m., they checked their equipment (20 rolls of film, four Nikon 35-mm cameras, two 300-mm lenses, a 200-mm lens, 150-mm lens, and 135-mm lens).[16] At halftime, they ate a sandwich, grabbed a soft drink or cup of coffee, and re-checked their equipment.[17]

After the game, they drove the hour and a half back to Port Washington. During dinner, Vern's wife "Frankie" fielded calls from publications wanting shots from that day's game action. By 8:00 p.m., they went down to the family's basement where Vern's darkroom was located.[18] They dumped all 20 rolls of film into developing fluid and chose 150 out of 540 or so total shots to print. The promising ones would be blown up to 11 × 14 for magazines.

All of the film developed in the darkroom became black and white prints. Not only did Vern prefer black and white as a style choice, but he earned enough interest and business with black and white. When magazines or other interested parties requested color, the film would be delivered to a local drugstore and sent to a lab in Chicago.[19] The best 20 action photos were sent to the Packers. This remained part of the agreement between Biever and the Packers.

A letter to Chuck Lane, the Packers' public relations director in 1966, explains the situation. "When you do get requests for material I might have, I would appreciate your referring these people to me," Biever wrote. "This hobby is so interesting I would do all of it at a loss."[20] Although he was not being paid by the team, referrals of his work to publications allowed Vern to break even in the photography business.

Because of the success of Lombardi's Packers, the photos Vern took during the 1960s made his work popular and recognizable around the country. Not only did numerous books, magazines, and documentaries request photos of the championship Packers, but people wanted photos for their own personal collections. Found in Vern's personal papers were several letters from people requesting photos of different players and Coach Lombardi.

During the 1970s and 80s, when most of these letters arrived, Vernon Biever was no longer photographing a championship team. The Packers did not experience significant success, only making the playoffs twice in these two decades. Regardless of the team's ineptitude, Vern's photos continued to be exceptional. Steve Sabol of NFL Films summed it up by saying, "In the Packers' lean years, it's almost that the team did not live up to Vernon."[21] That statement seemed to apply in 1984, when the Packers went 8–8 and missed the playoffs but Vernon earned NFL Photographer of the Year honors from the Pro Football Hall of Fame.[22]

Of the team's down years, Vern said: "During down periods, I've almost lost interest, but finally what I'm interested in is the photography. It was photography itself that always kept me going. As long as I've been covering the Packers, I'm always hoping they will win, but more than that, I'm always looking for the one picture. If I can get one good picture a year, I'm happy."[23]

During the 1990s and 2000s, Vernon continued to add accomplishments to his long career. In 1994, he received a distinguished alumni award from his alma mater St. Norbert College, a proud moment for a man who treasured his education from the institution.[24] One recognition which displayed Vern's longevity in sports photography was acknowledgement by the NFL as a member of the "Super Club." The NFL created the club to honor the members of media and the league who attended every Super Bowl.[25] Because Vernon attended and photographed the first 35 Super Bowls, Vernon was part of a very select and distinguished group, including his son John.

While Vernon shared the sidelines of Super Bowls with elder son John, he spent many more Sundays with younger son Jim, who succeeded Vern as the Packers' official team photographer. Today, the Biever name continues to be a strong presence at Packer games with Jim and his own son Michael photographing the team. Including Vern's father Emil who worked as an assistant, four generations of the Biever family have captured Packers history.

Many first introductions to the Packers occur through the photography of the Biever family. Knowing the impact that these photos have on the brand and recognition of the team, the Packers honored the elder Biever. In 2002, he was inducted into the Green Bay Packer Hall of Fame, as a contributor to the franchise. Bart Starr, whom Vernon photographed as a quarterback and a coach, nominated then inducted Vern claiming, "You wouldn't have a Packer Hall of Fame without Vern Biever."[26] Former Packers president Bob Harlan said of Vern: "I can't tell you how many times through the years we've called him to get this shot or that shot and he's always got it. He's a godsend to this organization, because he's captured this history. I love the tradition of this franchise, and Vern Biever has kept a record of it."[27]

Although declining mobility forced Vern to shoot games from a press box, he never stopped trying to get "the one picture." It was after the 2007 season when he finally hung up his camera bag. Every day, visitors to the Lambeau Field Atrium and the Green Bay Packer Hall of Fame see his work. Although Vernon Biever passed away in October 2010, his photos live on, preserving the aura of Packers football.

Notes

1. Matt Foss, "The Man Behind the Camera: Vernon Biever," *Wisconsin Magazine of History,* Vol. 97, no. 1, Autumn 2013, 30.

2. *Ibid.*

3. *Ibid.*

4. John Zimmerman, Mark Kauffman, and Neil Leifer, *Photographing Sports: Capturing the Excitement of People in Action* (Los Angeles: Alskog, 1975), 21.

5. John Biever and George Vecsey, *Young Sports Photographer with the Green Bay Packers* (New York: W.W. Norton, 1969), 27.

6. Foss, 31.

7. *Ibid.*

8. *Ibid.*

9. Biever, 29.

10. *Ibid.*, 27.

11. *Ibid.*

12. Foss, 31.

13. Vernon J. Biever, *The Glory of Titletown: The Classic Green Bay Packers Photography of Vernon Biever*, ed. Peter Strupp (New York: Taylor Trade, 2003), 43.

14. *Ibid.*, 101.

15. Biever, *Young Sports Photographer with the Green Bay Packers*, 109.

16. *Ibid.*, 113–114.

17. *Ibid.*, 121.

18. *Ibid.*, 122–123.

19. *Ibid.*, 123–124.

20. Vernon J. Biever to Chuck Lane, September 12, 1966, personal papers of Vernon J. Biever, private collection, Port Washington, Wisconsin.

21. Biever, *The Glory of Titletown*, 133.

22. Foss, 34.

23. Biever, *The Glory of Titletown*, 137.

24. Foss, 34.

25. *Ibid.*

26. *Ibid.*

27. Biever, *The Glory of Titletown*, 265.

About the Contributors

Michael D. **Benter** is a freelance writer and lives in Milwaukee, Wisconsin. He is the author of three books, including *The Badgers: Milwaukee's NFL Entry of 1922–1926* and *The Green and Gold Glory Year's Quiz Book.*

George **Bozeka** grew up within walking distance of the Pro Football Hall of Fame and is a retired attorney living in Akron. He is the author of a number of articles published in the Professional Football Research Association's *The Coffin Corner.* He was the recipient of the Professional Football Researchers Association's Bob Carroll Memorial Writing Award in 2011.

Ed **Bryant** is a lawyer. A Patriots season ticket holder since 2003, he writes and delivers a new song before most New England games and is writing a book he is calling *The Songs, the Notes, and the Games That Inspired Them!*

Denis M. **Crawford** of Boardman, Ohio, is a freelance writer who has written articles extensively for Bucpower.com and *The Coffin Corner.* He is the author of three books: *McKay's Men: The Story of the 1979 Tampa Bay Buccaneers, Hugh Culverhouse and the Tampa Bay Buccaneers* and *All the Fun Life Would Allow: The Life of Johnny F. Bassett.*

Kenneth R. **Crippen** is the current president of the Professional Football Researchers Association and has been a member since 1989. He is the author of two books, *Turmoil vs. Triumph* and *The Original Buffalo Bills,* and the editor of a third, *The Early History of Professional Football.*

Mark L. **Ford** is the current executive director of the Professional Football Researchers Association. He is the author of *A History of NFL Preseason and Exhibition Games,* a two-volume set covering the years 1960 to 2013. He is a lawyer in Harlan, Kentucky.

Matt **Foss** earned an M.A. in history from the University of Wisconsin–Eau Claire in 2009. He interned for the Pro Football Hall of Fame and curated two temporary exhibitions for the Green Bay Packers in their Hall of Fame. He is the project coordinator for the Leigh Yawkey Woodson Art Museum in Wausau, Wisconsin.

Neal **Golden,** a high school teacher of mathematics and computer science since 1963, wrote the first high school computer programming textbook published in the United States (1965). He lives in New Orleans.

John **Grasso** has written books on basketball, football, boxing, wrestling, tennis, bowling and the Olympic Games. He serves as treasurer for the International Society of Olympic Historians (ISOH) and the Professional Football Researchers Association (PFRA) and was the founder of the International Boxing Research Organization (IBRO) in 1982.

Joe **Marren** is a professor and the chair of the communication department at SUNY Buffalo State. Before entering academia, he was an award-winning newspaper reporter and editor for various publications in western New York. He is the author of numerous book chapters and journal articles on subjects ranging from sports to media theory.

John **Maxymuk** is a reference librarian at Rutgers University. He has written ten books on professional football and four on libraries and computers. His first football book was *Packers by the Numbers*, and his latest is *Prime Packers*. He lives in Cherry Hill, New Jersey.

Jeffrey J. **Miller** is the author of several books on the history of football, including *Rockin' the Rockpile, Buffalo's Forgotten Champions, 100 Things Bills Fans Should Know & Do Before They Die, Game Changers: The Greatest Plays in Buffalo Bills Football History* (co-written with Hall of Fame coach Marv Levy), and *Pop Warner: A Life on the Gridiron*.

Rupert **Patrick** is a pro football historian and writer whose work has appeared in the PFRA's *Coffin Corner* and the *Wall Street Journal*. He lives in Greenville, South Carolina.

Matt **Reaser** has been a member of the Professional Football Researchers Association for seven years and has served on a number of PFRA committees.

Gary **Sarnoff** of Alexandria, Virginia, is a member of both the PFRA and SABR (Society for American Baseball Research). He is the author of two books, *The Wrecking Crew of '33* and *The First Yankees Dynasty,* and is writing a book about Vince Lombardi.

Rick **Schabowski** is a retired machinist from Harley-Davidson who teaches for the Wisconsin Regional Training Partnership. He is also president of the Wisconsin Old Time Ballplayers Association, president of the Ken Keltner Badger State Chapter of SABR and a member of the Hoop Historians. He has contributed to a number of SABR book projects.

Greg **Selber** is an associate professor of communication at the University of Texas–Rio Grande Valley, and the author of books on high school football and college basketball. He was the 2011 Putt Powell Award winner as Texas state sportswriter of the year, and has more than 30 years of sports reporting experience in print and broadcast.

Rich **Shmelter** is a writer and researcher specializing in sports history and American crime history. He is the author of several books, including *The Browns: Cleveland's Team, Chicago Assassin: The Life and Legend of Machine Gun Jack McGurn and the Chicago Beer Wars of the Roaring Twenties, The Raiders Encyclopedia,* and *The USC Trojans Football Encyclopedia*.

Randy **Snow** lives in Kalamazoo, Michigan, and has been a member of the PFRA since 2011. He has written more than 300 football-related articles for various newspapers and websites. He also lectures on football history and runs a website called the World of Football.

John **Vorperian** is the host and executive producer of *Beyond the Game*, a nationally syndicated sports cable television program. A member of the PFRA and the Sports Lawyer Association, who has taught sports management and law topics at Manhattanville College and Concordia College (New York), he lives in New York.

Chris **Willis** has been head of the research library at NFL Films since 1996. He is the author of several books, including four on early pro football. He was awarded the PFRA's 2012 Ralph Hay award for Lifetime Achievement in Pro Football Research and Historiography. He lives in Audubon, New Jersey.

Joe **Zagorski** is a former sportswriter for the *Daily Record* of Coatesville, Pennsylvania, and the *Evening Phoenix* of Phoenixville, Pennsylvania. He is writing his first book on the 1970s in the NFL. A park ranger for the National Park Service, he resides in Oak Ridge, Tennessee.

Jay **Zahn** is a lifelong Packers fan and Wisconsin resident. He is a member of the PFRA and has had articles on the 1969 Raiders–Cowboys Rookie Game and the Futility Bowl published in the PFRA's *Coffin Corner*.

Index

313